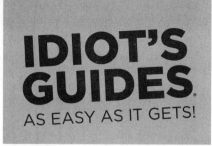

IDIOT'S GUIDES.
AS EASY AS IT GETS!

The Middle East Conflict

by Alan Axelrod, PhD

D1379298

ALPHA

A member of Penguin Group (USA) Inc.

For Anita and Ian

ALPHA BOOKS

Published by Penguin Group (USA) Inc.

Penguin Group (USA) Inc., 375 Hudson Street, New York, New York 10014, USA • Penguin Group (Canada), 90 Eglinton Avenue East, Suite 700, Toronto, Ontario M4P 2Y3, Canada (a division of Pearson Penguin Canada Inc.) • Penguin Books Ltd., 80 Strand, London WC2R 0RL, England • Penguin Ireland, 25 St. Stephen's Green, Dublin 2, Ireland (a division of Penguin Books Ltd.) • Penguin Group (Australia), 250 Camberwell Road, Camberwell, Victoria 3124, Australia (a division of Pearson Australia Group Pty. Ltd.) • Penguin Books India Pvt. Ltd., 11 Community Centre, Panchsheel Park, New Delhi—110 017, India • Penguin Group (NZ), 67 Apollo Drive, Rosedale, North Shore, Auckland 1311, New Zealand (a division of Pearson New Zealand Ltd.) • Penguin Books (South Africa) (Pty.) Ltd., 24 Sturdee Avenue, Rosebank, Johannesburg 2196, South Africa • Penguin Books Ltd., Registered Offices: 80 Strand, London WC2R 0RL, England

IDIOT'S GUIDES and Design are trademarks of Penguin Group (USA) Inc.

International Standard Book Number: 978-1-61564-639-5
Library of Congress Catalog Card Number: 2014938382

16 15 14   8 7 6 5 4 3 2 1

Interpretation of the printing code: The rightmost number of the first series of numbers is the year of the book's printing; the rightmost number of the second series of numbers is the number of the book's printing. For example, a printing code of 14-1 shows that the first printing occurred in 2014.

Printed in the United States of America

Most Alpha books are available at special quantity discounts for bulk purchases for sales promotions, premiums, fundraising, or educational use. Special books, or book excerpts, can also be created to fit specific needs. For details, write: Special Markets, Alpha Books, 375 Hudson Street, New York, NY 10014.

Publisher: *Mike Sanders*
Executive Managing Editor: *Billy Fields*
Senior Acquisitions Editor: *Brook Farling*
Development Editor: *Ann Barton*
Production Editor: *Jana M. Stefanciosa*

Cover Designer: *Laura Merriman*
Book Designer: *William Thomas*
Indexer: *Angie Martin*
Layout: *Brian Massey, Ayanna Lacey*
Proofreader: *Sara Smith*

Contents

Appendixes

Introduction

Every place on Earth has meaning for someone. No place on Earth has more meaning for more people than the Middle East. Historians have long spoken of it as "the cradle of civilization." That familiar phrase may be debated, but only because of the definite article *the*. There can be no debate that the region is *a* cradle of civilization—and more than one civilization at that.

Moreover, the Middle East is the birthplace of the world's three major monotheist religions, all—despite their sometimes violent differences—worshipping the same God. Almost certainly, this makes it the birthplace of monotheism itself, and some scholars have suggested that the region may well be the source of the very concept of religion.

No place on the planet is richer in physical and intellectual evidence of the very ancient past, and few regions have had a more intense and profound impact on the recent past, exert more influence on the present, and are more anxiously watched for their possible effect on the future.

The Middle East has contributed immeasurably to the collective heritage of humanity, and yet much of that heritage is one of conflict—millennia of struggle among diverse peoples for hearts, minds, and resources, and for nothing less than a stake in this world and the next.

In recent history, from the era of World War I (1914–1918) to the present day, conflict has increasingly come to define the image of the Middle East and to shape its identity. When conflict becomes chronic, as is the case with this great region, perspective and objective understanding are soon numbered among the casualties of combat. Violence draws our interest, but tends to dull our comprehension. The human threads of history not only multiply, they become almost hopelessly tangled.

A truly detailed and comprehensive understanding of the region and its conflicts requires veritable libraries and multiple lifetimes to devote to their contents. Doubtless, acquiring such an understanding also calls for firsthand experience on the ground itself. But even the most thoroughly informed regional experts are overwhelmed by a welter of conflicts that change on a daily basis.

The realistic aim of this book is to tease out the main threads of the Middle Eastern narrative. At the very least, the discussion presented here will help readers to understand the seemingly endless torrent of reports, video images, sound bites, claims, and counter claims that emerge throughout today's relentless 24-hour digital, cable, and broadcast news cycles.

We can also hope for even more. We can hope that the discussion moves readers to dig deeper and, most of all, to understand that, whatever else the "Middle East Conflict" is, and no matter how violently divisive, it is the product of spiritual, emotional, and material needs, dreams, and aspirations all people share. In this realization, as the likes of such Middle Eastern heroes as Anwar Sadat and Menachem Begin understood, is the hope not only of the region but of all humanity.

How This Book Is Organized

Part 1, Clash of Empires, narrates the key conflicts between the *caliphate*—the Muslim empire centered in the Middle East—and Christian Europe during the Crusades, the Mongol horde of Genghis Khan and his successors, and the Ottoman Empire, which straddled Europe and Asia.

Part 2, Peoples in Conflict, explains how what is today perceived as a conflict between Muslims and Jews was shaped by and, in turn, came to shape much of the history of the twentieth and twenty-first centuries through European Zionism, the dissolution of the Ottoman Empire following World War I, the rise of "political Islam," and the impact of the Holocaust associated with World War II.

Part 3, A History of Violence, begins with the central role oil has played in the modern history of the Middle East and then presents chapters outlining the region's major twentieth-century wars: the Arab-Israeli War of 1948–1949, the Suez Crisis of 1956, the conflicts associated with the Arab Palestinian struggle for statehood, the Six-Day War of 1967, and the Yom Kippur War of 1973.

Part 4, Global Battleground, documents events that have linked the fate of the Middle East to that of the rest of the world, especially the United States and its Western partners. The chapters in this part treat the Islamic Revolution, including the U.S. embassy hostage crisis of 1979–1981; the Gulf War of 1990–1991; the evolution of Islamic terrorism, including the attacks of 9/11; and America's controversial wars in Afghanistan and Iraq.

Part 5, Risings and Revolutions begins with the grim struggle between Israel, founded to end the statelessness of the Jewish people, and the Arab Palestinians of Gaza and the West Bank, stateless people in search of a state. From this dark situation, the last two chapters turn to the mixture of hope, fear, and hopelessness that has characterized what the Western media calls the "Arab Spring," an extraordinary regional outbreak of popular revolutionary fervor, new alliances, and old enmities.

Extras

Throughout *Idiot's Guides: The Middle East Conflict,* you'll find three types of sidebars:

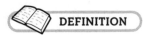
DEFINITION

Here are the most significant vocabulary items relating to Middle East history, culture, religion, and conflict.

VOICES

This sidebar offers telling quotations from key documents and the region's leading personalities.

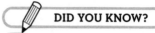 **DID YOU KNOW?**

Here are facts, factoids, and statistics of special interest and significance.

Also included are brief biographical sketches of key figures in Middle East conflict.

But Wait! There's More!

Have you logged on to idiotsguides.com lately? If you haven't, go there now! As a bonus to the book, we've included four additional chapters providing in-depth coverage of early history in the Middle East. Point your browser to idiotsguides.com/mideast, and enjoy!

Acknowledgments

My thanks to editors Brook Farling, Phil Kitchel, and Ann Barton at Alpha Books, and to Sam McNeil from the University of Arizona School of Middle Eastern & North African Studies, who served as technical editor for the book and provided much insight into the complex currents of the Middle East conflict throughout history.

Trademarks

All terms mentioned in this book that are known to be or are suspected of being trademarks or service marks have been appropriately capitalized. Alpha Books and Penguin Group (USA) Inc. cannot attest to the accuracy of this information. Use of a term in this book should not be regarded as affecting the validity of any trademark or service mark.

Prologue

The modern conflicts in the Middle East are rooted in the region's ancient past, a span of history that would require many volumes to narrate comprehensively. By way of prologue, we can only sketch the centuries of context in which the conflict has developed. You can find a more complete discussion of this period, beginning in prehistoric times and ending with the close of the tenth century C.E., online at idiotsguides.com/mideast.

Prehistory

In a high school textbook published in 1914, Professor James H. Breasted of the University of Chicago coined the phrase *Fertile Crescent* to define a region of western Asia and northeastern Africa in which many of the earliest civilizations rose. The phrase caught on to encompass the ancient lands of Mesopotamia—the territory between and adjacent to the Tigris and Euphrates rivers. Some authorities extend the region to include ancient Assyria, to the north of Mesopotamia; Phoenicia, west of Assyria and Mesopotamia and fronting, on the east, the Mediterranean Sea; and Egypt, along the lower reaches of the Nile. Today, the modern nations of Iraq, Syria, Lebanon, Jordan, Egypt, Israel, and the Palestinian territories, together with extreme southeastern Turkey and the western fringes of Kuwait and Iran, occupy this historical region.

Often called the "cradle of civilization," the region is *an* origin—not always *the* unique origin—of some of the earliest examples of the wheel, irrigation, glass, writing, and law, as well as many religions and (as far as we can tell) the idea of monotheistic religion, the faith in a single god.

Cradle of Civilization

About 4500 B.C.E., Sumer arose on territory that is part of modern Iraq. It is presumptuous to say that civilization began with Sumer, but it is accurate to trace the longest *continuous* line of civilization from those ancient people. About 2340 B.C.E., Sargon the Great, ruler of Akkad, invaded Sumer, his neighbor to the south, creating the first empire of Mesopotamia, the heart of what we call the Middle East.

Like many ancient rulers, Sargon proved far better at conquest than at sustainable government. Within about two centuries, rule in the Akkadian Empire broke down, and the realm created by conquest in turn fell prey to conquest when, about 1760 B.C.E., Hammurabi—the "Sun of Babylon"—saw that Sumer and Akkad were ripe for plucking. Babylon, the city-state Hammurabi ruled, now became the center of Babylonia, a new empire encompassing all of southern Mesopotamia and, along the Euphrates, extending well to the north.

Hammurabi created the first enduring set of laws, the so-called Code of Hammurabi, covering many aspects of human behavior in society, ranging from rules of trade and commerce to criminal matters. Among the most enduring principles in the code is the concept known in Latin as *lex talionis,* the "law of retaliation," a principle the authors of the Old Testament book of Leviticus (24:19–20) called "eye for eye, tooth for tooth." *Lex talionis* has been influential throughout civilization, but it remains particularly durable in many cultures of the Middle East and some have seen in it a trigger of the present-day conflict in the region.

Cradle of Religion

During the period dominated by Sumer, Akkad, and Babylonia, Mesopotamians worshipped many gods. Continuities between ancient Mesopotamian religious beliefs and Judaism, Christianity, and Islam suggest that the early traditions influenced the latter. Equally important, however, is what the three dominant modern religions rejected—namely, polytheism. For all of their differences, which have been the source of much violent conflict over the centuries, Judaism, Christianity, and Islam share belief in a single god—ultimately, the same god, that of Abraham.

Assyrian Terrorism and Babylonian Renaissance

To the north of Babylonia lay three cities along the Tigris—Assur, Nineveh, and Nimrud. The first of these gave its name to Assyria, an empire dominated for many years by the more powerful Babylonians. Then, in the ninth century B.C.E., the Assyrian warlord Shalmaneser III invaded Babylon and adjacent Palestine. Ultimately, Assyria extended its dominion into the western part of present-day Iran, northern Turkey, and as far south as Thebes, in Egypt.

The dominance of Babylon was often brutal, but also brought concepts of law. In contrast, Assyrian conquest conferred few civilizing benefits and brought much misery. If a population proved resistant to brutality, the Assyrians broke up tribes by dispersing members to far-flung parts of the empire. This is the fate Israel suffered in 722 B.C.E., when tens of thousands of Hebrews were sent into exile as the "10 lost tribes of Israel."

Rule by terror proved impossible to sustain, and in 612 B.C.E., Nabopolassar, king of the Chaldeans—the ethnic group that had come to dominate Babylonia—made an alliance with the Medes, a people of what is today western Iran. The allies attacked Ninevah, inflicting a major defeat on Assyrian forces there. Nabopolassar's son, Nebuchadnezzar II, completed the defeat of the Assyrian Empire and, in the course of his reign over the Neo-Babylonian Empire (ca. 605–562 B.C.E.), led the conquest of Egypt, Syria, and Palestine. As the Old Testament book of Daniel relates, Nebuchadnezzar destroyed Jerusalem, together with Solomon's Temple (the First Temple), in 586 B.C.E. and, like the Assyrians before him, implemented ethnic cleansing by sending Hebrew captives into Babylonian exile and slavery.

Under Nebuchadnezzar, Babylon became an international economic powerhouse. Babylonian religion was polytheistic, but it did introduce an element common to Judaism, Christianity, and Islam: a concern for the relationship between human beings and the divine. Babylonian religion traced the direct connection between humanity and its gods even as it emphasized the essential inferiority of human beings.

On the Iranian Plateau

The empires that rose and fell, up to and including the rise of Neo-Babylonia, were Semitic peoples, meaning that the languages they spoke shared certain characteristics. From this group, arose another distinctive people: the Arabs. They would ultimately lend their name to Arabia, a region that includes the peninsula bounded by the Mediterranean Sea to the northwest, the Tigris River to the northeast, the Persian Gulf to the southeast, the Arabian Sea to the south, and the Red Sea to the west, and also encompasses Egypt west of the Red Sea.

Perhaps because Iran—until 1935 known as Persia—has long figured prominently in the turmoil of the Middle East, many modern Westerners think of it as another Arab country. It is not. The history, language, and culture of Iran—and Persia before it—are all very distinct from those of the Arab nations.

A nomadic tribe called the Medes arose and allied itself with the Neo-Babylonians. Together, they defeated the Assyrians, and beginning about 678 B.C.E., the Median Empire came to dominate what is now Iran.

The Persian Empire

In 559 B.C.E., Cyrus II ascended the throne of Persia's Achaemenid Dynasty. His father was a Persian, his mother a Median princess. About 550 B.C.E., Cyrus rebelled against his mother's father, who was king of the Medes. This drove the momentum of a great conquest, in which "Cyrus the Great" took Asia Minor and then Babylonia.

Cyrus was succeeded on his death in 530 B.C.E. by his son Cambyses II, who extended the Persian Empire into Egypt. Cambyses II was followed by Darius I the Great, who conquered Thrace and Macedon, making Persia the greatest empire on the planet, extending from Afghanistan to the fringes of Greece and encompassing perhaps 50 million people. Yet neither Darius I nor his son and successor, Xerxes I, succeeded in their greatest ambition, which was to add the city-states of Greece to their empire. Instead, their aggression provoked Alexander the Great to lead the forces of a Greek confederation against Persia in 333–331 B.C.E. After conquering Persia, Alexander went on to add Mesopotamia, Palestine, Pakistan, a portion of India, and most of Egypt to his empire.

Alexander died suddenly in 323 B.C.E., at 33, having conquered much of the ancient world, but also having come up short in his effort to transform it. This would be left to the Romans, whose empire was on the rise by the early first century B.C.E.

Egypt

Like Mesopotamia, Egypt was a civilization sustained by a river. The Nile was a means not only of transportation, but of fertility in a desert land. Recorded civilization in Egypt dates to about 3100 B.C.E., but not until between 2700 and 2200 B.C.E. does the record becomes more complete, in the period known as the Old Kingdom. After passing through the Middle Kingdom period (2050–1800 B.C.E.) and enduring a period of conquest, Egypt entered the New Kingdom (1550–44 B.C.E.), becoming the dominant empire in the region until it fell to Alexander the Great in 332 B.C.E.

The Israelites

The ancient Middle East, from Persia in the east to Egypt in the west, was a vast stage on which great empires rose, fought, and fell. Into this drama came a tribal people who, never having created a vast empire, would likely have sunk into archaeological obscurity were it not for the religion associated with them and the telling of their story in the founding document of that religion: the Old Testament.

Around the twentieth century B.C.E., Abraham left Ur, in Mesopotamia, for Canaan, near modern Palestine. This was a journey from polytheism to monotheism, undertaken (according to the Old Testament) at the command of Yahweh, the one true God, who promised Abraham that He would protect and guide him and his descendants forever. Those descendants, the chosen of God, were the Hebrews, or Israelites, or Jews.

They lived modestly in Canaan until about 1600 B.C.E., when drought and famine forced them to migrate to Egypt, where they settled east of the delta in Goshen. After a period of well-being, the pharaoh pressed the Jews into slave labor to build the pyramids and other monuments. This enslavement lasted some 400 years until Yahweh, in fulfillment of his covenant with Abraham, intervened, commanding Moses to lead his people into freedom.

For 40 years, the Jews lived in 12 loosely confederated tribes in the Sinai wilderness until God summoned Moses to Mount Sinai and gave him the Ten Commandments, which became the basis of the Hebrew Torah, the central text of Judaism.

From the wilderness, Moses led his people back to Canaan, the Promised Land. A cornerstone of Judaism is the doctrine that God set this land aside for the Jews and the Jews alone. Canaan, however, was occupied by Hittites, Amorites, and others. The book of Exodus relates that God commanded the Hebrews to wage war on the interlopers, even to the point of their extermination: "For ... the LORD thy God hath chosen thee to be a special people unto himself, above all people that are upon the face of the earth." (Deuteronomy 7:6)

The Jews fought the Canaanites for some 200 years, first under King Saul and then, after he was killed in combat, under his lieutenant, David. It was David who led a decisive victory against the Philistines, the most formidable among those contesting for possession of Canaan. It was David, too, who forged a kingdom—Israel—out of the 12 disparate tribes that had settled in Canaan, and it was David who wrested Jerusalem from the Jebusites and made the city his capital.

David died about 970 B.C.E., having ruled some 40 years, and was succeeded by his son Solomon, who made Israel an important center of copper mining and foreign trade and who institutionalized Judaism by building a great temple in Jerusalem. Yet the kingdom barely survived Solomon's death in 931 B.C.E. Following civil war, it divided in two, Israel to the north, with its capital in Samaria, and Judah to the south, centered on Jerusalem. Israel prospered while Judah languished.

Unfortunately for Israel, prosperity made it a target for Assyrian invasion in 722 B.C.E. Most of the Israelites were exiled in a *diaspora*—a scattering. Many were simply absorbed into the Assyrian Empire as uprooted members of the "10 lost tribes." Suddenly, humble Judah became the center of Judaism and Hebraic culture. The very name *Jew* is derived from *Yehudi,* "man of Judah."

As mentioned, under Nebuchadnezzar II, the Neo-Babylonian Empire rose, conquering (among much else) Judah. Over the course of Nebuchadnezzar's reign, Judah underwent four mass deportations between 605 and about 582 B.C.E., and in 586 B.C.E., Babylonian forces sacked Jerusalem and destroyed Solomon's Temple. The Jews underwent a new diaspora (usually called, however, the First Diaspora), and were exiled into the Babylonian captivity commemorated in Psalm 137, which begins, "By the rivers of Babylon, / there we sat down, yea, we wept, / when we remembered Zion," *Zion* being a synonym for Jerusalem.

Persia's Cyrus the Great liberated the Jews from their captivity after he conquered Babylonia in the sixth century B.C.E. The Jews began to return to Judah, which, after 450 B.C.E., flourished as a quasi-autonomous nation within the Persian Empire. They lived once again in the Promised Land, but that land was no longer absolutely theirs. An enduring sense of exile and loss was planted at the heart of the Jewish religion. As the covenant had united the Hebrews for centuries, now the sense that it had been lost and was in need of restoration formed an even stronger bond.

The Birth of Christianity

After he defeated Persia in 332 B.C.E., Alexander the Great began remodeling Judah in the Greek image. Under those who followed Alexander, including the monarchs of the Seleucid Empire (which encompassed much of modern Turkey, the Levant, Mesopotamia, Kuwait, Persia, Afghanistan, Turkmenistan, and northwestern India), the "Hellenizing" process continued. This prompted a successful Jewish revolt in 166 B.C.E., in which Judah was renamed Judea and became an independent Jewish kingdom.

In 63 B.C.E., Pompey, consul of the Roman republic, sent his formidable legions to take and occupy Jerusalem. Judea soon earned a reputation as the most unruly province of the Roman Empire, and in 37 B.C.E., Rome forcefully annexed it to the empire and installed Herod, a convert to Judaism from Idumea (a region just south of Judea), as a Roman puppet king.

The Gospel According to Saint Matthew portrays Herod as a tyrant who, hearing of the birth of a destined "king of the Jews," preemptively ordered the mass execution of all male infants in and around Bethlehem, on the assumption that one of them had to be the infant Jesus, a future usurper of the Judean throne.

The story of the life and teachings of Jesus—or Jesus Christ, *christ* being the Greek word for "anointed one"—is found mostly in the New Testament gospels of the apostles Matthew, Mark, Luke, and John, with additional material included in the Epistles, 1 Corinthians, Acts, and 1 Timothy. The consensus among *secular* historians is that Jesus was a Galilean Jew, born between 6 and 4 B.C.E.—near the very end of Herod the Great's life and reign. It is generally believed that Jesus died, by judicial crucifixion, between 30 and 36 C.E., as authorized by the Roman provincial prefect (governor) Pontius Pilate.

When Jesus reached the age of about 30—sometime between 27 and 29 C.E.—he began a career of itinerant preaching in Judea. Presenting himself as the son of God (the one and only God of the Jews) as well as the Messiah, he preached God's love for humankind and proclaimed that the "kingdom of God" existed in the here and now, not in some heavenly realm. He charged his followers to love God and to love their fellow man as they loved themselves. In contrast to the long-prevailing doctrine of *lex talionis*, Jesus taught forgiveness, charity, humility, and a general pacifism.

Jesus won followers even as he stirred the opposition of local authorities, both Roman and Jewish. He was arrested, tried, convicted, and crucified, ostensibly for the treasonous and heretical claim to being the king of the Jews. But the story of Jesus Christ did not end with his death. The New Testament holds that he rose from his tomb three days after interment. The resurrection persuaded his followers of their teacher's divinity and became the catalyst for a new monotheistic religion.

Surviving early Roman attempts to suppress it, Christianity became not only the state religion of Rome, but one of the world's most influential religions and a major force in history and civilization.

The Jews Go to War Against Rome

Although the life, death, and reported resurrection of Jesus would, in the fullness of time, have a profound effect, for most Judeans and their neighbors, Christ's ministry and execution had little to no immediate impact. Of far greater consequence was the growing unrest in Rome's Jewish province. Many Judeans were unhappy with both Roman rule and the Jews Rome had installed to administer it. Some were profoundly outraged over being compelled to live under an empire based in the polytheistic worship of false gods. The most militant among these were the Zealots, who came into being in 6 B.C.E. as a group of protesters against Roman taxation. They believed that paying tribute to Rome denied the exclusivity of their acknowledgement of God alone as their ruler. They staged anti-Roman revolts in the years following Jesus's execution, culminating in the Great Jewish Revolt of 66–73, also known as the First Roman War.

In 70, the Roman emperor Vespasian sent an army under his son Titus to retake Jerusalem and restore order. Titus reduced Jerusalem to rubble. The Second Temple, built to replace the First Temple, which had been destroyed in 568 B.C.E., was also destroyed. (The so-called Wailing Wall is still located in the Old City of Jerusalem and is part of the ancient wall that surrounded the courtyard of the Second Temple.)

The desolation ended the Great Jewish Revolt, except among the Zealots, who took a desperately heroic stand at a fortress called Masada, committing mass suicide there in 73, just before Roman legionnaires overran it. To this day, inductees into the Israel Defense Forces (IDF) swear an oath: "Masada shall not fall again."

In 117 c.e., Simon bar Kokhba led a new Jewish rebellion against Roman domination, which provoked a massive response from Emperor Hadrian, whose legions killed (according to Roman sources) 580,000 Jews—a genocidal toll. Those who survived were exiled in yet another diaspora. The Jews were once again stateless.

The Rise of Islam

Islam was the last of the three major monotheistic religions to rise. Like Judaism and Christianity before it, Islam was born in the Middle East, but whereas the two earlier religions had their origin to the west of Mesopotamia, Islam came into being on the Arabian Peninsula, occupied today by Saudi Arabia, Kuwait, Qatar, the United Arab Emirates, Oman, Bahrain, and Yemen.

As the founding of Christianity is identified with a single personality, Jesus Christ, so Islam began, some 600 years later, with Muhammad. The precise year of his birth is disputed, but Islamic tradition places it in 570, in Mecca—today a city of two million in Saudi Arabia.

Islamic tradition holds that, shortly after his birth, Muhammad was sent out of Mecca to live with Bedouins in the desert, an environment considered healthier for infants than the teeming city. The same tradition says that he did not return to Mecca and his birth mother until he was two. Recently, some scholars have rejected this traditional biographical narrative. What is known for certain, however, is that the boy's mother, Amina, died when he was six and that he was put under the guardianship of his paternal grandfather, who, however, died just two years later. The eight-year-old was then taken into the care of his uncle, Abu Talib ibn Abdul-Muttalib, whom he accompanied on trading trips to Syria.

Muhammad became a merchant and, in 605, played a central role in setting the Black Stone. The stone—possibly a rare black meteorite—was revered as a sacred symbol of Allah. At this time, Arabs worshipped many gods, among whom Allah was considered supreme. The Black Stone was housed in Mecca, within a monument called the Kaaba (now Islam's most sacred mosque). The stone had been removed during repairs and renovations to the Kaaba, after which the leaders of the disputatious clans could not agree on who should have the honor of resetting it. At length, they agreed to await the arrival of the next man to come through the gate and ask him to make the choice. That next man was Muhammad, and his response to the leaders' request was inventive, diplomatic, and wise. He asked for a cloth, placed the Black Stone in its center, and then gave each clan leader a corner of the cloth to hold. Muhammad accompanied them to the Kaaba wall, lifted the stone from its cloth, and set it in place—to the satisfaction of all, who thus enjoyed a share of the honor.

At about this time, Muhammad began to feel that shallow materialism had come to replace Arab traditions of charity and unity. Seeking enlightenment, he took several weeks out of each year to retire to the solitude of a cave on Mount Hira, outside of Mecca. During one of these retreats in 610, the angel Gabriel—the same figure who is mentioned in the Old Testament of Judaism as well as the New Testament of Christianity—appeared to him, commanding that he recite certain sacred verses—unknown to Muhammad (who, according to Islamic tradition, was illiterate), yet miraculously now familiar. These would become a part of the Quran, the holy book of Islam.

During the next three years, Muhammad continued to engage in solitary contemplation. This prepared him to receive additional revelations and visions, the totality of which would inform his teachings and ultimately be set down in the Quran.

Gradually, Muhammad was accepted as a prophet, winning a few converts to *Islam,* a word meaning "submission to Allah's will." The first were poor people at the margins of society, but eventually Muhammad's teachings entered the mainstream, and the rich and powerful saw Muhammad as an economic and cultural threat. His message was that Allah was the very God, the God of Abraham, who had already revealed himself to Moses and, later, to Jesus. To worship this one true lord required renunciation of all others. Many Arabs were loath to abandon those gods, and some merchants approached Muhammad with bribes, offering to admit him—a fellow merchant, after all—into their inner circle, provided that he renounce his teachings. He refused and was subjected to insults and shunning. Only his membership in the esteemed Banu Hashim clan protected him from physical assault. This protection did not extend to his followers from the lower classes, especially slaves, some of whom were tortured or killed by their angry masters. In 617, leaders of two powerful mercantile clans commenced a boycott against trading with the Banu Hashim. For three years, Muhammad's clan stood by him, ultimately outlasting the boycott.

Discouraged by resistance in Mecca and hearing of an assassination plot against him, Muhammad, together with his closest supporters, journeyed north in 622 to Yathrib—a town later to become known as Medina, usually translated as "the city of the Prophet." This departure—the Arabic word for which is *Hijra*—became recognized as Year One in the Islamic calendar.

The people of Yathrib—Medina—welcomed Muhammad as a prophet and arbitrator of disputes. Muhammad accordingly instructed his followers to move from Mecca to Medina. The combination of Medina converts (called the *Ansar*) and Muslim immigrants from Mecca (the *Muhajirun*) transformed Medina into the world's first Islamic city.

Muslims believe Muhammad is the prophet of Allah because he was chosen to receive—through the revelations of Gabriel—the Quran, which is the word of God and the central book of Islam. The revelation was made to the prophet verbally—the word *Quran* means "the recitation"—and spanned some 23 years of Muhammad's life, beginning on December 22, 609, when he was 40, and ending in 632, the year he died.

The revelations of Gabriel, together with the Hijra and the conversion of Medina, certified Muhammad as a prophet and a major religious leader. His subsequent acts, undertaken to create an enduring resolution of the bloody grievances among the clans and tribes of Medina, revealed his brilliance as a political leader.

Muhammad set about drafting what has come to be known as the Constitution of Medina, which forged a federation among the tribes of Medina and the Muslim emigrants who had arrived from Mecca. The Constitution of Medina created the precedent and pattern of an Islamic state, the fusion of secular and spiritual order in a single polity (community or state). This would have a profound effect through history—especially the recent history of conflict in the Middle East.

Muhammad the religious and political leader went on to become a military leader as well, leading a far-reaching campaign of conquest. In no other major religion is the founder of the faith so intimately, personally, and directly involved in prophecy, religious teaching, civil government, and military conquest.

Muhammad's first conquest was Mecca in 630, which won the majority of Meccans to Islam. After this, many tribes in the region were drawn to Islam. The prophet did not wait passively for conversion, however, but sent military parties to persuade holdouts, especially among the Bedouin nomads.

In 632, Muhammad led the first *Islamic* pilgrimage to Mecca. (Called the *Hajj*, such a pilgrimage is still observed as the duty of all faithful Muslims, who make at least one pilgrimage to Mecca in a lifetime.) Muhammad ascended Mount Arafat, east of Mecca, from which he delivered what came to be known as the Farewell Sermon. In it, the prophet elevated Islam as a faith above class, ethnicity, and race, declaring all of the faithful to be equal, except for how they might distinguish themselves in terms of faithfulness, piety, and good works. Muhammad sought to create a clean slate for Islamic society, declaring void the old blood feuds based on centuries of tribal dispute.

Islam After Muhammad

Muhammad died from an illness on June 8, 632. He had not, in the Farewell Sermon nor on his deathbed, definitively designated a *caliph*, or leader of the Islamic community, to succeed him. If he'd had a son, the choice would have been clear. But he had only daughters, and no male successor could be identified in his immediate bloodline. A *shura* (council) of Ansar leaders convened to select a new caliph. Ali ibn Abi Talib, Muhammad's cousin and son-in-law, and the first male to accept Islam, seemed to many an obvious choice, but he was a young man at 34 and widely considered insufficiently experienced to follow the great man. Instead, by a very close vote, the shura settled on the prophet's father-in-law, Abu Bakr—the sobriquet of Abdullah ibn Abi Quhafa—who, at 60, possessed the gravitas of age deemed appropriate for succession to leadership.

The Muhajirun (Muhammad's original followers) did not accept the credentials of the new caliph and, with the passing of Muhammad, the seed of crisis was planted. The Ansar and others who accepted Abu Bakr's succession became known as "Ahl-al-Sunnah wa al-Jama'ah"—"the people of tradition and unification"—or, more simply, the Sunnis.

To this day, the Sunnis hold that all the Muslims of Medina—including Ali ibn Abi Talib, Muhammad's first cousin and son-in-law—accepted the succession of Abu Bakr. However, among the Muhajirun, the original emigrants from Mecca, who did not take part in the Ansar council, were those who believed that Allah chose Ali, the prophet's closest male relative, to be Muhammad's successor. This group came to be called the *Shiat Ali*—"faction" or "followers"—commonly abbreviated to Shia.

This dispute between Sunnis and Shia, the two principal branches of Islam, is an enduring source of social and political upheaval and violence to this day within many Muslim communities and Islam in general. It did not explode at the time of Abu Bakr's succession, however. Both sides agreed that Islam was facing an urgent danger of civil war and that, for the sake of unity, it was best to approve Abu Bakr's leadership. For rebellions—known as Al-Ridda, the apostasy—had broken out among some who renounced Islam, believing that their "conversion" was a personal oath sworn to Muhammad, and his death released them from the oath. In addition, a number of self-proclaimed prophets came forth after Muhammad's passing and also incited apostasy and revolt.

Not only did Abu Bakr prove effective in suppressing Al-Ridda, he also launched offensive campaigns against Persia (under the Sassanid Empire) and the Byzantine Empire in an effort to expand Islam. In 634, however, Abu Bakr fell desperately ill and, as he lay on his deathbed, seeking to avoid repeating the discord created by Muhammad's failure to designate a successor, he named Umar ibn Al-Khattab to succeed him.

During Umar's reign, the Islamic conquest of Syria was completed and almost all of Sassanid Persia was annexed to the Islamic Empire, along with the Levant, Egypt, Cyrenaica, Tripolitania, Fezzan, and Eastern Anatolia. Included in his conquests was Jerusalem, which fell to Umar's forces in 637 without a fight.

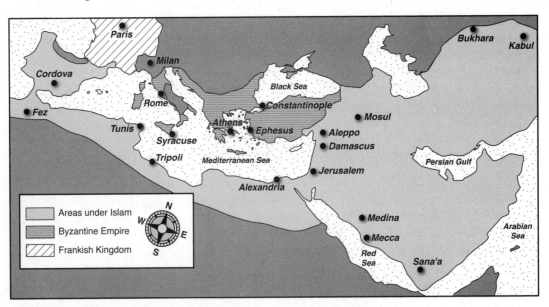

Umar was at the height of his power when, on November 3, 844, a Persian soldier, captured by Muslim forces and enslaved, attacked him with a dagger, stabbing him six times in the belly as Umar led morning prayers. Before he died, Umar composed a final testament of tolerance, enjoining the Muhajirun and Ansar to treat each other kindly. Umar did not name a successor, however, but appointed a six-man shura to choose the caliph from among themselves.

Once again passing over Ali ibn Abi Talib, the shura chose Uthman, an early Meccan convert and the husband of one of Muhammad's daughters. An able leader, Uthman presided over a wave of prosperity in the Muslim community. He also assembled a committee of scholars that produced multiple copies of the Quran, thereby establishing the text as it exists today. Uthman launched military campaigns to suppress rebellion among the lands Umar had conquered, and he positioned forces for further expansion of the caliphate. Nevertheless, rebellion was widespread throughout the Muslim empire, and on June 20, 656, Egyptian rebels assassinated Uthman. Ali ibn Abi Talib was chosen to succeed him.

Ali was faced with fighting a *fitna* (civil war), which spanned 656–661. On or about January 27, 661, members of a faction called the Kharijites ("those who leave") assassinated Ali as he prayed in the Great Mosque of Kufa (in Iraq). Fatally wounded, he commanded there to be no retaliation against the Kharijites.

Ali's eldest son, Husayn, succeeded him, but was opposed by Muawiyah bin Abi-Sufyan, who had been appointed governor of Syria by Uthman. Muawiyah bribed Husayn's top commanders to mutiny, whereupon Husayn had no choice but to yield the succession to Muawiyah. Muawiyah immediately named his son Yazid to succeed him—and thus the Umayyad Dynasty was founded, the Umayyads being the subclan of the Quraysh clan, to which Muawiyah belonged.

By this point in Islamic history, Muslims viewed the world as divided among three groups. The *dar al-Islam* ("the realm of Islam") consisted of all Muslim territory controlled by the caliph. Those territories deemed ripe for conquest were designated as the *dar al-harb* (the "realm of war"), and those non-Muslim nations that coexisted with Islam but were deemed unavailable for conquest were the *dar al-sulh* ("realm of truce"). Muawiyah was intent on transforming more of the *dar al-harb* into the *dar al-Islam,* and sent annual military expeditions into the territory of the Byzantine Empire.

Muawiyah fell ill and died in 680, but not before enjoining Yazid to treat Husayn with reverence. No sooner did Muawiyah die, however, than Husayn laid claim to the caliphate. He, after all, was directly descended from the prophet, Muhammad, and his faction—the Shia—were prepared to assert anew their belief that only a direct male descendant of Muhammad could rightfully rule as caliph.

Supported by the Sunni (who had accepted Abu Bakr as Muhammad's successor over the prophet's nearer relative, Ali), Yazid felt that his father's dying command concerning Husayn no longer applied. On October 10, 680, forces loyal to Yazid defeated Husyan and his followers at the Battle of Karbala (in Iraq). Yazid's commander captured Husayn and his brothers, summarily executing them, Husayn's six-month-old son, and many of Husyan's followers.

The slaughter of Husayn, grandson of Muhammad, and his close companions, far from consolidating Yazid's control of the Islamic Empire, turned many Muslims against him and the Sunnis. It brought to a crisis the long-simmering dispute between the Shia and the Sunnis, creating a schism that has endured as a source of violent strife within Islam. To this day, the events are commemorated in Shia Islam as the Mourning of Muharram—the tenth day of which, the day of the slaughter, is known as Ashura.

Yazid was killed in a riding accident in 683 and was succeeded by his son Muawiyah II, who abdicated just 40 days later. He was succeeded by Marwan I, who reigned for little more than a year amid civil war. His successor, Abd al-Malik ibn Marwan, proved far more capable and reigned from 685 to 705, expanding the Islamic Empire eastward into what is today Afghanistan, Turkmenistan, and Uzbekistan. His successor, Al-Walid I, pushed the *dar al-Islam* westward, into Europe. By the time of his death in 715, the Iberian Peninsula (modern Spain and Portugal) was under Islam, and the Muslims were on the verge of advancing into France at the heart of Western Europe. (In 732, Charles Martel, king of the Franks, defeated an Umayyad military expedition at the Battle of Tours—also known as the Battle of Poitiers—in France, arresting the Muslim advance into Western Europe.)

Eight more caliphs would rule before the Umayyad Dynasty ended with the defeat of Marwan II in 750 at the hands of the Abbasid commander Abdallah ibn Ali in the Battle of Zab (near the Great Zab River in Iraq).

As-Saffah (full name, Abu al-Abbas Abdullah ibn Muhammad as-Saffah) became the first caliph of the Abbasid Dynasty, which endured until 1258 and marked a long period of Islamic expansion, often called a "Golden Age," which saw tribalism yield to a greater degree of imperial unity and the Arab world rise as a center of learning, art, and culture even as Europe languished in what later historians called the Dark Ages.

Under the Abbasids, the Islamic Empire would come into bitter conflict with Christian Europe in the Crusades, the subject of Chapter 1.

Clash of Empires

The present-day Middle East conflict is a complex of geopolitical, economic, and cultural as well as religious causes in which conquest, colonialism, and nationalism have played major roles. The conflict is, however, rooted in the three major monotheistic religious traditions—Judaism, Christianity, and Islam—all of which were born in, developed in, and struggled with one another in the Middle East. Once the influence of Islam came to dominate the region, the caliphate—the Muslim empire—came into direct military conflict with Christian Europe during the Crusades (Chapter 1), with the Mongol horde of Genghis Khan and his successors (Chapter 2), and, yet again, with Europe during the rise and fall of the Ottoman Empire (Chapter 3).

The Crusades

"Europe cringes at Bush 'crusade' against terrorists," read the headline of a *Christian Science Monitor* story published on September 19, 2001, eight days after the deadliest attack on American territory in the nation's history. The article noted that the reference to a "'crusade' against terrorism ... raised fears that the terrorist attacks could spark a 'clash of civilizations' between Christians and Muslims, sowing fresh winds of hatred and mistrust."

Westerners have long used the word *crusade* to describe any serious campaign—whether military or nonmilitary. In the context of attacks by Islamic extremists, however, the word inevitably recalled the bloody religious campaigns waged during the eleventh through thirteenth centuries by Christian forces against Muslim territories in and near Jerusalem in an effort to gain control of the so-called Holy Land. Medieval Islamic leaders proclaimed that the proper response to such campaigns was a jihad, a holy war in defense and furtherance of Islam. A call to a crusade against terrorism could easily be interpreted in 2001 as a call to a new crusade against Islam—and could well justify the waging of jihad in response.

In This Chapter

- The influence of the medieval Christian Crusades on the twenty-first-century War on Terror

- The triumph of the First Crusade and the failure of the following eight

- Saladin's unification of the Middle East

- The bitter fruit of the Crusades

What Were the Crusades?

A decade ago, the Crusades seemed to most Westerners a vague page out of history. But suddenly, on September 11, 2001, Americans and other Westerners discovered that there remained many people in the world willing to kill and be killed for their religion. Who were these people? Why were the attacks greeted with joy and dancing in many urban streets of the Middle East? Editorial pages and TV news anchors asked: "Why do they hate us?"

Some, Christian and Muslim alike, believed the answers were to be found in the Crusades. They pointed out that this series of medieval conflicts had never really stopped. Some Muslim leaders specifically charged that the West had not only sought to destroy Islam for centuries, it continued to do so today.

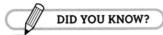

DID YOU KNOW?

While TV and other Western mass media often depicted celebrations in Muslim countries following 9/11, the terrorist acts also sparked mass demonstrations *against* Al-Qaeda in Cairo, Tehran, and many other Muslim cities across the world.

Whatever the validity of this charge, one fact is inescapable: with 9/11, the medieval Crusades came to seem painfully relevant. For some Muslims and Christians alike, the events of roughly 1095 (when Pope Urban II proclaimed the First Crusade) through 1291 (when the last of the Crusader states fell) came to seem just as immediate.

Prelude

Simply put, the Crusades were religious wars, mainly between Christians and Muslims, declared by papal authority, aimed at recovering the Holy Land and other so-called Christian realms from Islamic control, and spanning the late eleventh century through the end of the thirteenth.

Although the First Crusade was not officially proclaimed until 1095, the European effort to retake formerly Christian territory conquered by Muslims began in 722 (or possibly 718—sources differ) with the Battle of Covadonga in Asturias, on the northwestern coast of the Iberian Peninsula. Some 300 Asturian knights, led by Pelagius, defeated a force of Umayyad Muslims that may have numbered as many as 1,400 (by modern estimate) or 187,000 (by medieval estimate). The victory went to the Asturians, who thereby reclaimed for Christianity a stronghold in northern Iberia, over which Pelagius subsequently ruled as king. The cost of victory was great. According to Asturian sources, all but 10 or 11 of the knights were killed. Medieval estimates, however, put Muslim losses at a staggering and highly unlikely 124,000.

The Battle of Covadonga began the *Reconquista*, the campaign to reconquer Iberia from Islam. The effort spanned nearly 800 years, ending only with the fall of Granada, the last Islamic Iberian state, in 1492, and thus it preceded, coincided with, and lasted long beyond the period of the Crusades.

 **DEFINITION**

The **Reconquista,** meaning "reconquest," spanned roughly 711 to 1492 and is the label for the Christian military campaigns by which control of the Iberian Peninsula was wrested from Muslim powers.

Abbasid Decline, Fatamid Rise, and Seljuk Explosion

Although Islam rapidly expanded under the Ummayad and Abbasid dynasties, the Islamic realm rarely experienced the stability of internal peace. By the middle of the tenth century, Abbasid control over the caliphate was being effectively challenged by the Fatamid Dynasty, which, headquartered in Cairo, dominated North Africa. This was no mere struggle for power, but, rather, a contest of religious belief. The Fatamids were Shia, the Abbasids Sunni. Once again, this fundamental rift in Islamic theology drove bloody political and military action. The Fatamids never fully overthrew the Abbasids, but they did overtake their cultural influence in the Muslim world. Having done this, however, the Fatamids in turn faced a new threat.

The Seljuk Turks, Central Asian converts to Islam, were warriors by tradition as well as inclination. They thrived during the rivalry between the Ummayads and Fatamids, serving both sides as mercenaries. There came a time when the Seljuks were no longer content to be mere employees of the caliphs. They wanted their own stake in the Islamic Empire.

In 934, the Persian Buywayhids captured Baghdad from the Abbasids. The Seljuks conquered Persia in 1044, then took Baghdad from the Buywayhids 11 years later, in 1055. Although they pledged loyalty to the Abbasids, the Seljuk leaders wielded the real power in and around the city. Having marginalized the Abbasids, the Seljuks then turned their forces against the Fatamids. At the same time, Seljuk forces looked beyond the *dar al-Islam* (Muslim-controlled territory) and made war against the Christian Byzantine Empire.

The Pope Calls a Council

At least two Byzantine emperors requested aid from the Catholic Church in fighting Muslim forces on their territory. Three years after suffering a costly defeat at the hands of Seljuks in the 1071 Battle of Manzikert, Emperor Michael VII called on Pope Gregory VII for military aid, but nothing came of the plea. In 1091, Byzantine Emperor Alexios I Komnenos successfully expelled Seljuk forces from the Danube River area; four years later, he requested the help of Pope Urban II to continue the fight against a new wave of Seljuk invaders.

Urban convened the Council of Clermont, in Clermont, France, and issued a momentous call to Christians of the West to march to the aid of their Eastern brethren in Byzantium. His reason for the call was simple—*God wills it*—but he offered an added incentive. According to some sources, it was nothing less than "remission of sins"—a complete wiping of the moral slate, as it were. Fight, and you will go to heaven—guaranteed. Other sources say that Urban offered nothing more or less than a holy "indulgence"—remission of any *penance* due from sins, not remission of the sins themselves. Either way, many heeded the call.

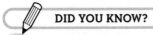

DID YOU KNOW?

In calling on Western Christians to come to the aid of Eastern Christians, Pope Urban II was not just waging a war to reclaim "Christian" lands from the Muslims, but was also desperately trying to reunite a Christian Church that was badly split. In 1054, Pope Leo IX in Rome and Patriarch Michael Cerularius of the Byzantine church reciprocally excommunicated each other. The Roman Catholic Church and the Eastern Orthodox Church have gone their separate ways ever since.

A Crusade Out of Control

As the pope outlined it, the First Crusade was, first, a *defensive* war against the Seljuks to drive them out of Byzantium, and, second, an *offensive* war to "free" the Holy Land—seen as the land of Christ—from the grip of Islam.

As actually fought, however, the First Crusade and the Crusades that followed were often campaigns of extermination—and not just of Christian against Muslim, which would have been horrific enough, but of Christian against Jew and, frequently, against fellow Christians. The Crusades became "crusades" for a vague and often arbitrary ideal of religious absolutism, and thus atrocities were committed—in the name of God.

It is easy, therefore, to see the Crusades as acts of evil committed in the name of Christianity. In many cases, this perception is all too accurate. The idea that only Christians and not Muslims (or anyone else) had a right to occupy the Holy Land is arbitrary, self-righteous, and unjustified. On the other hand, the notion that the Crusaders invaded the peaceful realm of Islam, where everyone was minding their own business, is equally distorted and misguided. As it existed in the Middle Ages, Islam divided the world into territory it held, territory it intended to take—the *dar al-harb*, or realm of war—and territory with whose people it intended to coexist. In the era of the Crusades, no side had a monopoly on aggression and inhumanity.

VOICES

The Crusades—the most signal and most durable monument of human folly that has yet appeared in any age or nation.

—David Hume, *The History of England* (1754-1761)

The Crusades of 1095–1149

Modern Westerners are deeply disturbed by the Islamic idea of *jihad*, or holy war, the linking of religion, international politics, and combat. This seems alien to Western traditions, but the fact is that Pope Urban II never used the word *crusade* in his call to action, but framed the military expedition as a pilgrimage, a religious duty. In this, his approach was virtually identical to how the caliphs rallied military action. Moreover, while the pope called on Western Christians to march to the aid of their Eastern coreligionists, he also emphasized that the ultimate destination was the Holy Land—most specifically Jerusalem.

Like Muslims who believed in the sacred nature of certain holy places—Mecca, Medina, Karbala—medieval Christians conceived of holiness in very physical terms. Piety and good works were one thing, but actually journeying to the epicenter of the religion, Jerusalem, was the ultimate "spiritual" journey. Indeed, both before and after the era of the Crusades, many thousands of Europeans made the extremely expensive and hazardous trip.

 **DEFINITION**

> **Jihad** is a holy war waged on behalf of Islam and undertaken as a religious duty. Jihad accurately describes the Muslim response to the Crusades, but the Arabic word itself is not recorded until the mid-nineteenth century. **Crusade** originally applied to a holy war fought under sanction from the pope and to the military expeditions into the Holy Land conducted by European Christians during the eleventh through thirteenth centuries. The word was not coined until the sixteenth century, from the French *croisade*, derived from *croisée*, meaning "marked with the cross."

The First Crusade

Inspired by a French priest known as Peter the Hermit, a so-called People's Crusade, consisting mostly of peasants, embarked for the Holy Land just after Easter 1066. When they reached the Byzantine Empire, Emperor Alexios pleaded with them to await the arrival of the "official" army of knights and nobles, so that they might be most effectively led into combat. Instead, the members of the People's Crusade pushed on—and were ambushed by Turkish forces. Of perhaps 20,000 (the number is uncertain), all but 3,000 were killed or captured.

The "official" armies did not leave France and Italy until August and September 1096, respectively. The total strength of these forces may have reached 100,000. Emperor Alexios did not greet their arrival in Constantinople with unalloyed rejoicing. It occurred to him that so large an army of *Western* Christians might just as well decide to act against his own Eastern forces. But the leaders pledged to restore to his empire all territories Byzantium had lost to the Turks.

The armies were led by members of the principal nobility of Western Europe. Notably absent, however, were Philip I, king of France, and Holy Roman Emperor Henry IV, both of whom were in dispute with the pope. Like the Muslims, the Christians were far from unified.

The first major engagement of the Crusades was the Siege of Antioch, an ancient city straddling the Orontes River in what is today Hatay Province, Turkey. Begun in October 1097, the siege lasted until June 1098, when the Crusaders finally breached the city's walls. As happens most often after a prolonged siege, those who entered the city indulged in an orgy of pillage and mayhem. Muslims were slaughtered wherever the Crusaders found them.

The fabled Turkish commander Kerbogha led a countersiege against the Crusaders who now occupied the city. Under Bohemond, prince of Taranto (in Italy), the Crusaders rallied to defeat Kerbogha on June 28. Having won Antioch—twice—they confirmed Alexios's worst fears when they refused to restore the city to Byzantine control. Instead, Bohemond named himself prince of Antioch.

From Antioch, a contingent of the Crusader force—mostly Franks, much reduced by battle and disease—marched on to Jerusalem, reaching the city walls on June 7, 1099. In defense of the city, Jews united with Muslims, but to no avail. On July 15, 1099, the Franks entered Jerusalem and slaughtered the Muslims along with their Jewish allies. They also targeted the sacred symbols of Islam, looting and then razing the city's mosques.

 VOICES

Wonderful sights were to be seen. Some of our men (and this was more merciful) cut off the heads of their enemies; others shot them with arrows, so that they fell from the towers; others tortured them longer by casting them into the flames. ... [I]n the temple and the porch of Solomon, men rode in blood up to their knees and bridle reins. Indeed it was a just and splendid judgment of God that this place should be filled with the blood of unbelievers since it had suffered so long from their blasphemies.

—Raymond D'Aguilers, chronicler of the First Crusade, account of the Battle of Jerusalem in *Historia Francorum qui ceperunt Iherusalem*, 1099

Aftermath of the First Crusade

Not only did the Crusaders withhold Antioch and Jerusalem from Byzantine control, they proclaimed the creation of four so-called "Crusader states": County of Edessa, Principality of Antioch, County of Tripoli, and the Kingdom of Jerusalem. Moreover, the success of the First Crusade opened the floodgates of radical Christian rhetoric and preaching directed not solely against Muslims but everyone perceived as outside the faith. Throughout Europe, anti-Jewish pogroms were unleashed, resulting in the massacre of entire European Jewish communities. And far from uniting Western and Eastern Christians, the post-First Crusade rhetoric stirred massacres of Eastern Orthodox Christians as well.

Additional efforts followed the First Crusade, though none came close to achieving the success of the first. When three of the cities captured by the Crusaders—Mosul, Aleppo, and Edessa—were retaken by Islamic forces in 1127, 1128, and 1144, respectively, Pope Eugenius III, early in 1145, proclaimed a new crusade, which historians refer to as the Second Crusade, spanning 1147–1149.

In response to the new onslaught, Nur ad-Din, the *atabeg* (crown prince) of Aleppo, proclaimed a jihad against the Crusaders, who were quickly defeated in their attempt to capture Damascus. A Crusader contingent that passed through Portugal, however, was successful in retaking Lisbon from the Muslims in 1147, and in 1148, the Spanish city of Tortosa was reclaimed as well.

Those Crusaders who limped back from the Holy Land, having achieved nothing, took out their frustration in a new series of pogroms directed against the "Christ-killing Jews" of Europe.

Saladin Triumphs

Despite setbacks, the Crusader states waged a vigorous war against Egypt's Fatamid caliph, who called on Nur ad-Din for help. He responded by dispatching Shirkuh, his most celebrated commander, to Egypt. By the time Shirkuh and his nephew, a timid young man named Yusuf, arrived to do battle, however, the Christians, daunted by the resistance they had encountered at Cairo, had already withdrawn. The grateful caliph nevertheless credited Shirkuh with the victory and appointed him vizier (prime minister) of Egypt.

The only thing Shirkuh was more famous for than his military prowess was his gluttony. Within two months of becoming vizier, he dropped dead following an eating binge. Nur ad-Din replaced him with, of all people, the timid Yusuf, who interpreted his selection as nothing less than a sign from Allah and instantly transformed himself from a frightened youth into a pious Muslim and fearless commander. Casting aside his former name with his former self, he took the name Salah ad-Din— "Righteousness of the Faith"—and became known in the English-speaking world as Saladin.

Nur ad-Din commanded his new vizier to replace Egypt's Shiite Islam with Sunni. It was a tall order indeed, but such was Saladin's powerful presence that the people simply accepted the transformation. Saladin then led Egyptian forces in renewed attacks against the Crusaders. In 1174, when Nur ad-Din succumbed to a heart attack, Saladin succeeded him.

Saladin conducted a new kind of combat, which combined brilliant tactics ferociously executed with honor and compassion for his enemies. He also thoroughly inculcated religious values in his soldiers, creating an army guided by skill and driven by religious fervor. They took Aleppo from the Crusaders in 1181. Crusader commander Reynauld of Chantillon responded by mounting an attack on Mecca and Medina, an assault Saladin used as the occasion to mount a massive jihad. In 1183, he began a determined offensive against the Kingdom of Jerusalem. After two years, Reynauld and Saladin concluded a truce—which Reynauld quickly violated by ambushing caravans. At this, Saladin renewed his attacks on Jerusalem, which fell to him in 1187.

Saladin

Saladin (ca. 1138–1193) was born in Tikrit, Mesopotamia, the son of an influential Kurdish family. As a young man, he accompanied his uncle on a military expedition to liberate Egypt from the Frankish domination brought by the First Crusade. When his uncle died, about 1169, he became vizier of Egypt and the commander of Syrian troops. Within two years, he established himself as the sole ruler of Egypt.

Saladin set as his goal bringing the entire Middle East under the standard of Islam. To achieve unification, he either negotiated with or fought various Islamic rulers. As part of his effort, he transformed the Muslim lands into a haven for religious scholars and teachers, to whom he assigned responsibility for instilling the tenets of Islam in the masses.

By 1187, Saladin had so consolidated the Islamic Empire that he now felt prepared to turn from battle against his Muslim rivals to wage war on the Crusader states. In northern Palestine, on July 4, 1187, Saladin and his magnificently trained army met a poorly equipped Frankish army near the city of Tiberius. Within hours, the Islamic forces had routed the Franks. Three months later, Saladin was in control of Acre, Toron, Beirut, Sidon, Nazareth, Caesarea, Nabulus, Jaffa, Ascalon, and Jerusalem. In victory, Saladin typically treated the defeated Christians far better than the Crusaders ever treated those whom they had conquered.

When news of the fall of the Kingdom of Jerusalem reached Europe, Richard I the Lionheart of England, Philip II of France, and Frederick I Barbarossa of Germany took their armies to the Holy Land in a Third Crusade. Frederick drowned while trying to cross the Saleph Göksu River in Turkey, and Philip returned to Europe before committing to combat. On his own, Richard concluded a peace with Saladin, which left the Muslim leader with his Islamic Empire intact, Jerusalem included.

Throughout his reign, Saladin exercised great diplomatic and military skill. His unification of Islamic nations into a single military power strengthened the culture and religion of the Muslim world. He died in Damascus on March 4, 1193, shortly after the end of the Third Crusade.

The Crusades of 1187–1272

Profoundly shaken by news of Saladin's victories, Pope Urban III was felled by a massive heart attack on October 19, 1187. His successor, Pope Gregory VIII, promulgated the bull *Audita tremendi* on October 29, calling for a Third Crusade.

In response to the papal call, Emperor Frederick I Barbarossa of Germany, King Philip II of France, and England's King Richard I—soon to be known as Richard the Lionheart—assembled armies.

An Abortive Campaign

From the beginning, the new crusade did not go well. Barbarossa died en route, leading to mass desertions before his forces ever approached the Holy Land, and although the other two armies arrived intact, they were torn by political dispute. King Philip abandoned most of his soldiers in the field, returning to France with a few loyal followers.

Left to carry on alone, Richard captured Cyprus in 1191—not from Muslims, but from the Orthodox Christians of the Byzantine Empire. He did retake Acre (in modern Israel) from the Muslims, however, and, defeating Muslim forces again, recaptured the important port of Jaffa (in present-day Tel Aviv, Israel). This put him and his men in sight of Jerusalem, but supply problems prevented their taking the city. Richard I negotiated peace with Saladin, winning the right of Christian merchants to trade in the city and Christian pilgrims to visit it, but leaving Jerusalem under Saladin's control. With that, the Third Crusade simply petered out.

Christian Against Christian

Not surprisingly, the Third Crusade tore Western and Eastern Christianity even farther apart, and when the Fourth Crusade was launched in 1201, it never even reached the fringes of the Holy Land. The Crusaders got as far as Constantinople—which they sacked and occupied, not only seizing control of the Byzantine capital from the Byzantine Empire, but transforming Constantinople and environs into yet another Crusader state. The Fourth Crusade ended in 1204, but the Byzantine army would not retake the city until 1261.

The Final Crusades

There would be five more Crusades important enough to be numbered by historians, but they accomplished little beyond bloodshed. Pope Innocent III proclaimed the Fifth Crusade in 1217, and his call was answered mostly by German, Flemish, and Frisian nobility in addition to a large contingent from Hungary. Damietta, a Lower Nile city in Egypt a short distance inland from the Mediterranean, fell to the Crusaders in November 1219, but the Christian armies made no further gains. After suffering defeat at the hands of Al-Kamil, sultan of Egypt, Damietta was returned to Egyptian control, an eight-year truce was concluded, the Crusaders withdrew, and the Fourth Crusade ended in 1204.

Following the failure of the Fifth Crusade, Holy Roman Emperor Frederick II promised to organize a sixth, but reneged so often that Pope Gregory IX excommunicated him in 1228. Undaunted, Frederick at last sailed that year, landed at Saint-Jean d'Acre (in modern Israel) in September 1228 but, instead of fighting, made a treaty with Al-Kamil. It gave Christians ruling power over most of Jerusalem in addition to a strip of land running from Acre to Jerusalem. Certain sacred areas of the city were reserved to Muslim control, and Frederick pledged his protection of Al-Kamil against all his enemies, Christians included.

In 1244, Al-Kamil's son al-Salih Ayyub led an army of tribal warriors from the Khwarezmid Empire—Sunni Muslims centered in Persia and often called Mamluks—in a successful invasion of Jerusalem. Ayyub's uncle Ismail joined forces with the Franks and with the emir of Homs to fight the Khwarezmians in Gaza. The Mamluks quickly defeated the troops of the Christian/Muslim alliance, an event that prompted King Louis IX of France to organize a Seventh Crusade.

Recruitment consumed years, and Louis did not sail from France until May 1249. He and his Crusaders landed near Damietta in June and then had to await the end of the seasonal Nile flood before they could commence their march inland. Reaching Al Mansurah, Egypt, they found themselves massively outnumbered. Louis's 15,000 men were overwhelmed by some 70,000 Ayyubid fighters. The entire French army was annihilated, except for the king, who was captured and ransomed for a vast sum, whereupon a 10-year truce was called.

In 1270, 20 years after his defeat at the hands of the Mamluks, Louis IX launched an attack against the Arabs in Tunisia. Plagued by disease and his own inept leadership, the men of this Eighth Crusade either died or withdrew. Louis himself perished in Tunis on August 25, 1270, a victim of bubonic plague or of dysentery. He was canonized as Saint Louis in 1297, but his ill-conceived final expedition was the last major Crusade. In a bloody campaign, the Mamluk leader Baibars drove all the Franks out of the Holy Land. Edward Longshanks—the future King Edward I of England—arrived in Acre in May 1271 but, vastly outnumbered, he and his "Ninth Crusade" did nothing other than broker a truce between Baibars and Hugh, the Frankish king of Jerusalem.

Bloody Legacy

Christians and Muslims alike drew blood and were bloodied by the Crusades. In 1291, nearly 20 years after the abortive Ninth Crusade ended, Al-Ashraf Khalil, Mamluk sultan of Egypt, overran Acre, the last major outpost of Christianity in the Holy Land. Christian soldiers, knights, and civilians were slaughtered indiscriminately, women and children included. Those Christians who heard the accounts of the few survivors branded all of Islam brutal and bloodthirsty. In doing so, however, they forgot the slaughters perpetrated earlier by Crusaders—against Muslims (in 1099, for example, Richard I the Lionheart slaughtered all 2,700 of his Muslim prisoners of war), against Jews, and against those fellow Christians deemed to be insufficiently or incorrectly faithful. Today, some 800 years after the last Crusade, both Muslims and Christians have an ample store of horrific stories with which to demonize one another.

The Least You Need to Know

* Although the words *crusade* and *jihad* did not come into use until many years later, the concept of war in the name of religion was indelibly etched by the Crusades—for both Christians and Muslims.

* Historians recognize nine numbered Crusades, but the period 1096 to 1285 was marked by nearly continuous warfare between Muslims and Christians, as well as among Muslims and among Christians.

* Both Muslims and Christians committed horrific atrocities in God's name. Only one warrior-leader emerged from this period as just and capable of both tolerance and even mercy—the founder of the Ayyubid Dynasty, Saladin.

* Of the nine numbered Crusades, only the first ended in substantial Christian victories. The rest were either Muslim triumphs or bloody draws.

The Mongol Invasions

In our post-9/11 world, it is all too easy to see a "clash of civilizations" between the nations of Islam and those predominantly Christian. It's also tempting to believe this clash began during the Crusades. Beyond question, the Crusades scarred Muslim/Christian relations painfully, deeply, and, evidently, indelibly. They did not, however, directly transform the Middle East into a modern battleground on which Muslims and Christians inevitably feel compelled to fight. Rather, the Crusades were a product of mutual religious conviction and intolerance, and they created a compelling metaphor that strongly influences—in predominantly Muslim as well as predominantly Christian nations—the rhetoric that has been used to justify European imperialism and colonialism in the Middle East and has guided numerous conflicts in the nineteenth, twentieth, and twenty-first centuries.

Yet, even in this limited metaphorical sense, the history of conflict that has long unfolded in the Middle East is not a just a matter of Christian versus Muslim or of West versus Middle East. Although many Westerners think of the modern Middle East as the product of its many clashes with the West, the region's early history was, if anything, even more profoundly shaped by its encounter with a figure who vies with both Jesus and Muhammad for his impact on history.

In This Chapter

- The struggle of Temujin
- The rise of Genghis Khan
- The Mongol conquest of the caliphates
- Mongol shamanism
- Why Genghis Khan is a hero among many Muslims

From Outcast to Universal Ruler

Genghis Khan—the Great Khan, or the "Universal Ruler"—founded the Mongol Empire, the largest contiguous empire history has ever known. His birth name was Temujin, and he was born into the Borjigin clan of the Khiyad tribe in the middle of the twelfth century. His origins are actually so obscure that the year of his birth is too uncertain even to debate, and historians content themselves with assigning it somewhere between 1155 and 1167.

Temujin's grandfather was Khabul Khan (reigned 1130–1146?), founder of the Khamag ("Whole") Mongol confederation of tribes, and his father was Yesukai the Strong, a prominent member of the Khamag royal clan. Temujin was thus positioned for power, but, when he was just eight or nine years old, a *Tartar* cabal poisoned his father. The motive of these nomads was nothing more or less than the settling of some old score, but Yesukai's murder made room for a rival family to muscle into leadership of the clan, whose members refused to be led by Temujin, a mere boy. Worse, the entire Khiyad tribe turned its collective back on all of Yesukai's heirs, including Temujin, his four siblings (three brothers and a sister), and their mother, Hoelun, in addition to a pair of half-brothers.

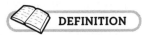   DEFINITION

> During the Middle Ages, Europeans applied the term **Tartar** to anyone from the Great Steppe (the region stretching from the Caspian Sea and the Ural Mountains to the Pacific Ocean), a region Europeans called Tartary. Those who lived here included Cossacks and Mongols as well as a variety of Turkic peoples. The so-called Tartars who poisoned the father of Genghis Khan, were undoubtedly of Turkic origin.

The family's reversal of fortune ignited within Hoelun a determined passion to see her eldest son claim his birthright as a Mongol chief. Accordingly, she taught him to surround himself with a loyal band of men. It was a lesson Temujin never forgot and endeavored always to implement.

Guided by his mother's tutelage and driven by desperate poverty, Temujin developed his prodigious natural talent for the hunt, and thus the family was saved from starvation. Hunting also led to his development as a skilled and fearless warrior. His feats of the hunt rapidly won him an impressive following—not that family life was all loving and peaceful. When Temujin and his half-brother Bheter fell out over division of a hunting catch, Temujin killed him.

Hoelun

Hoelun, the mother of Genghis Khan, was born into the Olkhunut tribe, from which she was abducted about 1159 by Yesukai, a prominent member of the Borjigin clan of the Khiyad tribe. Hoelun was quickly reconciled to her fate when Yesukai made her his chief wife, which meant that she was eligible to bear the heirs to power and position within the Borjigin clan. These included five children, the oldest son being Temujin—the future Genghis Khan.

After Yesukai was assassinated by poisoning, the Khiyad tribe spurned Hoelun and her children. Forced into exile, she struggled to raise her family on the Mongolian steppes. She taught her children the value of loyalty and self-reliance, and she encouraged Temujin in the development of his hunting and martial skills. She also never let him forget that his birthright was to lead his clan and tribe. Even after Temujin married Börte—a union that had been arranged by his late father—Hoelun remained his closest confidant and counselor. Neither the date of her birth nor death is known.

The Legend Begins

Temujin found an opportunity to exercise power when Börte, his bride by an arranged marriage, was abducted and ravished by the Merkit clan. The young man struck a sly alliance with an acquaintance of his father's and was thereby able to borrow from him an entire army, which he led against the Merkit in 1180. Not only did Temujin redeem his bride, he annihilated the enemy clan in the process—a deed of arms that instantly won him a very large following, including his *own* private army of some 20,000.

Early Conquests

While Temujin fought the Merkit, another clan, the Jurkin, exploited his absence to plunder the small store of treasure he had begun to accumulate. On his return, Temujin turned this misfortune to his advantage, using it to create a reputation for utter ruthlessness.

He set about swiftly exterminating all of the Jurkin nobility, an act that made him both feared and respected. It also determined his future strategic course. Henceforth, he would leave no enemy or potential enemy at his back, but would destroy or neutralize all rivals before advancing to the next conquest. Opponents had either to be entirely subjugated or totally annihilated.

After a series of conquests carried out on this principle, Temujin maneuvered for a showdown with the Tartars—the very people who had killed his father and were the chief obstacle to further conquests. Although an alliance with the eastern Mongols had made them more formidable than ever, Temujin routed the Tartar army in 1201. Having defeated the Tartars militarily, he then systematically slaughtered every adult taller than the height of a cart axle. He reasoned that adults were already set in their ways and therefore impossible to convert into loyal subjects. Rather than trying to coerce loyalty, he killed them, so that they could not pass on their enmities to their children. In this way, Temujin believed he could cultivate a generation completely loyal to himself.

 **VOICES**

The greatest happiness is to vanquish your enemies, to chase them before you, to rob them of their wealth, to see those dear to them bathed in tears, to clasp to your bosom their wives and daughters.

—Genghis Khan

Temujin Becomes Genghis Khan

In 1203, Temujin conquered the Naiman and Karait tribes, and by 1204 he built a capital city at Karakorum and was universally acknowledged master of Mongolia. It was during this period, at a grand assembly of clans by the River Onon, that Temujin took the name by which he is known to history: Genghis Khan, "universal ruler."

Beyond Mongolia

Having unified all of the Mongolian clans under his rule, Genghis Khan next led the Mongols to conquests beyond the *steppes* of Central Asia. As effective as he had been in conquering Mongolia, it was only now that the full extent of his military genius manifested itself. When fighting tribal wars, he had relied exclusively on swift but lightly armed cavalry, riding tough Mongolian ponies against nomadic peoples. He recognized that such cavalry tactics were of little use in assaulting cities, such as those of China. So he quickly mastered the art of the siege, learning the use of works, catapults, ladders, burning oil, and even accomplishing such engineering feats as diverting rivers to either flood a city or deprive it of water.

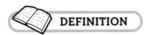

DEFINITION

The Central Asian **steppe** is prairie-like savannah grassland, insufficiently watered to support a forest but not sufficiently dry to be a desert. The so-called "Great Steppe" stretches from Ukraine through parts of Russia, Kazakhstan, Turkmenistan, and Uzbekistan.

Genghis Khan used siege tactics in his invasions of the Western Hsia Empire in 1205, 1207, and 1209. He recruited Chinese engineers to help him breach city walls. In April 1211, he crossed the Great Wall of China itself to begin his conquest of the realm of the Chin Dynasty of northern China. By 1215, Peking (Beijing) fell to him, and within the space of two more years, the last Chin resistance was neutralized.

Into the Caliphate

From China, Genghis Khan turned to Khwarezm, a large oasis region—center of the Khwarezmian Empire—that today is partly in Uzbekistan, Kazakhstan, and Turkmenistan. Taking as his pretext for invasion the fact that a minor Khwarezmi official had killed a Mongol trading envoy, Genghis led an invasion of 200,000 troops, who simply consumed everything in their path. From here, he rode into the rest of the imperial realms, on to Transoxiana (Bukhara and Samarkand), Khorasan, Afghanistan, and northwestern India, all of which fell to him in quick succession.

In 1220, he defeated the forces of Muhammad II of Khwarezm, shah of the Khwarezmian Empire, and sacked the cities of Samarkand, Bukhara, Otrar, and others. Muhammad II's son, Jalal as-Din Mingburnu, attempted a stand against Genghis at the Indus River in a battle of November 24, 1221, but was defeated.

Genghis Khan now held a large portion of the Muslim caliphate, but he was forced to turn his attention in 1225 to northwestern China in order to crush a rebellion against him. Although he won a great battle on the Yellow River in December 1226, a new Chin rebellion broke out the following year. Genghis Khan succumbed to an illness on August 18, 1227, before this latest uprising was suppressed.

 DID YOU KNOW?

> Genghis Khan died at roughly the age of 65 from causes that historians have debated. Most believe that he fell from his horse while hunting and later succumbed to internal injuries. A traditional folktale holds that, when Genghis attempted to ravage a Tangut (Western Xia Dynasty) princess, she castrated him with a knife she had hidden in her vagina. He never recovered from the "operation."

After Genghis

The death of Genghis Khan did not end the Mongol invasion of the Middle East. On the contrary, his campaigns were only the beginning of Mongol conquests in the caliphates.

Anatolia

Anatolia, today also known as Asia Minor or Asian Turkey, makes up most of the territory of modern Turkey. It is strategically located at the doorstep of Europe, with the Black Sea to its north, the Mediterranean to its south, and the Aegean to its west. Far from being an impediment to conquest, the vast extent of this region perfectly suited the highly mobile tactics of the Mongols. Indeed, recent historical climate studies suggest that an unusually wet weather pattern in the steppes predated Genghis Khan's westward expansion. It may be that this climate anomaly increased the grass yield of the typically meager steppes, enabling the horde to ride greater distances than ever before. In any event, the Mongols completed the conquest of Anatolia between 1241 and 1243, when the Seljuks surrendered. From 1243 to the end of the first third of the fourteenth century, Anatolia was ruled by Mongols, who were repeatedly obliged to put down rebellions raised by the Seljuk sultans.

Syria

In the thirteenth century, Syria spanned most of the eastern shore of the Mediterranean Sea. Beginning in the 1240s, Mongol armies repeatedly invaded Syria. Although they were often unsuccessful in taking the key fortified cities of the region, their reputation for brutality was such that regional rulers submitted to Mongol authority rather than risk annihilation. The leaders of Aleppo, in the north, agreed to pay a heavy tribute, as did Bohemond VI, Christian prince of Antioch and count of Tripoli. Sultan Saleeh offered no resistance to the invaders elsewhere in Syria, and in 1251, Sultan Nasir concluded a peace by formally making Syria a Mongolian vassal state.

Siege of Baghdad

On January 29, 1258, Hulagu Khan, grandson of Genghis, laid siege to Baghdad, capital of the Abbasid Caliphate and the cultural center of the Muslim world. He demanded of Caliph Al-Musta'sim continued submission to the Mongol khan as well as troops to support the ongoing Mongol campaigns in Iran. When the caliph refused, Hulagu continued the siege until Baghdad fell on February 10, 1258.

For a week, the Mongol warriors sacked the city, not only committing a variety of atrocities against residents, but looting and vandalizing the great libraries that represented learning far beyond that of medieval Europe. Slaughter was general, and the great city was left severely depopulated.

 **VOICES**

> They [the Mongols] swept through the city like hungry falcons attacking a flight of doves, or like raging wolves attacking sheep, with loose reins and shameless faces, murdering and spreading terror ... beds and cushions made of gold and encrusted with jewels were cut to pieces with knives and torn to shreds. Those hiding behind the veils of the great Harem were dragged ... through the streets and alleys, each of them becoming a plaything ... as the population died at the hands of the invaders.
>
> —Abdullah Wassaf, Persian historian and contemporary of Marco Polo

A Surprising Legacy

The terror and destruction wrought upon the Islamic realm by Genghis Khan and his successors was far more intense than anything that the Europeans had perpetrated during the Crusades. Indeed, the siege and sack of Baghdad marked the end of Islam's so-called Golden Age, during which the caliphates stretched from the Iberian Peninsula (Spain and Portugal) to the Sindh (in what is today Pakistan), and when Islamic culture, art, and learning were shining beacons piercing the so-called Dark Ages of Europe.

And yet, whereas the legacy of the European Crusades remains bitter and intensely provocative throughout the modern Middle East, Genghis Khan is respected—even revered—as a role model, the equivalent of Alexander the Great, a conqueror so successful that he must have been blessed by God himself.

What accounts for this surprising legacy, so different from what the Crusaders created? For one thing, while Genghis Khan and those Mongol leaders who followed him were extraordinarily good at conquest, they were miserably unsuccessful at long-term occupation. The *Ilkhanate*, the breakaway state of the Mongol Empire established by Hulagu over Persia and its neighbors in Mesopotamia and present-day Turkey, lasted only from 1256 to 1335. And then it was gone, along with most of its cultural influence. The Mongol Empire itself did not last much longer, dissolving by 1368.

DEFINITION

> The **Ilkhanate** was an independent Mongol state—it broke away from the Mongol Empire—and was ruled by Hulagu and his descendants from 1256 to 1335. It encompassed Persia, its near neighbors, and central and eastern Turkey.

Second, while Genghis and his successors conquered much Muslim territory, they also hit the non-Muslim world very hard, especially Europe and Asia. Vassals of the Mongol Empire ultimately included Korea, China, Russia, the Caucasus, and much of Eastern Europe, in addition to the Middle East. The Muslim world has always understood that, in the Mongol conquests, it was hardly a lone victim. Muslims also blame internal conflict—the Ridda wars and the Umayyad decadency of the eighth century—for weakening the *dar al-Islam* before the Mongol invasion.

Finally, and perhaps most of all, whereas the Christian Crusaders were intent on wiping out Islam, the Mongols had no such religious agenda. Their own religious tradition was shamanistic—a term applied to spiritual traditions that, lacking a formal theology or doctrine, are more a collection of magico-religious practices than a compelling and cohesive religious faith.

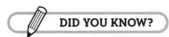
DID YOU KNOW?

> The royal courts of Genghis Khan and the Mongol khans who followed him included Buddhists, Christians, and Muslims, in addition to shamanist Mongols.

If anything, the Mongols tended to absorb the culture of those they conquered rather than impose their own culture upon them. It is a testament to the weak hold their own shamanism had over them that, in Muslim territories where the Mongols lingered, they almost always converted to Islam. Indeed, in the Crimea, on the fringes of European Russia, the Mongol invaders were heralds of Tartar tribal groups who were enthusiastic Muslims. In Uzbekistan, Timur—also known as Tamerlane—combined Turkish and Mongol bloodlines and founded during the first half of the fifteenth century a hybrid Mongol/Islamic empire that included parts of Iran, India, Russia, Turkey, and Syria. Thus, by the beginning of the fifteenth century, the Mongol invasion of the caliphates came full circle, ending in a new rising of Islam.

Historically, whereas the Christian/Islam conflict of the Crusades resolved nothing, the clash between Muslims and Mongols ended in a total power vacuum. Genghis Khan and those who followed in his footsteps created no central religious authority or tradition. The vacuum would be filled by the leaders of a yet another empire—that of the Ottoman Turks, the subject of the next chapter.

The Least You Need to Know

- Although many Westerners think of the Crusades as the defining early conflict in the Muslim Middle East, of arguably even greater contemporary impact were the Mongol invasions of the thirteenth and fourteenth centuries.

- Temujin rose from obscurity to become Genghis Khan, founder of the largest contiguous empire in history and conqueror (for a time) of most of the Muslim caliphates.

- In contrast to the Christian-led Crusades, the Mongol invasions of the Middle East, destructive as they were, did not create an enduring legacy of bitterness and retribution—probably because the Mongols imposed neither their culture nor their religion on those they conquered.

The Ottoman Era

Mesopotamians, Arabs, Persians, or Mongols—any of these might have become the dominant power in the Middle East during the latter Middle Ages. But none of them did. Instead, a most unlikely people prevailed. Like Genghis Khan and the hordes who followed him, these people came from Central Asia, but not as conquerors—not at first. At first, they were slaves.

The Rise of Osman Bey

The Turkic tribes that became the origin of the Ottoman Empire first encountered Islam as it expanded from the Middle East into Central Asia during the twelfth century. Like the Mongols of Genghis Khan, these Proto-Turks originally practiced a shamanist religion rather than a "revealed" religion, like Judaism, Christianity, or Islam. Driven by highly organized religious zeal, the Muslims overran the Proto-Turks and enslaved many of them. The conquerors were particularly interested in the warriors: although many of the Turkic tribespeople were insufficiently organized to resist the Muslim onslaught, these fighters were extraordinary cavalrymen, capable of hitting moving targets at a full gallop.

In This Chapter

- The birth of the Ottoman Empire under Osman I

- Osman's creation of a strong central government and powerful state military

- A European coalition is defeated at Nicopolis—the "final Crusade"

- Timur defeats the Ottoman Empire—temporarily

- The reign of Suleiman I the Magnificent—apogee of Ottoman power

- The Ottoman Empire transitions from sultanate to republic

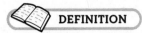

The term **Proto-Turkic** is used to describe predecessor languages to the modern Turkic languages spoken today mainly in Anatolia and the Balkans. *Proto-Turk* applies to a speaker of these historical languages and, by extension, a predecessor of the modern ethnic Turks.

Osman's Father

By the close of the twelfth century, the members of the Turkic Kayi tribe had, under Muslim influence, converted to Islam. Now they faced a new invader: the Mongols. A Kayi chief named Ertugrul led the Kayi west from Central Asia into Anatolia, the area that corresponds to modern Asian Turkey. Seeking protection against the Mongols, he vowed his allegiance to the Seljuk sultan Kayqubad I, who gave Ertugrul his blessing to establish a principality (called a *beylik*)—provided that he carved it out of the Byzantine territory adjoining Anatolia. He did just that in 1231, conquering the Byzantine town of Thebasion, which, renamed Sogut, became the capital of his beylik.

Fifty years after creating his principality, Ertugrul died, leaving his oldest son, Osman, to become prince—*bey*—of the beylik.

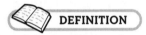

Beylik is a Turkish word designating the territory ruled by a **bey**. In Western European terms, it may be understood as a principality, and the bey as the equivalent of a prince.

Birth of an Empire

Osman came into power at the right place and the right time. Islamic troops poured into his beylik, looking to expand the Muslim realm deeper into the territory of Orthodox Christian Byzantium, which was well into its long decline. Osman's principality also benefitted from an influx of Turkic refugees in flight from the Mongols. Among these were skilled Ghazi warriors.

Osman rallied, organized, and—to a remarkable degree—united the newcomers, creating one of the most formidable armies in the Middle East.

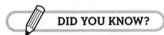

Some names are custom-made for ferocity: Ivan the Terrible, Stalin (meaning, in Russian, "Man of Steel"), and Osman—which means, in Turkish, "Bone-breaker."

In 1302, Osman defeated a Byzantine army at Nicaea (in northwestern Anatolia) and immediately settled more of his people on what had been Byzantine territory. So weakened was the Byzantine Empire that, instead of resisting, the Christian population withdrew, yielding more and more of Anatolia to Osman.

Having essentially given up on confronting Osman's forces on land, Byzantine leaders turned to their navy, hoping to block, by sea, his westward push into Europe. The strategy proved futile, however, and Osman relentlessly led Ottoman forces against the major Byzantine city of Ephesus, near the Aegean Sea. After this city fell to him, he drew upon his growing immigrant army to overrun Byzantine territory all along the Black Sea.

Osman spent the rest of his life and reign taking Anatolia from the Byzantine Empire. The culminating campaign of his career was the Siege of Bursa, in northwestern Anatolia, which fell to him on April 6, 1326, after more than six years under siege.

Osman I died at 68, shortly after the city fell. He had outlived the princes of the Alaeddin family, who had given him his initial beylik. This meant that no one contested his leadership of the Turks in his beylik and in the territories he had added to it. Only the emir of Karamanids, a beylik to the east of his, in south central Anatolia, offered himself as a rival.

The Conquests of Orhan and Murad I

Because Osman paid little attention to the Karamanid beylik, preferring instead to seize the much weaker Byzantine territories, the Karamanids remained rivals of the Ottomans long after his death. Nevertheless, when Osman's son, Orhan, succeeded his father, a large portion of the Turkish people were calling themselves "Osmanli"—or *Ottoman*—in honor of Osman.

Under Orhan, the government of the Ottoman Empire rapidly took shape. While Orhan assumed leadership of the military and was officially the head of state, he delegated most administrative authority to his brother Alaeddin as *vizier*. Technically, the Ottomans were still vassals of the Seljuk Turks, but Alaeddin immediately ended this subordination, removing the image of the Seljuk rulers from coinage and banning the invocation of their names in prayers.

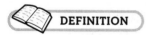 **DEFINITION**

> **Vizier** is the highest ranking adviser (in Turkish, *vezir* means "counselor") to the caliph or sultan. As the Ottoman government matured, a vizier became the equivalent of a cabinet minister, and grand vizier was, in effect, prime minister. A vizier might also serve as viceroy of a large province.

Either Alaeddin or Orhan himself decreed the creation of a standing professional army, which included the Janissaries, a force raised from the children of Christians the Ottomans had conquered. The Janissaries were not treated like prisoners or slaves; they lived well, were well trained, and were often given the opportunity to rise to posts of political power. The Janissaries remained a mainstay of the Ottoman military up to the reign of Sultan Mehmet IV in the seventeenth century.

Under Orhan, the Ottoman armies routed mercenary Byzantine forces at Darica (in the Marmara region of modern Turkey) in the 1329 Battle of Pelekanon. Byzantine Emperor Andronicus III was so thoroughly shaken by the defeat that he never again offered armed resistance against the Ottomans.

The next major Byzantine city to fall to Orhan was Nicaea (modern Iznik, Turkey) in 1331, after a marathon siege of three years. This prize was second only to Constantinople itself. From here, Orhan expanded in three directions, pushing the boundaries of the Ottoman Empire to the shore of the Aegean Sea to the west, the Sea of Marmara to the northwest, the Black Sea to the north, and the neighboring beylik of Candar in the east and the beylik of Aydin in the south. In terms of geography, this represented nearly fourfold growth.

 DID YOU KNOW?

> Under Murad I, troops for the Janissary corps were levied from Christian families throughout territories conquered by the Ottoman Empire under a system called *devşirme* ("collecting"). Conscripts were scouted by imperial agents, who designated some boys for military service in the Janissary corps, others for nonmilitary palace service, others for religious service, and still others to serve as scribes. Officially called "Slaves of the Porte" or "door servants," the Janissaries were salaried, allowed to retire on a government pension, and free to marry. Over the years, they became a distinct community within the Ottoman Empire, amassing power comparable to the aristocratic classes, and many Christian Ottoman families freely volunteered their children for recruitment because it offered the potential of influence, power, and wealth.

Like Father, Like Son

Upon Orhan's death in 1362, his son Murad succeeded to what was now not merely a beylik but a sultanate, a realm ruled by a sultan, or emperor. Although the Byzantine city of Constantinople still loomed as the crowning prize for the rising empire, Murad I chose to bypass it and instead swept through the Balkans in 1385. He captured much of Bulgaria, but was unable to overcome resistance in Serbia. At the same time, he pushed Ottoman territory far to the south, driving a wedge between the beyliks of Aydin and Karaman to seize a portion of the Mediterranean shoreline anchored by the important city of Antalya.

The Battle of Kosovo

In 1389, Murad turned once more against the Serbs, who had earlier defeated him. At the Battle of Kosovo, on June 15, 1389, he led possibly as many as 40,000 men (estimates rise from a low of 27,000) against a Serbian-Bosnian army of 12,000 to 30,000 men. In the ensuing combat, both sides lost most of their troops, and both leaders—Murad and Serbia's Prince Lazar—were killed. In immediate tactical terms, the battle was a catastrophically bloody draw, but, in the long term, it was a strategic victory for the Ottomans because it brought Islam into the European Balkans.

In the even longer term, however, the Battle of Kosovo became a symbol of Serbian Christian patriotism, leading to a nationalist movement in the nineteenth century and an intense desire to break away from both Ottoman rule and domination by the Austro-Hungarian Empire. A Serbian nationalist secret society trained and funded Gavrilo Princip, the Bosnian Serb whose assassination of the Austrian Archduke Franz Ferdinand and his wife, Sophie, in 1914 triggered World War I. In the early 1990s, memories of the Battle of Kosovo were invoked when Serbia's dictator Slobodan Milosevic stirred a genocidal campaign against Muslim Kosovars during the breakup of Yugoslavia.

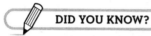

DID YOU KNOW?

Murad I was killed during the Battle of Kosovo, but just who killed him remains a mystery. A frequently cited Western source reports that, early in the battle, he was knifed to death by a Serbian knight named Miloš Obilić. Ottoman chroniclers report that he was assassinated after the battle ended, while he was inspecting the battlefield. Still others believe that a man he admitted to his tent on the night after the battle, who had come on pretext of seeking a favor, treacherously killed him. The last two accounts do not identify the assassin, and no one was ever captured or punished.

Murad's elder son, Bayezid, who commanded the left flank of the Ottoman forces during the battle, succeeded to the throne upon his father's death. Bayezid summoned his younger brother, Yakub Bey (commander of the right flank), to the headquarters tent, ostensibly to inform him of their father's death. When Yakub Bey arrived, however, he was waylaid and strangled, almost certainly at Bayezid's command. This left Bayezid as the sole heir.

Europe Stumbles at Nicopolis: 1396

In addition to ordering the strangulation of his brother, Bayezid further secured his power by making a political marriage to Princess Olivera Despina, daughter of the slain Serbian leader Prince Lazar. Bayezid recognized Lazar's son as the new Serbian prince, but also ensured that he would rule as a vassal of the Ottoman Empire. Thus the Ottoman hold on Eastern Europe became both strong and extensive.

From 1389 to 1395, Bayezid I led campaigns into Bulgaria (to capture what his predecessors had left unconquered) and into northern Greece. He attacked Wallachia (in modern Romania) in 1394 or 1395, but the enemy stopped his advance at the Danube.

Undaunted, Bayezid also laid siege to Constantinople, hitherto the most elusive European prize the Ottomans coveted. The Byzantine Emperor Manuel II Palaeologus revived the Crusade tradition by organizing the so-called Crusade of Nicopolis. This brought together an army of Hungarians, Bulgarians, Wallachians, French, Burgundians, and Germans—in addition to ships of the Venetian navy—in an effort to raise the Ottoman siege of Constantinople. This coalition did battle against the Ottoman army at Nicopolis, in Bulgaria, on September 25, 1396.

The two sides were about equally matched at some 15,000 men each, and both took heavy casualties, but the Crusaders suffered almost total annihilation. Only a very small portion of the Christian army survived to retreat. As many as 3,000 prisoners of war (estimates vary from a low of 300) were put to death by the Ottomans in retaliation for an atrocity the Crusaders had committed on the eve of the battle—the slaughter of a thousand or more Muslim civilian hostages.

Constantinople did not fall to the Ottomans at this time, but Bulgaria remained firmly under Ottoman control, and Europe declined to mount any new Crusade against the Muslim invaders.

The Ottoman Rout at Ankara: 1402

Although the Crusade of Nicopolis failed to halt the advance of Islam into Europe under the Ottoman banner, and even though the Ottoman Empire now controlled virtually all Byzantine lands around Constantinople, the city itself—a citadel surrounded by great stone walls that were the most formidable and complex fortification system of antiquity and the Middle Ages—still remained under Byzantine control.

On July 20, 1402, Bayezid I led an army against the Turko-Mongol forces of Timur (also known as Tamerlane), ruler of the Timurid Empire. Between 1370 and 1507, this Sunni Muslim empire controlled most of what is today Iran, Afghanistan, much of Central Asia, and parts of India, Pakistan, Mesopotamia, the Caucasus, and portions of Anatolia. Bayezid and Timur clashed at Cubuk, near Ankara (the present-day capital of Turkey). Some have estimated that Timur brought 140,000 men against Bayezid's 85,000, and there's no question that the sultan was substantially outnumbered. He boldly took the offensive, but was met by a withering barrage of arrows from Timur's expert archers, which terrified and quickly wore down the Ottoman forces. After suffering some 50,000 killed, the Ottomans retreated—and Bayezid himself was captured as he fled into the mountains.

Timur

Timur, also known as Tamerlane, was born at Kesh (modern Sahrisbaz, Uzbekistan) in 1336, most likely the son of a Tartar chieftain. Appointed vizier to Khan Tughlak Timur of Kashgar in 1361, he left that post to join his brother Amir Hussain in an expedition to conquer Transoxiana in 1364. For nearly six years, the brothers raided the region until, in 1369, Timur succeeded his father as amir of Samarkand. After more than a decade battling the khans of Khwarizm and Jatah, in 1381 he invaded Persia, capturing Herat. In 1382, he began several years of raids into Khurasan and eastern Persia. From 1386 to 1387, Fars, Armenia, Azerbaijan, and Iraq fell to him in rapid succession.

Toktamish, descendant of Genghis Khan and a former ally, invaded Samarkand in 1385–1386 and again in 1388 and 1389. Timur defeated him all three times, and in 1390–1391, pushed him back into Russia. He had to break off the offensive, however, to put down a rebellion by Shah Mansur in Persia. After defeating the shah, Timur went on to reconquer Armenia, Azerbaijan, and Fars in 1393 and 1394. In 1393, he captured Baghdad, and within two years held all of Mesopotamia as well as Georgia.

When Toktamish invaded his realm yet again in 1395, Timur defeated him at the Battle of Terek the following year, and then rampaged through southern Russia and the Ukraine in a punitive raid. Taking no prisoners, he slaughtered all of the Mongols he encountered. He interrupted this orgy of slaughter to return to Persia to suppress a new rebellion there in 1396 and 1397. A year later, he launched a massive cavalry invasion of India, cutting a broad and bloody swath on his way to Delhi.

On the outskirts of Delhi, he routed the army of Sultan Mahmud Tughluq and entered the city on December 18, 1398. He turned his troops loose upon its citizens for some two weeks, allowing them to kill tens of thousands. Although he did not seek to occupy or hold India, he gutted and looted it, severely undermining the Delhi sultanate, which soon fell.

Following the Indian expedition, Timur invaded Syria, where he annihilated the Mamluk army at the Battle of Aleppo on October 30, 1400. After sacking Aleppo and Damascus, he returned to rebellious Baghdad, which he utterly destroyed in 1401 as retribution for revolt.

Awash in blood, Timur invaded Anatolia, smashing the army of Sultan Bayezid I at Ankara on July 20, 1402. Going on to capture Smyrna from the Knights of Rhodes, he also collected tribute from the sultan of Egypt as well as from John I, emperor of the Byzantines. He then returned to his capital at Samarkand, and set about planning a massive invasion of China. He was stricken with illness and died on January 19, 1405, before putting his plans into operation.

The catastrophe at Ankara not only forced the Ottomans to break off their siege of Constantinople, but resulted in loss of territory in Anatolia itself and, even worse, triggered 11 years of chaotic civil war, which threatened to bring down the whole empire. Europe rejoiced—although princes, kings, and Christian religious leaders soon feared Timur as an even worse threat than the Ottoman Empire. Bayezid I died in captivity in 1402, leaving no successor as his sons fought among one another during the violent Ottoman *Interregnum.*

 **DEFINITION**

> In Latin, **interregnum** means, literally, "between the kings" and describes a gap in regular government, often implying disorder.

Recovery

The turmoil of the Interregnum ended in 1413 when Mehmet I became sultan and began the restoration of Ottoman power. Timur had died in 1405 and, with his death, the Timurid Empire—briefly so very powerful—stepped toward a collapse that was total by the start of the sixteenth century. With both the Byzantine and Timurid empires in their death throes, Mehmet was able to begin restoring to the Ottoman Empire the territories it had lost. His successor, Murad II, won back most of the Balkans, and on November 10, 1444, defeated the combined Hungarian, Polish, and Wallachian armies at the Battle of Varna, thereby bringing more Europeans under Ottoman control and setting the stage for the long sought-after capture of Constantinople.

Imperial Apogee

In 1444, Murad II abdicated the throne to his 12-year-old son Mehmed II, whose intense devotion to Islam revitalized the religion throughout the royal court. At his request, Murad II returned to the throne and ruled until his death in 1451, whereupon Mehmed II again ascended.

Without delay, he enlarged the Ottoman navy and built a fortress on the European side of the Bosphorus Straits to complement the fortress built earlier on the Asian side. Thus prepared, in 1453, Mehmed II laid siege to Constantinople, believing he was fulfilling a command of Muhammad himself. The conquest of this Christian citadel on the cusp of Europe and Asia was a long-cherished goal of Islam.

The city fell to Mehmed and his huge army (estimated at between 80,000 and 200,000 troops) on May 29, 1453. As zealous as he was in taking Constantinople, the sultan practiced great restraint in dealing with the populace. He permitted the Orthodox Church to continue worship and even to retain the land it owned. In exchange for these considerations, Mehmed sought and received acknowledgment of Ottoman authority.

It was, in fact, a brilliant piece of statesmanship. The sultan understood that relations between the Roman and Orthodox Christian churches were so bitterly strained that most of Constantinople actually preferred living under Ottoman authority than chafing under the yoke of Venice, which had dominated the city since the late twelfth century. In the end, Constantinople submitted meekly to Mehmet and his successors.

Selim and Suleiman

The fifteenth and sixteenth centuries became a period of new expansion for the Ottoman Empire, and new heights were reached under Sultan Selim I (reigned 1512–1520) and his successor Suleiman I the Magnificent (reigned 1520–1566).

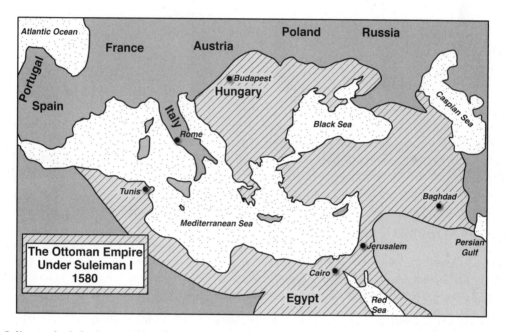

Selim pushed the imperial borders eastward and southward, at the expense of Persia and Egypt. He extended the empire's naval power to the Red Sea. His successor, Suleiman, took Belgrade in 1521, and then overran much of Hungary, bringing it almost entirely under Ottoman control as a result of his victory at the Battle of Mohács in 1526.

 **VOICES**

> What men call sovereignty is a worldly strife and constant war. Worship of God is the highest throne, the happiest of all estates.
>
> —Suleiman I the Magnificent

Established in Hungary, Suleiman turned next against Austria, laying siege to Vienna in 1529. Repulsed, he returned in 1532, but again failed to capture the city. Nevertheless, he made vassals of Transylvania, Wallachia, and—for a time—Moldavia.

Suleiman also turned to the Muslim world, retaking Baghdad in 1535 and reclaiming as well most of Mesopotamia, extending the empire's holdings all the way to the Persian Gulf.

A sophisticated geopolitician, Suleiman made common cause with the court of France to oppose the Habsburgs, who, in 1547, officially recognized Ottoman suzerainty over Hungary. Turning back to the Muslim world, Suleiman defeated the Adal Sultanate and extended Ottoman rule into Somalia and throughout the Horn of Africa. By the end of Suleiman's long reign, 1566, the Ottoman Empire contained some 15 million souls and spread over three continents.

 DID YOU KNOW?

> During 1949 and 1950, when the U.S. House of Representatives was remodeled, 23 marble relief portraits were installed over the doors of the House gallery. They depicted historical figures who had established principles underlying American law. In addition to the likes of the Roman Emperor Justinian I and Pope Gregory IX is Suleiman I the Magnificent.

Tipping Point

By the end of Suleiman's reign, the Ottoman Empire was the most powerful and influential force in the Muslim world. Unfortunately for the empire, however, the many sultans who succeeded Selim and Suleiman fell far short of their genius for leadership and governance. Although the empire continued to expand for 100 years or more after Suleiman's death, the Ottoman military increasingly lost its tactical and technological edge, even as military art and science made significant strides in Europe. Moreover, the religious zeal that had been instrumental in driving conquest hardened into a more passive spiritual conservatism dedicated to preserving the status quo.

Even as Ottoman martial prowess declined, so did the empire's long-held monopoly on maritime trade between Europe and Asia, as European powers pioneered new trade routes that simply bypassed Ottoman-controlled regions. The result, by the sixteenth century, was a sharp decline in revenues, which brought, among other things, a devaluation of Ottoman currency and an economic crisis throughout the empire.

From 1593 to 1606, the Ottomans fought the aptly named Long War against Austria, ruled by the house of Habsburg. Increasingly desperate for troops, Ottoman military leaders recruited just about anyone with a pulse. The result was a mutinous army that triggered widespread revolt. By the end of the sixteenth century, former Ottoman soldiers looted the Anatolian countryside, creating chaos and anarchy.

Murad IV, who reigned from 1623 to 1640, used brutal methods to restore central authority, and as the century approached its final decades under Sultan Mehmed IV, a new attempt was made to capture Vienna during the so-called Great Turkish War.

On September 11 and 12, 1683, a vast Ottoman army (estimated between 90,000 and 300,000 soldiers) under Grand Vizier Kara Mustafa Pasha attacked Vienna after having held it under siege for two months. Assembled against the Ottomans were the forces of the Holy League, an alliance consisting of Poland, the Holy Roman Empire, Bavaria, Saxony, Franconia, Swabia, and Royal Hungary. Combat losses on both sides were horrific. During the siege, some 12,000 members of the Vienna garrison died, along with a large number of civilians living in and around Vienna. At least 30,000 Christian captives were executed by the Ottomans. During the culminating battle, however, Ottoman forces suffered disproportionate losses. Forty thousand fell during the battle—in addition to some 20,000 killed during the two-month siege that had preceded it.

The Battle of Vienna put an end to Ottoman expansion into Europe. Within two decades, Hungary and a large portion of the Balkans came back into European—and Christian—control.

The Long Twilight

The triumphant Holy League fought the Great Turkish War to a victorious conclusion at the Battle of Zenta (in what is today Serbia) on September 11, 1697. With a loss of just 429 men, Holy League forces inflicted 30,000 casualties on the Ottomans. Two years later, the Treaty of Karlowitz (January 26, 1699) formally ended the Great Turkish War, forcing the Ottoman surrender of most of its remaining European holdings; Transylvania, Hungary, Croatia, and Slovenia all became part of the Austrian Empire. During the eighteenth century, in 1783, a resurgent Russia seized the Crimea from Ottoman hands, and in 1812 added Bessarabia (modern Moldavia, now an independent republic).

By the nineteenth century, the growing Christian minority within the shrinking Ottoman Empire pulled ahead of the Muslim minority in level of education and economic prosperity. Christians (as well as Jews) served as intermediaries in trade with Europeans, often in free-trade zones established in major cities like Smyrna, Istanbul, and Cairo. The growing inequality created resentment, but the Christians became so powerful an economic force that their influence over the empire was disproportionate to their numbers.

The *Sublime Porte*—the traditional Ottoman government—mired in corruption and out of touch with the realities of the disintegrating empire, was increasingly incapable of holding it all together. Serbia won initial independence in 1817, as did Greece in 1830. The Crimean War (1853–1856) resulted in a mass exodus of Crimean Tartars and others, along with an economic crisis so profound that the nations of Western Europe took to calling the tottering empire "the Sick Man of Europe." They eyed its decline hungrily, waiting to grab more of the empire's pieces as they fell away.

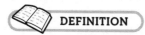 **DEFINITION**

> **Sublime Porte** is the name by which the central government of the Ottoman Empire was long known. It is derived from the great gate that opens onto the principal administrative buildings of the government in Constantinople (modern Istanbul). Today, these buildings accommodate the governor of Istanbul, the Turkish capital having moved to Ankara.

As a result of the Russo-Turkish War of 1877–1878, Bulgaria became independent, as did Romania and Montenegro. Serbian independence was also ratified by the war. That same year, Austria-Hungary occupied the Ottoman provinces of Bosnia-Herzegovina and Novi Pazar (now part of Montenegro, Serbia, and Kosovo). Not to be left out, Britain stepped in to assume administration of Cyprus and dispatched troops to Egypt—thus getting a foothold that would eventually transform that country into a British client state until the mid-twentieth century.

The Young Turks

In 1908, a group of young army officers and other progressives led the Young Turk Revolution. The movement reinstated the General Assembly (the Ottoman parliament), which had been suspended by Sultan Abdul Hamid II in 1878. This restoration ended the absolute rule of the sultans and marked the beginning of the dissolution of the Ottoman Empire.

The end, however, would come neither easily nor bloodlessly.

Genocide

Throughout what remained of the Ottoman Empire, many non-Turkish ethnic groups fled—some in eager voluntary exodus, others as the victims of ethnic cleansing and outright genocide. Between 1894 and 1896, as many as 300,000 (some estimates put the number as low as 100,000) Armenians—the vast majority of them Christians—were killed in the Hamidian massacres, named after Sultan Abdul Hamid II.

Even more devastating in terms of numbers was the Armenian Genocide of 1915–1923, in which 1 to 1.5 million were killed following an Armenian revolt. Concentration camps characterized by mass starvation and execution proliferated, foreshadowing the Jewish Holocaust of World War II.

 DID YOU KNOW?

> To this day, the government of Turkey rejects claims of an Armenian genocide. Twenty-two nations worldwide, most prominently Russia and France, have officially recognized the 1915-1923 events as genocide. U.S. presidents Ronald Reagan and Barack Obama, as well as the U.S. House Committee on Foreign Affairs, have all used the word *genocide* to describe the events of 1915. Although the federal government has not made this official, 43 of the 50 state governments have issued proclamations recognizing the genocide.

Regional and World Wars

From 1911 to 1912, war with Italy cost the ailing Ottoman Empire possession of Libya. The war, in turn, prompted the Balkan League (an alliance among Greece, Bulgaria, Serbia, and Montenegro) to declare war against the empire. These Balkan Wars resulted in the loss of remaining Ottoman holdings in the region, with the exception of East Thrace (today often called European Turkey).

Desperate to regain something of Europe, the Ottoman Empire allied itself with Germany in World War I—an action that backfired disastrously. During the war, Britain and the other Allies opposed to Germany encouraged Arab nationalism and independence from the Ottomans. With Germany's defeat in 1918, the victorious Allies not only stripped the Ottoman Empire of everything it held in the Middle East, but, by the 1920 Treaty of Sèvres (one of several treaties concluded at the end of World War I), the Ottoman Empire was effectively dissolved.

From Islamic Empire to Secular Republic

In the immediate aftermath of World War I, before the Treaty of Sèvres made the dissolution of the empire official, a crippled and humiliated Ottoman Empire was invaded by Greek forces even as Sultan Mehmed VI was confined by the Allies under house arrest in Constantinople (the name of which would officially be changed to Istanbul in 1930).

Into the chaos stepped Mustafa Kemal, a Turkish military officer who now led a new nationalist movement and a war of independence that ensured Mehmed VI would be the last sultan of the Ottoman Empire, and that the *empire* would become the *Republic* of Turkey. For his leadership in the nationalist movement and his success in driving the Greek invaders out of Anatolia in 1922, Kemal was given the name Atatürk—"Father of the Turks"—and served as the new nation's first president from 1923 until his death in 1938.

As far as the modern Middle East conflict is concerned, the transformation of Turkey from an Islamic theocracy to a predominantly Muslim but secular republic—with a constitutional guarantee of freedom of religion—has been crucial. Atatürk and his followers blamed the sultanate's unquestioning attachment to Islam for holding the nation back. Atatürk sought to revitalize Turkey with what he regarded as the best of Western secular influences.

Throughout most of the twentieth century, Turkey has been governed as a moderate secular Islamic state, in which the government does not sponsor religion or religious activism. The installation of Recep Tayyip Erdogan as prime minister in 2003 has seen a rise in so-called Neo-Ottomanism, a foreign policy that seeks to restore Turkish presence throughout the territories of the former Ottoman Empire.

Despite a degree of geopolitical uncertainty the Erdogan government has introduced, many throughout the world see in the transformation of Turkey from history's biggest Islamic empire to a prosperous, majority-Muslim republic a model for integrating all the states of the Middle East into the global family of nations—fully, peacefully, and productively.

The Least You Need to Know

- The Ottoman Empire began when Osman I unified various Turkic tribes and began the acquisition of territory, especially from the weak and declining Byzantine Empire.

- Beginning under Murad I in the late fourteenth century, the Ottoman Empire developed a strong and efficient central government along with one of the best militaries of the late Middle Ages.

- Under Suleiman I the Magnificent, the Ottoman Empire reached its greatest power and extent, making territorial gains in all directions.

- No truly great imperial leader succeeded Suleiman I, which doomed the Ottoman Empire to stagnation and decline, culminating in disastrous wars late in the nineteenth century and early in the twentieth.

- Following World War I, Mustafa Kemal Atatürk led a nationalist movement of democratic and secular reform that replaced the Ottoman Empire with the modern Republic of Turkey—a highly successful secular Islamic nation.

PART 2

Peoples in Conflict

The four chapters of this part focus principally on the conflict between Zionists (and their heirs), who sought a homeland to escape a history of persecution, and Muslims, who had lost, would lose, or feared losing their homelands to the forces of Western colonialism, which, in their view, included Zionism.

The conflict has come to define much of the twentieth and twenty-first centuries, both within the Middle Eastern region and far beyond.

Chapter 4 explores the history of Zionism, the movement among Europe's persecuted Jews to exchange their perpetual statelessness for a "return" to the homeland promised in the Old Testament. Chapter 5 explains how World War I affected and was affected by the struggle of the Muslim Ottoman Empire in its long decline, the imperial powers of Europe in what would prove to be the twilight of their far-flung empires, and the contest between stateless Jews and tribal Arabs for possession of Palestine. Chapter 6 shows how the pressures exerted by all these forces combined to create a new phenomenon, "political Islam," which has exerted profound influence on the course of modern global history. Chapter 7 brings the pressure of change to the point of explosion in World War II's Holocaust and the resulting postwar "Exodus" that followed as survivors of Hitler's genocide fought to create a new Israel in Palestine.

Visions of Zion

The ancient Jews were repeatedly exiled from their Middle Eastern homeland. The Assyrians sent them out of Israel between 740 and 722 B.C.E., the Babylonians in 587 B.C.E., and the Roman Empire in 70 C.E. Each of these exiles is often described using a Greek word meaning scattering or dispersion: *diaspora*. Historians customarily speak of *the* Diaspora, with a capital *D*, to denote any or all three of the major Jewish exiles in ancient times, and the word has also been applied, with a lowercase *d*, to subsequent exiles of the Jews—and others—in more modern times, as when King Ferdinand and Queen Isabella of Spain expelled the Jews from their Iberian realm in 1492.

The Jews of the ancient world were not empire builders, and their repeated scattering or dispersion might well have relegated them to a very obscure place in history were it not for the way they defined themselves in the Old Testament: they were God's chosen people, and Israel was the land God had chosen for them.

In This Chapter

- Judaism—a history of exile and persecution

- Hess, Pinsker, Herzl, and the emergence of Zionism

- The early "aliyahs" (Jewish migrations to Palestine)

- Impact of the Dreyfus Affair on Zionism

- Theodor Herzl crystallizes the Zionist movement

- The Balfour Declaration

Persecution and Pogrom

Persecution has marked the long history of the Jews. Under Christianity throughout Europe, anti-Semitism was driven by a widespread belief that the Jews had killed Christ and so deserved a range of persecution and punishment up to and including death.

In the cities of Western Europe during the Middle Ages, it was common for Jews to be confined by law to segregated neighborhoods today called *ghettos*. In Russia and elsewhere in Europe, *pogroms* were staged. These violent riots directed against Jews were sometimes spontaneous results of mob violence, sometimes decreed by government authorities and carried out by government forces, or often a combination of the two.

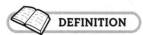

DEFINITION

Today, **ghetto** means a poor urban neighborhood inhabited by people of the same race, ethnicity, or religion—usually due to discrimination. When the word first appeared in the late Middle Ages or early Renaissance, however, it applied specifically to an urban quarter to which Jews were restricted by law. The word was first applied to the Jewish quarter in Venice and may derive from the Italian *borghetto*, the diminutive of *borgo*, the word for a settlement outside of a walled city.

A **pogrom** is a violent persecution—sometimes a massacre—of a particular minority group. Most often, the word is applied to the officially encouraged (sometimes even sanctioned) military, police, and/or mob actions directed against Jewish communities, especially in czarist Russia.

The Holocaust

The culmination of organized, culturally and politically institutionalized anti-Semitism was the policy of Nazi Germany (1933–1945), which decreed a "final solution to the Jewish question"—namely, total annihilation in what has come to be called the Holocaust (Chapter 7).

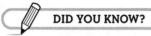

DID YOU KNOW?

The phrase "final solution"—derived from the more complete "final solution to the Jewish question"—is infamous for its use by Adolf Hitler and other Nazi leaders before and during World War II as an allusion to the genocide of German, European, and ultimately world Jewry. With tragic irony, however, the phrase in both its short and long forms was first used by the pioneering Zionist writer Moshe (Moses) Hess in his 1862 book, *Rome and Jerusalem: The Last Question*. For Hess, the "final solution to the Jewish question" was the creation of a Jewish national homeland.

Jews in Muslim States

Nor is the history of Jewish persecution confined to the ancient world and to Christian Europe. By the mid-twentieth century, at the outbreak of World War II, a little less than half of the world's Jews lived in the Middle East and North Africa, where Muslim governments generally treated them with much more respect than they received in Europe. Some recent scholars have pointed to the fact that Jews (as well as Christians) could rise to the highest levels of power in, for example, the Ottoman sultanate as a recognition among Muslim political leaders that there was much to be gained in "Abrahamic cohesion" solidarity among peoples who shared a reverence for the patriarch Abraham.

Nevertheless, Jews living in Muslim lands were, along with Christians, *dhimmis*—non-Muslim citizens of an Islamic state, subject to a head tax (the *jizya*) and deprived of some rights and privileges. They were marked as "other" and, accordingly, felt themselves perpetually vulnerable.

Anti-Semitism: The Role of Statelessness

Over many years, Jews and many non-Jews alike saw statelessness as a major source of the vulnerability of the Jewish people. Not only did many come to feel that establishing a Jewish homeland was a political, moral, and humanitarian necessity, some believed that Palestine—the Old Testament's Israel—was the divinely ordained homeland from which the Jews had been expelled in ancient times and to which they were entitled (even divinely destined) to return and to possess.

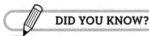

DID YOU KNOW?

The desire for a Jewish state has not been unanimous among Jews. Many Orthodox and traditional religious Jews opposed the idea of a Jewish homeland as either secular ideology or as a violation of two of the Talmudic "Three Oaths." God adjured Jews not to return from exile to Israel en masse or to rebel against other nations. Although most Jews, including most Orthodox Jews, now accept the religious legitimacy of Israel, some groups still oppose the existence of a Jewish state as a rebellion against God. The strongest early critics of the movement were Jews within the Mizrahi communities of the southern and eastern Mediterranean, specifically in Baghdad, Istanbul, and Cairo.

Prelude to Zionism

Although the idea of creating a Jewish state was periodically discussed throughout history, the movement known as *Zionism*, the quest for a Jewish state, did not begin to crystallize until 1862 when Moshe (Moses) Hess, a German-born Jewish philosopher and socialist, published *Rome and Jerusalem: The Last Question.* In this volume, Hess argued for a Jewish return to Eretz Yisrael—the Land of Israel—by which he meant a tract of the Southern Levant corresponding to the boundaries of Israel, the Jewish homeland, as described in the Old Testament. Hess further argued that the nation to be established there should be governed on socialist principles according to which the citizens would live agrarian lives and thereby be "redeemed" by the soil.

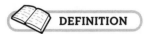 **DEFINITION**

> **Zionism** is a word of nineteenth-century origin applied to a political movement to establish a national Jewish homeland. *Zion* is an alternative name for Israel, and most (but not all) Zionists insisted that the homeland be established in Palestine, site of Old Testament Israel. Since the establishment of the State of Israel in 1948, Zionism has also been applied to the continued survival and development of the Jewish nation.

Hess articulated three principles of Zionism:

1. Without an actual homeland, Jews are destined to be strangers among the people of Europe and therefore subject to persecution or, at the very least, an absence of respect.

2. The "Jewish type"—the Jewish self-identity—is persistent and enduring, and a Jewish national longing cannot therefore be extinguished through assimilation into the society and culture of those places in which Jews happen to live.

3. If the "emancipation" (freedom from discrimination) of the Jews requires assimilation, it is irreconcilable with Jewish nationality; therefore, Jews must sacrifice emancipation to nationality—which means that the "final solution" to what Hess called the "Jewish question" is a return to the Land of Israel.

About a decade after Hess published *Rome and Jerusalem*, Leo Pinsker, a Russian Jew who turned from the study of law to medicine when he realized that czarist Russia's discriminatory laws would bar his ever practicing in the legal profession, concluded that the "Jewish question" could be answered if Jews enjoyed equal rights. His first approach toward this end was urging Jews to assimilate into European society, but the Odessa Pogrom of 1871, which triggered a wave of anti-Semitic violence throughout Russia, persuaded him that assimilation was a lost cause.

In 1881, therefore, he published *Auto-Emancipation*, which argued that the Jews of Europe should address their destiny by organizing to take positive steps toward founding their own homeland. This led to the creation of an organization called Hibbat Zion—Lovers of Zion—which advocated Hebrew education, embracement of Jewish culture and heritage, and the ultimate reversal of the Diaspora through a revival of the Jewish nation.

 DID YOU KNOW?

> Repeatedly during the nineteenth century and into the early twentieth, the Black Sea port city of Odessa in Ukraine (at the time a part of czarist Russia) was the scene of violent pogroms. Early pogroms were perpetrated by ethnic Greeks, but later pogroms were the work of both Greeks and Russians. Czarist police and other officials were complicit in the mob violence. The early Zionist Leo Pinsker was among many Jewish social thinkers who viewed the 1871 Odessa Pogrom as a tipping point in the history of Russia's Jews. Pinker and others believed it demonstrated that assimilation of Jews into Christian society was impossible, leaving the creation of a national homeland as the only option for the Jewish people.

The First Aliyah

The early work of Hess, Pinsker, and others initiated an immigration movement to Palestine. It was mostly a trickle, so that by the end of the 1870s, only some 25,000 Ashkenazi Jews had taken up residence in Palestine. In 1882, after publication of *Auto-Emancipation* and amid the activities of Hibbat Zion, the migration increased significantly in volume. Between 1882 and 1903, more than 35,000 Jews, mostly Russians, immigrated to establish agricultural communities that included Rishon le-Ziyyon, near Tel Aviv, and Zikhron, near Haifa. This migration was dubbed the *First Aliyah*, from the Hebrew word for "ascent." These newcomers were Zionists, whereas the Ottoman Jews, long resident in Palestine and far outnumbering the First Aliyah, were not.

DEFINITION

Aliyah, Hebrew for "ascent," is the word applied to a series of migrations of Jews from Europe and elsewhere to Palestine or Israel beginning during the late nineteenth century. The word implies that the progressing toward Jerusalem is the act of "going up" to the Promised Land.

The Dreyfus Affair

Anti-Semitism was so deeply ingrained in European life that it usually passed unremarked and unprotested among those who harbored no anti-Semitic sentiments and even among the majority of Europe's Jews.

This status quo changed dramatically at the end of the nineteenth century when powerful forces conspired to convict an obscure French artillery captain, an Alsatian Jew named Alfred Dreyfus, of high treason.

It all began, really, with the fall of the Second French Empire of Napoléon III after France's ignominious defeat in the Franco-Prussian War of 1870. In place of the Second Empire, the Third French Republic was founded, which, although generally popular, was vehemently opposed by a group of reactionary monarchists, including a powerful clique of senior military officers. Failing to get much support for their return-to-monarchy movement, this group took a new tack. If the French people could not be rallied in *support* of a return to monarchism, perhaps they could be organized *against* a group long portrayed in French society as alien: the Jews. The monarchists deliberately identified Jews with republicanism and portrayed them as using the republic to destroy France. Organizations such as the Antisemitic League of France and the League of Patriots accused French Jews of being Jews first and citizens second.

VOICES

> I see just one figure and it is the only one I wanted to show you: the figure of Christ, humiliated, insulted, lacerated by thorns, crucified. Nothing has changed in 1800 years.... He is everywhere, hanging in cheap shop windows, abused by caricaturists and writers in Paris full of Jews, as obstinate in their deicide as in the time of Caiaphas.
>
> —Antisemitic League of France founder Edouard Droumont, in *La France Juive* (*Jewish France*), 1885

Against the growing background noise of French anti-Semitism, Alfred Dreyfus earnestly pursued a military career. The son of a Jewish textile manufacturer, he was 11 years old in 1871 when his native Alsace—he was born in the Alsatian town of Mulhouse—was annexed by the German Empire. The Dreyfus family remained in Mulhouse, but chose to retain their French citizenship after the annexation, and the patriotic Alfred graduated from the prestigious École Polytechnique in 1880 with a French army officer's commission. By 1893, he graduated from the École supérieure de guerre (Superior War College), an institution reserved for those promising young officers earmarked for the highest commands.

That is when Dreyfus came to the attention of the army's supreme headquarters, a bastion of right-wing monarchism and anti-Semitism. Despite his distinguished record, Dreyfus was turned down for a career-making assignment to the general staff after a key officer declared that Jews were undesirable for posts at the highest levels. Instead of submitting to the decision, Dreyfus protested. In October 1894, he was suddenly arrested on charges of passing military secrets to the German embassy in Paris.

The only physical piece of evidence against him was a note detailing the specifications of the army's brand-new Modèle 1890 120-mm Baquet howitzer, which was discovered by French counterintelligence in the wastepaper basket of the German military attaché assigned to the embassy. Based on the fact that Dreyfus came from Mulhouse, now a German town, and on an assertion that the handwriting in the note looked like his, Dreyfus was subjected to a high-speed show trial that convicted him in December 1894, dishonorably discharged him, and bundled him off to the infamous Devil's Island prison colony off the coast of French Guyana.

Although the headquarters officers hoped that the public would write Dreyfus off as an example of Jewish treachery, others, outraged by the obvious injustice, worked behind the scenes to uncover the truth behind his conviction. Eventually, they revealed that prosecutors failed to disclose evidence that the incriminating note had been written and delivered not by Dreyfus, but by one Major Ferdinand Walsin Esterhazy, a French-born infantry officer of Hungarian descent.

While Dreyfus languished in captivity, his brother Mathieu, a Jewish journalist named Bernard Lazare, Senate Vice President Auguste Scheurer-Kestner, and an incorruptible French cavalry officer, Lieutenant Colonel Marie-Georges Picquart, disclosed to Émile Zola, one of the most popular, esteemed, and controversial writers of turn-of-the-century France, the details of the false conviction. On January 13, 1898, Zola published an open letter to French President Félix Faure under the headline "*J'accuse!*"—"I accuse!"

Published worldwide, Zola's letter named names in the government and military hierarchy, provoked his own prosecution for libel, and ignited the Zola Affair, which divided France (and much of the world) into the "Dreyfusards," who believed in the innocence of Dreyfus, and the anti-Dreyfusards, who persisted in the belief that a Jew must also be a traitor.

As the international community watched, an appeals court overturned Dreyfus's conviction and ordered a new court-martial. Despite presentation of the evidence implicating Esterhazy, the officers of the tribunal closed ranks and reconvicted Dreyfus—whereupon the new French president, Émile Loubet, pardoned him.

 DID YOU KNOW?

Although some of his defenders urged Dreyfus to refuse the presidential pardon and demand full exoneration, he himself believed that a return to Devil's Island would kill him and settled for the pardon. An official exoneration did come, in 1906, whereupon Dreyfus rejoined the army and was even elevated to knighthood in the Légion d'Honneur. He served in World War I (1914-1918), attaining the rank of lieutenant colonel of artillery.

Publication of *The Jewish State*

The sensational Dreyfus Affair awakened much of the world to the depth and breadth of anti-Semitism. Among the legion of journalists who covered the Dreyfus story was Theodor Herzl, a reporter for Vienna's *Neue Freie Presse*. He was also a Jew, and what he saw and heard moved him to publish in 1896 *Der Judenstaat* (*The Jewish State*), a book that dramatically chronicled anti-Semitism as a thoroughly institutionalized and inescapable fact of European life. Building on the earlier work of Hess and Pinsker, he argued that the creation of a Jewish state was necessary to the survival of the Jewish people and, for that matter, the satisfaction of gentile Europe, which did not want Jews living among them.

 VOICES

Everything tends to one and the same conclusion, which is clearly articulated in that Berlin phrase, 'Juden raus!' ['Out with the Jews!'] . . . Let sovereignty be granted us over a portion of the globe large enough to satisfy the rightful requirements of a nation. The rest we shall manage for ourselves.

–Theodor Herzl, *The Jewish State*, 1896

Herzl wanted to establish the Jewish state in Palestine, which was, in 1896, part of the Ottoman Empire. He therefore proposed addressing a petition to the sultan for the territory to be granted in exchange for Jewish financial expertise to rehabilitate the precarious economy of Turkey.

The First Zionist Congress: 1897

Although nothing came of Herzl's notion of petitioning the Ottoman sultan, *The Jewish State* did create momentum for a First Zionist Congress, convened in Basel, Switzerland, during August 29-31, 1897.

The congress established the term *Zionism* for the movement to create a Jewish state, and the meeting also adopted an anthem, "Hatikvah" ("The Hope"), with lyrics by the Ukrainian Jewish poet Naphtali Herz Imber set to a seventeenth-century Italian tune, "La Mantovana." Years later, in 1948, the Knesset (Parliament) of the newly founded Israel would adopt it as a national anthem.

Most important of all, the congress adopted the Basel Declaration, which set out the "program" of Zionism:

> Zionism aims at establishing for the Jewish people a publicly and legally assured home in Palestine. For the attainment of this purpose, the Congress considers the following means serviceable:
>
> 1. The promotion of the settlement of Jewish agriculturists, artisans, and tradesmen in Palestine.
>
> 2. The federation of all Jews into local or general groups, according to the laws of the various countries.
>
> 3. The strengthening of the Jewish feeling and consciousness.
>
> 4. Preparatory steps for the attainment of those governmental grants which are necessary to the achievement of the Zionist purpose.

Zionism Pro and Contra

"Were I to sum up the Basel Congress in a word," Herzl confided to his diary, "it would be this: At Basel I founded the Jewish State."

Within two decades of the First Zionist Congress, some 3,000 Jews were immigrating to Palestine annually. Yet, at the time of the Basel Congress and for years afterward, the dream of creating a Jewish state was shared by only a very small number of the world's Jews.

Jewish objections to creating a Jewish state in Palestine included a prediction of intractable conflict between the Jews and the Palestinian Arabs. These critics pointed out a flaw in the Zionist assumption that Palestine was essentially vacant land actually awaiting a population to occupy it and render it fruitful, productive, and useful.

Many conservative and Orthodox Jews were, at the very least, offended by the secular, strongly socialist tone of the Zionist movement. The two waves of immigration that followed the First Aliyah—the Second Aliyah of 1904–1914 and the Third Aliyah of 1919–1923—were dominated by socialists, a fact that offended both the religious and political sentiments of conservative Jews. Moreover, the truly Orthodox saw the creation of a Jewish state as a sinful rebellion against God. They believed that the Jewish return to the Promised Land would come only under the leadership of the true Messiah—not Theodor Herzl or a bunch of socialists.

Some, Jews as well as non-Jews, criticized Zionism as old-fashioned European colonialism in a new guise.

Yet the Zionist movement found an increasing number of supporters. Among Jews, even those who had no intention of ever immigrating to Israel themselves, many believed that the mere existence of a Jewish state would be an invaluable safeguard for the entire community. Statelessness meant that a Jew had no place to go if the country in which he lived persecuted him or cast him out. The existence of a Jewish state ended that vulnerability by providing a refuge and a resort.

Among some Christians—especially Protestants—Zionism accorded perfectly with biblical prophecy. For them, Zionism was actually "Restorationism," the divinely decreed return of the Jews to the Promised Land.

Even among some Muslims, "self-determination" for the Jewish people seemed both just and desirable—a means of promoting justice as well as enhancing regional stability. Moreover, some Muslims saw an opportunity to profitably sell land to Jewish settlers and to benefit from the wealth, skills, and education they brought with them.

Chaim Weizmann and the Balfour Declaration

Chaim Weizmann was born in 1874 near Pinsk, Belarus, into the family of a timber merchant. A brilliant youngster, he left his village in 1892 to study chemistry in Germany and was ultimately awarded a doctorate in organic chemistry from the University of Fribourg, Switzerland. He taught at the University of Geneva before moving to the University of Manchester in 1904. Six years later, he became a British subject.

While living in Switzerland, Weizmann became interested in Zionism, and although he missed the first conference in Basel, he attended all those held subsequently. After his move to Britain, he became prominent among that nation's Zionists and presented the case for a Jewish homeland to Arthur Balfour, who was Britain's prime minister and member of parliament for Manchester.

A Homeland in Africa?

Balfour listened to Weizmann sympathetically and agreed with him on the desirability of a Jewish state. Balfour, however, spoke in favor of the so-called Uganda Scheme, an offer made in 1903 by British Colonial Secretary Joseph Chamberlain to Theodor Herzl. Despite the name, the actual offer was for some 5,000 square miles of British East Africa (in modern Kenya, not Uganda) to serve as a Jewish homeland—or, at least, as a refuge from Russian pogroms. Herzl favored the offer and introduced it at the Sixth Zionist Congress in Basel. Although some Zionists agreed, others believed that accepting the African land would rule out a more desirable Jewish state in Palestine. Weizmann was among these, and he patiently persuaded Balfour that only a homeland in Palestine would be spiritually meaningful and historically legitimate.

Balfour ultimately agreed, but took no immediate action. In the meantime, in 1907, Weizmann visited Jerusalem, where he helped to establish the Palestine Land Development Company the following year. Its purpose was to privately acquire agricultural land in Palestine on which Jews could be settled. It was, in effect, an immediate and *practical Zionism*.

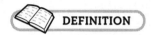 **DEFINITION**

Practical Zionism was the name given to various private or small-scale negotiations to acquire land in Palestine to be used for Jewish settlement. This form of Zionism required no diplomatic or legislative action—merely sufficient financing to acquire sizable parcels of property.

Weizmann in World War I

The outbreak of the Great War—World War I—in 1914 saw Weizmann join the British war effort as head of the Admiralty Research Laboratories, a scientific establishment whose efforts were mainly directed at creating antisubmarine technologies. This brought him close to wartime Prime Minister David Lloyd George, to whom he proposed a strategy for defeating the German-allied Ottoman Empire in the Middle East.

An enthusiastically loyal British subject, Weizmann wanted Britain to win the war. A dedicated Zionist, he also wanted Britain to capture Palestine from the Ottomans, reasoning that he could far more easily and honorably negotiate the acquisition of the territory from the British government than from the Sublime Porte. Indeed, when a grateful Lloyd George asked what he could give Weizmann in return for his services to the Admiralty and for his winning advice concerning Middle Eastern strategy, the Zionist declined monetary reward and a knighthood, asking instead for "a national home for my people."

Balfour Again

Lloyd George listened and gave his blessing to talks with Arthur Balfour, who was now secretary of state for foreign affairs in his cabinet. The result of these talks was the Balfour Declaration of November 2, 1917, a letter addressed to Walter Rothschild, Second Baron Rothschild, a prominent British Jew, and intended for him to transmit to the Zionist Federation of Great Britain and Ireland:

Dear Lord Rothschild,

I have much pleasure in conveying to you, on behalf of His Majesty's Government, the following declaration of sympathy with Jewish Zionist aspirations which has been submitted to, and approved by, the Cabinet.

"His Majesty's Government view with favour the establishment in Palestine of a national home for the Jewish people, and will use their best endeavours to facilitate the achievement of this object, it being clearly understood that nothing shall be done which may prejudice the civil and religious rights of existing non-Jewish communities in Palestine, or the rights and political status enjoyed by Jews in any other country."

I should be grateful if you would bring this declaration to the knowledge of the Zionist Federation.

Yours sincerely,

Arthur James Balfour

The text of the Balfour Declaration was widely published in the world press, and, over Arab dissent, it was incorporated into both the 1920 Treaty of Sèvres, by which the Ottoman Empire was dissolved, and the mandate over Palestine the League of Nations awarded to Britain (see Chapter 5).

The Balfour Declaration became a cornerstone of the eventual establishment of the State of Israel, but it fell substantially short of what Weizmann and other Zionists had hoped for, which was a proclamation of the forthright reconstitution of Palestine as *the* Jewish national home or, better yet, Jewish state. The wording of the declaration, however, merely voiced sympathy—support—for *facilitating* Jewish efforts to establish *a* national home in Palestine. As we will see in the next chapter and in Chapter 7, the Balfour Declaration created as much ambiguity as clarity on the subject of the Jewish claim on a Palestinian homeland.

The Least You Need to Know

- Zionism—the movement to create a Jewish national homeland in Palestine—was born of a positive desire for a biblically sanctioned home and by what came to be seen as an urgently needed alternative to perpetual intolerance and persecution by European peoples and governments.

- European Jewish political writers—especially Moshe (Moses) Hess, Leo Pinsker, and Theodor Herzl—created and popularized Zionist doctrine in the second half of the nineteenth century.

- Driven and guided in part by a series of Zionist congresses held in Europe, Jews began a series of organized migrations (called *aliyahs,* or "ascents") from Europe (especially pogrom-plagued Russia) to agricultural settlements in Palestine.

- During World War I, the Russian-born British Zionist Chaim Weizmann enlisted the aid of Prime Minister David Lloyd George and Secretary of State for Foreign Affairs Arthur Balfour to throw British support behind the creation of a Jewish homeland in Palestine. This resulted in the Balfour Declaration, a cornerstone on which the nation of Israel would later rise.

A "War to End All Wars"

At one time the chief contender against the Ottoman Empire for control of southeastern Europe, the corrupt and inefficient Austro-Hungarian Empire was, like its former rival, ailing in 1914. As the Ottoman realm had been picked apart by Balkan provinces seeking independence, now these same provinces beat against the Austro-Hungarian Empire. When an adolescent Bosnian Serb nationalist assassinated the heir to the Austro-Hungarian throne, along with his wife, on June 28, 1914, the leaders of the moribund empire thought they saw a way to cling to life. It required magnifying the assassination into a cause for war.

Americans—who would not get involved until April 1917—initially referred to the conflagration of 1914 to 1918 as the "European War," but it was, in fact, a *world* war virtually from the very beginning.

In This Chapter

- The Young Turks take the Ottoman Empire to war

- The Armenian Massacre—a genocide of Turkey's "indigenous Christians"

- The Turks prevail at Gallipoli

- Lawrence of Arabia: an Englishman leads an Arab war for independence

- The Ottoman Empire falls, a secular Turkish republic rises

- Jews and Arabs clash in Palestine

The Young Turks Rise

The Ottoman Empire had the toe of one foot in Europe, but had most of its weight on the other foot, planted squarely in Asia. As most of the rest of the world saw it, the Turks need not have gotten involved in the "European" War, but, secretly, they had already tied themselves to one of the major combatants: Germany. And as Austria-Hungary regarded war as a means of staving off imperial decay, so the Turks gambled on an alliance with Germany as a means of transforming its European toehold into a foothold and injecting new life into a disintegrating empire and economy.

The Spirit of Reform

As we saw in Chapter 3, the decline of the great Ottoman Empire was long, turbulent, and marked by frequent attempts at reform. Most of these political movements died aborning, but the Young Turk Revolution of 1908 was different. It elevated to power within the government a number of charismatic, progressive-minded young men, most of them military officers, who looked to Europe for new ideas. They saw the salvation of their failing nation in two things. The first was ending the archaic absolute authority of the sultan by reinstating modern representative constitutional government, originally introduced in 1876 but dismantled just two years later by Sultan Abdulhamid II. The second was connecting to the great powers of Europe. Now, being military men, the Young Turks most admired Europe's greatest military power, Germany—even though Germany was ruled not as a progressive republic but as a regressive empire, under Kaiser Wilhelm II.

The German Connection

Within a year of the 1908 revolution, with the constitution restored, the Muslim Ottoman government was extensively controlled by secular Young Turks. They reached out to Germany, which eagerly seized an opportunity to acquire a pliable ally at the southeastern doorstep of Europe. The German army sent the Turks a substantial cadre of Prussian military instructors, and Enver Pasha, the Turkish officer who emerged as the leader of the Young Turks, became increasingly convinced that an outright alliance with Germany would do wonders to rehabilitate the "Sick Man of Europe." Most immediately, it would provide protection against the continual threat posed by its traditional enemy, Russia, which (as it often did) hungrily eyed the Bosphorus and the Dardanelles.

 DID YOU KNOW?

Anchored by the city of Istanbul (in the early 1900s, still called by some Constantinople), the Bosporus is a narrow strait between European and Asian Turkey. It connects the Black Sea with the Sea of Marmara. At the southwestern end of the Sea of Marmara, the Dardanelles is an even longer strait that connects to the Aegean Sea and continues the separation of the Balkans (Europe) from Asia Minor. Russia, with important Black Sea ports, long coveted control of the two straits as a means of passage to the Aegean and thence to the Mediterranean. Such access would be Russia's only warm-water outlet (not subject to a seasonal hard freeze) to the rest of the world. It seemed worth fighting for.

Enver Pasha persuaded Said Halim Pasha, who, as grand vizier (prime minister) was effectively the head of the post-revolutionary Ottoman government, to conclude a secret treaty with Germany binding Turkey to come to Germany's aid in the event that Germany sided with Austria-Hungary in a war against Russia.

The Wild Card

As World War I erupted, the secret alliance was a wild card unsuspected by the *Allies*—the nations opposed to Germany and Austria-Hungary. Historically, the Ottoman Empire and the Austro-Hungarian Empire had been bitter enemies, on geopolitical as well as religious grounds. Austro-Hungary, traditional center of the Holy Roman Empire, was staunchly Catholic, whereas Ottoman Turkey hosted the Caliphate in Istanbul. True, Russia (dominated by Eastern Orthodox Christianity) and Turkey frequently fought, but the Allies took it on faith that the animosity between Austria-Hungary and the Ottoman Empire ran far deeper.

 **DEFINITION**

The **Allies** and **Central Powers** were the names given to the main opposing alliances in World War I. At the height of the war, the principal Allies were Russia, France, the British Empire, Italy, the United States, Japan, Rumania, Serbia, Belgium, Greece, Portugal, and Montenegro, and the Central Powers were Germany, Austria-Hungary, the Ottoman Empire (Turkey), and Bulgaria.

Indeed, at the outbreak of the war, many in the Turkish government hesitated to honor the secret alliance with Germany. The reluctance became strongest after Britain entered the conflict, since the Royal Navy had (out of self-interest, of course) long defended Turkish trade routes in the Mediterranean Sea and via the Suez Canal. Had the British government behaved with respect and sensitivity toward the Turks at the outbreak of World War I, the Ottoman Empire would likely have remained neutral. Instead of respect, however, His Majesty's government delivered a rude slap in the face.

Before the war, as part of the Young Turk program of modernizing the Ottoman military, the government contracted with British shipyards to build two dreadnought-class battleships. Purchase of these vessels was wholly financed directly by the Turkish people, who made voluntary donations as a grand gesture of renewed national pride. On August 3, 1914, however, with the war under way and the two ships almost ready to launch, the British Admiralty high-handedly seized possession of them. Worse, it did so without any apology or payment to Turkey.

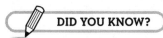 **DID YOU KNOW?**

The British Royal Navy's HMS *Dreadnought*, launched in 1906, revolutionized naval warfare in terms of firepower (huge 12-inch guns), speed (21 knots), power plant (steam turbine), and armor (4- to 11-inch belt plate). Similar battleships built by all navies after it were called dreadnought-class battleships, while those before, called pre-dreadnought-class battleships, were rendered obsolete.

While second thoughts over the German alliance were evaporating in Turkey, German troops on August 4 crossed the Belgian border, thereby defying Britain's ultimatum insisting that Germany respect Belgium's neutrality. The British were propelled into the war, and a Royal Navy squadron in the Mediterranean gave chase to the German *battle cruiser Goeben* and *light cruiser Breslau*. Seeing that escape from the Mediterranean was impossible, Vice Admiral Wilhelm A. T. Souchon, commanding the *Goeben*, decided to take refuge with the Turks via the Dardanelles. En route, he bombarded the French North African ports of Bone and Philippeville, where French colonial soldiers were embarking for transfer to the Western Front in Europe.

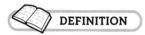 **DEFINITION**

> The **battle cruiser** was an important warship type in the first half of the twentieth century. Similar in size and armament to a battleship, the battle cruiser was less heavily armored, which made it lighter and faster. Germany's *Goeben* had a top speed in excess of 28 knots. A **light cruiser** was a medium-sized warship that was more maneuverable and faster than a standard battleship (Germany's *Breslau* had a top speed of 27.5 knots), though less heavily armed and armored.

The German warships reached the Dardanelles on August 10, brazenly violating international treaties that barred ships of war from transiting the straits. But acting on instructions from his government, Souchon made the Turks an offer they couldn't refuse. He presented both *Goeben* and *Breslau* to the Ottoman navy—along with the services of their highly trained German crews.

Enver Pasha Plays the Wild Card

Despite the German gift, Turkey continued to hesitate to enter the war. Most of the cabinet, Young Turks included, thought it prudent to bide their time until the likely victor became clear.

Enver Pasha, now minister of war, did not want to wait. He believed that achieving a victory now would not only boost national pride and enhance Turkey's status among nations, but would position it to recover some of what it had lost during the long imperial decline. He therefore authorized *Goeben* and *Breslau* to lead the Turkish fleet across the Black Sea on a mission to bombard, without warning, the Russian ports of Odessa, Sevastopol, and Theodosia.

No one in the government stopped him, and the attacks of October 29–30 damaged the ports and sank several Russian ships. The cabinet's doubts notwithstanding, it was Turkey's de facto declaration of war. On November 1, Russia declared war against Turkey, and the Western Allies followed suit on November 5.

Enver Pasha

Less famous than Mustafa Kemal Atatürk, the "father of Turkey," Enver Pasha (1881–1922) was nevertheless even more central to the Young Turk Revolution of 1908. Born Enver Ismail into a modest family in Bitola (then called Manastir), Macedonia, at the time an Ottoman province, the young man had a military education and rose quickly through the ranks. With the outbreak of the revolution, he immediately became one of the movement's military leaders.

During the Italo-Turkish War of 1911–1912, he organized the ultimately fruitless Ottoman resistance in Libya, and in 1913 was a leader of the coup in Constantinople that propelled him to the position of chief of the general staff of the Ottoman army. His first action was to lead it to defeat in the Second Balkan War (1913), but he nevertheless was elevated to minister of war in 1914 and was instrumental in bringing Turkey into World War I on the side of Germany.

Enver's objective in joining Turkey's fate to Germany's was the defeat of Russia through a union of the Turkic peoples of Russian Central Asia with the Ottoman Turks. This moved Enver to launch a campaign in the Caucasus, which cost most of the Third Army, a disaster from which the Turkish military never recovered. Nevertheless, he used the military to lead infamous genocidal campaigns against rebellious Armenians and Assyrians within the Ottoman Empire, beginning mainly in 1915.

Within the Turkish government, Enver was saved from immediate disgrace by the defeat of the Allies in the ill-fated Gallipoli Campaign in 1916, but the surrender of Germany and the other Central Powers, including Turkey, in 1918, sent Enver into flight to Germany. There he met the Bolshevik leader Karl Radek and traveled to Moscow to seek a Soviet military alliance against the British. Although the beleaguered Soviets rejected the proposal, they endorsed an expedition to Turkistan, where Enver was to help organize the Central Asian republics. In 1921, however, Enver Pasha suddenly turned coat and joined an anti-Soviet rebellion. He was killed in action against the Red Army.

Discounting Turkey

Despite instruction and advice from Germany, Turkish military performance was singularly unimpressive in 1914. The army came into World War I having lost its three most recent wars—and badly.

Allied leaders discounted the threat of what seemed an anachronistic and decaying Muslim empire. What this assessment failed to take into account, however, was the power possession of the Dardanelles and Bosporus conferred. Whoever controlled this passage controlled communication with Russia. And since the Turks controlled it, Russia—on whose giant army France, Britain, and the other Western Allies now pinned so many of their hopes—was cut off, unable to maneuver by sea and unable to receive supplies from the West.

Enver's Ambition: A Muslim Rebellion in Russia

Enver Pasha appreciated the importance of controlling the southern passage to and from Russia, but he was not content to defend it passively. Instead, he planned a massive assault against Russia via the Caucasus Mountains, which formed a natural border between the two nations. The chief German military advisor to the Turks, General Otto Liman von Sanders, pleaded with Enver to give up the idea of an invasion through some of the most forbidding terrain on the planet, but neither the German government nor the German high command raised an objection.

The fact was that Germany also had little faith in the Ottoman army, but, at this stage in the war, Germany was fighting on two fronts—against France and Britain in the west and against Russia in the east. German strategy called for quickly defeating France and, only when that was accomplished, transferring major strength to the Eastern Front; therefore, any campaign that drew Russian troops away from Germany's eastern borders was seen as valuable—no matter how militarily flawed.

Interpreting German strategic exploitation as a vote of confidence, Enver Pasha took personal command of 95,000 Ottoman troops and led them, during November and December 1914, into the mountains. His belief was that a quick Turkish victory in South Georgia would ignite a broad Muslim uprising throughout Russia's southern provinces.

The Caucasus rise to an average elevation of 6,500 feet, with numerous peaks topping 16,000 feet. Half the year, the entire region is snowbound—frozen and barren. Although the Russian army faced the same hostile conditions, the Russian commanders led it far more effectively than Enver Pasha led his men. Outgeneraled, he was soundly defeated at the Battle of Sarikamish on December 29, and the Turkish advance over the mountains was stopped in its tracks.

The Caucasus Campaign finished the Turkish army as an offensive force in World War I.

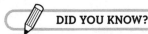

DID YOU KNOW?

Of the 95,000 men who had marched with Enver Pasha, only 12,000 returned from the defeat at Sarikamish. Most of the casualties were suffered in the hellish retreat down ice-clogged mountain passes.

Modern War in Ancient Places

Although Sarikamish was a disaster, one of Enver Pasha's subordinate commanders, Abdul Kerim, triumphed over a Russian corps at the Battle of Malazgirt, north of Lake Van, near the Ottoman Empire's Persian frontier. This victory, however, was followed by defeat at Cossack hands in the Battle of Kara Killisse, on the Turkish side of the Caucasus.

Amid these reversals, Enver Pasha led the military against the Ottoman Empire's own Armenian population. Long-oppressed, Armenians from the Caucasus eagerly formed volunteer battalions to aid the Russian army. In response, Enver persuaded the government to order the mass deportation of some 1,750,000 Armenians to Syria and Mesopotamia. Of this number, about 600,000 died of exposure and starvation en route through the desert.

While their kind were being deported and killed, Armenian rebels seized the key Turkish fortress of Van on April 20, 1915. For the next several months, possession of this prize passed back and forth between Turks and Russians.

 **VOICES**

> Turkey is taking advantage of the war in order to thoroughly liquidate its internal foes, i.e., the indigenous Christians, without being thereby disturbed by foreign intervention. What on earth do you want? The question is settled. There are no more Armenians.
>
> —Talat Pasha, Turkish minister of finance and the interior, in conversation with a German government official, June 1915

Egypt and Palestine

Early in 1915, the Great War expanded elsewhere in the old Ottoman Empire, to Egypt and Palestine. In military terms, the most valuable strategic prize in the region was the Suez Canal, the shortest maritime route between Europe and all the lands around the Indian and western Pacific oceans.

On January 14, 1915, Djemal Pasha, a Turkish military leader known to the Arabs as al-Saffah (The Bloodletter), with German General Friedrich Kress von Kressenstein as his chief of staff, led 22,000 men in a secret march across the Sinai Peninsula from Beersheba, bound for the canal. Advance elements were beaten back on February 2, and, from then on, the Suez Canal remained firmly under British control—albeit at the cost of tying down large numbers of British troops who had been intended to reinforce the faltering campaign against the Dardanelles at Gallipoli.

Tragedy Straddles the Continents

Winston Churchill, at the time First Lord of the Admiralty, pushed hard for a campaign to seize the Dardanelles, hoping thereby to open an avenue of aid to beleaguered Russia, provide the West access to the vast grain fields of Ukraine, and defeat the Ottomans once and for all.

 **VOICES**

> This is one of the great campaigns of history. Think what Constantinople is to the East. It is more than London, Paris, and Berlin rolled into one are to the West. Think how it has dominated the East. Think what its fall will mean. Think how it will affect Bulgaria, Greece, Rumania, and Italy.... You cannot win this war by sitting still.
>
> —Winston S. Churchill, speaking in support of the Dardanelles campaign

The principal French army commander, Joseph Joffre, and Lord Horatio Herbert Kitchener, senior-most commander of the British army, refused to take troops from the Western Front to fight at Gallipoli. This should have killed Churchill's proposal, since many prewar studies had shown that an amphibious operation—navy *and* army—was necessary to capture the Dardanelles. Obstinately, however, Churchill persuaded Royal Navy leaders that ships *could* do it alone, and in February 1915, Admiral Sir Sackville Carden led an Anglo-French naval squadron of a dozen obsolescent battleships plus the *Queen Elizabeth*, one of the newest super dreadnoughts, and various smaller ships on a mission to bombard the forts at Cape Helles at the southern tip of the Gallipoli Peninsula and Kum Kale on the Asiatic shore.

The expedition was launched on a mixture of wishful thinking and the customary Western underestimate of the Ottoman army. At Gallipoli, the Ottomans, led by Atatürk, had skillfully reinforced and manned some 20 forts, fire from which did heavy damage to the assaulting fleet and greatly slowed its progress.

On March 18, when Carden was finally ready to mount a breakthrough assault on the Dardanelles, he collapsed with an attack of ulcers and nerves. Rear Admiral John de Robeck replaced him and rushed forward with the attack—but in the chain-of-command chaos created by Carden's sudden illness, someone neglected to give the order to fully clear the strait of mines. As a result, the French battleship *Bouvet*, striking a mine on March 8, sank with the loss of 700 sailors. The British battle cruiser *Inflexible* struck a mine next, as did the battleships *Irresistible* and *Ocean*. Two smaller British ships were also badly damaged by mines. Robeck felt he had no choice but to retreat.

Even as the naval assault was failing, Lord Kitchener relented and released a few divisions (including one French unit)—78,000 troops—for land operations against the Dardanelles. Preparations were so haphazard, however, that the first contingent of troops and their weapons were loaded into separate ships, so that—incredibly—the soldiers landed minus their weapons. It took a full month before the land assault could begin. The delay gave the Turks ample time to deploy some 60,000 men in strongly defended positions.

The result, when the attack began on April 25, was slaughter of British, Australian, and New Zealand troops, who were pinned down, under fire and helpless, along a thin sliver of beach located below steep, heavily defended cliffs. Incredibly, the bloody siege dragged on through the summer when, on August 6, a second landing was made to reinforce the first. It likewise failed, and the survivors of the long and utterly fruitless assault on the Dardanelles were evacuated between December 10, 1915, and January 9, 1916.

 DID YOU KNOW?

The Allies lost 252,000 soldiers in the Dardanelles Campaign. Astoundingly, this was only a thousand more than the Turks lost—but with the Dardanelles still in Turkish hands, Russia was entirely and permanently cut off from France and Britain. This situation doubtless contributed to the desperate combat situation that accelerated Russia's headlong plunge toward revolution, the overthrow of the czar, and the nation's "separate peace" with Germany in 1917.

A Turkish Reprieve

Costly as it was, the Ottoman strategic victory at the Dardanelles gave Europe's "Sick Man" a reprieve, keeping the Ottoman military in the war. Turning away from Gallipoli, the British directed their efforts to another corner of the Ottoman Empire.

Although the world's navies ran chiefly on coal in 1915, oil was rapidly emerging as another strategically vital commodity. Accordingly, an Anglo-Indian force was dispatched to protect the flow of oil from the great Anglo-Persian pipeline. After the expedition efficiently brushed aside Ottoman resistance at Qurna, Iraq, on April 12–14, British command ordered the unit to advance on Baghdad, with the objective of taking the city.

What at first appeared to be a relatively soft target proved far more formidable after the Turks reinforced it. The Anglo-Indian forces conducted a fierce offensive, but were shocked by the ferocity with which the Ottoman soldiers counterattacked, and Baghdad remained under Ottoman control.

Going after Baghdad was yet another instance of underestimating the Ottoman military. In a war whose principal front—the Western Front, running from the English Channel down to the Swiss border—was heartbreakingly stalemated, commanders on all sides were looking for morale-lifting "easy" victories elsewhere. The British assumed Baghdad would be a pushover. It was not, and soon it became apparent that a more urgent threat loomed, yet again, against the Suez Canal. Accordingly, early in 1916, General Sir Archibald Murray began work on extending the Suez Canal defenses eight miles into the Sinai Desert to defend against Ottoman attempts to bombard the canal with artillery.

Lawrence of Arabia and the Arab Revolt

In the midst of British efforts to enlarge Suez Canal defenses, the Senussi tribes of western Egypt rebelled against the British presence. Suddenly, it became clear to British high command that it needed to win the hearts and minds of the locals if any real progress was to be made against the Ottomans. Accordingly, in the autumn of 1915, British and French officials negotiated an agreement with Hussein, the grand sherif (chief magistrate) of Mecca, pledging to help him gain territory and to support Arab independence from the Ottoman Empire, in the countries now known as Saudi Arabia, Iraq, Jordan, Palestine, and Syria. Hussein, in return, promised to cooperate with the Allies in operations against Ottoman forces.

On June 5, 1916, Hussein attacked the Ottoman garrison at Medina, proclaimed independence for all Arabs, and then stormed the Ottoman garrison at Mecca, which surrendered to him on June 10. Although Medina withstood Hussein's onslaught, General Murray was pleased because Hussein's operations significantly hampered the Ottoman war effort in the region.

Attached to Murray's staff was a young captain named T. E. Lawrence. Assigned to observe the Arab operations at Medina, Lawrence reported that the Arab cavalry could not reasonably challenge the well-defended Ottoman positions. With the permission of his superiors, he persuaded Hussein's third son, Feisal, field commander of the Arab army, to break off the direct attack against Medina and instead use his forces to disseminate anti-Ottoman, pro-British propaganda among the Arabs and to raid the Ottoman lines of communications. These guerrilla-style tactics proved highly effective, forcing the Ottomans to cease offensive operations south of Medina. They also compelled Ottoman command to assign valuable troops to defend long stretches of the Hejaz Railway.

Lawrence would go on to become Feisal's chief adviser, earning the unofficial title "Lawrence of Arabia" for his leadership of the Arab struggle for independence from the Ottoman Empire.

Stalemate on the Turkish Fronts

Lawrence's unconventional tactics would prove far more effective than many of the major British army operations in the Middle East. For most of 1916, the Ottoman and Anglo-Indian forces fought each other to a standstill in Mesopotamia. In 1917, activity intensified on all of the far-flung so-called Turkish fronts. After the Russian czar was overthrown in the Russian Revolution of March 1917, Russian forces withdrew from the Caucasus, leaving Ottoman troops on this front free to bolster operations elsewhere, especially the Middle East. Nevertheless, the Battle of El Magruntein (January 8–9, 1917) resulted in the defeat of all Ottoman forces in the Sinai Peninsula. This put General Murray in position to invade Palestine.

Murray's first objective was to dislodge the Ottoman troops from their strong positions along ridges between Gaza and Beersheba, which formed a natural portal into Palestine. On March 26, 1917, Sir Charles M. Dobell began the First Battle of Gaza, which resulted in the loss of 4,000 men out of his force of 16,000 and sent him into retreat.

To higher headquarters—astoundingly—Murray portrayed this tactical draw and strategic defeat as a British victory. Accordingly, he was ordered to advance immediately against Jerusalem. Murray in turn ordered Dobell to once again attack the Ottoman positions at Gaza. Fought on April 17–19, this Second Battle of Gaza began with a suicidal frontal assault against Ottoman defenses that resulted in 6,444 dead and wounded among the Anglo-Indian forces. A stunned British high command relieved Murray and replaced him with the far abler General Edward Allenby.

"Jerusalem Before Christmas"

The British War Office issued Allenby a simple order: "Jerusalem before Christmas." The new commander began by moving his headquarters out of the luxury Cairo hotel Murray had commandeered to the fighting front. After scraping together seven infantry divisions and a cavalry unit, consisting of horses and camels, he had some 88,000 men to throw against the 35,000 of the Ottoman Seventh and Eighth Armies.

The Third Battle of Gaza, also known as the Battle of Beersheba, began early in the morning of October 31, 1917. Allenby eschewed a frontal attack on Jerusalem, and instead made a surprise attack against nearby Beersheba, exposing the Ottoman Seventh Army and splitting it off from the Eighth. Divided, the Ottoman forces were defeated in detail—although at great cost. Allenby suffered a 20 percent casualty rate (18,000 killed or wounded out of 88,000) but inflicted 25,000 casualties on the smaller Ottoman force—a catastrophic 71 percent casualty rate. On December 9, Allenby occupied Jerusalem, subsequently defeating an Ottoman counterattack on the day after Christmas.

Allenby Turns to Lawrence

Once he had taken Jerusalem, Allenby was forced to relinquish many of his men to serve on the Western Front in Europe. Left with insufficient forces to mount major operations, he approved T. E. Lawrence's request to lead Faisal's small force of tribal warriors—some 6,000 men—in raids against the Hejaz Railway, principal supply line for the Ottoman armies. These operations tied down some 25,000 Ottoman soldiers, effectively taking them out of the war.

Thomas Edward Lawrence

Thomas Edward (T. E.) Lawrence (1888–1935) was the illegitimate son of Sir Robert Chapman by his daughters' governess, Sara Maden. A brilliant student at Oxford, he first traveled to the Middle East as a scholar in 1909 to study the Crusader castles of the Holy Land. Lawrence's archaeological interests gave him perfect cover as a British agent, reconnoitering the northern Sinai early in 1914 as the world hovered near war. Soon after the outbreak of hostilities, he was dispatched to Cairo as an intelligence officer attached to the Arab section.

In November 1916, he was assigned as political and liaison officer attached to the army of Sharif Husein (commanded by Husein's son Faisal). Working closely with Faisal, Lawrence molded the ongoing Arab revolt into a force that would aid the British cause in the Middle East. Ultimately, Faisal's men virtually became Lawrence's personal army, which he led very effectively against the Ottoman desert garrisons.

After the war, Lawrence was chosen as member of the British delegation to the Versailles peace conference, in which he struggled in vain to promote Arab independence. Beginning in 1921, he served as adviser on Arab affairs to the Middle Eastern Division of the British Colonial Office, but, disillusioned, left government service in 1922.

Disdaining the public attention his wartime exploits had earned for him, Lawrence enlisted in the Royal Air Force (RAF) under a pseudonym in August 1922. When a newspaper revealed his secret in January 1923, he resigned and enlisted in the Royal Tank Corps in March, calling himself T. E. Shaw. (In 1927, he made the name change legal.) Lawrence transferred back to the RAF in 1925, and the following year published his wartime memoirs, a massive literary masterpiece entitled *The Seven Pillars of Wisdom*.

Lawrence left the RAF in 1935 and was fatally injured in a motorcycle accident near his home, Cloud Hill, in Dorset.

In August 1917, Lawrence decided to take more aggressive action by leading a small camel force in the capture of the port of Aqaba. Successful in taking this strategic prize, he presented Allenby, early in the fall of 1918, with a proposal that the Arabs be given a role in an offensive the British general intended as the decisive campaign of the war in the Middle East. Lawrence asked to lead the Arabs as the right flank of the entire British army's advance through Palestine to Damascus, Syria.

Impressed with the plan, Allenby agreed. He did so, however, in ignorance of Lawrence's ulterior motive, which was less to help the British win the war than it was to aid the Arabs in achieving enduring independence from the Ottoman Empire. Allenby knew that the British pledge of support for Arab independence had been made under false pretenses. On May 16, 1916, British diplomat Sir Mark Sykes concluded with his French counterpart François George-Picot the Sykes-Picot Agreement, which, with Russian acquiescence, effectively divided the Arab provinces of the Ottoman Empire (outside of the Arabian Peninsula) between future British and French areas of influence or outright control. This clearly meant that neither Britain nor France intended to honor the full and genuine independence of any new Muslim countries. Lawrence intended to lead the Arab contingent ahead of Allenby, taking Damascus before the main body of British troops arrived. This would give Faisal a claim to Damascus as the capital of an independent Arabia, thereby forcing Britain to honor its promise.

As Allenby and Lawrence advanced toward Damascus later in the campaign, Allenby at last perceived Lawrence's intentions and ordered him to halt. Disobeying the general's direct order, Lawrence marched on and entered the city on September 30, 1918, three hours ahead of Allenby.

Outraged though he was, Allenby declined to court-martial Lawrence, whose exploits were by then legendary and, in an otherwise overwhelmingly dismal war, uplifting. In any case, Lawrence rendered moot any question of court-martial by suddenly resigning his commission at the very moment of his greatest triumph.

All too predictably, Allenby and his superiors did forsake the Arabs once the Armistice ending World War I went into effect on November 11, 1918. Hoping to rescue the Arabs' hard-won independence, Lawrence attempted to intercede at the highest levels of government, in both England and France. His efforts came to nothing.

Empires Fall, Nations Are Born

The Great War, World War I, may have ended in November 1918, but the Ottoman Empire was finished as a military power by September 30, when Lawrence—soon followed by Allenby—marched into Damascus.

It was the culmination of a campaign that began, for Allenby, with the Battle of Megiddo, fought due north of Jerusalem, on September 19, 1918. By the next day, the entire Ottoman Eighth Army seemed to dissolve as the British forces advanced. The Ottoman Seventh Army retreated from the destruction of its brother force in complete disarray.

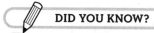 **DID YOU KNOW?**

Although the Middle East was something of a sideshow in World War I, the Battle of Megiddo was by far the most spectacular British success in the entire war. Allenby annihilated three Ottoman armies and took 76,000 prisoners. His own losses were 853 killed, 4,482 wounded, and 385 missing. The battlefield itself was the site of the very first battle recorded in history, about 1469 B.C.E., which pitted Egypt's King Thutmose III against forces led by the Mitanni king of Kadesh. Many believe that this first Battle of Megiddo is the Battle of Armageddon referred to in the Old Testament.

Mandate for Palestine

Although the Armistice ended the shooting in the Great War at the eleventh hour of the eleventh day of the eleventh month of 1918, formal treaties were concluded much later, during 1919 and 1920. The principal treaty, the Treaty of Versailles (1919), created (among many other things) the League of Nations, which awarded Great Britain administrative rights over Palestine under the British Mandate, assigned on April 25, 1920. Shortly after this, on August 10, the Treaty of Sèvres effectively dissolved the Ottoman Empire. It continued to exist, essentially in name only, until it was legally replaced on October 29, 1923, by the Republic of Turkey.

As Zionists like Chaim Weizmann understood it, the Balfour Declaration (Chapter 4) meant that the British would turn over Palestine to the Jews for their national homeland. But during the war, even as the British government made what certainly sounded to the Zionists like solemn promises, they also made promises to the local Muslims, especially the Arabs, from whom the Allies needed close cooperation to defeat the Ottoman armies.

Following a series of tortuous conferences and negotiations involving numerous parties, Winston Churchill, now Britain's colonial secretary, issued, on June 3, 1922, the so-called White Paper of 1922 to "clarify" (*his* word) the British view of the Balfour Declaration. Essentially, Churchill walked back the scope of the Balfour document. The White Paper denied that the British government ever intended to "create a wholly Jewish Palestine," but only that "a Jewish National Home ... should be founded 'in Palestine.'"

Palestine, the White Paper stated, "in the eyes of the law shall be Palestinian," but the Jewish community existing there—"a community, now numbering 80,000"—was to be "internationally recognized as the Jewish National Home in Palestine" and its right to exist "should be internationally guaranteed." Moreover, Churchill wrote, "the Jewish community in Palestine should be able to increase its numbers by immigration," albeit immigration not "so great in volume as to exceed whatever may be the economic capacity of the country at the time to absorb new arrivals."

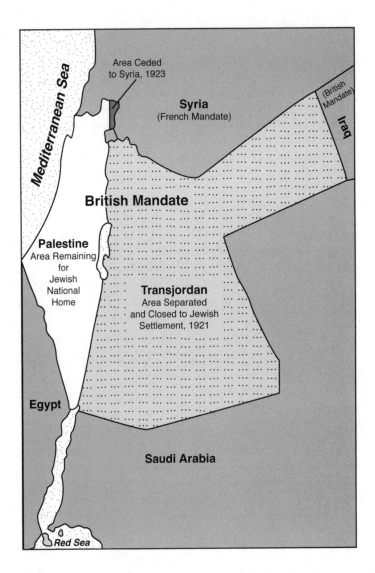

The Jewish Return

Unsurprisingly, the White Paper did not end the controversy. Under the British Mandate, Jewish immigration steadily increased the Jewish population in Palestine, beginning with the Third Aliyah of 1919 to 1923. In 1929, the British government officially gave the World Zionist Organization a role in Palestine by creating the Jewish Agency, which both assisted newly arrived Jewish immigrants and promoted further immigration.

Clashes in Palestine between Arabs and Jews were frequent and bloody. After Arabs repeatedly attacked Jewish homes and businesses in 1919, the immigrants formed Haganah ("The Defense") in 1920. Outlawed by British mandate administrators, Haganah nevertheless functioned as a paramilitary force that went on to become, in 1948, the Israel Defense Forces (IDF)—the Israeli army, air force, and navy.

Palestine became a most violent place as Arabs attacked and killed Jewish settlers and as Haganah, its numbers swelling, retaliated forcefully and at times disproportionately. Amid the bloodshed, the Jewish immigration continued, reaching an influx of approximately 100,000 between 1919 and the early 1930s, as Germany and the world were, as yet unknowingly, poised on the brink of Adolf Hitler's genocidal Third Reich.

The Least You Need to Know

* In 1908, after centuries of territorial and economic loss, the Ottoman Empire underwent the Young Turk Revolution, which began the empire's transformation from a Muslim theocracy to a "modern" secular republic.

* Part of the Young Turks' program was to align Turkey with Europe's most aggressive military power, Germany, in an effort to recover at least some of the European holdings lost to the Ottoman Empire.

* Despite some victories, World War I proved disastrous for Turkey, ending in the fall of the Ottoman Empire.

* Although the remarkable T. E. Lawrence attempted to help the Arabs win independence from both the Ottoman Empire and Europe, the European powers ultimately sought to exercise colonial control over Arabia and other Muslim realms in the Middle East.

* Awarded by a League of Nations a mandate over Palestine, Britain sought to balance both Arab and Jewish demands for sovereignty over the region (in part, surely, to further its own geopolitical ambitions). The result was epidemic and endemic violence.

The Power of Political Islam

The three Abrahamic religions—Judaism, Christianity, and Islam—all regard as sacred the region known historically as Palestine (and now including modern Palestine as well as modern Israel). All three religions identify it as the Holy Land. The three have shared the region over time, respecting each other's traditions to varying degrees. Too often, however, and under many circumstances, they have fought over it.

In the early Middle Ages, Muhammad and his successors brought the Holy Land under Muslim control, and during the later Middle Ages, European Christians sought to reclaim it as the site of Christianity's founding. Beginning in the late nineteenth century, an influential minority of mostly European Jews, calling themselves Zionists, looked to Palestine as the divinely sanctioned location for the establishment of a Jewish national homeland.

After Britain assumed control of Palestine and other regions of the Middle East following the defeat of the Ottoman Empire in World War I, Jewish Zionist immigration to the Holy Land dramatically increased. Many Arabs resisted, violently and nonviolently, against both the British and the Jews. In 1928, an Egyptian schoolmaster and Islamic scholar created an organization he hoped would unite disaffected Islamic populations, such as the Arabs of Palestine, with Muslims everywhere in a movement to re-create and even magnify the Caliphate as it existed during Islam's political zenith.

In This Chapter

- The Caliphate concept in history and modern times

- The founding of the Muslim Brotherhood and its role in the development of political Islam

- The Egyptian Revolution of 1952

- The assassination of Anwar Sadat

- The Egyptian revolutions of 2011 and 2013

Visions of the Caliphate

From the days of its founding by Muhammad, Islam was a religion as well as an ambitious political movement. It sought not only to convert people to belief in the one true God, but to use that belief as the foundation for states and empires.

The Rashidun, Abbasis, and Fatamid Caliphates

At its greatest extent, the Rashidun Caliphate (632–661), the first to be established, encompassed the Arabian Peninsula and the Levant, the Caucasus, North Africa from Egypt to modern Tunisia, the Iranian highlands, and part of Central Asia. It was succeeded in the seventh and eighth centuries by the Umayyad Caliphate, which came to occupy large portions of Africa, Europe, and Asia, becoming the fifth largest empire the world has ever known. Next, the Abbasid Caliphate, spanning the eighth through thirteenth centuries, moved the capital from Mecca to Baghdad as the Abbasids continued to rule over a vast region. During the tenth through twelfth centuries, the Abbasid realm coexisted with the Fatamid Caliphate, which (at its height) controlled territory from the Red Sea in the east to the Atlantic Ocean in the west, including Egypt and the Mediterranean coast of Africa as well as parts of the Maghreb, Sudan, Sicily, Yemen, Hijaz, and the Levant.

Ottoman Geography

After the Abbasid and Fatamid dynasties, the Muslim territories passed through Ayyubid rule and Mamluk rule until the sixteenth century, which saw the emergence of the Ottoman dynasty. Centered in what is today Turkey, the Ottoman Caliphate—also known as the Ottoman Empire—endured into the early twentieth century. At its greatest extent, in the 1500s and 1600s, it contained 32 provinces and controlled many *vassal states* throughout southeastern Europe, western Asia, the Caucasus, North Africa, and the Horn of Africa. It dominated most of the Mediterranean basin. Although Muslim possession of Iberia had been ended by 1492, the Ottoman Empire pushed the Muslim Caliphate well into southeastern Europe and planted Islamic religious and political influence in both the Western and Eastern worlds.

 **DEFINITION**

> A **vassal state** differs from a colony by enjoying some degree of autonomy and independence in conducting its internal affairs, yet, like a colony, it is wholly subject to another state in its foreign relations.

As the Caliphate rose to its greatest extent during the early epoch of the Ottoman Empire, so it ended, in 1924, with the replacement of that Islamic empire by the secular Republic of Turkey. The first president of Turkey, Mustafa Kemal Atatürk, constitutionally abolished the Caliphate.

No sooner did Atatürk end the Caliphate than Hussein bin Ali, self-proclaimed king of Hejaz, the man who, aided by Lawrence of Arabia, led the 1916–1918 Arab Revolt against the Ottoman Empire, claimed the title of caliph for himself. The very next year, 1925, Ibn Saud captured Mecca, capital of Hejaz, bringing about the overthrow of Hussein. In January 1926, Ibn Saud was proclaimed king of Hejaz.

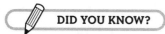

DID YOU KNOW?

In 1932, Ibn Saud united his various Arabian dominions with Hejaz, and the resulting state became the kingdom of Saudi Arabia, the name by which it is known today.

Later in 1926, Arab leaders convened a summit in Cairo, to debate reviving the caliphate. Although the summit voted to take action to resurrect the defunct Islamic empire, few Muslim countries sent representatives to the summit, and the proposal died from lack of substantive support. Nevertheless, visions of a new caliphate persisted.

Hassan al-Banna Founds the Muslim Brotherhood

Hassan al-Banna was born and raised in a rural Egyptian backwater called Mahmudiyya, the son of an imam, mosque teacher, and Muslim scholar. Even as al-Banna absorbed his father's spiritual piety, he also became politically active at a young age and an enthusiastic supporter of Egyptian nationalism.

As close as he was to his father, Hassan al-Banna left him and his village to enroll in a Cairo college specializing in the instruction of schoolteachers, with an emphasis on "modern" (that is, secular and Western) subjects. His conservative father objected, but, in fact, al-Banna had no intention of compromising his religious beliefs. Rather, he believed that engagement with the modern secular world was the most effective way to reintroduce into it the values of traditional Islam.

He soon found that he had his work cut out for him. After graduating from the four-year training institution in 1927, al-Banna moved to Ismailia to teach school. Cairo was an intensely cosmopolitan city, but Ismailia, as Egyptian headquarters for the Suez Canal, was so thoroughly exposed to Western influence that it often seemed more European than Egyptian.

Thanks to the Suez Canal, Egypt existed essentially as a British vassal state. In 1875, after leading Egypt into catastrophic debt, Kehdive (viceroy) Isma'il Pasha had no alternative but to sell Britain its share of the Suez Canal in order to pay his country's bills. The sale gave Britain a financial strangle-hold on the Egyptian government, which made the British the country's de facto rulers. After World War I, Egyptian nationalist politicians led a revolt that prompted the British government to declare Egypt independent on February 22, 1922. Nevertheless, Britain continued to exert such a powerful cultural and financial influence over Egyptian affairs that the country still felt and functioned like a colony of Europe.

To Hassan al-Banna, Ismailia seemed the epicenter of British influence. And he feared that this was only a foretaste of what Egypt would soon become: a Europeanized, secularized cultural colony of the United Kingdom, independent in name only. Already prominent in Islamic social and political organizations, including the Islamic Society for Nobility of Islamic Morals and the Young Men's Muslim Association (YMMA), al-Banna, with six Suez Canal workers, founded what they called the Muslim Brotherhood in 1928.

The mission of the Brotherhood was educational and charitable, but it also espoused the renewal of Egyptian society through a return to the values of traditional Islam. More controversial was its position on *sharia* as the foundation for secular civil and criminal law.

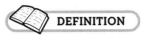 **DEFINITION**

Sharia is, in essence, a law-based Islamic society. As generally used, sharia law denotes the application of religious reasoning in place of secular criminal and civil law. Sharia law is much debated within the Islamic world, and very few predominantly Muslim nations have actually instituted it.

Al-Banna believed that the values of conservative Islam were inherently opposed to the social and political injustices of life under British domination. The connection between a return to Islam and opposition to British authority positioned the Muslim Brotherhood as a force for social equality between the working classes and upper classes as well as for Egyptian independence. By linking Muslim values with nationalism—the struggle against colonialsm—the Brotherhood sought to bridge the gap between tradition, with its idle nostalgia for the great days of the Caliphate, and progressive modernity. Independence was clearly the wave of the future, but al-Banna intended that this future be defined in traditional Islamic terms.

The Brotherhood Grows

When it was introduced, the Muslim Brotherhood hardly seemed revolutionary. It was an Islamic-oriented welfare organization, not all that different from many others of the era. It offered social assistance programs for the needy, it raised funds and provided volunteers for repairing mosques and even building new ones, and it opened several schools. Although these schools were religious in orientation, they also emphasized the basic literacy skills so badly needed in a society with an 80 percent illiteracy rate in the late 1920s and early 1930s. As the Brotherhood grew, it opened additional benevolent and aid institutions, including pharmacies and clinics, all of which were available to the public—not just Muslim Brotherhood members. Adult education became a priority as well.

Unlike many other political and religious organizations, the Muslim Brotherhood focused on practical matters and tended to avoid overt ideology and politics. Because of this, the government greeted its activities favorably—at least in the early years.

By 1932, the Muslim Brotherhood expanded from Ismailia to Cairo, to which al-Banna moved, transferring the organization's headquarters to the bigger city. The move touched off explosive growth, from three branches at the end of 1931 to 300 all across Egypt by the end of 1938.

DID YOU KNOW?

In 1936, the Anglo-Egyptian Treaty created a military alliance by which Egypt essentially consented to be permanently occupied by British forces. For Egyptian nationalists, including members of the Muslim Brotherhood, the 1936 treaty seemed yet another form of European Christian imperialism, and it created great resentment.

The Brotherhood Becomes a Political Force

As we will see in Chapter 7, by the mid-1930s, with the full establishment of Nazism in Germany and fascist regimes elsewhere in Europe, Jewish immigration to Palestine increased sharply. Accordingly, Zionism became an increasingly pressing issue for Muslims throughout Egypt and the Middle East.

As more Zionist Jews immigrated, conflict between Jews and Arabs in Palestine intensified, as did the membership in military operations of the Haganah. In response to the growing Palestinian violence, which pitted Arab nationalism against both Zionism and the British administration of Palestine, al-Banna steered the Muslim Brotherhood in a more overtly political direction.

Following the lead of various other Egyptian organizations, the Brotherhood raised money to support Palestinian Arab workers who had gone on a marathon strike during the anti-British Arab uprising of 1936–1939. Al-Banna and other Brotherhood leaders gave speeches and led demonstrations in favor of Arab nationalist activists in Palestine. The Muslim Brotherhood did not attack Jews in Egypt, either physically or verbally, but it did lead a boycott of Jewish businesses in Cairo, arguing that prosperous Egyptian Jews were financing Palestinian Zionist organizations.

DID YOU KNOW?

In the middle to late 1930s, the Muslim Brotherhood occasionally published articles overtly hostile to Jews and Judaism. More usually, however, writers associated with the Brotherhood took pains to distinguish Jews and Judaism from Zionists and Zionism, directing their attacks exclusively against the latter. It may well be that the organization wanted to distance itself from the violent anti-Semitism that was coming to characterize *European* behavior.

To those who criticized the Brotherhood's new political turn, arguing that social welfare, charity, and ethical religious instruction were laudable, but politics was the business of political parties, al-Banna countered with the historically accurate observation that Islam was inherently political and had always concerned itself with the conduct of government and "the happiness of this world."

If anything, the criticism encouraged al-Banna to continue down the path of *political Islam*. The scope of the organization's activity enlarged beyond opposing Zionism to cover a range of issues that were then current in Egyptian society, including vice (alcohol, prostitution, gambling, and so on), the excessive influence of Christian missionaries in Egypt, and the struggle for Egyptian independence. An increasing political emphasis began to differentiate the Muslim Brotherhood from other Islamic organizations, which typically went out of their way to remain apolitical. More and more, the political empowerment the Brotherhood offered drew young, educated, politically progressive Egyptians to membership.

 **DEFINITION**

The Muslim Brotherhood played a key role in the creation of **political Islam** in the twentieth century, which is the practice of Islam driven by the proposition that the religion should guide collective political and social life in addition to the spiritual life of the individual.

A Hierarchy of Power and Influence

As the Muslim Brotherhood grew in membership, the need for administrative organization became apparent. Al-Banna designed a simple hierarchy. At the top, he placed himself as "General Guide." Below him, within the organization's central headquarters, was a deputy and a General Guidance Bureau.

On the branch level, individual membership was also subject to a hierarchy. A new member was an "assistant" and could rise through several levels up to "activist." The rise was based on individual merit as measured by performance of Islamic duties and demonstration of knowledge acquired through the Brotherhood's various study groups. Recognition of merit was rare in both the Egyptian bureaucracy and social organizations, in which position was typically a function of socioeconomic status. Indeed, while Brotherhood members paid dues, they did so on a sliding scale, depending on their means. No one was turned away. If a member was too poor to afford dues, none were collected from him.

Political Islam and Geopolitics During and After World War II

In the next chapter, we will detail how Nazi persecution of European Jews, culminating in genocidal Holocaust, impacted the Middle East conflict. Here we will trace the development of the Muslim Brotherhood just before, during, and following World War II. During this period, the Brotherhood functioned in the cause of political Islam and Muslim nationalism much as Zionism functioned for the cause of Jewish nationalism: as the leading edge of a revolutionary political movement.

A Hesitant Militancy

As Europe marched to the verge of world war in the late 1930s, the Muslim Brotherhood exhibited ambivalence about two things. The first was whether to begin an *armed* struggle against British rule. The second was whether to focus its actions—whatever form they took—on the forces of British imperialism or on Zionism in Palestine.

Hassan al-Banna counseled the members of the Brotherhood to refrain from military action, arguing that the organization was not yet ready for it. On the other hand, he immediately set about organizing zealous young members into what he called "Battalions," designating them for special religious and physical training. Even as he instituted this militaristic initiative, however, al-Banna specifically banned what he called terrorism as well as outright revolution. When the time came—and only if peaceful measures failed—he believed that the Brotherhood should openly declare war on Britain's "imperial occupation" of Egypt.

Some members were sufficiently discontent with this prepare-but-wait strategy that they broke away from the Muslim Brotherhood to create, in 1939, an organization called Muhammad's Youth. In response to this schism, the Muslim Brotherhood created a secret military wing, which, however, saw no significant action during the war. Indeed, when the war broke out in September 1939, al-Banna declared that the Brotherhood's official position was that Egypt should simply stay out of the conflict.

After the War

The Muslim Brotherhood was not very active during World War II, although individual members may have been saboteurs and spies. It was only after the war that that the organization was labeled a terrorist organization by British authorities.

Ban, Renunciation, and Revival

As we will read in Chapter 7, pursuant to a United Nations resolution, Palestine was formally divided between Arabs and Jews in November 1947, and, the following year, on May 14, 1948, British forces withdrew from Palestine. The very next day, May 15, David Ben-Gurion, Israel's first prime minister, officially proclaimed the State of Israel, in defiance of the UN partition plan. Palestinians call this day *Nakba*, "the tragedy," when 80 percent of them were either forced out of their homes or fled out of fear of Israeli troops. On this day, most of the Arab world went to war with Israel.

 **VOICES**

> If the Jewish state becomes a fact, and this is realized by the Arab peoples, they will drive the Jews who live in their midst into the sea.
>
> —Hassan al-Banna, *New York Times* interview, August 3, 1948

Although Egypt was not directly affected by the partition of Palestine and the subsequent establishment of Israel, *pan-Islamist* activists carried out a number of bombings and assassination attempts during 1947 and 1948. At the time, the Muslim Brotherhood was the best-known pan-Islamist organization, and, in November 1948, Egyptian police seized an automobile that contained documents relating to what officials called a "secret apparatus" of the Muslim Brotherhood, which officials now implicated in the bombings and attempted assassinations. Immediately, 32 persons named in the seized documents were rounded up and imprisoned while police simultaneously raided the Cairo offices of the Brotherhood.

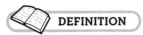 **DEFINITION**

Pan-Islamism may be seen as a movement advocating the creation of a single great Islamist state—or a Caliphate—that unites Muslims of all nationalities. Alternatively, it describes a movement promoting political unity among Muslims.

In December, the month after the arrests of Muslim Brotherhood members, Egypt's Prime Minister Mahmud Fahmi Nokrashi ordered the organization dissolved. Before the month was out, on December 28, Nokrashi was assassinated by a young student of veterinary medicine, Abdel Meguid Ahmed Hassan, a member in good standing of the Muslim Brotherhood.

Not surprisingly, it was widely assumed that the prime minister's assassination had been a retaliation against the ban on the Brotherhood, and, in a pattern as old as the *lex talionis* of Hammurabi, on February 12, 1949, Hassan al-Banna, founder and head of the Muslim Brotherhood, was gunned down by two unidentified men. He had been waiting on a Cairo street for a taxi after he left what was supposed to be a meeting with an Egyptian government minister. The minister failed to show up. It was, of course, widely assumed that the assassins were either government agents or supporters of the late Nokrashi.

Despite the government ban, the Muslim Brotherhood continued to exist under the leadership of Hassan Isma'il al-Hudaybi, a former judge.

Revolution

In 1952, a group of Egyptian military officers calling itself the Free Officers Movement and led by Gamal Abdel Nasser and Muhammad Naguib staged a coup d'état that not only overthrew Egypt's flamboyant and thoroughly corrupt King Farouk but replaced the constitutional monarchy in Egypt with a republic. In addition, the revolution ended the British occupation and made Sudan a separate republic independent of both Egypt and Britain.

Although the Muslim Brotherhood supported the coup, the military refused to share power with the Brotherhood, prompting some members to commit acts of arson directed mainly against nightclubs, restaurants, and hotels patronized by foreigners. To quell the outbreaks of violence and arson, the military junta imposed martial law, deepening the rift with the Brotherhood and prompting more clashes.

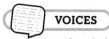 **VOICES**

The whole world is in revolt. Soon there will be only five kings left—the King of England, the King of Spades, the King of Clubs, the King of Hearts, and the King of Diamonds.

—King Farouk I, shortly before his overthrow

Under the Nasser Regime

In 1954, Gamal Abdel Nasser, then deputy prime minister of Egypt, was giving a speech commemorating the British withdrawal when Mohammed Abdel Latif, a member of the Muslim Brotherhood, fired eight shots at him. Every bullet missed Nasser, who remained steadfast during the fusillade and then dramatically declared his willingness to die for the sake of the freedom and honor of the Egyptian people.

Far from eliminating him, the attempt on his life positioned Nasser for the presidency of Egypt, which he gained in 1956. He acted quickly to permanently abolish the Muslim Brotherhood. He ordered the arrest not merely of Brotherhood leaders, but of as many members as could be identified. Thousands were imprisoned or confined to concentration camps. Many were tortured.

Sayyid Qutb, an eminent Egyptian man of letters, Islamic political philosopher, and a leading member of the Muslim Brotherhood, was implicated in the failed assassination plot. Arrested in 1954, he was imprisoned under brutal conditions through 1957, when he was given a degree of freedom and even allowed to write. His writing was radically anti-secular and anti-Western, and his philosophy of government did much to shape an extreme form of political Islam named for him: "Qutbism."

To many, Qutb was the face of what the Muslim Brotherhood, under suppression, had become: utterly uncompromising in adopting the Quran as the only guide for government, and unwilling to compromise with any leader, any nation, or any people who thought otherwise.

Recognizing Qutb's influence and popularity in some quarters, Nasser thought it prudent to release him from prison as a goodwill gesture in 1964. Eight months later, however, he was again arrested. This time, he was tried for plotting to overthrow the state and to assassinate President Nasser.

Renunciation of Violence

Qutb's execution by hanging on August 29, 1966, along with six other prominent Brotherhood members, had a mixed effect on political Islam. In many parts of the Muslim world, the ideology of Qutbism became a popular and compelling driver of revolution based on the belief that modern Islamic states were irredeemably corrupt and had to be overthrown in order to restore Islam to its proper spiritual purity.

In Egypt, however, the surviving leaders of the Muslim Brotherhood, though they paid homage to Qutb, renounced his call to violent revolution. They agreed that modern Islam was in need of reform, but they advocated reform by peaceful means.

Return to Violence

Upon Nasser's death (of natural causes) in 1970, Anwar Sadat, like Nasser a former member of the Free Officers Movement, succeeded him as president. He came into office with secularist but anti-Western and anti-Israeli views aligned with those of Nasser. Soon, however, his thinking evolved toward a much more liberal stance. He began releasing imprisoned members of the Muslim Brotherhood and sought reconciliation with them. The organization remained under a legal ban, but Sadat made no arrests and quietly allowed the Brotherhood to function.

What drew the attention of the West, however, was Sadat's bold move toward peaceful coexistence with Israel, culminating in the breakthrough Egypt/Israeli peace agreement known as the Camp David Accords, brokered in 1978–1979 by U.S. President Jimmy Carter, who followed up on initiatives begun during the Nixon administration. Under both Presidents Nixon and Carter, Egypt became a major recipient of U.S. economic and military aid in an effort to lure Egypt out of the Soviet sphere of influence to which it had gravitated during the Nasser years. Both Nixon and Carter let it be known to the leaders of Egypt as well as Israel that continued good relations with the United States was, however, contingent on the two adversaries negotiating a path to peaceful coexistence. (Today, among nations, only Israel receives more U.S. military aid than Egypt.)

Tragically, Sadat's open attitude toward the Muslim Brotherhood encouraged the development of other radical and violent groups of Islamic extremists. Close relations with the United States and the accord with Israel put Sadat in the crosshairs of the Muslim Brotherhood and those other extremists, including a group known as Tanzim al-Jihad. On October 6, 1981, a member of this organization, Khalid Islambouli, an Egyptian army lieutenant, gunned down Sadat and 11 others as they attended an annual victory parade.

 DID YOU KNOW?

> The Camp David Accords are named after the U.S. presidential retreat located in Catoctin Mountain Park, Frederick County, Maryland. Here, Egyptian President Anwar Sadat and Israeli Prime Minister Menachem Begin were closeted for 13 days of secret negotiations, which produced two framework agreements for the Egypt-Israeli Peace Treaty that followed. The two leaders shared the 1978 Nobel Peace Prize.

Brethren Against Mubarak

Anwar Sadat was succeeded by his vice president, Hosni Mubarak, who was recovering from serious wounds sustained during the October 6 assassination.

Born in 1928, Mubarak was a graduate of the Egyptian Air Force Academy, who, during the presidency of the pro-Soviet Nasser, also received advanced flight and command training in the USSR. On his return to Egypt, he rose rapidly within the air force, became politically well connected, and, in 1975, was appointed vice president of Egypt by Anwar Sadat.

As vice president, he supported Sadat's peacemaking efforts with Israel, but was later critical of some aspects of the Camp David Accords. Nevertheless, as president, Mubarak maintained peaceful relations with Israel as well as Israel's ally and supporter, the United States. During the Persian Gulf War of 1991, he even took Egypt into the U.S.-led coalition against the Iraqi invasion of Kuwait.

Democracy and the Brotherhood

Mubarak's alignment with the West and his continued tolerance of Israel alienated many young Egyptian Islamists, who, in consequence, joined the Muslim Brotherhood. By the 1980s, the Brotherhood became Egypt's most important political association among students and professionals. Early in the 1990s, an alarmed Mubarak took brutal steps to suppress the organization by ordering police harassment and mass arrests. These ruthless acts of repression backfired by associating the Muslim Brotherhood with elements of Egyptian society advocating greater democracy and condemning the Mubarak regime as a dictatorship. In parliamentary elections during the 1990s, numerous candidates supported by the Brotherhood fared well.

Even as the Muslim Brotherhood became increasingly identified with a movement toward democratic transformation in Egypt, its leaders called for closer identification of the government as a *Muslim* government, upholding Muslim values for a Muslim country instead of capitulating to foreign domination and economic subservience. This stance created conflict among many Westerners, who were accustomed to defining democracy in terms of religious freedom and the separation of church and state. Nevertheless, although the secular Mubarak was a U.S. ally, it became clear to many Americans and other Westerners that he was also a corrupt autocrat.

Yet the 15 Muslim Brotherhood leaders elected to the Egyptian parliament in 2000 were unabashed in their advocacy of conservative Muslim values and the suppression of Western cultural expressions they deemed contrary to Islam. The Brotherhood's parliamentary leader, Hamdy Hassan, spoke out against what he called a "U.S.-led war against Islamic culture and identity."

Many Americans asked how such rhetoric could be compatible with democracy. It was a valid question, which, however, overlooked the fact that U.S. aid had, for some 43 years, propped up Mubarak, whose approach to government was very far from democratic.

The Kefaya Movement

Kefaya (Arabic for "enough") was the popular nickname for the Egyptian Movement for Change, a bottom-up coalition that came together in 2004 to protest the Mubarak presidency and initiate progress toward democracy.

The Muslim Brotherhood enthusiastically participated in the Kefaya movement and evaded the government's "emergency" ban on Muslim Brotherhood political candidacy by running as independents in 2005—albeit under a slogan that unmistakably identified them: "Islam Is the Solution."

Despite police attempts to suppress the opposition vote, the Brotherhood candidates took 20 percent of parliamentary seats, making them the largest bloc opposed to the Mubarak government.

The Muslim Brotherhood was keenly aware that, although the United States and the rest of the West feared political Islam, they favored any move toward democracy, almost certainly because Westerners tended to equate "democracy" with secular government and held a belief that democracies generally do not perpetrate violence against other democracies. Accordingly, the Brotherhood members of parliament addressed a number of pro-democracy issues that had little or nothing to do with Islam. Among these was a plea for tolerance of all religions. Moreover, although many Islamist groups shunned outsiders, the Brotherhood launched an English-language website and made a concerted public-relations effort to correct what they called "Western misconceptions" about Islam and the Muslim Brotherhood.

The Mubarak regime fought back by warning the West that the Brotherhood represented radical Islam and was determined to create a global Caliphate to "Islamize" the world. In Egypt, the government cracked down even harder on the Brotherhood. The harassment was not unusual, but the regime now went much further. It proposed a constitutional amendment that would have the effect of ending Islam as the state religion of Egypt. This prompted the Brotherhood members to walk out of parliament, and it sent a cadre of Brethren (students at Cairo's Al Azhar University) marching through city streets in ominous masks and militia-style uniforms.

The show of militancy actually emboldened the government in 2008 to amend the constitution to disqualify "independents" from running for parliament. This effectively barred Brotherhood political representation. At the same time, new arrests were made, and thousands of Brethren were jailed. In 2010, all but one of the Brotherhood members lost their parliamentary seats.

The Arab Spring Comes to Egypt

In Chapter 19, we will see how the so-called Arab Spring, which began as a grassroots movement in Tunisia in 2010, toppled repressive regimes and strongman dictatorships in the Arab world by December 2013.

Mubarak and Egypt were not immune. In 2011, a popular uprising swelled in Egypt, growing into a revolution that overthrew Hosni Mubarak, Egypt's longest-serving president. Westerners generally welcomed this, but they also feared that the subsequent legalization of the Muslim Brotherhood would transform a secular Egypt into a hostile state.

For its part, the Brotherhood again embraced the rhetoric of democracy, creating a new political party called the Freedom and Justice Party, which took nearly half the seats in parliament and won the presidency in 2012, narrowly defeating a former army officer.

Mohamed Morsi

Mohamed Morsi was born in a village north of Cairo in 1951, the son of a farmer. He went on to earn a bachelor's and a master's degree in engineering at Cairo University, and then studied at the University of Southern California in Los Angeles, receiving in 1982 a PhD in materials science. He taught engineering and worked as an engineer during the 1980s, even participating in the development of materials for U.S. Space Shuttle engines.

Morsi returned to Egypt in 1985 and became head of the Engineering Department of Zagazig University, continuing to teach there until 2010.

A leading member of the Muslim Brotherhood, Morsi was elected to the Egyptian parliament in 2000 and served until 2005. During the 2011 revolution, Morsi was briefly held as a political prisoner, but managed to escape two days after his arrest. He was appointed chairman of the Brotherhood's Freedom and Justice Party and was named its presidential candidate in 2012.

Morsi won 51.7 percent of the vote in a presidential runoff election against former army officer Ahmed Shafik, who had served as Mubarak's last prime minister. He was Egypt's first democratically elected president.

Although Morsi came into office promising a moderate regime, he soon encountered militant opposition, which prompted his "temporary" assumption of "unlimited powers." When he presented an Islamist-backed constitution and called for a referendum on it, he was widely accused of perpetrating an "Islamist coup." Amid increasingly repressive measures taken against those who opposed him, Morsi was swept out of office by a military coup on July 3, 2013. The action took place amid a popular uprising against him—the so-called Revolution of 2013—which was supported by General Abdel Fattah el-Sisi, chief of the armed forces.

On September 1, 2013, Morsi was formally charged with "inciting deadly violence." Prosecutors referred Morsi to trial on charges of inciting deadly violence, to which espionage charges were later added. As of February 2014, his trial is in progress. If found guilty, he faces possible execution.

From Cooperation to Counterrevolution

The new president, Mohamed Morsi, was a member of the Muslim Brotherhood, but presented himself as a democrat first and foremost and claimed to harbor no radically ideological agenda. The new regime at first seemed to garner considerable cooperation, but within its first several months was increasingly assailed by popular and military opposition.

Late in November 2012, the "democrat" Morsi suddenly declared that he was granting himself temporary unlimited powers to protect Egypt from falling back into the clutches of Mubarak and his supporters. Opponents now spoke of "an Islamist coup," and the same Cairo streets that had earlier filled with the anti-Mubarak, pro-democracy demonstrators of the Arab Spring were now jammed with those protesting Morsi as a radical Islamist usurper.

Egypt, a year earlier nearly united behind the idea of democratic reform, now split into two apparently irreconcilable factions. On one side were the Islamist supporters of Morsi and the Brotherhood. On the other were the political moderates—moderate Muslims, Christians, and liberal secularists—who wanted a democracy without either a secular or a religious dictator.

In the spring of 2013, a full-on counterrevolutionary movement, called the Tamarod ("The Rebellion"), came into being to secure the recall of President Morsi. On June 29, Tamarod presented some 22 million petition signatures, and, on June 30, an estimated 17 to 33 million Egyptians fanned out in protest all over the nation, demanding that Morsi step down.

The Military Intervenes

The power of ideas, people, and religion is great. In modern Egypt, the power of the military has often been even greater. Certainly, no modern Egyptian leader has long endured without the support of the military, and, on July 3, 2013, General Abdel Fattah el-Sisi, chief of the armed forces, did not simply voice the end of military support for Mohamed Morsi, he announced the removal of Morsi himself.

The constitution was suspended pending new elections, and a state of emergency was declared, in which troops raided Brotherhood facilities and meetings and broke up pro-Brotherhood, pro-Morsi protests. In retaliation, Muslim Brotherhood members attacked and burned police stations and many churches throughout the country.

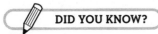

DID YOU KNOW?

During the summer of 2013, violence swept Egypt, especially the larger cities. In all, 638 people (595 civilians, 43 police officers) were killed and more than 4,000 injured.

In the end, the Muslim Brotherhood was left in shambles, its leaders in prison or in flight. Once again, the organization was outlawed, and its now considerable assets confiscated. On September 25, the newspaper of the Freedom and Justice Party was shut down. In 2014, the crackdown went far beyond these measures as an Egyptian court in the town of Minya, on March 24, sentenced 529 Brotherhood members to death on charges that included attacking a police station and killing a policeman. Little more than a month later, on April 28, the same court handed down death sentences for 683 Muslim Brotherhood members, including the organization's supreme guide, Mohamed Badie, after they were convicted of attacking a police station and killing an officer. At this time, the Minya court also upheld 37 of the earlier death sentences, commuting 429 to life terms.

Egyptian Outlook

Since the end of World War II, Egypt has been one of the most powerful forces in the Arab world and among the most strategically important links between the nations and peoples of the Middle East and those of the West. Since the 1970s, and especially following the Camp David Accords, Egypt has been a beacon of hope for peaceful and productive relations between the Muslim world and the secular West. Its future is therefore of intense international concern.

In January 2014, 98.1 percent of Egyptian voters approved a new constitution, which guarantees equality between the sexes and proclaims freedom of religion while nevertheless affirming Islam as the state religion. In an effort to curb, among other things, political Islam, the new constitution forbids basing political parties on "religion, race, gender, or geography." The constitution establishes a presidency and a parliament, limiting the president to two four-year terms and giving the parliament the power to impeach the president. It also allows the military, not the president, to appoint the nation's minister of defense for the next eight years, which has drawn criticism from leftist groups.

Until the mass capital sentences handed down in March and April 2014, most Western observers cautiously greeted the strong popular approval of the new constitution as a sign that Egyptians have confidence in a future marked by their desire to retain the nation's Islamic identity while engaging fully with the family of nations, both in the region and throughout the world. The May 2014 election of Abdel Fattah el-Sisi as president sent a highly ambiguous message. Although el-Sisi received more than 96 percent of the vote, fewer than half of the electorate chose to cast ballots. Was the election a retreat from both Islamic rule as well as secular democracy in a return to government by military dictatorship? And was this retreat an expression of popular will or, given the low voter turnout, the result of popular resignation?

The Least You Need to Know

- Founded in Egypt in 1928, the Muslim Brotherhood has spearheaded the creation of "political Islam," the doctrine that the beliefs, laws, and values of Islam should guide not only individual conduct, but collective politics and national leadership.

- Political Islam is often associated with the Pan-Islamist movement and Arab nationalism.

- Another way to view political Islam as represented by the Muslim Brotherhood is as the counterpart to Zionism, which may accordingly be seen as "political Judaism."

- The Muslim Brotherhood played important role in Egypt's democracy movement, which began as the Kefaya movement in 2004 and culminated in the Egyptian Revolution of 2011, which resulted in the election of Mohamed Morsi, a prominent member of the Muslim Brotherhood, to the presidency in 2012.

- Less than a year after he became Egypt's first democratically elected president, Morsi gave himself "temporary" unlimited power—a step that instigated his being overthrown by a combination of popular uprising and military coup.

The Holocaust and the Exodus

Theodor Herzl called the Dreyfus Affair an expression of intractable European anti-Semitism and identified it as the personal turning point that moved him in 1896 to present the theory of Zionism in *The Jewish State*, but he also said that the principal motive for creating a Jewish national homeland was not to escape persecution. It was, he insisted, to fulfill a profound spiritual and cultural imperative; Zionism was born of a basic human need and human right.

And yet it was the Jews' history of persecution that won over many of the world's non-Jews to the support of Zionism. In the nineteenth and early twentieth centuries, the worst persecution occurred in Russia. In the 1930s, the epicenter of European anti-Semitism moved to Adolf Hitler's Germany. This not only dramatically increased the volume of Jewish immigration to Palestine, but also stirred support from much the world's non-Jewish population.

In the Middle East, however, among Arabs and other Muslims, and in Palestine especially, the new influx of Jewish Zionist immigrants raised the Arab-Jewish conflict to a state of bloody civil war. Arabs not only protested their displacement from Palestine, they deemed Zionist settlement a new form of European colonialism. Even granting that Jews were fleeing Nazi persecution, many Arabs protested the injustice of giving up their homes to atone for the murderous sins of Christian Europe. The new migration brought fresh urgency—indeed, desperation—to the long-simmering "Palestinian question."

In This Chapter

- The dramatic increase of Jewish immigration to Palestine during the 1930s due to Nazi persecution

- Germany's shift from a policy of persecution to a program of genocide

- The chronic riots and revolt in Palestine during the 1930s

- The partition of Palestine

- Postwar "Exodus" and the founding of Israel

Anti-Semitism Becomes Law

Adolf Hitler did not invent anti-Semitism when he and his Nazi Party assumed power in Germany in 1933, but his policies enshrined it in German law, and what the Nazis called the "final solution to the Jewish question" became a national mission and a cornerstone aim of World War II.

From 1933 on, reports of anti-Jewish persecution continuously flowed out of Germany. Much of the world turned a blind eye, but on September 15, 1935, the *Third Reich* put its anti-Semitism on violent display for all the world to see.

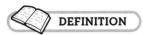 **DEFINITION**

Third Reich is the name for the government Adolf Hitler introduced when he took power in 1933. The First Reich was the Holy Roman Empire of 800 to 1806. The Second Reich was the German Empire, which was founded in 1871 with Prussia's victory over France in the Franco-Prussian War and ended in 1918 with Germany's defeat in World War I.

That evening, two laws were announced at the annual Nazi Party rally held in Nuremberg. The Law for the Protection of German Blood and Honor barred marriage as well as extramarital sexual intercourse between what the law called "Germans" and "Jews," thereby explicitly excluding Jews from being identified as Germans. Furthermore, the law prohibited the employment of "German" women and girls under age 45 in "Jewish" households. The second law, promulgated at the same time, was called the Reich Citizenship Law. It distinguished between persons of German blood and those of non-German blood. The former were classified as "Aryans" and, by virtue of their Aryan race, were citizens of the Third Reich. The latter, non-Aryans, were not citizens, but "state subjects." Although this second law did not use the terms *Jew* or *Jewish*, Jews—including those of Jewish lineage (Jewish "blood")—were by definition non-Aryans. In effect, the law summarily stripped Jews of German citizenship.

 DID YOU KNOW?

The Nazi definition of *Jew* and *Jewishness* had nothing to do with religion, but was instead a matter of "race" or "blood." A Mischling ("crossbreed" or "mixed breed") was a person who combined Jewish and "Aryan" ancestry. Whether a particular Mischling was legally a Jew or an Aryan was resolved by an addendum to the Nuremberg Laws, issued on November 14, 1935. A person with three or four Jewish grandparents was legally a Jew. A person with two Jewish grandparents was either a Jew or a "Mischling of the first degree" (for most legal purposes, a Jew). A person with only one Jewish grandparent was a Mischling of the second degree (for some legal purposes, a Jew).

The Nuremberg Laws were used to legalize discrimination against Jews, who were barred from voting and running for political office as well as prevented from practicing most professions, including teaching, the law, medicine, and journalism. Public education was denied to Jews past the age of 14, and such public amenities as parks, beaches, and libraries were closed to Jews. The names of Jews were ordered to be removed from all war memorials in Germany, and the passports of Jews were stamped with a capital *J*, meaning that they could be used to leave Germany—but not to return.

 DID YOU KNOW?

> In September 1939, Nazi officials ordered Jews in German-occupied Poland to sew a so-called "yellow badge," a Star of David, onto their outer garments. In September 1941, this order was extended to all Jews living in Germany or other German-occupied territories. Requiring Jews to wear badges or other distinctive articles of clothing was not unique to the Nazi regime. During the Middle Ages, Jews in some Muslim countries were required to distinguish themselves in these ways (as were, at some times and in some places, all non-Muslims, including Christians). Throughout Medieval Europe, Jews and Muslims alike were obliged to display clothing that marked them as non-Christian.

Emigration and Exile

Beginning in 1933, two years before passage of the Nuremberg Laws, rural Jews were subjected to internal exile, driven off of their farms or out of their villages and forced to find homes in urban Germany. This policy coincided with the official encouragement of voluntary emigration abroad. Those who left, however, did so at enormous sacrifice. New German laws prevented Jews from leaving the country with most of their money. Just about everything they owned was confiscated.

 DID YOU KNOW?

> More than half of Germany's 500,000 Jewish citizens voluntarily emigrated between 1933 and 1938. About 100,000 settled in the United States, 63,000 in Argentina, 52,000 in Great Britain, and 33,000 in Palestine.

The Jewish exodus from Germany spread the word of the growing horrors of Jewish life under the Nazi regime.

A Night of Shattered Glass

In addition to organized discrimination, the German government sanctioned, encouraged, or instigated persecution. The first phase of truly organized persecution culminated in Kristallnacht ("Crystal Night") during November 9 and 10, 1938. This Night of Shattered Glass was a nationwide pogrom, during which more than 1,000 synagogues were burned and some 7,500 Jewish businesses looted, their windows smashed—the shattered glass giving the act of terrorism its name. At least 91 Jews were killed outright by mobs during Kristallnacht, and Jewish homes, hospitals, schools, and cemeteries were vandalized.

The pretext for Kristallnacht was the November 7 shooting, in Paris, of German diplomat Ernst von Rath by Herschel Grynszpan, a Jewish student from Poland. Hitler and his minister of propaganda, Joseph Goebbels, exploited the incident to ignite a mass reprisal against Germany's Jews, and Goebbels secretly called on the Storm Troopers (the paramilitary wing of the Nazi Party) to orchestrate "spontaneous" demonstrations, which were, in fact, coordinated by the Gestapo (secret police) throughout the Reich.

No Aryans were arrested during the riots, but, in their wake, approximately 30,000 Jews were rounded up and sent to *concentration camps*. Moreover, Reich officials seized insurance settlements Jewish victims obtained and levied fines against Germany's Jewish community totaling some one billion Reichsmarks.

 **DEFINITION**

> A **concentration camp** is a place where masses of people—usually political prisoners or members of some persecuted minority—are gathered (concentrated), typically under terrible conditions. Some concentration camps were also forced-labor camps. In Germany during World War II, some were death camps: places of mass murder.

Concentration Camp Nation

By May 1934, the beginning of the second year of Nazi government in Germany, about 80,000 people were incarcerated in a growing number of concentration camps throughout the country. Until 1938, however, after the Reich created the Central Office for Jewish Emigration, headed by an *SS* (*Schutzstaffel*) officer named Adolf Eichmann, the camps held mostly communists and those judged by the government to be undesirable, including Gypsies, homosexuals, and habitual criminals. In November 1938, Jews were increasingly added to the concentration-camp population.

 **DEFINITION**

> The **SS** (*Schutzstaffel*) was an elite corps of German combat troops originally constituted as a personal bodyguard for Adolf Hitler.

The Anschluss, Germany's annexation of Austria, on March 12, 1938, followed by the annexation of the Czech Sudetenland, Bohemia, and Moravia later in the year, brought a quarter-million Austrian and Czech Jews under Nazi control. By 1939, an estimated 1,000 Jews had been murdered in concentration camps. Of Austria's 160,000 Jews, about 100,000 emigrated, but by this time many nations had enacted policies restricting Jewish immigration.

The German invasion of Poland in September 1939 not only ignited World War II, it brought under Reich control another three million Jews, Poland having the largest Jewish community in Europe. The resulting influx into Nazi concentration camps was massive, and of the 10,000 Polish civilians killed during the opening phase of the invasion of Poland, 3,000 were Jews—many of them herded into synagogues and then burned alive.

Because the concentration camps could not handle three million new prisoners all at once, most Polish Jews were forcibly moved into ghettos, neighborhoods walled off from the non-Jewish portions of the Polish cities. These areas were severely overcrowded—the Warsaw Ghetto, for example, occupied 2.4 percent of the city's area, but held 30 percent of its population—and food was rationed at starvation levels. The purpose of the ghettos was not just containment, but death. By the early summer of 1941, half a million Jews were confined in the Warsaw Ghetto, and starvation and disease were claiming about 2,000 persons per month.

The Polish ghettos proved to be only an intermediate step to mass murder—genocide—in large camps designed and built as death camps.

Palestine: Riots and Revolt

Between 1933 and the outbreak of World War II in 1939, 170,000 European Jews immigrated to Palestine, bringing its Jewish population to nearly 500,000, compared with more than a million Arabs. Amid ongoing violence between Arabs and Jews, the Arab High Commission, a body of Arab representatives in Palestine, formally petitioned the British authorities in 1935 to halt Jewish immigration.

The Arab response to Jewish immigration was by no means anti-Semitic. Indeed, during the nineteenth century, when the Jewish population of Palestine was about 25,000, rising to 60,000 by the start of the twentieth century, relations between Arabs and Jews were both cordial and respectful. To many Arabs, particularly those in Palestine, the influx of the 1930s seemed not like a flow of refugees from genocidal persecution, but a European invasion—for the people Europeans saw as *Jews*, the Arabs saw as *Europeans*. From the perspective of Arab Palestinians, the influx was a colonization, which threatened them with physical dispossession as well as spiritual and cultural extinction.

The Peel Commission Report

When British authorities rejected the 1935 Arab petition and refused to end Jewish immigration, Arab resistance escalated into a bloody civil war between Arabs and the ever-expanding Haganah. After a particularly bloody year in 1936, the British government appointed Lord Robert Peel to head a commission to study the problem and make recommendations. The Report of the Palestine Royal Commission—commonly called the Peel Report—was issued in July 1937.

The Peel Report identified the causes of the ongoing violence as the Arabs' desire for national independence and their fear and hatred of the prospect of a Jewish national homeland in Palestine. Concluding that the interests of the Jews and the Arabs could not be reconciled under the British Mandate for Palestine, the report recommended partitioning Palestine. A Jewish state was to consist of Galilee, the Yezreel Valley, and the Coastal Plain to a point midway between Gaza and Jaffe. This constituted about 20 percent of the area of Palestine. Except for Jerusalem, Bethlehem (plus a corridor connecting them to the sea), and (possibly) Nazareth and the Sea of Genezareth—all of which were to remain part of a British mandatory zone—the rest of Palestine, the report recommended, should be given over to Arab control and joined to Transjordan (modern Jordan).

Surprisingly, the Zionist Congress substantially accepted the Peel proposal (over the objection of a large minority of those participating in the Congress), but the representatives of the Arabs rejected it flat, protesting the injustice and persecution of usurping Arab homes and homeland to redress injustice and European persecution of Jews in Europe.

 VOICES

> To foster Jewish immigration in the hope that it might ultimately lead to the creation of Jewish majority [in Palestine] and the establishment of a Jewish State with the consent or at least the acquiescence of the Arabs was one thing. It was quite another to contemplate, however remotely, the forcible conversion of Palestine into a Jewish state against the will of the Arabs.
>
> —The Peel Report, 1937

Peel Repealed

In November 1938, five months after issuing the Peel Report, the British government issued a "Policy Statement against partition," concluding that "the political, administrative, and financial difficulties involved in the proposal to create independent Arab and Jewish States inside Palestine are so great that this solution of the problem is impracticable." This being the case, the government decided to continue the mandate until an "alternative means of meeting the needs of the difficult situation" described in the Peel Report could be found.

Britain Issues a New "White Paper"

Amid unceasing violent conflict in Palestine and with war clouds darkening over Europe, a conference was convened in London during February–March 1939 to find an alternative to the partition of Palestine. When this collapsed, the British government issued on May 17, 1939, a new "White Paper."

In a stunning repudiation of the Balfour Declaration of 1917, the British sought to prevent the Arabs from siding with Germany by meeting almost all of their demands. Jewish immigration was to continue for just 5 more years, capped at 15,000 people per year. After this, immigration was to cease altogether. In addition, Jewish purchase of Arab-owned lands would be barred in some areas and restricted in others.

 VOICES

> ...His Majesty's Government believe that the framers of the [League of Nations Palestine] Mandate in which the Balfour Declaration was embodied could not have intended that Palestine should be converted into a Jewish State against the will of the Arab population of the country.... His Majesty's Government therefore now declare unequivocally that it is not part of their policy that Palestine should become a Jewish State.
>
> —White Paper of 1939, May 17, 1939

Unsurprisingly, the Zionists rejected the White Paper. The Jewish Agency called the White Paper a "breach of faith and a surrender to Arab terrorism. Far from bringing peace, the Agency predicted that the new British policy would "lead to a complete breach between Jews and Arabs which will banish every prospect of peace in Palestine" and threatened that "the Jews would fight rather than submit to Arab rule."

Most tellingly, the Jewish Agency accused the British government of proposing "to deprive the Jews of their last hope and to close the road back to their Homeland" and, what is more, to do so "in the darkest hour of Jewish history."

As for the Arab leaders, in what must have been for the British government a stunning response, they, too, rejected the new policy. They demanded nothing less than an immediate and total end to Jewish immigration and the review of every Jewish immigration since 1918 with an eye toward deportation.

The "Darkest Hour of Jewish History"

On August 23, 1939, the world's democracies were stunned by news that the Soviet Union and Germany had concluded a non-aggression pact. Had those democracies been aware of the secret portions of the pact, they would have been more than stunned. The devastating truth was that Joseph Stalin and Adolf Hitler had made an alliance.

It proved short lived. On June 22, 1941, Hitler betrayed Stalin by invading the Soviet Union. Accompanying his troops were cadres of special soldiers, the Einsatzgruppen ("task forces"). Their mission was to kill Jews, and they did so in Russia and in other Eastern European countries conquered by the Germans.

It is estimated that Einsatzgruppen soldiers killed about a million Jews, many by shooting followed by burial in mass graves. But this method of murder was deemed too labor-intensive and slow for a program of genocide, and thus Reinhard Heydrich, head of the Reichssicherheitshauptamt (Reich Security Central Office) convened on January 20, 1942, a secret conference at Wannsee, a villa on Lake Wannsee in southwestern Berlin.

Here SS officials and administrators of the German civilian government agreed to cooperate in carrying out the Final Solution—the total annihilation of all the Jews of Europe. The minutes of the conference, recorded by Heydrich's lieutenant, Adolf Eichmann, outline a shift in policy from emigration to deportation, forced labor, and outright mass murder. Extermination of Europe's Jews was not an objective incidental to the war, but a top war aim. It was decided that death would be accomplished by factory-style methods using Zyklon-B, a pesticide agent consisting of prussic acid crystals that produced deadly cyanide gas when dissolved. If death was the product of this factory, corpses were the byproducts, which would be disposed of by burning in industrial-scale crematoriums.

Germany and the 21 German-occupied countries were swept by what was later called the *Holocaust*. Before it began, Europe had a Jewish population of about nine million. When it was over, six million were dead—two-thirds of Europe's Jews.

The Mufti and the Chairman

The horrors of Nazi Germany put tremendous moral and humanitarian pressure on all parties—Jewish, Arab, and British—who had a stake in Palestine. One major Arab leader, the Grand Mufti of Jerusalem, Haj Amin al-Husseini, even made a direct alliance with Adolf Hitler.

Husseini Seeks Common Cause with the Führer

On November 28, 1941, Husseini met with Hitler, his foreign minister, Joachim von Ribbentrop, and others. According to the German minutes of the meeting, he told Hitler that the "Arab countries were firmly convinced that Germany would win the war and that the Arab cause would then prosper." Husseini explained that the "Arabs were Germany's natural friends because they had the same enemies as had Germany, namely the English, the Jews, and the Communists." For this reason, he continued, the Arabs were "prepared to cooperate with Germany with all their hearts and stood ready to participate in the war, not only negatively by the commission of acts of sabotage and the instigation of revolutions, but also positively by the formation of an Arab Legion." He spoke of the "suffering inflicted upon [the Arabs] by the English and the Jews," and he promised to raise a German-allied legion not only from among Arabs, but also Algerians, Tunisians, and Moroccans. Husseini requested that Hitler "make a public declaration" of support so that the "Arabs would not lose hope" in their struggle for independence.

Hitler greeted Husseini's sentiments warmly, replying to him that "Germany stood for uncompromising war against the Jews" and that this "naturally included active opposition to the Jewish national home in Palestine, which was nothing other than a center, in the form of a state, for the exercise of destructive influence by Jewish interests." The German dictator explained that his nation was "resolved, step by step, to ask one European nation after the other to solve its Jewish problem," and would "at the proper time direct a similar appeal to non-European nations as well." But, he continued, "Germany was at the present time engaged in a life and death struggle with two citadels of Jewish power: Great Britain and Soviet Russia." Although it "went without saying that Germany would furnish positive and practical aid to the Arabs," it could only do so after it had made further progress against the British and the Soviets.

Husseini thanked Hitler and expressed understanding of why he could not yet make a public proclamation of support, but then he asked instead for a secret agreement. Hitler replied "that he had just now given the Grand Mufti precisely that confidential declaration."

Ben-Gurion's Plan

Even in the absence of a formal agreement with Hitler, the Arabs in Palestine stepped up attacks against both the British and the Jews. Indeed, the British were in a precarious position in Palestine, the 1939 White Paper having outraged the Jews while also leaving the Arabs profoundly dissatisfied.

By this time, the Palestine Jews—or *Yishuv*, as they called themselves—had organized three military forces to fight against Arab attacks. In addition to the original Haganah, there was the Irgun ("The National Military Organization in the Land of Israel"), which broke away from the Haganah in 1931. Whereas the Haganah defined itself as a self-defense force, the Irgun embraced a doctrine of "active retaliation" rather than mere defense. Irgun leaders believed that the state of Israel had to be established by any means necessary, including acts of terrorism.

Even more aggressive than Irgun was Lehi ("Fighters for the Freedom of Israel"), which the British referred to as the Stern Gang, after its founder-leader Avraham Stern. This group broke off from the Irgun in August 1940.

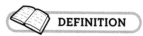 **DEFINITION**

> **Yishuv** is a Hebrew word meaning "settlement." From the 1880s to the creation of Israel in 1948, it was the name Jewish residents of Palestine collectively applied to themselves.

David Ben-Gurion, chairman of the executive committee of the Jewish Agency in Palestine, had long advocated working peacefully and patiently with the British to achieve an independent Jewish state. The publication of the 1939 White Paper, however, forced him to change his mind. Proclaiming that "Peace in Palestine is not the best situation for thwarting the policy of the White Paper," he now advocated preparing the Yishuv to go to war. With the outbreak of World War II, however, he encouraged Yishuv young men to volunteer for the British army, quietly arguing that this would build the core of a "Hebrew army" capable (some day) of defeating both the Arabs and the British. In the meantime, however, Ben-Gurion recognized that prominent Arab leaders were aligning with the Germans and that anything that could be done to defeat the Germans would not only contribute to the salvation of Jews everywhere, but would diminish Arab military prospects in Palestine. Once the Germans had been defeated, the "Hebrew army" that had been created to serve the British could be turned loose on whatever forces presented themselves as enemies to the creation of the Jewish state.

 **VOICES**

We will fight the White Paper as if there is no war, and fight the war as if there is no White Paper.

—David Ben-Gurion, 1939

The Jewish Brigade

Both the Haganah and the Irgun followed Ben-Gurion's lead and assisted the British war effort in Palestine. Chaim Weizmann, president of the World Zionist Organization, offered Britain the full cooperation of the Yishuv community, appealing to the British military to authorize a distinctive Jewish formation fighting under a Jewish flag. The appeal was deferred, but in September 1940, 15 Jewish battalions were created as part of the regular British army. Only much later in the war did the British government finally create the "Jewish Brigade" on July 3, 1944. It consisted of 5,000 Yishuv volunteers fighting under the Zionist flag.

 **DID YOU KNOW?**

Although raised in Palestine, the Jewish Brigade did not fight in the Middle East but instead participated in the Italian Campaign as part of the British Eighth Army. During the final offensive of the European war, brigade troops searched for Holocaust survivors, rendered aid to them, and facilitated their emigration to Palestine.

The Stern Gang Deals with the Devil

Irgun member Avraham Stern refused to follow Ben-Gurion and Weizmann. Instead, the young Zionist militant founded Lehi (the so-called Stern Gang) after Irgun leadership decided to suspend anti-British military operations to assist the British in defeating the Germans. Declaring that there was "no difference" between Hitler and British Prime Minister Neville Chamberlain, who had approved the White Paper of 1939, nor any difference "between [the Nazi death camps] Dachau or Buchenwald and sealing the gates of Eretz Israel," Stern argued that Jews should fight the British who, as far as the creation of a Jewish state in Palestine was concerned, were an even greater enemy than the Nazis. Incredibly, Stern even sought an alliance with the Nazis against the British, offering to fight alongside Germans in return for the transfer to Palestine of all Jews in German-occupied Europe.

The British labeled the Stern Gang a terrorist organization, and, thanks to Stern's reaching out to the Nazis, Lehi was intensely unpopular with most Yishuv. British authorities hunted Stern down, and on February 12, 1942, police arrested him in Tel Aviv—and then shot him dead when (according to the police) he attempted to escape. Many believe the police simply assassinated him.

Lehi continued to operate under other leaders, including Ytzhak Shamir, who went on to serve two terms as Israeli prime minister from 1983 to 1984 and from 1986 to 1992. The group was responsible for the November 1944 assassination of Lord Moyne, British Minister Resident in the Middle East; the October 1946 bombing of the British embassy in Rome; the January 12, 1947, bombing of a British police station in Haifa (in which 4 died and 140 were injured); and several subsequent failed bombing attempts in the UK. During the Arab-Israeli War of 1948, Lehi operatives mined the Cairo-to-Haifa train several times and participated with the Haganah in an attack on the Palestinian Arab village of Deir Yassin, in which at least 100 Arab civilians were killed (the Arab League reported 254 killed in addition to the perpetration of mass rapes).

 DID YOU KNOW?

Lehi was officially dissolved on May 31, 1948, when its members were integrated into the newly formed Israel Defense Forces. Nevertheless, some Lehi members continued to function in Jerusalem and were responsible, on September 17, 1948, for the assassination of United Nations mediator Count Folke Bernadotte. This prompted the Israeli government to declare Lehi a terrorist organization.

Exodus

The end of World War II in 1945 created a refugee crisis of unprecedented proportions. Between 11 million and 20 million persons were "displaced"—uprooted from their original homes and families, which in many cases no longer even existed. Among these were more than a quarter million Jews, survivors of the Holocaust, living in camps and urban centers in Germany, Austria, and Italy.

On May 1, 1946, a special Anglo-American Inquiry Committee issued a recommendation that 100,000 certificates be immediately authorized for the "admission into Palestine of Jews who have been victims of Nazi and Fascist persecution." This was of course far in excess of the 1939 British White Paper quotas—a problem the committee tried to get around by renouncing the idea of Palestine as *either* an Arab *or* a Jewish state.

"Palestine shall be neither a Jewish state nor an Arab state," the committee recommended, but shall adopt a "form of government ... under international guarantees [to] fully protect and preserve the interests in the Holy Land of Christendom and of the Moslem and Jewish faiths."

Well-intended as it was, this solution—effectively an indefinite continuation of the British Mandate—satisfied no one, and on February 14, 1947, British Foreign Secretary Ernest Bevin put to rest any further attempt to extend the mandate. He announced that Britain had decided to refer the Palestinian problem to the United Nations. As of May 14, 1948, His Majesty's Government would officially withdraw from Palestine.

Aliyah Bet

While British, American, and other officials debated how to handle Jewish displaced persons, some European Jews took matters into their own hands, organizing an underground network they called Brichah (Hebrew for "Flight"). The network moved thousands out of displaced persons camps to Mediterranean port towns, where they were to board ships of the Aliyah Bet, the "illegal immigration fleet."

While U.S., Italian, and French officials turned a blind eye to this activity, thereby silently sanctioning it, the British insisted on enforcing the 1939 White Paper and its regulations against illegal immigration. They mobilized the Royal Navy and the army to turn back illegal immigrants.

In all, British forces interdicted about half of the 142 voyages of Aliyah Bet vessels, sending some 50,000 would-be immigrants to internment camps. The most famous of the immigrant ships, an old American steamer launched in 1928 as the SS *President Warfield* and renamed by Aliyah Bet the *Exodus 1947*, carried 4,515 hopeful immigrants when it put to sea on July 11, 1947. On July 18, 20 miles off the Palestine coast, Royal Navy sailors boarded the ship and, after a skirmish, took command and sailed it, with its passengers, to Haifa. From here, all aboard were transferred to three vessels, which took them to a port near Marseilles, France, the designated country of their deportation.

French officials, however, suddenly announced that they would allow disembarkation only if it was voluntary. For three weeks, the passengers refused to leave the ships, which were then sailed to Hamburg, Germany, at the time occupied by British forces. From here, passengers were forcibly removed and sent to internment camps. But Brichah managed to smuggle more than half of the detainees out of the camps and out of the British occupation zone. From the U.S. zone, they boarded other Aliyah Bet vessels bound for Palestine. The remaining detainees did not reach their destination until January 1949, after the creation of the state of Israel.

The United Nations Acts

The UN accepted from Britain the hand-off of responsibility for Palestine and, in November 1947, passed Resolution 181, which partitioned Palestine, dividing it into an Arab state of 4,500 square miles and a Jewish state of 5,500. Jerusalem was designated an international city, belonging to neither population.

The Yishuv were divided on the resolution. Hardline Zionists wanted all of Palestine. Moderates, however, believed that the partition was the best deal the Jews were going to get—and they persuaded most of the hardline minority.

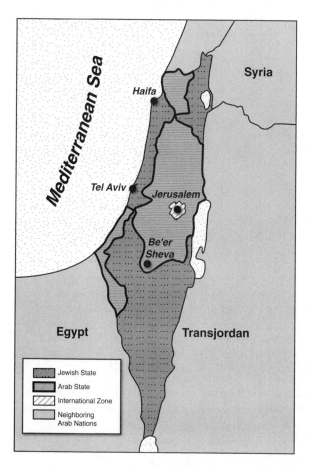

Arab leaders, in contrast, were united in rejecting the resolution. They argued that the United Nations had no authority to give away half of an Arab nation. Although they expressed sincere sympathy with the fate of Jews in the Holocaust, they yet again pointed out what seemed self-evident: that the Arabs of Palestine could not, in justice, be obliged to provide a Jewish homeland for an act of European genocide. The lawful and just thing to do, they proposed, was to allocate land in Europe—presumably in Germany—to be used for a Jewish homeland.

A product of the World War II alliance against Nazism and Fascism, the United Nations had been created to prevent war through negotiation, adjudication, and consensus. On the allocation of a little more than half of Palestine for a Jewish homeland, the members of the UN agreed. The Yishuv agreed as well. The dissent of the Arabs who actually lived in Palestine was dismissed.

And so the Arabs of Palestine went to war. From all over the Arab world, volunteer fighters—many called them terrorists—poured into Palestine to join in the attacks against Jewish settlers and settlements.

Israel Is Born

Amid the violence, on May 14, 1948, the day the British withdrew from their Palestinian mandate, Prime Minister David Ben-Gurion read the Declaration of the Establishment of the State of Israel. Fifteen minutes after this, President Harry S. Truman, over the objection of his own esteemed secretary of state, George C. Marshall, announced the United States as first among the nations of the world to recognize the new nation's existence.

 VOICES

> This government has been informed that a Jewish state has been proclaimed in Palestine, and recognition has been requested by the provisional government thereof. The United States recognizes the provisional government as the de facto authority of the new State of Israel.
>
> —President Harry S. Truman, May 14, 1948

Israelis called the event "independence"—a word with extraordinary depth of meaning for post-Holocaust Jews. The Arabs called it *al-Nakba:* "the Tragedy." Accordingly, Israel's declaration of independence was immediately followed by a war for that independence.

The Least You Need to Know

- In the run-up to World War II, Nazi Germany's program of anti-Semitic persecution culminating in genocide drove many German Jews to immigrate to Palestine, thereby provoking increased violence from the Arab majority there.

- As mandated administrators of Palestine, Great Britain struggled to resolve the conflict between Arabs and Jews, first calling for partition of Palestine, then rejecting partition, then repudiating its support for a Jewish homeland.

- After World War II, while refugee immigration into Britain and the United States was strictly limited, Jewish refugees commenced an "Exodus" to Palestine, defying British attempts to block immigration the British government deemed illegal.

- When the British renounced its mandate and turned over the Palestinian problem to the United Nations, that body's General Assembly passed a resolution partitioning Palestine between the Arabs and Jews, thereby enabling the creation of the state of Israel and igniting full-scale war between the Arab world and the new nation.

A History of Violence

The combination of history and faith, seared in the crucible of persecution and genocide, created a generation of Zionist European Jews determined to claim a national homeland in the Middle East—whatever the price.

As it turned out, that price included challenging the Arabs for possession of the land. It pitted one religious, cultural, and political tradition against another, and it was a price exacted not only from Arabs and Jews, but from all people who had a stake in a region that was the sacred source of three major religions, the nexus of communication among three teeming continents, and the fountainhead of a substance on which nations, economies, and wars all ran: oil.

Chapter 8 begins with oil as the coveted treasure that thrust the Middle East front and center in the geopolitics of the modern world. Chapter 9 narrates Israel's war of independence, which was also a war for its very right to exist, and follows up with the inescapable consequences of that war. Chapter 10, devoted to the Suez Crisis of 1956, explains how the Middle East became a battleground in the 50-year Cold War between the "Free World" (dominated by the United States) and the "Communist Bloc" (dominated by the Soviet Union). Chapter 11 turns to the Palestinian Arabs, the people rendered stateless by the creation of a Jewish state by once-stateless European Jews.

The final two chapters of Part 3 document the two major wars between Israel and the Arab world that followed the war for Israeli independence. Chapter 12 is about the so-called Six-Day War of 1967, and Chapter 13 covers the Yom Kippur War of 1973, in which Israel came perilously close to losing its right to continued existence.

Oil, Autocracy, and Revolt

During World War I, the Middle East was a strategic transportation nexus between African, Asian, and European combat theaters, providing access to southern Russia, the Balkans, and Turkey, and containing the vital Suez Canal linking the Red Sea with the Mediterranean. Desperate to maintain control of the region and its strategic assets, the British made conflicting promises to the Zionists and Yishuv on the one hand and to the Arabs on the other. When World War I ended, the British assumed responsibility for much of the Middle East, including Palestine. They were left to deal not only with the conflict between Arabs and Jews there, but with the consequences of their own contradictory pledges and policies.

With the outbreak of World War II, internal regional conflict became even more important to the European combatants, as did overall control of the Middle East, which provided direct access to the southern European front in the war.

In This Chapter

- The discovery of vast Middle Eastern oil resources

- 1947: America forges an oil partnership with Saudi Arabia

- 1953: Craving Iranian oil, Britain and the United States overthrow Iran's nationalist prime minister

- Gamal Nasser's starring role in oil politics

- The rise of OPEC and its limitations

The "Greatest Single Prize in All History"

Executive, consultant, and oil scientist Everette Lee DeGolyer served the U.S. government in several petroleum-related defense posts during World War II. In 1943–1944, he led a mission from the federal Petroleum Reserves Corporation to the Middle East. In this capacity, he prepared a report to the State Department in which he concluded that the region lay atop some 25 billion barrels of untapped crude oil. Unofficially, he confided to the Roosevelt administration that the true figure was probably closer to 300 billion barrels, and he called the "oil in this region ... the greatest single prize in all history."

Suddenly, the Middle East's importance loomed very large, to the industrial and political leaders of the West.

 DID YOU KNOW?

Middle Eastern oil was first discovered in 1908 at Masjed Soleyman in southwestern Iran, and its importance was instantly recognized. No one at the time dreamed, however, that this discovery was but a tiny part of the region's petroleum resources. The explosive growth of the automobile industry following Henry Ford's introduction of mass production in 1913 created an increasing demand for oil. As for World War II, it ran on petroleum, and the combined civilian and strategic demand made DeGolyer's 1944 report a true turning point for the role of the Middle East in world geopolitics and economics.

Oil Boom

World War II was a historic lesson in the central strategic importance of oil. Germany and Japan were defeated for many reasons, but high on the list was the fact that both essentially ran out of gas.

The war's intense strategic demand for oil was followed by the postwar era's even greater consumer demand. Discharged soldiers, especially in the nations of the victorious Allies—and nowhere more than in the United States—demanded cars to drive and wanted the consumer goods whose manufacture as well as delivery depended on petroleum.

During World War II, American oil drove the Allied victory. By 1948, however, just three years after the war's end, the United States ceased to be a net oil exporter, as the center of the petroleum industry shifted to the Middle East.

 VOICES

We cannot stress too strongly the importance of Middle East oil resources to us both in peace and war.

—British Chiefs of Staff memorandum, July 10, 1946

International Oil Politics

During World War II, the United States instituted, under the Lend-Lease Act, a policy of aiding countries whose well-being and friendship the president deemed vital to U.S. national security. Saudi Arabia, ruled by a fundamentalist sharia-minded monarchy still in power today, was in deep financial crisis. It benefitted from Lend-Lease assistance intended to secure Middle Eastern oil production and access for American strategic purposes. The U.S. government also created the Petroleum Reserves Corporation (with which DeGolyer was associated) to help secure to U.S. oil companies controlling interests in Saudi Arabian and other Middle Eastern oil concerns. In 1944, Prime Minister Winston Churchill and President Roosevelt concluded an Anglo-American Petroleum Agreement, mainly to ensure continual strategic access to Middle Eastern oil. Driven by the demands of the war, Aramco (today called Saudi Aramco, or Saudi Arabian Oil Co.), an international spin-off financed mainly by Texaco and Socal (today's Chevron), made huge investments in developing Saudi Arabian oil fields. After the war ended, however, the company needed to supplement its American sales with European sales in order to pay off its investment. Aramco designed a massive pipeline project to carry oil across the desert to Mediterranean ports, where it could be transferred to tankers for shipment to European markets. This Trans-Arabian Pipeline ("Tapline") not only traversed multiple countries, it terminated in Palestine—at the time in the thick of the Arab-Jewish conflict.

King Ibn Saud, the sovereign of Saudi Arabia, balked at a project that might support the cause of establishing a Zionist state with control over Jerusalem. Aramco overcame his opposition with a proposal to bypass Palestine. This, however, meant a much bigger construction and operating expense, which in turn required Aramco to join forces with two other U.S. oil companies, Standard Oil of New Jersey and Socony, to finance and operate the pipeline. The deal was concluded on March 11, 1947. Thanks to a great private-sector oil cartel, the United States was unofficially in the energy business with the Saudi king.

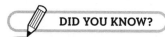

DID YOU KNOW?

Construction of the Trans-Arabian Pipeline ("Tapline") began in 1947 and was completed in 1950. Tapline was the world's largest oil pipeline system, 754 miles long, when it began operations in 1950. Partially closed down in 1976, it was shut down completely in 1990 by Saudi Arabia in response to Jordan's support of Iraq during the Gulf War. Today, it is obsolete and no longer in service.

Cold War Incentives

On March 12, 1947, the day after the Saudi deal was inked, President Harry Truman announced that the policy of the United States would henceforth be to "contain" the global spread of Soviet communism into democratic countries by means of economic and, if necessary, military aid. The so-called Truman Doctrine and the Marshall Plan (a massive, U.S.-funded recovery and reconstruction effort for Western Europe) that accompanied it required a steady flow of cheap oil to fuel Europe.

Boom times had indeed come to Saudi Arabia as well as other Middle Eastern oil countries, especially Kuwait, Bahrain, and Iraq. The leaders of these nations embraced their American partners. The Gulf Oil Company (like the companies of Aramco, American owned) partnered with the Dutch-owned Shell Oil Company to enter the Middle Eastern oil fields. Europe now relied largely on U.S. oil companies to supply them with Middle Eastern oil.

Tapline was completed in 1950 as a Saudi/Aramco joint venture. Instead of ending in Palestine, it terminated at Sidon, Lebanon, on the Mediterranean. At this time, the Iraq Petroleum Company, owned by a consortium of five U.S. oil companies and the Anglo-Persian Oil Company, was pumping oil to two Mediterranean outlets: one at Tripoli, Lebanon, and the other at Haifa, Palestine. The combined shipments contributed to the rapid postwar recovery of the European economy and created an economic boom in the oil countries of the Middle East. By 1951, 80 percent of Europe's oil was coming from Middle Eastern sources, which were largely financed by U.S. companies. In this way, the Middle East became intimately tied to both the United States and the nations of Western Europe.

Capitalism Clashes with Nationalization

Contrary to what some critics of American foreign and military policy in the Middle East have claimed, the United States of America never went into the oil business in the region. But American *companies* certainly did. Inevitably, this led to conflicts between U.S. capitalism and regional national ambitions.

The first challenge to American capitalism in the oil industry came not in the Middle East, however, but in another oil-rich location: Venezuela. In 1943, the Venezuelan government presented Standard Oil of New Jersey and its partner Shell with an offer they couldn't refuse: either split profits 50/50 with the state or face *nationalization*.

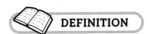 **DEFINITION**

> **Nationalization** is the act of government taking ownership of a private industry along with its assets. In some cases, the private owners are compensated—albeit often at levels below the value of the actual assets and far below their investment value. In many cases, however, the industry and assets are seized without compensation.

The prospect of a government suddenly swallowing up a company with all its assets was a major downside risk of doing big business in foreign countries. Understandably, the companies gave in to Venezuela's demands. This was a significant concession, not just in terms of the monetary value of the split, but because the 50/50 division transformed the companies' stake from an ownership interest in the oil fields to a renter's interest in them. In this way, the oil companies no longer had any legal dominion over foreign soil.

In 1949, a Venezuelan delegation took the 50/50 idea to the Saudis in an effort to persuade them to raise their prices. This would level the export oil market, prompting the Americans to make further investments in Venezuela. Despite the prospect of competition from Venezuela, the Saudis were impressed by the representatives' case, and in 1950 they renegotiated a 50/50 split with Aramco. Kuwait and Iraq almost immediately followed suit.

Iran stepped up next, but the 50/50 renegotiation with the Anglo-Iranian Oil Company was interrupted by internal strife, and Mohammad Mossadegh, at the time chairman of the Iranian parliament's oil committee, proposed full nationalization instead of any split. Challenged by Mossadegh's increasing popularity, the shah of Iran, Mohammad Reza Pahlavi, signed nationalization into law on April 28, 1951.

Britain threatened a military response, but almost instantly backed down and instead withdrew from Iran while also placing an embargo on British import of Iranian oil. In truth, the embargo was hardly necessary. Mossadegh had moved for nationalization without taking into account that Iran lacked the trained personnel to run a complex oil production, transportation, and refinery network. No sooner did the British leave Iran than oil production there ground to a halt.

Months passed, and the Iranian economy suffered. By late 1952, Mossadegh, now prime minister, had usurped most of the shah's power and was for all practical purposes governing Iran. Early in 1953, the British government secretly floated the possibility of supporting a coup against him—an idea that appealed to newly inaugurated U.S. President Dwight D. Eisenhower and his hardline anticommunist secretary of state, John Foster Dulles. They were nervous about overtures of alliance Mossadegh was making to the Soviets. CIA operatives were dispatched to undermine Mossadegh, an operation that emboldened the shah to turn against him. Dismissed as prime minister, Mossadegh was subsequently tried and sentenced to a term in prison.

Mohammad Mossadegh

Mohammad Mossadegh was born in Tehran in 1882, the son of a treasury official and his wife, who was related to the country's ruling Qajar Dynasty. Following Persian custom, young Mohammad Mossadegh succeeded to the treasury post upon the death of his father.

Mossadegh supported the Constitutional Revolution of 1906–1907 and was elected to the first parliament, which was designed after the French parliamentary system. At 25, he did not meet the minimum age for parliamentary membership, however. Unable to assume his seat, he pursued his education in Europe. On his return to Iran in 1914, he became a professor at the School of Political Science, wrote important treatises on a variety of financial and political issues, and gained appointment as undersecretary in the Ministry of Finance.

The post-World War I Anglo-Iranian Agreement of 1919, which made Iran something of a British client state, outraged Mossadegh, and by the mid-1920s, he earned a reputation as a champion of both national sovereignty and constitutionalism. He was among a small minority of Majles deputies who opposed legislation enabling Reza Khan to assume the throne as Reza Shah Pahlavi.

After the Pahlavi regime was established, Mossadegh continued his outspoken opposition. Barred from political life, he lived and wrote from his country home in Ahmadabad, north of Tehran. Reza Shah ordered his arrest in June 1940, and he was imprisoned in a remote town in southern Khorasan. The crown prince, Mohammad Reza, fearing that Mossadegh's popularity would incite an insurrection, interceded with his father, who released Mossadegh after six months and allowed him to return to Ahmadabad.

During World War II, Mossadegh was returned to the Majles and led the opposition to U.S., British, and Soviet demands for oil concessions. In 1950, he founded the National Front, which (among other things) worked to wrest control of Iranian oil resources from British hands. When British officials pushed back, Mossadegh and his party led the call for nationalization of the oil industry. This proved highly popular, forcing Mohammad Reza Shah (who succeeded to the throne following his father's death in 1941) to elevate Mossadegh to prime minister in May 1951.

Under Mossadegh, who assumed most of the shah's power, the oil issue became the center of a combined nationalist and democratic movement. In response to the nationalization of the oil industry, the British withdrew from Iran, embargoed Iranian oil, and then conspired with the U.S. CIA to destabilize the Mossadegh government.

Essentially paralyzed, Mossadegh resigned the premiership in July 1952, but almost immediately returned after a popular uprising. Both Britain and the United States raised alarms that Mossadegh supported and was supported by the officially banned Tudeh (Communist) Party. The vehemently anticommunist, pro-shah Iranian army refused to take orders from the prime minister. Although a majority of the Majles continued to back Mossadegh, the loss of military support made him highly vulnerable, and he lost parliamentary support. Desperate, Mossadegh called a popular referendum to dissolve the Majles and hold new elections. At this, the British MI6 and the U.S. CIA worked with Mossadegh's internal opponents (including the shah) to oust him by a coup d'état in August 1953. He had been Iran's first democratically elected prime minister.

Arrested and tried, Mossadegh was sentenced to three years of solitary confinement in prison. The term was followed by house arrest in his country home, where he died on March 5, 1967, at the age of 84.

With Mossadegh out of the way, the American government appealed to the major oil companies to venture into Iran as a way of preventing the country from falling into communist hands. To sweeten the deal, the Eisenhower administration dropped an antitrust lawsuit Ike's predecessor, President Truman, had brought against Big Oil. On September 17, 1954, Iran agreed to a deal with a consortium of Standard Oil of New Jersey, Socony, Texaco, Socal, Gulf, Shell, and a French company, CFP. A reorganized National Iranian Oil Company would own 40 percent of the consortium, and Iran would retain ownership of its resources and facilities.

Already rich, the shah of Iran became far wealthier as a result of the deal—but the close ties created between him and the United States would, in the fullness of time, lead to his downfall in a revolution combining nationalism and Islam.

Such was the double-edged sword of oil wealth throughout the modern history of the Middle East. For some Westerners, Middle Eastern oil was a brave new frontier that brought untold profit. For some in the Middle East, it brought both personal and national wealth, enabling struggling, newly independent countries to build themselves into strong nations. For others, however, admitting Big Oil opened the door to exploitation of the masses, tied national destinies to huge Western corporate entities and Western governments, and created economic, social, religious, and political conditions that spawned violent revolution.

The Spreading Influence of Oil

With no oil resources, Egypt is one of the Middle East's have-not countries. Nevertheless, while Egypt did not possess oil wealth in the 1950s—when Saudi Arabia, Kuwait, Bahrain, Iraq, and Iran were cashing in—the nation did have the Suez Canal, the passage through which two-thirds of Europe's oil supply was transported.

When Gamal Abdel Nasser rose to power in 1954, becoming instrumental in the overthrow of King Farouk, he stirred the Egyptian masses, and then the Arab world, with a call to Pan-Arabism. Pan-Arabism served to unite Muslims in opposition to the overpowering economic forces of the West and to one dramatic manifestation of those forces: the creation of a Zionist state in the very midst of the Arab world.

As we will see in Chapter 10, Nasser used the Suez Canal—the great artery of Europe's oil—to advance a Pan-Arab, anti-Israel agenda. Nasser's announcement of the nationalization of the Suez Canal in 1956 prompted President Eisenhower to cancel planned U.S. support for a loan to finance construction of the Aswan Dam, an ambitious project to give Egypt the ability to control Nile floods, provide much-need irrigation water, and generate hydroelectricity to promote industrialization. The cancellation drove Nasser into the arms of the Soviets, making the Middle East a major Cold War battleground between the United States and Western democracies on the one hand and the Soviet Union and its satellite nations on the other.

VOICES

As long as America is a major power, and as long as she is free of major war, anyone taking on the Jews will indirectly be taking on America.

—Hector McNeill, advisor to Britain's Secretary of State for Foreign Affairs Ernest Bevin, January 14, 1949

Nasser's decision to nationalize the Suez Canal was a stand against a tradition of economic vassalage, by which Britain and France used their control of the canal to "manage" Egypt. Nationalization and the global political realignments that followed it demonstrated the power of oil. The Egyptian leader saw oil as a weapon in the struggle to create an Arab federation, and indeed unified Syria and Egypt briefly for a time called the United Arab Republic (1958–1961). But the United States and the European nations that consumed Middle Eastern oil proved agile in their efforts to checkmate him.

First, they decided to find alternatives to dependence on the Suez Canal. New pipeline projects were planned, and a new generation of ships was designed. These were the *supertankers*, which would carry amounts of oil sufficiently large to justify the time and expense of navigating around Africa instead of relying on the Suez Canal connection between the Red Sea and the Mediterranean. Second, the United States and its European allies resolved to support independent Middle Eastern oil-producing states such as Kuwait, which had no interest in or actively resisted the call to Pan-Arabism.

DEFINITION

Supertankers are ocean-going petroleum transports built beginning in the late 1950s, largely in response to the Suez Crisis of 1956. Whereas the conventional T2 tanker was 532 feet long and carried 16,500 tons of oil, the new generation of supertankers (as built during the 1970s), called ultra-large crude carriers (ULCCs), were well over twice as long (more than 1,300 feet) and carried a half-million tons of crude.

OPEC Is Founded

The 1949 meeting between oil representatives from Venezuela and Iran laid the foundation for what, in 1960, would become OPEC—the Organization of the Petroleum Exporting Countries. Officially created at the Baghdad Conference of September 10–14, OPEC originally included Iran and Venezuela plus Iraq, Kuwait, and Saudi Arabia. Later, nine more oil producers joined—Libya, the United Arab Emirates, Qatar, Indonesia, Algeria, Nigeria, Ecuador, Angola, and Gabon. The organization established its headquarters in the very heart of Europe, Geneva, Switzerland, moving in 1965 to Vienna, Austria.

The founding purpose of OPEC was to maximize oil revenues by increasing the price of the crude oil produced by member countries. OPEC was also dedicated to combatting exploitation by the multinational companies of Big Oil. The organization asserted the right of every country to exercise sovereign control over its own natural resources. In the principle of unity, OPEC members believed they had found a way to maximize revenues while maintaining ownership of resources.

Defying Market Forces

Over the years, oil consumers have protested that OPEC is an unfair monopoly dedicated to keeping oil prices artificially high. Members do not deny this, but they point out that, in legal terms, they cannot be accused of monopolistic business practices. The reason is simple. They are sovereign nations, not private companies. Therefore, national and international antitrust laws do not apply to them.

Wielding the Weapon of Oil

In October 1973, OPEC stepped beyond the realm of business and squarely into global politics when it declared an oil embargo against the United States and the nations of Western Europe, which had supported Israel in the Yom Kippur War of 1973 (Chapter 13).

Energy Crisis

If OPEC members thought that the embargo would force the West to withdraw support from Israel, they were mistaken. Nevertheless, oil prices skyrocketed from $3 per barrel to $12—and still demand outpaced supply. Throughout the United States and Europe, gas rationing became the new normal, as did round-the-block lines at American gas stations, along with outright shortages.

The cost of fuel oil as well as natural gas for heating, industrial operations, and electrical generation also rose sharply during the embargo, limiting production and cutting into profits. A serious energy crisis developed, accompanied by a global recession that far outlasted the yearlong OPEC embargo.

Oil: The Fuel of Tyranny and War

In 1973, OPEC succeeded in creating economic pain, but never came close to changing the policy of its target nations with regard to Israel. The action nevertheless underscored the fact that oil, especially in times of relative scarcity and high demand, was a powerful weapon.

The popular *New York Times* columnist and author Thomas Friedman has theorized that the production of oil exists in inverse ratio to the state of democracy in a nation or a region. Rulers who command great oil wealth can essentially bribe their citizens into compliance and submission rather than democratically earn their consent. While Friedman's theory has drawn criticism as an oversimplification, it is true that the modern history of Iran, Iraq, and Saudi Arabia has hardly been marked by an excess of democracy. Oil may lift the general economy of a nation, but it also tends to support and promote an autocratic class.

Oil wealth in the Middle East has also financed extreme forms of Islam that sometimes promote terrorism. Apart from any religious agenda, oil has certainly financed armament and military enterprises.

Acquiring, protecting, and controlling sources of oil has also driven the West—particularly the United States—to go to war in the Middle East. President George H. W. Bush promoted the Gulf War of 1990 and 1991 (Chapter 15) as a just struggle to liberate Kuwait, an American ally, from an invasion led by Iraq's Saddam Hussein. But it was no accident that both Iraq and Kuwait are major producers of oil, in which American companies have major interests. Moreover, Saudi Arabia—an even bigger oil producer—appealed to the United States to help defend it against imminent Iraqi invasion. Little more than a decade later, President George W. Bush led the nation to a second war against Iraq partly on the promise that the military enterprise would be more than paid for by the access to oil that victory would achieve.

It is frequently said that oil has been both a blessing and a curse for the modern Middle East. That this formulation has assumed the status of cliché makes it no less true. On the contrary, it is all the more accurate for being so commonplace.

The Least You Need to Know

- The discovery of vast Middle Eastern oil resources during World War II thrust the region front and center in world geopolitics.

- Issues relating to control of oil have shaped governments and international relations in Saudi Arabia and Iran, as well as less directly in Egypt.

- The emergence of OPEC beginning in the 1960s gave the Middle Eastern states a powerful means of demanding resource sovereignty, and (among other things) put American support for Israel to a severe test.

- In the modern Middle East, the oil industry has been both a blessing and a curse.

The Arab-Israeli War, 1948–1949

On May 14, 1948, the Provisional State Council, forerunner of the Knesset (the Israeli parliament), published a Proclamation of Independence, bringing into existence the State of Israel.

Words matter. Unlike the Continental Congress of the United States in 1776, which published a *Declaration* of Independence, the Provisional State Council called its document a *Proclamation*. Whereas *declaration* implied a decision to create a change of status from dependence on the British Empire to independence, *proclamation* implied the statement of an existing right. The Provisional State Council's document is eloquent and moving. For the Arabs of Palestine and throughout the Middle East, it was also offensive and provocative. In fact, it was a call to arms.

Self-Proclaimed

The Proclamation of Independence explains the creation of Israel as both a "natural right" and a legal right. "The Land of Israel was the birthplace of the Jewish people," it begins, and goes on to speak of centuries of exile, during which the "Jewish people remained faithful to it [Israel] in all the countries of their dispersion, never ceasing to pray and hope for their return...." The Jews were "impelled by ... historical association ... to go back ... and regain their statehood," and in "recent decades, Jews actually did return" and "reclaimed the wilderness," bringing "the blessings of progress to all inhabitants" of Palestine.

So goes the claim to natural right. To many, especially in the West, that claim was persuasive. But it was hardly absolute. History, after all, is full of stories of conquest and exile; consider the history of Manifest Destiny and the Native Americans, for example. As for creating a culture of national and global value and bringing the "blessings of progress" to a place of immigration, these are laudable outcomes, but do they necessarily secure a right to live in that place—especially when others already live there?

And so the proclamation adds a legal claim to the natural one: "On November 29, 1947, the General Assembly of the United Nations adopted a Resolution requiring the establishment of a Jewish State in Palestine." Furthermore, the General Assembly "called upon the inhabitants of the country to take all the necessary steps on their part to put the plan into effect." As if the framers of the proclamation recognized that the assertion of a "natural" right could admit a plausible counterargument, they wrote that UN recognition "of the right of the Jewish people to establish their independent State is unassailable." It was, they argued, absolute.

A "Jewish State"? Yes...and No

The Proclamation of Independence proclaims the establishment of "the Jewish State in Palestine, to be called Medinath Yisrael (The State of Israel)." As a "Jewish State," Israel was to be "open to the immigration of Jews from all countries of their dispersion." And yet the "Jewish State" would not be exclusively Jewish. Following "the principles of liberty, justice, and peace as conceived by the Prophets of Israel," the state would "uphold the full social and political equality of all its citizens, without distinction of religion, race, or sex." It would guarantee "freedom of religion, conscience, education, and culture" and "will safeguard the Holy Places of all religions."

The proclamation appealed to "the Arab inhabitants of the State of Israel to preserve the ways of peace and play their part in the development of the state, on the basis of full and equal citizenship and due representation in all its bodies and institutions...." As for the rest of the Middle East, the framers extended their "hand in peace and neighbourliness," inviting all to cooperate "for the common good." Israel "is prepared to make its contribution to the progress of the Middle East as a whole."

The Arab Response

By the time of the Proclamation of Independence, the Jewish community of Palestine consisted of some 650,000 persons, including *sabras*—Jews born in Palestine—and immigrants, among them very recently arrived survivors of the Holocaust. What is more, Jews everywhere were guaranteed citizenship, if they chose to immigrate.

 **DEFINITION**

> **Sabra** is the modern Hebrew term for any Jew born in Israel or, before 1948, any Jew born in Palestine. Coined about 1945, *sabra* derives from the modern Hebrew word for the tough but sweet prickly pear native to desert Israel.

Under the leadership of David Ben-Gurion, a majority of these 650,000 agreed to the partition of Palestine as set forth in General Assembly Resolution 181.

The Arab League was founded in Cairo on March 22, 1945, as a regional organization consisting of Egypt, Iraq, Transjordan (renamed Jordan in 1949), Lebanon, Syria, and Saudi Arabia. On May 15, 1948, the day after the Proclamation of Independence was published, Abdul Razek Azzam Pasha, secretary general of the League of Arab States, cabled the UN secretary general requesting him to lay before the General Assembly and Security Council what he called the Arab position on the Israeli Proclamation of Independence and Resolution 181.

The cable stated that, under the Ottoman Empire, the Arab majority and Jewish minority in Palestine enjoyed full parliamentary representation, that the Jewish minority was not discriminated against, and that Holy Places were "protected and accessible to all without distinction." It continued by asserting that the "Arabs have constantly been seeking their freedom and independence" and that the British government, under its Palestinian mandate, ultimately asserted the Jews' right to establish a "spiritual abode" in Palestine "without there being any ulterior motives such as the creation of a Jewish State." Nevertheless, the cable argued, Great Britain "made it possible for the Jews to flood [Palestine] with waves of immigrants … thereby neglecting … the interests and the rights of its lawful inhabitants." The cable pointed to the charter of the Arab League, which "declared that Palestine had become an independent country since its separation from the Ottoman Empire, but that all the appertaining external rights and privileges attendant upon formal independence had to be subdued temporarily for reasons beyond the will of its people." The League, the cable continued, has attempted, through the United Nations, to "find a fair and just solution for the problem of Palestine … but such solution invariably conflicted with opposition from Zionists."

With the British mandate over Palestine ended, the cable asserted the right of the "Arab States" to "set up a Government in Palestine … under the principles of self-determination" recognized by both the League of Nations and the United Nations Charter. In so doing, the Arab States would do whatever is necessary to "administer law and order in the country and afford the necessary and adequate protection to life and property."

The Arab Call to Arms

The Arab League would become the basis of a military alliance between Arab Palestine and virtually all Arabs throughout the Middle East. In immediate response to Israeli independence, two irregular Arab armies formed. The Arab Liberation Army (ALA) was led by Iraqi General Ismail Safwat and by Syrian Commander Syr Fawzi Kaukji. It consisted of about 4,000 men. Another force, the Army of the Holy War, also numbering about 4,000, was commanded by Abd al-Qadir al-Husayni, a Palestinian nationalist born in Jerusalem when it was part of the Ottoman Empire. In addition to these principal formations, grassroots Palestinian militias were organized.

The Forces of Israel

Israel already had the Haganah as the basis of its national army, which would become the Israel Defense Forces. The elite unit within the Haganah was the Palmach (an acronym derived from *Plugot Mahatz*, meaning "strike forces"). The Palmach had been created in the spring of 1941; by 1948, it consisted of three small brigades for a total strength of 2,000 men and women.

In addition to Haganah and Palmach—early Israel's regular forces—were Irgun and Lehi (the Stern Gang), both discussed in Chapter 7. Irgun could justifiably be described as a paramilitary guerilla force, but Lehi, which broke from Irgun, was a paramilitary terrorist organization.

A War Already in Progress

Violence erupted during the run-up to independence, and outright atrocities were committed on both sides. Most infamous was the Deir Yassin Massacre of April 9, 1948, mentioned in Chapter 7. One hundred twenty Irgun and Lehi (Stern Gang) fighters swept into the Arab hamlet of about 600, killing, according to the most widely accepted account, 107 villagers (some accounts report 254), including women and children. Some were shot, others were blown to bits by hand grenades lobbed into their homes. Unconfirmed reports hold that some villagers were taken prisoner, marched through West Jerusalem, and then shot.

The atrocity was condemned by the Haganah—the regular Jewish military force—and by the two chief rabbis of Jewish Palestine. The Jewish Agency for Israel (formerly called the Palestine Zionist Executive) addressed a letter of apology to King Abdullah of Transjordan, who rejected it.

 VOICES

> The Jews ordered all my family to line up against a wall and they started shooting us. I was hit in the side, but most of us children were saved because we hid behind our parents. The bullets hit my sister Kadri (four) in the head, my sister Sameh (eight) in the cheek, my brother Mohammed (seven) in the chest. But all the others with us against the wall were killed: my father, my mother, my grandfather and grandmother, my uncles and aunts and some of their children.
>
> —Fahimi Zidan, Palestinian boy, age 12, recounting the Deir Yassin Massacre

Despite official condemnation of such terrorist tactics, as well as the revulsion of the majority of the Jewish community, their ruthlessness made an impact. Following Deir Yassin, many Arabs fled Palestine. Others, however, responded in kind. On April 13, Arab fighters fell upon a Jewish hospital convoy near Mount Scopus, east of Jerusalem, killing 76 civilians, mostly doctors and nurses. A month later, on May 14, Arab militia laid siege to and overran the four Jewish settlements at Kfar Etzion, south of Jerusalem. Of some 500 people, 148 were killed defending the settlements.

Abd al-Qadir al-Husayni Husayni

Abd al-Qadir al-Husayni Husayni was born into a prosperous Arab family in Jerusalem in 1907. He attended Cairo's American University, earning a degree in chemistry, and went on to found the Congress of Educated Muslims. As a young man, he accepted a post with the British Mandate government of Palestine, but during the 1936–1939 Arab revolt against British rule, he moved to Hebron and became a leading figure in the struggle against the Mandate.

Husayni was active in the Palestine Arab Party, becoming its secretary-general as well as editor-in-chief of *Al-Liwa'*, the party's official newspaper. He also edited other key Arab Palestinian papers.

British authorities exiled Husayni in 1938, prompting him to flee to Iraq the following year, where he became part of the coup d'état that overthrew the British-aligned Iraqi government of Regent 'Abd al-Ilah and installed, albeit briefly, Rashid Ali al-Gaylani as prime minister. Rashid Ali favored rapprochement with the Axis powers in World War II.

In 1946, Husayni moved to Egypt, and then slipped quietly into Palestine, assuming leadership of the Army of the Holy War in January 1948. By this time, Husayni was a self-taught military professional of courage and ability. A hands-on commander, he personally set out on April 8 to reconnoiter Qastal Hill in preparation for battle there. In the early morning fog, he was shot dead. His loss came as a significant blow to Palestinian Arab morale.

Husayni had married in 1934, and his son Faisal al-Husayni, born in 1940, went on to found the Arab Studies Society and to assume leadership of Fatah, which became the largest faction in the Palestine Liberation Organization (PLO).

The Cities Fall

Although Arabs were willing to fight and die to prevent the establishment of Israel, their most capable commander, Abd al-Qadir al-Husayni Husayni—a chemist by education, a committed Palestinian nationalist, and a natural military leader—was killed on April 8, 1948, during the Battle of al-Qastal, a Palestinian village five miles west of Jerusalem. His loss, before the "formal" start of the Arab-Israeli War, was a catastrophe for Arab morale.

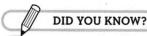 **DID YOU KNOW?**

> The early triumphs of their forces were heartening to the Israelis, but casualties were heavy. Twelve hundred Israeli soldiers and civilians were killed between November 29, 1947, and April 3, 1948. During the intense fighting between April 3 and May 14, 1948 (Independence Day), the Israelis suffered 753 military and 500 civilian battle deaths.

Five Arab Nations Rally

In the space of 6 months, 2,500 Israelis had been killed. The forces of Arab Palestine were defeated. Yet this was just the beginning of the Arab-Israeli War. Although volunteer fighters had already poured into Palestine to fight the Israelis, it was only after the Proclamation of Independence that the five major Arab nations of the Middle East—Lebanon, Syria, Iraq, Transjordan, and Egypt, all members of the Arab League—entered into a military alliance to invade Israel and wipe it out of existence.

From the international point of view, Israel, momentarily triumphant, now appeared doomed. Five populous nations were arrayed against a single fledgling state sharing a divided territory with a people hostile to it.

And yet appearances were deceiving. Although the Arab countries were much larger, they mobilized only a fraction of the troops Israel mustered, and received no substantial Western military aid. At the start of the invasion, the Arab Liberation Army fielded about 5,500 troops. The Army of Holy War and other Palestinian and Arab volunteer forces added another 5,000. Iraq deployed about 10,000 troops, but initially committed just one brigade, about 2,000 men. Egypt immediately sent 7,000 in a single infantry brigade, which also included a Sudanese battalion, three armored battalions, and a pair of air squadrons. Transjordan sent its Arab Legion of 7,500 troops, with another 2,500 available. The Legion was formed into three infantry brigades, including eight infantry battalions, four armored cavalry battalions, and one artillery regiment. Syria committed 5,000 men in two infantry brigades consisting of six infantry battalions, one tank battalion, and one air squadron. Lebanon sent 2,000 troops—four infantry and two artillery battalions. Added to this were volunteer forces—fewer than 1,000 men—from Saudi Arabia and Yemen, attached to the Egyptian contingent.

Opposing the initial Arab deployment of some 42,000 men were 30,000 Haganah troops (including 2,500 elite Palmach fighters), 3,500 Irgun members, 500 Lehi (Stern Gang) guerillas, and some 30,000 reserves in various stages of training. In addition to infantry, Israel had 40 tanks and 35 combat aircraft. Thus, the invasion of Israel began on May 15, 1948, with 42,000 Arabs against 34,400 Israelis who enjoyed the natural advantages of homeland defenders, were more ably commanded, and were augmented by elite forces as well as guerilla forces seasoned from paramilitary operations against British colonialists and Palestinian civilians.

   DID YOU KNOW?

Both sides would commit more forces as the war went on. By October 1948, Arab forces numbered 55,000. Of these 55,000, 20,000 came from Egypt (and Sudan), 10,000 from Jordan's Arab Legion, 10,000 from Iraq, 5,000 from Syria, and 2,000 from Lebanon, in addition to 3,000 Arab Liberation Army members, and some 5,000 irregular militia volunteers. Israel had 45,000 regulars supported by a mobilization of 45,000 reserves in so-called Home Defense Battalions.

A Question of Commitment

It quickly became clear that many of the troops from outside of Palestine were less than wholeheartedly committed to the fight. Israeli forces halted the advance of Syrian and Lebanese forces that entered Galilee within the first week of the invasion. The Iraqi contingent, which invaded Samaria, north of Jerusalem, scored a few quick victories, but soon lost momentum and failed to cut across Israel in an intended advance to the sea.

Early in June, the Syrians and Lebanese, stiffened by assistance from the Arab Liberation Army, rallied for a renewed offensive, which, at first, drove rapidly through a swath of northern Galilee. In fairly short order, however, it was, once again, bottled up by effective Israeli resistance.

The Arab Legion Hits Hard

Far more formidable was the Arab Legion of Transjordan. Its commander was a former British army lieutenant general, Sir John Bagot Glubb. Better known as Glubb Pasha, he took over the Arab Legion during World War II, in 1939, from another Briton, Frederick G. Peake. An able trainer and tactician, Glubb is credited with fashioning the Arab Legion into the strongest and most effective Arab army to fight in the Arab-Israeli War.

Glubb led the center of the invasion, while the Egyptians came in from the south, through Israel's Negev Desert. Glubb aimed his Legion squarely against Jerusalem, which was now home to some 100,000 Jews. The fighting in and near the ancient city was extremely brutal. For almost a month, Arab Legion artillery fired some 10,000 shells into the traditional Jewish quarter of the city. More than 1,200 civilians were killed and in excess of 2,000 houses destroyed.

In the epicenter of the assault, the Jewish quarter of the Old City, about 1,700 residents, held out day after day, week after week, defended by a mere 280 armed troops. By May 28, only 34 of the surviving Israeli soldiers weren't wounded. They surrendered, along with 153 wounded comrades. In all, 294 Israeli soldiers and civilians were made prisoners of war. Arab Legion losses were some 200 killed. Losses among Arab and Christian civilians are unknown. The Arab Legion expelled most of the rest of the Jewish inhabitants of the quarter, escorting them out and providing protection against Palestinian mobs.

Despite the loss of the old Jewish quarter, most of Jerusalem continued to withstand the onslaught of the Arab Legion, and the heaviest fighting moved from the city to the territory separating Tel Aviv from Jerusalem. The Arab Legion sought to cut off lines of communication and supply from Tel Aviv to the Holy City. The Israelis struggled to keep them open.

The Arab Legion dug in at Latrun, effectively blocking the route to Jerusalem. Against Latrun, the Israelis launched three major attacks—and as a result suffered their heaviest casualties of the war. On May 25, Israeli Colonel Shlomo Shamir led the 7th Brigade, a unit of recent immigrants, against Latrun. The Arab Legion commander holding Latrun, Colonel Hadis el-Majali, had two small regiments. He rebuffed the assault, inflicting on the Israelis more than 140 fatal casualties. Five days later, a second attack was also repulsed with heavy losses. Finally, on June 9 and 10, two fresh Israeli brigades made a third assault. Both units suffered heavy losses, one brigade losing half its strength.

While the offensives against Latrun were under way, David "Mickey" Marcus, a U.S. Army colonel advising the Haganah, assumed command of Israeli forces on the central front, the sector facing the Arab Legion. After repeatedly failing to clear the main highway into Jerusalem, he mobilized his forces to build a new road—thereby relieving the beleaguered city.

Marcus had little time to enjoy his triumph, however. On June 10, mere hours before a UN-sanctioned cease-fire was to begin, he fell victim to friendly fire. An Israeli sentry mistook him for an Arab infiltrator and opened fire.

The Egyptian Invasion

Major General Ahmed Ali al-Mwawi led two Egyptian brigade groups—7,500 men (later reinforced by an additional 12,000) against Negba, a fortified *kibbutz* founded in 1939 and forming the southern-most Jewish settlement in Mandate-era Palestine. The kibbutz held out, but following a siege from May 19 to 24, nearby Yad Mordechai fell—after its 200 defenders managed to kill or wound 300 Egyptians. The Egyptian attackers far outnumbered and outgunned the Israeli defenders.

 **DEFINITION**

Hebrew for "gathering" or "clustering," **kibbutz** is any collective community established in Israel in the course of a kibbutz movement that, beginning in 1909, established quasi-utopian communities founded on socialist and Zionist principles. As of 2010, 270 *kibbutzim* (the plural form) existed in Israel.

Egyptian forces went on to take several other Negev kibbutzim and defeated two Israeli task forces at Ashdod, north of Yad Mordechai on the Mediterranean shore. Not only did the Israelis suffer 400 casualties at Ashdod, their defeat allowed the Egyptians to advance to within 25 miles of Tel Aviv, where they might have succeeded in linking up with the Arab Legion. Israeli forces, however, managed to halt the advance.

A Cease-Fire and a Fresh Start

While the war raged, the United Nations acted, declaring a truce on May 29 to take effect on June 11. All sides agreed. By design, the truce was a mere 28 days, intended as a cooling-off period to provide an interval during which the sides could seek an alternative to further bloodshed. An arms embargo was put into place, and all combatants agreed to refrain from taking military advantage of the truce.

Both sides freely violated their pledges and worked feverishly to improve their positions. The Israelis worked harder. In blatant violation of the cease-fire and with financing from Jews all over the world, including many Americans, they covertly imported large arms shipments, especially from Czechoslovakia. During the 28 days of the cease-fire, the Israeli army far more than made up for its losses, nearly doubling its strength, from 35,000 regular troops to 65,000. This was made possible in part by the large number of immigrants who entered Israel immediately after the independence was proclaimed.

 **VOICES**

Without arms from Czechoslovakia [acquired during the cease-fire of June 1948], it is very doubtful whether we would have been able to conduct the war.

—Yitzhak Rabin, Israeli commander and (later) prime minister and peacemaker

On the Offensive

On July 9, with the cease-fire at an end, the Israelis burst into battle with a vigorous offensive that took the war to the invaders. Not only did they roll back the Arab advances, the Israeli air force sent three B-17s to bomb the Cairo airport, stunning the Egyptian government and people.

In the north, from July 9 to 14, a fight raged for Mishmar HaYarden, a *moshav* (village) in the Upper Galilee. Strategically, the battle ended in a draw. Tactically, however, it was an Israeli victory. At the cost of 150 killed and 500 wounded, the Israelis had killed some 800 Syrians.

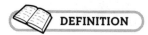 **DEFINITION**

A **moshav** is an Israeli village or settlement established by so-called Labor Zionists as a cooperative community, typically agricultural in nature. *Moshavim* (the plural form) are the products of the Second Aluyah, the wave of Zionist immigration into Palestine that spanned 1904 to 1914.

The Haganah did score a strategic victory at Nazareth, where it captured the Arab Liberation Army's base of operations. This took an old enemy out of the war. Nevertheless, the Arab Legion still proved a most formidable adversary. Latrun, target of three earlier Israeli assaults, withstood a renewed attack on July 15 and 16.

Despite defeat at Latrun, Haganah troops overran and captured Ramla and Lydda. In Lydda, the town's Arab residents rose up against the Israeli occupiers, prompting a ruthless Haganah response in which more than 200 residents were killed.

A Second Cease-Fire

On July 18, a second UN-sponsored cease-fire settled over Israel. It lasted three times longer than the first—about three months—but did not eliminate all fighting, as street-level violence was frequent. Worse, on September 17, Sweden's Count Folke Bernadotte, a United Nations mediator, was assassinated, presumably by members of Lehi.

The Israeli Offensive Resumes

On October 15, the second cease-fire was shattered by the resumption of Israel's offensive. General Moshe Carmel led four Israeli brigades in Operation Hiram, sweeping the Syrians, Lebanese, and Arab Liberation Army out of Galilee between October 20 and 31. Four hundred Arab fighters were killed, and 550 were captured.

Even more central to Israeli strategy in this phase of the war was the offensive in the Negev against the Egyptians, whose engaged forces now numbered 35,000, augmented by a Saudi battalion. The Egyptians anchored their main defensive line at Beersheba, which was garrisoned by 500 troops. A massive Israeli assault on October 21 overran the garrison, which resulted in a 4,000-man Egyptian brigade being cut off in the so-called Faluja Pocket. With land access blocked, the Egyptian navy sent a pair of destroyers to effect the amphibious landing of reinforcements. In a spectacular countermeasure, highly trained Israeli underwater demolition teams planted charges that sank both vessels. One, the *Emir Farouk,* went to the bottom with all 700 of the troops it carried.

In November, Egypt launched another attempt to relieve the Faluja Pocket, but failed. Still reeling from this disaster, the Egyptian army was hit late in December by Operation Horev, which pushed it all the way back into the Sinai and cut off the town of Rafah, in the southern Gaza Strip.

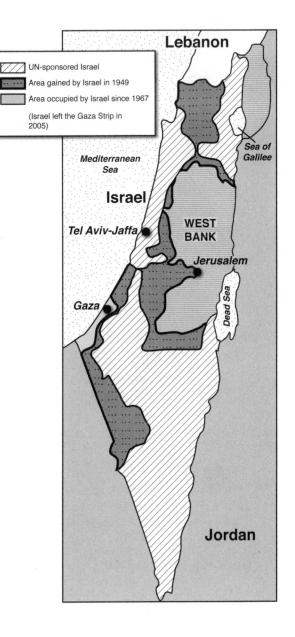

The War Winds Down

In November 1948, Transjordan agreed to a truce, thereby taking the most effective Arab force out of the war. One by one, the other Arab League armies quietly followed suit. Only Egypt remained in the fight, but its leadership finally ordered a cessation of combat, effective January 7, 1949.

With the fighting stopped, the United Nations directed Israeli forces to withdraw from the Sinai. When Britain dispatched military aircraft to enforce the withdrawal, Israeli pilots engaged the British planes, shooting six out of the sky.

Outcome

The Arab-Israeli War of 1948 and 1949 ended on March 10, 1949, with a final armistice concluded 10 days later. Israel not only prevailed, keeping the territory assigned to it by the United Nations partition of Palestine, but triumphed, capturing half the Palestinian territory originally allotted to the Arabs.

Jordan was allowed to occupy the West Bank, the area now ruled by a combination of the Palestinian Authority and the Israeli military. Egypt occupied the Gaza Strip, which borders Egypt on the south and Israel on the east and north. Today, the Gaza Strip is governed by the democratically elected political party Hamas, a revolutionary party allied to the Muslim Brotherhood in Egypt, classified as a terrorist organization by the United States government, and ideologically opposed to the State of Israel, instead favoring a greater Palestine including Gaza, Israel, and the West Bank.

 DID YOU KNOW?

> For Israel, total losses in the Arab-Israeli War were 4,074 military personnel and more than 2,000 noncombatant civilians killed. Some 15,000 soldiers and civilians were wounded. Of some 1,500 U.S. nationals who volunteered to fight on behalf of Israel, 45 died, 37 in combat. Arab losses can be determined only by estimate. Egypt suffered between 1,500 and 2,000 killed, and 4,231 wounded. Syria lost more than 1,000 killed, as did Transjordan's Arab Legion. Iraq and Lebanon each lost an estimated 500 killed, while Saudi Arabia, Yemen, and Sudan collectively lost a few hundred. It was the Palestinian irregulars and civilians who suffered most in the war. An estimated 15,000 died, some 25,000 were wounded, and most outside of the West Bank lost their homes.

The most dramatic and significant immediate outcome of the war was the departure of nearly 700,000 Palestinian Arabs from Israel—fully two-thirds of the territory's Arab population. The causes of this "exodus" are still hotly disputed. Some clearly fled—presumably in fear of the Israeli military—while others were forcibly expelled. About 156,000 Arabs chose to remain in Israel and became citizens.

The displaced Palestinian Arabs were housed in rapidly constructed refugee camps. The sentiments produced in these places of squalor and humiliation were despair, desperation, and rage—emotions that would drive the creation of the Palestine Liberation Organization (PLO), which, like Israel's own Stern Gang, has made extensive use of terrorist tactics in an ongoing effort to reclaim Palestine for the dispossessed Arab Palestinians.

Beyond the territorial adjustments and mass movement of population, there was no formal or official resolution to the 1948 conflict. The war ended with an armistice—a mere cessation—rather than a treaty, a resolution. Thus the end of the war was but the beginning of a violent conflict that waxes and wanes but has yet to end.

The Least You Need to Know

- Israel proclaimed independence on May 14, 1948, asserting both a natural and legal right to nationhood, provoking the nations of the Arab League to invade from the north, east, and south.

- On both sides, the Arab-Israeli War combined atrocities against civilians with large-scale conventional battles. The Israelis were outnumbered, but their forces were better led and equipped.

- Having begun the war on the defensive against a large-scale invasion, Israel was able to turn the tables on the invaders with an offensive strategy that not only preserved Israel's original UN-allotted territory but gained about half of the Palestinian territory originally assigned to the Arabs.

- The biggest losers in the war were the Palestinian Arabs, of whom an estimated 15,000 were killed and 25,000 wounded. Nearly three-quarters of a million left what was now Israeli territory, reducing the Arab population there by two-thirds and creating a refugee community determined to reclaim, by any means necessary, the land they lost.

Suez: Crisis and War, 1956

Egypt, though invaded from time to time and occasionally even conquered, remained a kingdom unto itself from almost the dawn of recorded history until the Roman victory at the Battle of Actium in 31 B.C.E. At last, in 1517, it became part of the Ottoman Empire; however, except for a brief period of occupation by Napoleon's army at the end of the eighteenth century, Ottoman Egypt was essentially a self-governing province.

These last vestiges of Egyptian autonomy began to erode in the nineteenth century and came to an end in 1882, when the British occupied the country.

Occupied

After Napoleon's withdrawal from Egypt on the cusp of the nineteenth century, the Ottoman-sanctioned rulers of the country became determined to modernize infrastructure and catch up to the technological and economic level of European nations. European tax structures were brought to the Nile delta, and the increased revenues in the central government coffers were spent on elaborate palatial complexes and, among other things, a greatly expanded industrial army. Combined with the inefficiencies of Ottoman-style government, this meant that government spending, though extravagant, created little improvement in the Egyptian civilian economy. Increasingly, the country became a debtor nation, an economic vassal to Europe—especially to France and Britain, who had invested most heavily in Egypt.

In This Chapter

- The European investment in Egypt and the Suez Canal

- The Anglo-Egyptian War of 1882 and the British occupation

- Nasser and the Free Officers Movement rise

- The Egyptian republic is born

- The Suez Crisis and its political fallout

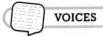

VOICES

Soldiers! Think how from the tops of these pyramids 40 centuries look down upon you!

—Napoleon in Egypt, addressing his troops before the Battle of the Pyramids, July 21, 1798

As discussed in Chapter 6, Egypt's debt to Europe became unsupportable after the massive British and French investment in the construction of the Suez Canal, which was completed in 1869. In 1875, the Egyptian khedive (viceroy), Isma'il Pasha, sought to settle the national debt by selling Egypt's share of the canal outright to Britain. Far from getting Britain off Egypt's back, the sale transformed it into a vassal state not just of the British Empire, but of Europe itself. By the latter nineteenth century, European financiers held the Egyptian purse strings.

This humiliating state of affairs provoked a combination of Islamist and Pan-Arab nationalist opposition to all European influence in Egypt and, indeed, throughout the Middle East. Within Egypt, it was the army, dominated by Albanian and Mamluk officers, that became the source of organized resistance. The military understood that the priorities of *European* financiers did not include them, and the top officers were—quite rightly—fearful of losing power and privilege.

Resistance

In September 1881, the army staged an intimidating demonstration, which prompted Khedive Tawfiq to fire his prime minister and rule by fiat and decree. He was powerless to prevent the military from instituting a reign of terror against Europeans and their Egyptian allies throughout the country. Many were murdered. In response, during April 1882, both France and Britain dispatched warships to Alexandria to back the khedive's efforts to rein in the military. The nationalists, in turn, warned their followers that the arrival of the European warships signaled an imminent invasion, and they used this threat to stir revolutionary fervor.

VOICES

"Egypt for the Egyptians" is the sentiment to which I would wish to give scope; and could it prevail it would I think be the best, the only good solution of the "Egyptian Question."

—William Ewart Gladstone, prime minister of Great Britain, speaking to his foreign secretary, January 4, 1882

Rebellion

Khedive Tawfiq had had enough. He departed Cairo for Alexandria, creating a power vacuum an army officer named Ahmed Urabi rushed to fill. Backed by the army, he assumed control of the government, which, by June 1882, was in anticolonial nationalist hands. Among the first acts of the revolutionary government was the seizure of European assets and the nationalization of European companies.

In the streets, some Egyptians took to violence. As European and Greek shops and homes were attacked in Alexandria, the British unleashed a naval bombardment from the harbor.

War

As is often the case, military action begat military escalation. The naval bombardment overcame all political inertia and prompted the British government to go all in. Fearful that either foreign powers would intervene or that a general Islamic uprising would be triggered—not only in Egypt but throughout the Middle East and also in British India—and concerned that nationalists would seize the Suez Canal, the government of Prime Minister William Gladstone dispatched in August an Anglo-Indian expeditionary force to cover both ends of the canal. This action was coordinated with a French landing at Alexandria and at the northern end of the canal.

The combined Anglo-French-Indian army advanced against the Egyptian army, handily defeating it at the Battle of Tel-el-Kabir on September 13, near the Suez Canal. This single battle was the sum and substance of the so-called Anglo-Egyptian War of 1882. It put Khedive Tawfiq back in control of Egypt—or, more properly speaking, it put Britain back in control, via Tawfiq.

 DID YOU KNOW?

The Anglo-Egyptian War of 1882 consisted essentially of a preparatory naval bombardment and a single major land battle. Nevertheless, it introduced three significant innovations that would shape military operations in the coming century. A special unit, the 8th Railway Company RE, was raised to operate railway transportation, which greatly accelerated the movement of troops. Telegraph lines were laid in advance of the Battle of Tel-el-Kabir to facilitate command and control. And to make this British intervention in faraway Egypt more palatable on the British home front, an Army Post Office Corps was created to deliver mail to troops on the front lines.

The Long Aftermath

With hindsight, it might appear that Britain, supported by France, intended the brief war to secure a permanent European occupation of Egypt. In fact, both Britain and France would much rather have continued to manage Egypt from afar through Tawfiq and succeeding khedives, rather than rule it close-up. It soon became clear to various influential figures in the British colonial administration, however, that the security of Europe's financial, trade, and strategic interests in Egypt depended on long-term administrative and fiscal stability. The only way to ensure this, the reasoning went, was to institute a full-scale occupation. Egypt thus became Britain's investment and its burden.

VOICES

As regards the Suez Canal, England has a double interest; it has a predominant commercial interest, because 82 percent of the trade passing through the Canal is British trade, and it has a predominant political interest caused by the fact that the Canal is the principal highway to India, Ceylon, the Straits, and British Burmah [sic] … and also to China, where we have vast interests [and] to our Colonial Empire in Australia and New Zealand.

—Sir Charles Dilke, British undersecretary of state for foreign affairs, justifying intervention in Egypt, July 25, 1882

In the Ottoman Twilight

After 1882, Egypt was a nation twice removed from sovereignty. A province of the Ottoman Empire, it was occupied by soldiers and officials of the British Empire. In 1914, Ottoman rule in Egypt faltered and failed as a result of the two Balkan wars that were a run-up to World War I. In December 1914, the British administration took advantage of Ottoman weakness to oust the khedive who had succeeded Tawfiq in 1892, Abbas II Hilmi Bey, and replace him with his uncle, Hussein Kamel.

The big difference between the two men was that Abbas II had been a lackey of the Ottoman Empire, whereas Kamel was more than willing to be a lackey of the British Empire—for which the British administration conferred upon him the lofty title of "sultan."

In the guise of defending the august *sultan* of Egypt, Britain imposed martial law on the country— a move that also ensured the continued strategic flow of Middle Eastern oil via the Suez Canal throughout World War I.

Rebirth of Rebellion

Hussein Kamel died in 1917, whereupon Ahmad Fuad, his ambitious brother, assumed the title of sultan as Fuad I of Egypt. Timing is often everything, and Fuad I succeeded to power—such as it was—at a time when Egyptians were straining under a British yoke that the demands of war had made heavier than ever. British policing was often brutal, and British wartime rationing was especially oppressive. It was enough to fan anew the flames of Egyptian nationalism.

As the Ottoman Empire ceased to be a presence in Egypt immediately following the war, Fuad I sent a nationalist delegation to London to petition His Majesty for autonomy, if not outright independence. The British government responded not merely by refusing to hear the delegation, but also arrested its leader, the popular revolutionist Zaghlul Pasha, and confined him to prison. In response, nationalist groups throughout Egypt staged paralyzing strikes and launched violent attacks against colonial officials and functionaries.

The political climate following World War I, the Treaty of Versailles (and related treaties), Woodrow Wilson's "14 Points" (with its emphasis on democracy and self-determination), and the creation of the League of Nations were all conducive to the dissolution of colonial empires. Responding to the winds of change, the British took a new tack in Egypt, looking for a way to grant the country at least a semblance of autonomy while actually retaining a high degree of fiscal control over it.

Field Marshal Viscount Edmund Allenby, architect of British victory in the World War I Sinai and Palestine Campaign, now negotiated a settlement with the nationalists, proclaiming, in February 1922, Egypt independent—albeit "with reservations." These included provisions to protect "foreign interests," namely the Suez Canal and the "rights" of European oil companies. Although the British occupation was formally ended, Great Britain continued to "supervise" Egyptian defense—which meant maintaining a significant military presence in the country.

To secure Fuad's compliance with the new scheme, the British crown recognized his elevation from sultan to King Fuad I, and Egypt was refashioned into a constitutional monarchy. Both the monarchy and the constitution were cynical fictions because of the looming presence of British troops, backing the autocracy of King Fuad I.

Nasser and the Free Officers Movement

Gamal Abdel Nasser was just four years old when Fuad I became Britain's handpicked king. Born in an Upper Egyptian village, he was more or less insulated from world, national, and local politics, growing up in a solid middle-class family. But he had an insatiable appetite for books and devoured the Quran and other Islamic texts, as well as the biographies of notable nationalists and expansionists, ranging from Napoleon to Bismarck to Garibaldi—and, of course, Atatürk.

Primed by his reading, he entered Egypt's Royal Military Academy in 1937, and came under the influence of an instructor named Aziz al-Masri, a committed and articulate anticolonialist. He also read and reread *The Return of the Spirit,* a 1933 novel by the Egyptian playwright and novelist Tawfiq al-Hakim, which spoke of Egypt's need for a strong leader in whom the people could recognize a symbol of all their patriotic feelings and desires.

In the army, Second Lieutenant Nasser befriended two other young academy graduates, Zakaria Mohieddin and Anwar Sadat. By the outbreak of World War II, this trio would become the nucleus of the Free Officers Movement, a group of nationalist military men who favored a revolution to create a fully independent Egyptian republic.

After serving in Sudan in 1941, Nasser became an instructor at the Royal Military Academy in 1943 and used his position to continue recruiting members of the Free Officers Movement. When he was promoted to the General Staff College, he gained access to increasingly senior officers, who were added to the movement. Soon, senior officers in every branch of the Egyptian military were enrolled.

Gamal Abdel Nasser

Born on January 15 or 16, 1918, in the village of Bani Morr in the Upper Egyptian province of Asyut, Gamal Abdel Nasser began his rise to power in 1937, when he entered Egypt's Royal Military Academy in Cairo. Graduating in 1938 as a second lieutenant, he served in the town of Mankabad, finding close friends in two other recent graduates, Zakaria Mohieddin and Anwar Sadat, both of whom would, with Nasser, become prominent in the Free Officers Movement that overthrew King Farouk in 1952.

Nasser returned to the academy in 1941 as an instructor and forged many more close alliances with young officers, whom he gradually recruited into the Free Officers Movement.

During the 1940s and early 1950s, deep social unrest spread through Egypt, as 20 percent of the land was owned by .01 percent of landowners, and most small landowners owned a mere acre or even less. Malnutrition and disease were rampant, and dismal conditions in rural areas sent many peasants to the cities, driving prices and unemployment steadily higher.

On July 22 and 23, 1952, Nasser was among the leaders of a military coup that overthrew King Farouk and established a new republican political order under Major General Muhammad Naguib. At first, Nasser remained in the background, but subsequently led an action to oust Naguib in the spring of 1954. Nasser then emerged as the new prime minister.

Nasser led a radical land reform, which redistributed land holdings and greatly raised the status of the middle class. In addition, he advocated construction of a massive public works project, the Aswan Dam, as a powerful stimulus to the languishing Egyptian economy. At first approaching Britain and the United States for financial backing, he was rebuffed on account of neutrality in the Cold War and rhetoric concerning the Palestinian conflict. He therefore secured Aswan Dam funding from the Soviet Union—and went a step further by nationalizing the Suez Canal. He announced that canal fees would no longer go to European bondholders, but to the construction of the dam.

Nasser's realignment with the Soviets and his seizure of the Suez Canal prompted Britain and France to collude with Israel in fomenting a war by which the British and French would regain control of the canal. Although Nasser suffered military defeat in this contest, he ended up reaping an international political victory, which solidified his support in Egypt and throughout the Arab world.

Using his newfound political capital, Nasser concluded a union with Syria to form the United Arab Republic (UAR) in 1958. It was the first step in what he envisioned as a union of all Arab countries. The UAR proved short-lived, however. Not only did the other nations fail to join, but Syria withdrew in 1961. Despite this, Nasser welcomed political refugees—Pan-Arab radicals and anticolonial revolutionaries—from other Arab countries. Yet even as he embraced foreign radicals, he became a repressive dictator at home, presiding over a domestic security apparatus that included concentration camps and a well-organized secret-police force. Although regular elections were held, they featured Nasser's handpicked candidates, who generally ran unopposed.

Despite his repressive regime, Nasser remained immensely popular. In 1967, however, when Nasser called for the withdrawal of United Nations Emergency Force (UNEF) troops from the Gaza Strip and blockaded Eilat, Israel responded with the brilliant, preemptive "Six-Day War," which (among other things) destroyed Egypt's air force on the ground.

On June 9, 1967, Nasser appeared on Egyptian television to announce his resignation in response to defeat at the hands of Israel. Hundreds of thousands of Egyptians staged demonstrations of protest, demanding that he remain in power. Perhaps Nasser expected this popular response, perhaps not. In any case, he withdrew his resignation and continued to govern until he was felled by a fatal heart attack on September 28, 1970.

The Shame of Farouk

On April 28, 1936, Fuad I died and was succeeded by his son Farouk. A monarch much given to the pleasures of the flesh, Farouk earned a reputation as an international playboy even as the majority of Egyptians languished in poverty, malnutrition, and disease. With land concentrated in the hands of a tiny wealthy minority, peasants fled rural Egypt for the squalid slums of Egypt's cities, where they found inflationary prices and boundless unemployment.

Turning a blind eye to the suffering and social unrest among his people, Farouk continued to indulge himself at the grand and gaudy watering holes of Europe. Years passed, and Nasser and the Free Officers grew in number and influence. At last, sensing that the times were ripe for revolution, they made their move.

In preparation for a coup d'état, Nasser took the bold step of informing both the governments of the United States and Britain that he and the senior military intended to overthrow Farouk's corrupt monarchy and install a democratic republic in its place. By this time, it was clear to the leaders of the West that Farouk's corrupt reign was untenable, and the Americans and the British agreed to lend no aid to him; however, the Americans demanded one condition: Nasser and his group not only must refrain from harming Farouk, they would exile him with a show of courtesy that included a formal ceremony.

On the night of July 22, 1952, 200 Free Officers led 2,000 troops in an assault on all government buildings, radio stations, and police stations in Cairo, along with army headquarters. The targets folded with little or no resistance, and, by morning, King Farouk abdicated in favor of his infant son, who was proclaimed King Fuad II. That hardly mattered. A new government—a new political order—was installed under Major General Muhammad Naguib. This was as Nasser had planned it. A mere lieutenant colonel, he did not believe the people would support him as head of government. He therefore remained in the background as a Revolutionary Command Council took control.

 DID YOU KNOW?

> Immediately upon abdicating the Egyptian throne, Farouk wasted no time in fleeing, first to Monaco and then to Rome, where he lived for the rest of his life, which ended on March 18, 1965, after he consumed a customarily sumptuous meal at a Roman restaurant. The reign of his son and successor, seven-month-old Fuad II, was brief, ending on June 18, 1953, after the Republic of Egypt was officially proclaimed. The boy grew up in Switzerland, lived for some years in Paris, was married and had three children, divorced, and returned to Switzerland, where he still resides.

The Republic Is Proclaimed

On June 18, 1953, the monarchy was officially abolished and the Republic of Egypt proclaimed in its place, with Muhammad Naguib as its first president. Within a short time, however, Nasser and other members of the Revolutionary Command Council accused Naguib of supporting the outlawed Muslim Brotherhood (see Chapter 6) and demanding dictatorial authority. On February 25, 1954, the council announced Naguib's "resignation," but mass street protests brought him back to the presidency the next day.

In fact, because Nasser was elevated to the posts of prime minister and chairman of the Revolutionary Command Council on the very day of Naguib's reinstatement, the presidency was relegated to a figurehead role, and Naguib, rendered effectively powerless, resigned in earnest on November 14, 1954.

Land Reform and Economic Stimulus

Even before Naguib's departure, Nasser, first as prime minister and then in the dual role of prime minister and president, turned his attention to land reform. His idea was to empower Egypt's farmers by giving them ownership of the land they worked. Yet even as he pushed land reform forward, Nasser was keenly aware that this step alone, momentous as it was, would not pull Egypt out of its long, steep economic decline.

Nasser needed to give his country an economic shot in the arm. A powerful economic stimulus was called for, and Nasser believed he found what he needed in the construction of the Aswan Dam on the Nile.

As he saw it, the project would accomplish four things. First, it would control Nile floodwaters. Second, it would irrigate huge swaths of land, making them arable for agriculture. Third, it would generate a great supply of hydroelectric power, which would drive the industrialization of Egypt. Fourth—and finally—building the spectacular dam would create tens of thousands of jobs for desperately poor Egyptians.

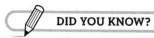

DID YOU KNOW?

> The Aswan High Dam is 12,570 feet long, 3,220 feet wide at its base, 130 feet wide at its crest, and 364 feet in height. It is capable of passing a maximum of 390,000 cubic feet of water per second and fills a reservoir, Lake Nasser, which is 340 miles long by 22 miles wide at its widest.

Nasser turned first to Britain and the United States for financial assistance with the dam. Initially, he was warmly received, but his courtship of Soviet support, his recognition of the People's Republic of China, and a recent arms deal with Czechoslovakia—the very nation from which Israel had purchased war-winning arms in 1948 (see Chapter 9)—prompted Britain, the United States, and also the World Bank to withdraw from the project.

Cold War Comes to Egypt

Nasser did not take the rebuff lying down. In June, he secured a $1.12 billion construction loan from the Soviet Union at 2 percent interest. (In 1958, the USSR would decide to fund the project outright, asking for neither interest nor payback of principal.)

Officially, Egypt was a *non-aligned* nation, owing allegiance neither to the West nor to the Soviet-dominated Eastern Bloc. But as American leaders saw it, Nasser was transforming Egypt into a Soviet satellite, and that made the Middle East potentially yet another battlefield—as a divided Germany and Korea already were—in the developing Cold War between the world's two thermonuclear superpowers.

DEFINITION

> A **non-aligned** nation was any state, typically in the Third World, not formally associated with either the U.S.-dominated West or the Soviet-dominated East. Egypt's Nasser was instrumental in the creation of the Non-Aligned Movement (NAM), first conceived by Nasser in association with India's Prime Minister, Jawaharlal Nehru, Indonesian President Sukarno, Ghana's President Kwame Nkrumah, and Yugoslavia's President Tito. Although less important than it once was, NAM continues to exist today and has 120 member nations in addition to 17 "observer" states.

Nasser Nationalizes the Suez Canal

On July 26, 1956, Nasser took a step the West had long feared: he nationalized the Suez Canal, preempting the lucrative operating proceeds that went to European bondholders. Henceforth, he declared, canal transit fees would go to building the Aswan Dam. He added to this the defiant prediction that the fees would pay for construction in five years.

 VOICES

> At this moment as I talk to you, some of your Egyptian brethren are proceeding to administer the canal company and to run its affairs. They are taking over the canal company at this very moment—the Egyptian canal company, not the foreign canal company.
>
> —Gamal Abdel Nasser, speech on the fourth anniversary of the 1952 revolution, July 26, 1956

A Three-Way War Cabal

Fearful that the "unpredictable" Nasser might decide at any moment to close the canal, thereby cutting off Western Europe's major source of oil, British and French diplomats laid plans to wrest the Suez Canal back from nationalization. Diplomatic means were proposed for regaining control of the canal, but this quickly emerged as a mission impossible. Ideas were secretly traded on how to undermine the new Egyptian government and depose Nasser. But Nasser was tremendously popular.

If diplomacy is an alternative to war, war is also an alternative to diplomacy. The French and British began to formulate a plan to take the canal by force.

Shadow War

The British government directed General Sir Hugh Stockwell, a testy, eccentric, but highly admired World War II commander, to formulate a plan for employing a joint Anglo-French expeditionary force to seize, hold, and protect the canal.

Neither British nor French leaders sought to engage U.S. participation in the military operation. First, they understood that President Dwight D. Eisenhower would be hesitant to commit America to any endeavor that smacked of British and French imperialism. Second, the British and French leaders also appreciated the fact that the president did not want to bring the United States into a direct military confrontation with the Soviet Union over Egypt.

On the other hand, both France and Britain wanted to avoid an outright provocation of their American ally. Therefore, to disguise the overt appearance of imperialist aggression, French and British diplomats entered into secret negotiations with Israel to explore the possibility of cloaking their planned invasion of Egypt as a fresh flare-up of the Arab-Israeli War.

Ultimately, the three countries agreed to a plan in which Israel would appear to threaten the Suez Canal, thereby furnishing England and France with a pretext for intervention. As scripted, the charade called for Britain and France to demand that *both* Israel and Egypt withdraw 10 miles from the canal. The conspirators were quite certain that Nasser would refuse to withdraw. Well, so much the better. That would provide a pretext to seize the prize.

Operation Musketeer

In the summer of 1956, General Stockwell was presented with a "Contingency Plan" the British Chiefs of Staff had prepared for fighting a war to take the Suez Canal. He didn't at all like what he saw and quickly submitted an alternative called Operation Musketeer. It prescribed a British assault on and occupation of Alexandria, followed by an advance by British tanks against the Egyptian army north of Cairo. As Stockwell envisioned it, this battle would be one of annihilation, its object to overwhelm, overrun, and destroy the Egyptian army in a single stroke.

Shortly before the operation was set to commence in early September, politicians in France and Britain decreed a modification, by which Port Said, just north of the Suez Canal, was substituted for Alexandria as the initial principal target of the invasion. Both Stockwell and his French deputy, General André Beaufre, strenuously objected to the modification as a dilution of the plan. But they nevertheless acquiesced.

Operation Kadesh

As if the drastic modification to Operation Musketeer were not bad enough, the French and English had to delay their invasion two months, pushing it from early September to early November, so as to allow time to coordinate their mobilization with that of Israel.

The Israeli portion of the planned engagement, a campaign in the Sinai, was called Operation Kadesh. Its stated objectives were to capture the Straits of Tiran between the Sinai and Arabian peninsulas in order to occupy the high ground just east of the canal, thereby posing a military threat to it. In addition, the Israelis had other objectives in view, the most important of which was occupying the Gaza Strip, the territory along the Mediterranean coast at Egypt's northeast border and Israel's northwestern border. Israel regarded the Gaza Strip as both a training ground for militant Islamic *Fedayeen* guerilla groups and as safe haven from which the Egyptian army could launch an invasion at any time. Finally, by attacking multiple objectives and menacing the canal, the Israelis hoped to create sufficient confusion within the ranks of the Egyptian army to bring about its collapse and, with it, the fall of President Nasser.

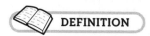 **DEFINITION**

> **Fedayeen** is an Arabic word that may be translated as "commandos," although it is rooted in a word meaning "sacrifice." It describes militant volunteers willing to fight (and die) for diverse causes, from local nationalism to perceived defense of the faith.

Nasser Falters

Thanks in large part to the delay of Operation Musketeer, President Nasser became aware that some military action was looming. Of its extent, however, he had no precise intelligence.

When reports reached him of Anglo-French forces massing on Malta and Cyprus, he reacted with a degree of panic, withdrawing nearly half his Sinai garrison and repositioning these troops to the Canal Zone Delta. Distracted by the Europeans, Nasser took his eye off the Israelis, leaving just 30,000 men under Major General Ali Amer to defend the Sinai. Moreover, these forces were deployed far to the northeast in a static defense of the triangle formed by Rafah, Abu Ageila, and El Ansh. In short, Nasser had made a tactical blunder, rendering the force an easy target for the Israeli army.

Curtain Up

The drama commenced on October 29, 1956, with an Israeli attack that steamrolled across the Gaza Strip, capturing it along with Sharm el-Sheikh (an Egyptian port city and naval base at the southern tip of the Sinai Peninsula) and other towns, before the British and the French—still acting from the same script—imperiously demanded that both Israel and Egypt cease fire and withdraw from the war zone. To enforce the ultimatum, they bombed Cairo.

Continuing to go along with the script, Israel announced its compliance with the demand. As expected, Nasser refused—apparently leaving the European allies no choice. On November 5, 1956, an Anglo-French paratroop force dropped near Port Said, which they attacked. This was followed by a Royal Marine landing and the occupation of the city.

British casualties were light (16 killed, 96 wounded), as were French (10 killed, 33 wounded). Israel, which was more heavily committed, lost 231 killed and 899 wounded. Egypt never revealed its casualties, but estimates vary from at least 1,000 killed to more than 3,000, in addition to some 4,000 wounded. In any case, Nasser had enough. He accepted a cease-fire arranged by the United Nations.

Curtain Down

Short and sharp, the war had been a military cakewalk for France and England and a harder-won but more extensive triumph for Israel. Politically, however, the "Suez Crisis" very quickly proved a disaster for the European members of the trio.

Soviet leaders were not in the least deceived by the charade. Soviet Premier Nikita Khrushchev threatened to intervene militarily. For his part, President Eisenhower, outraged by the deceit of the British, French, and Israeli leadership, warned of his intention not to come to their aid, should the Soviets take the action they threatened. Indeed, the Eisenhower administration pressured the Anglo-French forces to withdraw from the Suez Canal.

 **VOICES**

> If we had allowed things to drift, everything would have gone from bad to worse. Nasser would have become a kind of Moslem Mussolini, and our friends in Iraq, Jordan, Saudi Arabia, and even Iran would gradually have been brought down. His efforts would have spread westwards, and Libya and North Africa would have been brought under his control.
>
> —British Prime Minister Anthony Eden, attempting to justify the Anglo-Franco-Israeli Suez "cabal" to President Dwight D. Eisenhower, November 5, 1956

Eisenhower also pressed Israel to give up occupation of the Sinai and Sharm el-Sheikh, but the Israeli leadership refused to budge for more than a year. When it finally yielded, in March 1957, Israel turned these prizes over to the United Nations Emergency Force (UNEF) rather than to Nasser's Egypt.

The price the prime ministers of Britain and France paid was heavy. Accused of misleading Parliament, Britain's Anthony Eden resigned on January 9, 1957. Five months later, French Prime Minister Guy Mollet likewise stepped down.

As for Gamal Abdel Nasser, having endured a humiliating military defeat, his reputation among Egyptians and throughout the Arab world nevertheless soared after the Suez Crisis, the military loss more than compensated for by a political triumph.

Financed by the Soviet Union, he proceeded with construction of the Aswan Dam and rode the momentum of this great project toward what he hoped would be the realization of another goal: the unification of Arab countries. In 1958, the government of Syria merged with Egypt to form the United Arab Republic. From here, Nasser intended to recruit all the other Arab countries into one common alliance, which would not only destroy Israel at last but would put the Arab world on a par with the West. Such, at any rate, was his plan.

The Least You Need to Know

- European nations—especially Britain and France—manipulated Egypt's leaders and their Ottoman overlords to transform Egypt into a vassal of its European creditors.

- To protect its investment in Egypt—and especially the continued profitable operation of the Suez Canal—the British launched the Anglo-Egyptian War of 1882, which began a long occupation of the country.

- With the majority of the Egyptian people in ruinous poverty, conditions were ripe for revolt, which found its modern expression in the Free Officers Movement of the 1950s.

- After the Egyptian Revolution of 1952, which overthrew the corrupt King Farouk and create the Republic of Egypt in place of the monarchy, Nasser courted close relations with the Soviet Union and defied the West by nationalizing the Suez Canal.

- The Suez Crisis brought about the downfall of leaders in France and Britain and succeeded only in raising the popularity and influence of Nasser as a leader of the Arab world.

Palestinians Stand Up

The Middle East conflict appears vexing in its complexity, and yet one of the most painful and tragic aspects of the conflict, the struggle between Israelis and Palestinians, is at root starkly simple. What has been called at least since Israeli independence the "Palestinian Question" is actually quite a direct question: "who owns the land?"

Behind the Palestinian Question

The Palestinian Question goes back some 60+ years, to 1947, when the United Nations "settled" the partition of Palestine between Arabs and Jews with General Assembly Resolution 181, and to 1949, with the UN-brokered armistice agreements formally ending the Arab-Israeli War of 1948–1949.

The armistice gave Israel a third more territory than the UN apportioned to it before the Arab-Israeli War, so that Israel came to control more than 78 percent of the territory that had comprised "Mandatory Palestine"—Palestine as it was defined under the post-World War I League of Nations British Mandate. Known as the *"Green Line,"* the 1949 armistice borders added to Israel all of Galilee and the Jezreel Valley in the north and all of the Negev in the south, as well as West Jerusalem and the coastal plain in the center. The Gaza Strip was occupied by Egypt, and the West Bank, which included East Jerusalem, was occupied by Jordan.

In This Chapter

- The "Palestinian Question": who owns the land?

- The PLO story

- Black September: Arab conflict with the PLO

- The Munich Massacre and other terrorist acts

- Palestine declares independence

- Prospects for peace

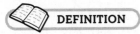 **DEFINITION**

> **Green Line** is the name for the borders of the State of Israel as laid down by the United Nations in the 1949 armistice ending the Arab-Israeli War of 1948-1949.

As noted in Chapter 9, about three-quarters of a million Palestinian Arabs fled or were expelled from their homes following the war. This massive departure was out of a total Palestinian Arab population of 1.2 million. Some 156,000 Arabs chose to remain in Israel after the war and became Israeli citizens.

After the armistice, the UN quickly established the United Nations Relief and Works Agency for Palestine Refugees in the Near East (UNRWA) to provide humanitarian assistance. But the agency's efforts were overwhelmed, and most refugees were settled in camps, typically squalid, throughout the Arab world. These Arab nations, like Jordan and Lebanon, refused to accept the refugees as residents, let alone citizens, insisting instead that they be allowed to return to Palestine as their homeland.

In short, the Palestinian refugees were people without a country. It is even possible to see their situation as analogous to that of the stateless Jews prior to the creation of Israel.

Sixty Years or Four Thousand?

But the date of origin for the Palestinian Question ultimately depends on how you define *Palestinian* and *Israeli*. Again, there is a deceptively simple issue at root. Both the Jews and the Palestinians believe that, regardless of the outcome of war and the force of UN resolutions, the territory of modern Israel is theirs both by right of history and inheritance. Both Muslims and Jews claim direct descent from Abraham, the original "owner" of Palestine/Israel. The Jews see themselves as descended from Isaac, Abraham's younger son and designated heir. The Muslims claim descent from Ishmael, who, as Abraham's oldest son, they see as the rightful and true inheritor of Abraham's land.

Like so many other conflicts in the Middle East, the Palestinian Question—the Israeli-Palestinian conflict—is a modern conflict founded on the most ancient of sources.

The Jewish Exodus from Arab Countries

During the 1948–1949 war, some 10,000 Jews were forced to flee their homes in Arab-controlled parts of what had been Mandatory Palestine. And thus the war made refugees of Jews as well as Palestinian Arabs, albeit in far smaller numbers. Moreover, during the 3 years immediately following the armistice, some 700,000 Jews immigrated to Israel, settling near or in formerly Arab neighborhoods, villages, and houses. The influx doubled Israel's Jewish population and almost equaled the number of Palestinian Arabs who had left or were forced out of the country.

Yet it must be noted that about 300,000 of the 700,000 Jews who came to Israel after the 1948–1949 war were themselves from Arab and Muslim countries. Some of these people had been forcibly expelled by Arab and Islamic governments. Others, though not officially expelled, fled to escape anti-Semitic persecution. Most recent scholars of *Mizrahim*, as the Arab Jews call themselves, see the principal drivers of the migration as colonialism, nationalism, and the search for economic opportunity simply unavailable in the Arab countries.

Although most intense during 1949–1951, the so-called Jewish exodus from Arab countries lasted into the early 1970s. In all, about a million Jews emigrated from Islamic countries, the largest single source being Iraq, from which 100,000 Jews fled. Not all of the million immigrated to Israel. Some 300,000 settled in Europe (especially France), the United States, Canada, and South America. (Jews who left Iran and North Africa were mostly of ancient, non-European stock and typically settled in Europe and North America rather than Israel.)

The influx into Israel was such that refugees had to be accommodated at first in tent camps. In contrast to the squalid camps the Arab Palestinians occupied, however, those for Jews were well run by the Jewish Agency. By the 1950s, Quonset huts replaced the original tents, and the Jewish Agency strategically withdrew its support, compelling the newcomers to provide for their own sustenance. Aided by the established Israeli population, they did just that, and by the early 1960s, the Quonset hut settlements had evolved into towns and cities with permanent housing. In this way, new Jewish settlements were built in Israel, either on land that had once been Arab or on the frontiers of such lands. Moreover, some Jewish settlers were given the homes formerly owned by Palestinians.

Right of Return

Zionism was founded on the principle that all Jews have an ancient *"right of return"* to their ancestral homeland, Israel. Once Israel was established as an independent state, that right became a cornerstone of Israeli law. Citizenship was open to any Jewish immigrant from anywhere in the world.

DEFINITION

Right of return is a cornerstone of Israeli law, enshrined in the country's constitution. It opens Israeli citizenship to all Jews, everywhere, who decide to return to their ancestral homeland. The Palestinians later claimed the same right, applying it to the property they or their parents abandoned or were forced to leave during the Arab-Israeli War of 1948-1949.

Taking their cue from Israeli law, the Palestinians likewise claimed a right of return, asserting that first-generation refugees and their descendants had a right to the property they lost during the 1948–1949 war. This right would be reasserted following the Six-Day War of 1967.

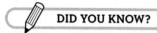

DID YOU KNOW?

Today, many Palestinians, no matter where they may live, keep a key to their family's home in prewar Palestine as a token of their wish and hope to return and reclaim what they believe is theirs.

The Arab League Meets

The Arab League—more formally, the League of Arab States—was founded in Cairo on March 22, 1945, by representatives from Egypt, Iraq, Transjordan (Jordan), Lebanon, Saudi Arabia, and Syria. It was not until 19 years later, in 1964, that Gamal Abdel Nasser convened the league's first summit, in Cairo. The league's purpose was twofold—to unify Arab nations in their response to "imperialism," by which was mostly meant interference in Arab affairs by Western European nations, and to unite against what league members called the "aggressive policies" of Israel.

Representatives from Syria and the Palestinian Fedayeen went further, calling for a renewal of the Arab-Israeli War of 1948. Nasser led the other members in objecting that the time was not right for military action against Israel. The Egyptian leader instead proposed to divert the headwaters of the Jordan River outside of Israeli territory in order to prevent Tel Aviv from using it for large-scale irrigation. Nasser secured the summit's approval of his plan, which was to have a momentous effect he never expected—Israel's lopsided triumph in the 1967 Six-Day War.

Founding the PLO

Of more enduring impact was the league's resolution to empower Palestinian diplomat Ahmad al-Shuqaryri to create a Palestinian "entity." This became the Palestine Liberation Organization (PLO), established on May 28, 1964, with as-Shuqaryi as its first chairman.

The Palestinian National Charter (renamed in 1968 the Palestinian National Covenant) was promulgated on the day of the organization's founding. It set down five principles:

1. Palestine, as bounded "at the time of the British mandate is an integral regional unit."

2. The establishment of the state of Israel was and is "entirely illegal."

3. The "existence and activity" of Zionism are to be prohibited.

4. Palestinians have a right of return.

5. Palestinians have a right of self-determination.

The 1964 charter did not specifically mention Palestinian statehood, however, and it was only 10 years later, in 1974, that the PLO called for establishing an independent state in the former territory of Mandatory Palestine.

A Parliament of Factions

Within the PLO is the Palestinian National Council (PNC), which is supposed to function as a legislative body, but is actually far less powerful than the much smaller PLO Executive Committee, consisting of 18 members elected by the PNC. The committee makes policy and other key decisions. However, neither the PNC nor the Executive Committee has absolute control over the many factions and non-affiliated "independent" members that make up the organization.

At its founding, members were unified in their violent opposition to Israel, determination to regain control of Palestine, and their generally secular approach to political ideology. The PLO was born of Nasser's Pan-Arab philosophy—the idea that, ultimately, all Arabs should be part of a single state. This may seem reminiscent of the Islamic idea of a caliphate, but Nasser, like his hero and model, Atatürk, was a secularist, and both Pan-Arabism and the PLO are generally secular. They are dedicated to republican goals, not political Islam.

Despite the organization's factionalism, the Arab League has always recognized the PLO as the legitimate representative body of the Palestinian people. As such, the PLO functioned as a kind of shadow state, a legislative and diplomatic body for a nation that had yet to exist.

Arab League members have never been unanimously enthusiastic about the creation of a Palestinian state. From the beginning, Egypt and Jordan supported it, provided the state existed entirely on land "occupied" by Israel. Egypt and Jordan refused to grant Palestinian sovereignty over the territory those nations occupied—the Gaza Strip in the case of Egypt, and the West Bank in the case of Jordan. Together, this territory amounted to 53 percent of what the UN Partition Plan had allotted to the Arabs.

 DID YOU KNOW?

It was one thing for the Arab League to recognize the PLO as the legitimate representative of the Palestinian people, but quite another for the United Nations to do so. In 1974, the General Assembly not only extended such recognition, it also granted the PLO observer status at the UN. Two years later, the General Assembly voted to allow the PLO to participate in Security Council debate, albeit without voting rights. After the Palestinian Declaration of Independence was promulgated on November 15, 1988, the UN renamed the PLO's representation "Palestine," and on November 29, 2012, the General Assembly passed Resolution 67/19, upgrading Palestine's status within the UN from "observer entity" to "non-member observer state." Many interpret this as de facto UN recognition of Palestinian state sovereignty. Palestine still has no voting rights in the UN.

Aspiring State or Terrorist Organization?

From the beginning, the PLO employed tactics some described as "militant" and many others as "terrorist." In January 1965, just months after its founding, the organization attacked the National Water Carrier of Israel, which conveys water from the Sea of Galilee in northwestern Israel via canal, pipeline, and tunnel to the southwestern region, near the border with Egypt. Indeed, the United States formally designated the PLO a terrorist organization in 1987, but through a presidential waiver issued in 1988, permitted official contact with the organization. Israel also branded the PLO as terrorist.

 VOICES

> It is not as though there was a Palestinian people in Palestine considering itself as a Palestinian people, and we came and threw them out and took their country away from them. They did not exist.
>
> —Israeli Prime Minister Golda Meir, in *The Sunday Times* (London), June 15, 1969

The School Bus Massacre

On May 22, 1970, two bazooka shells hit an Israeli school bus on the road to Moshav Avivum, near the Israel-Lebanon border. Twelve Israelis were killed, including nine children, first through third graders. Of 25 more who were wounded, 19 suffered permanent crippling disabilities.

The attackers were members of the Popular Front for the Liberation of Palestine—General Command (PFLP-GC), a breakaway group from the Popular Front for the Liberation of Palestine (PFLP). Both organizations were represented in the PLO.

 DID YOU KNOW?

> The PFLP-GC also carried out the bombing of Swissair Flight 330, on February 12, 1970. Carrying 38 passengers and 9 crew members, the plane was bound from Zurich to Tel Aviv. The explosive device was planted in luggage in the cargo compartment. All aboard were killed.
>
> Another bomb detonated the same day aboard a flight from Frankfurt, Germany, to Vienna, Austria; however, the aircraft landed safely.

Israel Defense Forces (IDF) responded to the massacre by shelling four villages in Lebanon, killing 20 and wounding twice that number. The artillery bombardment prompted many residents living near the border with Israel to flee their homes. In addition, the IDF began patrols in southern Lebanon. This and the shelling prompted the Dawson's Field hijackings.

The Dawson's Field Hijackings

The Popular Front for the Liberation of Palestine, second largest (after al-Fatah) of the factions making up PLO membership, carried out a number of attacks and, especially, aircraft hijackings during the late 1960s and early 1970s. These included the so-called Dawson's Field hijackings of September 6 and 9, 1970, in which four commercial jetliners were hijacked and three of them landed at Dawson's Field, a former British RAF airstrip in the Jordanian desert, near Zarka; the PFLP renamed the remote airstrip "Revolutionary Airport."

The aircraft included a TWA flight from Frankfurt am Main, a Swissair flight from Zurich, a Pan Am flight from Amsterdam, and a BOAC (now British Airways) flight from Bahrain. (A hijacking attempt against a fifth aircraft, an El Al flight from Amsterdam, was ended when one hijacker was killed and another subdued shortly after takeoff.)

In the four hijackings, 310 hostages were taken, all of them soon released—except for 56 identified as Jews, who remained in custody longer. The hijackers blew up the empty aircraft on the ground.

Black September

Whatever else they may have done, the Dawson's Field hijackings tested the limits of Pan-Arabism versus national sovereignty. King Hussein of Jordan responded to PFLP's actions at Dawson's Field as a challenge to the *Hashemite* monarchy. Declaring martial law on September 16, 1970, he dispatched military forces throughout areas of Jordan controlled by Palestinians. This, in turn, sparked a civil war extending from September 1970 to July of the following year.

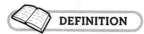 **DEFINITION**

A **Hashemite** is a member of an Arab royal family claiming direct descent from Hashim, the great-grandfather of Muhammad. Hashemite monarchs ruled in Iraq and Yemen and still rule in Jordan and Saudi Arabia.

Called "Black September," the conflict not only pitted Palestinians against native Jordanians, it nearly triggered a regional war involving Jordan, Syria, Iraq, and Israel. Moreover, because the PLO/PLFP was supported by both Syria and the Soviet Union, whereas the United States supported Jordan, the Black September conflict became yet another *proxy war* in the 45-year-long Cold War between the Soviet Union and the United States.

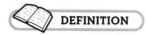 **DEFINITION**

A **proxy war** is a war instigated or backed by a major power that does not itself become directly involved. Proxy wars were typical of the Cold War, in which the United States and the Soviet Union, unwilling to fight one another directly, supported states or factions as they fought one another.

Early in the conflict, on September 27, 1970, King Hussein concluded an agreement with PLO Chairman Yasser Arafat, pledging to treat both sides in the war as equals and granting Palestinian organizations the right to operate in Jordan, albeit outside of the cities. The very next day, however, Egypt's Gamal Abdel Nasser, champion of Pan-Arabism and protector of the PLO and its factions, succumbed to a heart attack. With Nasser out of the picture, Hussein resumed the assault on the Palestinians operating within Jordan.

In the end, the civil war in Jordan resulted in a lopsided victory for the Hashemite monarchy. Better armed and more numerous than the Palestinian and Syrian forces arrayed against it, the Jordanian armed forces suffered 82 killed (out of some 74,000 men deployed) while inflicting at least 3,400 fatal casualties among the Palestinians, with some estimates running as high as 20,000. More than 600 Syrian troops were also killed. Only the rout of Palestinian and allied forces brought Black September to an end.

Munich Massacre

Black September may have ended in 1971, but it inspired the founding of the Black September Organization (BSO), made up mostly of dissidents within al-Fatah.

At 4:30 A.M. on September 5, 1972, eight members of Black September, dressed in track suits and carrying duffels loaded with Soviet-made assault rifles, military pistols, and hand grenades, scaled the security fence surrounding the Olympic Village in Munich, West Germany, site of the Summer Olympic Games. Using stolen keys, they entered two apartments occupied by the Israeli Olympic team. In efforts to resist the attackers, a wrestling coach and a weightlifter were shot and killed, but the kidnappers (two of whom were wounded) captured nine Israeli hostages, among them a wrestling referee, sharpshooting coach, track and field coach, fencing master, weightlifting judge, two wrestlers, and two weightlifters.

Black September offered to release the hostages in return for the release of 234 prisoners held by the Israelis, as well as the release of Andreas Baader and Ulrike Meinhof, the founders of the infamous Red Army Faction (a.k.a. Baader-Meinhof Gang), a German left-wing militant group, who were in German prisons.

German police made an abortive attempt at a rescue before feigning agreement to the kidnappers' demand that they be flown to Cairo with their hostages. The German police planned to ambush the group at Fürstenfeldbruck, the NATO airbase from which the kidnappers and their victims were supposedly to be flown to Cairo. In addition to police sharpshooters deployed at the air base, six police officers, disguised as flight crew, were positioned in a parked Boeing 727 the kidnappers were told would fly them out. Incredibly, however, these officers, without consulting their commanders, voted among themselves to abandon their mission. All that remained arrayed against the Black September group, therefore, were five sharpshooters positioned on the tarmac.

Predictably, the hastily modified ambush was executed in chaos. In an exchange of gunfire, two kidnappers and a German policeman were killed. The hostages, bound hand-and-foot in the helicopters that had taken them to the air base, were powerless to resist or flee.

A standoff developed and, apparently feeling desperate, at 12:04 A.M., September 6, 1972, the kidnappers began murdering their helpless hostages. One kidnapper, Luttif Afif—who called himself Issa, Arabic for "Jesus"—leaped from the helicopter that held some of the hostages, lobbed a hand grenade into the aircraft, and ran across the tarmac, where he was gunned down. The bound hostages were blown to bits and incinerated in the grenade blast.

Three kidnappers were captured on the tarmac; another was killed in a subsequent gun battle in the parking lot of the air base. In all, 11 Israelis were killed, along with the German police officer and five of the eight Black September members.

The three surviving kidnappers were released by German authorities on October 29, 1972, after Palestinian sympathizers of the Black September Group hijacked Lufthansa Flight 615 and held eleven passengers and seven crew members hostage. In accordance with the hijackers' demand, the Black September members were handed over at Zagreb (Croatia) Airport and flown to Tripoli, Libya. There the hostages were released and the Black September members granted asylum by Libyan President Muammar Gaddafi.

Israeli Mossad (intelligence service) and special forces mounted two secret operations, "Spring of Youth" and "Wrath of God," both tasked with hunting down and killing all Palestinians involved in the Munich Massacre. The first operation, carried out in Lebanon on April 9 and 10, 1973, killed between 12 and 100 Palestinians, including three high-level PLO leaders. The second was carried out over a period of more than 20 years and included the assassination of PLO leaders and other Palestinians in various locations, including Rome, Paris, London, Athens, as well as Cyprus and Lebanon.

Two of the three gunmen released by Germany are widely believed to have been killed in Operation Wrath of God. One, however, Jamal al-Gashey, is very possibly still alive somewhere in North Africa or Syria.

Terrorist Attacks of 1974–1978

In 1974, another PLO faction, the Democratic Front for the Liberation of Palestine (DFLP), attacked an elementary school in the Israeli village of Ma'alot, killing 22 children ages 14 to 16, and 2 adults. More than 70 other persons were wounded in the assault.

The following year, on the night of March 4, Fatah members attacked Tel Aviv's Savoy Hotel, killing three persons in the initial onslaught and taking most of the guests and staff hostage. On the morning of March 5, an Israeli counterterrorism unit stormed the hotel, killing seven Fatah members and capturing the eighth. Five hostages were freed, but eight were killed, as were two Israeli soldiers. Another soldier, a private on leave from the IDF, had been shot and mortally wounded earlier, when he rushed to the hotel after hearing gunfire.

Al-Fatah also carried out the Coastal Road Massacre on March 11, 1978. Eleven of thirteen Palestinian Fatah militants landed by boat (two having drowned in rough weather) on a beach near a kibbutz north of Tel Aviv. Disoriented and encountering an American woman, Gail Rubin, taking nature photographs on the beach, they demanded to know where they were. She answered, whereupon the militants shot her dead. They then hijacked a bus on Israel's Coastal Highway, tossing hand grenades at passing cars, shooting bus passengers, and throwing at least one body off the moving vehicle. After hijacking a second bus, they forced the passengers on the first to board it. Stopping briefly, one of the Fatah militants shot and killed a teenager in a passing car, also wounding his father. The hijacking ended in a shootout with police.

A total of 38 civilians were killed and 76 wounded in the murderous spree. Of the eleven attackers, nine were killed and two arrested. They were released in a prisoner exchange after serving seven years.

The Death of Klinghoffer

Given the factional nature of the PLO, it is debatable whether we can assign full responsibility for these and other acts of terrorism to the member organizations (some clearly breakaway groups) or to the PLO umbrella group. In either case, by the mid-1970s, most nations—with the notable exceptions of America and Israel—overlooked the organization's association with terrorism and deemed the PLO the legitimate representative of the Palestinian people.

Yet one act in 1985 eroded the PLO's standing in the global community more than any other. The first half of the 1980s saw numerous attacks by the Palestine Liberation Front (PLF) and other PLO factions, almost always followed by (often disproportionate) Israeli reprisals. On October 1, 1985, an Israeli air raid demolished the PLO headquarters in Tunis, Tunisia, killing 60 PLO members in a reprisal for a PLO attack on an Israeli yacht. Possibly in response to the reprisal, on October 7, 1985, PLF militants hijacked the cruise ship MS *Achille Lauro* off the coast of Egypt.

The hijackers took passengers and crew hostage, demanding the release of 50 Palestinians who were in Israeli prisons. Because a number of the hostages were American tourists, President Ronald Reagan put Navy SEAL Team Six and Delta Force on alert. In the meantime, the hijackers ordered the ship to sail to the Syrian port of Tartus, but were refused Syria's permission to dock there.

At this point, the hijackers committed what can only be described as a brutally senseless murder. Leon Klinghoffer, an American Jew, retired from the appliance business, was celebrating his 36th wedding anniversary with a cruise on the *Achille Lauro*. At 69, he was confined to a wheelchair. The hijackers shot him at pointblank range in the forehead and chest, and then forced, at gunpoint, the ship's barber and a waiter to throw his body, still in the wheelchair, into the sea.

 DID YOU KNOW?

> Initially, the PLO denied responsibility for the Klinghoffer murder, claiming through its Foreign Secretary Farouq Qaddumi that the victim's wife, Marilyn Klinghoffer, had killed him to collect a life-insurance settlement. In April 1996, PLF leader Muhammad Zaidan admitted the obvious truth, and two years later the PLO made a financial settlement with the Klinghoffer family.

Following negotiations that stretched over two days, the hijackers obtained safe conduct to Tunisia; however, their aircraft, an Egyptian commercial airliner, was intercepted by U.S. Navy fighter jets and forced to land at Naval Air Station Sigonella, Sicily. There, Italian authorities arrested the hijackers, but permitted other passengers, including PLF leader Muhammad Zaidan, to go free.

Joseph Stalin supposedly once observed, "A single death is a tragedy. A million deaths, a statistic." The Arab-Israeli conflict had resulted in thousands of deaths on both sides, and the PLO and Mossad have both been implicated in numerous acts of terrorism. But it was the image of a wheelchair-bound elderly man shot and dumped into the sea that was permanently linked to the PLO. For many in the West, it indelibly stained the Palestinian cause.

Arafat Leads

Leon Klinghoffer's was not the only image associated with the PLO by 1985. Although the organization consisted of numerous factions, by 1969 one man emerged as its public face.

Yasser Arafat was a Palestinian from Gaza, who graduated from Cairo University with a civil engineering degree and became active in the Palestinian nationalist movement, including the founding of al-Fatah. Following Israel's humiliating defeat of Egypt, Syria, and Jordan in the Six-Day War in 1967, Arafat found PLO members receptive to his message of radical guerrilla warfare. He led al-Fatah to dominance within the PLO, and on February 4, 1969, was elected PLO chairman, the third to hold that position, after Ahmad Shukeri and Yahya Hammuda. He would remain in office, serving also as the first president of the Palestinian National Authority, until his death in 2004.

Arafat presided over an era of PLO militancy, but ultimately also of diplomatic and political compromise. Whereas many Palestinian leaders had called for the destruction of Israel as the only solution to the Palestinian Question, Arafat, throughout his early chairmanship, refused to either absolutely reject or accept the idea of coexistence with Israel—the so-called two-state solution. Later, he positively acknowledged Israel's right to exist. Nevertheless, most of the period of his PLO chairmanship was a time of war.

Yasser Arafat

Mohammed Yasser Abdel Rhaman Abdel Raouf Arafat al-Qudwa—Yasser Arafat—was born in 1929 in Gaza, Palestine, one of seven children in the family of a wealthy merchant. He immigrated to Egypt after the state of Israel was created and attended the University of Cairo, where he became involved in the Muslim Brotherhood and the Union of Palestinian Students, serving as president of the latter from 1952 to 1956. Commissioned in the Egyptian army, he served in the Suez Campaign of 1956. While working as an engineer in Kuwait, Arafat cofounded the anti-Israeli guerrilla group al-Fatah, of which he became the principal leader.

After Fatah became the leading military component of the PLO and Arafat was named PLO chairman in 1968, he presided over a campaign of guerrilla action and out-and-out terrorism against Israel.

In 1973, Arafat's focus shifted from military action to political strategy and diplomatic persuasion. By 1974, when he addressed the United Nations General Assembly, Arafat was widely recognized by the nations of the world as the chief spokesman for the Palestinian people.

With Lebanon embroiled in civil war and fearful of rebellion from factions opposed to him, Arafat moved PLO headquarters from Beirut to Tunisia in August 1982, and then to Baghdad, Iraq, in 1987. In November 1988, he boldly persuaded the Palestine National Council to declare Palestinian independence—and simultaneously issued a formal renunciation of terrorism and accepted United Nations General Assembly Resolution 242, affirming Israel's right to exist.

In 1989, Arafat was named president of the Palestinian government-in-exile, and, despite continual opposition from radicals and Syrian-backed factions within the PLO, he carried on an extended dialogue with Israeli leaders in an effort to establish a Palestinian state as well as peaceful relations with Israel.

Yet Arafat could not overcome his reputation as a terrorist, and his peace proposals were greeted with skepticism in Israel. He became increasingly isolated diplomatically, particularly after the 1990–1991 Gulf War. Nevertheless, Arafat retained great influence among a majority of the Palestinians, and in 1993 signed the Oslo Accords, for which he subsequently shared the Nobel Peace Prize with Israeli leaders Shimon Peres and Yitzhak Rabin. In 1994, he became the first president of the Palestinian National Authority.

Arafat fell ill on October 25, 2004, and was flown to a French hospital outside of Paris for treatment. His condition deteriorated, however, and on November 11, 2004, he died. Although the official cause of death was a stroke, some evidence exists of poisoning with radioactive polonium.

"The War of Attrition," 1967–1970

The Six-Day War was followed by chronic low-level combat between Israel and Egypt, the latter backed by Soviet and Jordanian military aid. The PLO also participated, but when PLO artillery shelled settlements and kibbutzim in the Beit She'an Valley of northern Israel and launched guerrilla attacks against IDF forces, Israel responded with raids on PLO camps inside Jordan.

Unable to control PLO military activities and having no desire to see Israeli soldiers within its borders, Jordan expelled the PLO from its territory in 1971 during the Black September civil war. The PLO then moved its operational headquarters to Lebanon.

The Lebanese Conflicts

Conflict between Lebanon's Westward-leaning Christian minority and its Sunni Muslim majority (many of whom were also pan-Arab nationalists) erupted into full-on civil war in the late 1950s, transforming the once prosperous and cosmopolitan country into one of the world's most violent hotspots.

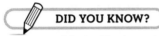

DID YOU KNOW?

> Moshe Sharett, prime minister of Israel during 1954–1955, wrote extensively about Israel's early efforts to foster a breakaway Christian Lebanese state, which would be an ally of Israel in the region. The efforts came to nothing, except to create resentment among many Muslim Lebanese.

On April 13, 1975, four members of Lebanon's Christian Phalange Party were killed during the attempted assassination of Phalange leader Pierre Jumayyil. Assuming that the failed assassins were Palestinian, Phalangist forces retaliated on April 14 by attacking a bus carrying Palestinians through a Christian neighborhood. Twenty-six passengers died and, before the end of the day, fighting was widespread though disorganized throughout Lebanon. Over the next several months, the government proved incapable of responding decisively or effectively to the violence, and a bloody pattern of action and retaliation developed among rival militia groups. The violence grew into outright civil war, not only between Christians and Muslims, but also among various Christian and Muslim factions.

The Palestine Liberation Army (PLA), which had been established at the founding of the PLO in 1964 as the organization's military wing, was never entirely under PLO control. In 1975, the PLA exploited the chaos prevailing in Lebanon to establish a strong political and military presence in the country. Despite attempts from Syria to bring order with a reform program called the Constitutional Document in February 1976, a mutiny swept the Lebanese Army in March, leading to the formation of a Lebanese Arab Army, which penetrated Christian-controlled Beirut, then attacked the presidential palace, forcing President Franjiyah to flee.

After the Lebanese National Movement made further gains, Syrian President Hafez al-Assad authorized an invasion of Lebanon, which forced all sides to meet at a peace conference convened in Riyadh, Saudi Arabia, on October 16, 1976. This brought a formal end to the civil war, only to give rise to warfare between the Syrian occupying and peacekeeping force and the Lebanese Arab Army.

Complicating the situation further was an invasion of southern Lebanon in March 1978 by the Israel Defense Forces (IDF) in retaliation for Fatah's March 11, 1978, Coastal Road Massacre. The United States endorsed a United Nations call for Israeli withdrawal. Despite intervention by a UN force, conditions in Lebanon continued to deteriorate through 1980–1982, and on June 6, 1982, Israel invaded Lebanon for a second time, in retaliation for a PLO-sponsored assassination attempt on the Israeli ambassador to Britain. Israel's objective in this second invasion was to force the removal of PLO forces from the country. In August, an agreement was reached for the evacuation of Syrian troops as well as PLO fighters from Beirut and the subsequent deployment of a three-nation Multinational Force (MNF), tasked with keeping the peace during the period of the evacuation.

 VOICES

> The Israeli invasion of Lebanon ... was designed to destroy once and for all any hope among the people of the West Bank and Gaza that the process of shaping the Palestinian people into a nation could succeed.
>
> —Harold H. Saunders, assistant U.S. secretary of state for Near Eastern and South Asian Affairs, in *Foreign Affairs* 61 (Fall 1982)

By late August, the MNF, consisting of U.S. Marines as well as French and Italian military units, arrived in Beirut. When the evacuation ended, the MNF withdrew, the U.S. Marines departing on September 10, 1982. On September 14, Bachir Gemayel, who had been elected president in August, was assassinated, and on September 15, Israeli troops yet again entered west Beirut. In the meantime, during the next three days, Lebanese militiamen massacred hundreds of Palestinian civilians in the Sabra and Shatila refugee camps in west Beirut.

 DID YOU KNOW?

> On February 21, 1983, *Time* published a story implying that Israeli minister of defense (and future prime minister) Ariel Sharon "discussed with the Gemayels the need for the Phalangists to take revenge" for the assassination of Bachir. Sharon sued *Time* for libel, but lost because of his failure to prove the magazine acted out of malice. Relatives of massacre victims sued Sharon in 2001, but the case was dismissed in 2003 by the Belgian court in which the action had been brought.

Bachir Gemayel's brother, Amine, elected president by a unanimous vote of the parliament, took office September 23, 1982, and MNF forces returned to Beirut at the end of September to support the new government. In February 1983, a small British contingent joined the U.S., French, and Italian MNF troops in Beirut.

President Amine Gemayel called for the withdrawal of Israeli, Syrian, and PLO forces from Lebanon, and in late 1982, Lebanese-Israeli negotiations commenced with U.S. participation. On May 17, 1983, an agreement was concluded, providing for Israeli withdrawal, but Syria declined even to discuss the withdrawal of its troops. While negotiations stalled, a series of terrorist attacks during 1983 and 1984 were aimed at American interests in Lebanon. Most significantly, on April 18, 1983, the U.S. embassy in west Beirut was bombed, with the loss of 63 lives.

In the meantime, during 1982–1983, Druze (a mystic Islamic sect) and Christian forces clashed. When Israeli forces withdrew from the Chouf region southeast of Beirut at the beginning of September 1983, Syrian-backed Druze attacked the Christian Lebanese Forces (LF) militia as well as the Lebanese Army. The United States and Saudi Arabia brokered a cease-fire on September 26, 1983, which left the Druze in control of most of the Chouf.

Less than a month later, on October 23, 1983, two U.S. and French MNF buildings in Beirut were hit by suicide truck bombs, resulting in the loss of 298 lives, the majority of them U.S. Marines in a barracks building. On November 2, U.S. Secretary of Defense Caspar Weinberger announced that the suicide attack had been carried out by Iranians with the "sponsorship, knowledge, and authority of the Syrian government."

U.S. Marines came under attack again on December 4, at Beirut International Airport, fired upon from gun positions in Syrian-held territory. Eight Marines were killed and two wounded. U.S. Navy ships fired on the Syrian positions in retaliation, and 29 U.S. Navy aircraft raided Syrian antiaircraft positions in the mountains east of Beirut. After two aircraft were downed in these attacks, the battleship USS *New Jersey* delivered a massive artillery bombardment against the antiaircraft positions.

On January 13, 1984, Marines patrolling the Beirut International Airport area were engaged in a half-hour battle with gunmen firing from a building east of their perimeter. Two days later, Druze gunners attacked the airport, drawing a response from Marines and from the USS *New Jersey* as well as the destroyer USS *Tattnall*. There were no American casualties.

February saw heavy fighting in the suburbs of Beirut between the Lebanese Arab Army and Shiite militiamen, and on February 6 Druze and Muslim militiamen seized much of Beirut, demanding the resignation of President Gemayel. The next day, U.S. President Ronald Reagan announced his decision to redeploy Marines from Beirut International Airport to ships offshore, leaving behind only a contingent to protect the U.S. embassy and other American interests.

On February 8, the *New Jersey* bombarded Druze and Syrian gun positions, and on February 10 and 11, American civilians and other foreign nationals were evacuated from Beirut by navy helicopters. From February 21 to 26, the Marines withdrew to ships of the Sixth Fleet, which remained offshore. This ended the U.S. military intervention in Lebanon, where fighting continued with considerable intensity through most of 1990 and sporadically in 1991 and 1992, as the government gradually reasserted its control over Lebanese territory.

All of the warring militias, except for Hezbollah, were dissolved in May 1991, and government forces began mopping up PLO elements in Sidon, Lebanon's third-largest city, during July 1991. In May 1992, various Western hostages, held since the mid-1980s by Islamic extremists, were released.

The First Intifada

On December 9, 1987, an Israeli Army truck collided with a car, killing four Palestinians. Instantly, word circulated throughout the Jabalia Palestinian refugee camp that the "accident" had been a deliberate attack. From the camp, the rumors spread throughout Gaza, the West Bank, and East Jerusalem, triggering a wave of Palestinian strikes, boycotts, and demonstrations of civil disobedience, sometimes violent.

Israel responded with an iron fist, rushing in 80,000 troops, who did not hesitate to use live ammunition against civilians. Between the outbreak in December 1987 and the end of the First *Intifada* on September 13, 1993, the IDF killed more than a thousand Palestinians. Palestinians killed some 100 Israeli civilians and 60 IDF personnel; 1,400 Israeli civilians and 1,700 soldiers were wounded. Palestinian-on-Palestinian violence was another ugly product of the First Intifada. It is estimated that 822 Palestinians were targeted for death, justly or not, as collaborators with Israel.

 **DEFINITION**

Although usually translated as "uprising" or "resistance," **intifada** literally means "a shaking off."

Accord?

The First Intifada was brought to a close by the Oslo Accords, signed in the Norwegian capital in 1993. Modeled on the Camp David Accords, concluded between Egyptian President Anwar Sadat and Israeli Prime Minister Menachem Begin on September 17, 1978, and brokered by U.S. President Jimmy Carter, the Oslo Accords were based on UN Security Council Resolutions 242 and 338, aimed at fulfilling the "right of the Palestinian people to self-determination."

The Oslo Accords created the Palestinian Authority—of which Yasser Arafat was voted president—which administered a degree of self-government over a portion of the Occupied Palestinian Territories. The PLO, which was also still under Arafat's chairmanship, agreed to collaborate with Israel in achieving a permanent solution to the Palestinian Question.

The Second Intifada

The Oslo Accords ended the First Intifada, but they did not create a Palestinian state, and the entire "Oslo process" broke down in 2000 during a summit at Camp David. With this, a Second Intifada commenced on September 29, 2000, after Israeli Prime Minister Ariel Sharon visited the Muslim holy site Haram Sharif in Jerusalem. In the intensely symbolic environment of the Holy Land, Palestinians interpreted the visit as a deliberate insult to a sacred Muslim site, home of the Dome of the Rock and revered as the place of Muhammad's ascent to heaven. Demonstrations began, violence developed, and when the IDF used live ammunition on the demonstrators, the violence escalated.

In the course of the Second Intifada, which did not end until January 1, 2005, PLO personnel and other Palestinians used guns and homemade bombs, while the IDF responded with tank deployments, gunfire, and air attacks, as well as assassinations targeting specific Palestinian leaders. At least 3,000 Palestinians died, along with 1,000 Israelis and 64 foreigners.

On February 8, 2005, Mahmoud Abbas, who, on May 8, 2005, had succeeded Yasser Arafat as president of what was now called the State of Palestine, met with Israeli Prime Minister Ariel Sharon at Sharm el-Sheikh and agreed not only to a cease-fire, but to pursue the "roadmap for peace" outlined as part of the Oslo process.

The Unanswered Question: Palestine Today

The PLO unilaterally declared Palestinian independence on November 15, 1988, and was granted United Nations General Assembly observer-state status on November 29, 2012. On January 3, 2013, the UN officially redesignated the Palestinian Authority as the State of Palestine. However, Israel has not yet recognized Palestine's statehood.

In 2004, Israel promulgated its Disengagement Plan Implementation Law, which mandated the withdrawal of the Israeli army from Gaza as well as the removal of all Israeli settlements in the Gaza Strip. In addition, the law called for the evacuation of four modest settlements in the West Bank. Today, all of the Israeli settlers and almost all of the Israeli military presence are gone from the Gaza Strip, but Israel continues to control Palestinian air space and the Gaza coast.

The greatest concentration of Palestinian Arabs—2.1 million—now occupy the West Bank, which has a land area of just 2,178 square miles. In addition, about a half-million Jewish Israelis live here as well, in settlements that most of the international community considers illegal.

In 2004, Israel began construction of a massive West Bank barrier, intended to separate the West Bank—80 percent Arab Palestinian—from Israel and to prevent the territory from being used to mount terrorist attacks against the country. At present, 134 of 193 UN member states recognize the State of Palestine and deem the West Bank a territory of that state. In the meantime, as of spring 2014, construction of the barrier proceeds.

The Least You Need to Know

- Although complex and torturous, the conflict between Jews and Palestinian Arabs, the so-called Palestinian Question, may be expressed with stark simplicity: who controls the land?

- The Palestine Liberation Organization (PLO) was formed to lead the struggle of a stateless people toward the establishment of a Palestinian state.

- Under the leadership of Yasser Arafat, the PLO increased its commitment to militancy and terrorism, and then, after achieving UN recognition as the State of Palestine, turned increasingly toward finding a political solution to peaceful coexistence with Israel—despite skepticism, suspicion, and the looming specter of continued violence.

- As subsumed within the Palestinian Authority led by Mahmoud Abbas, the PLO has increasingly come under criticism for complacency toward Israel as Israelis build extensively in the West Bank and continue a military campaign against Gaza.

The Six-Day War, 1967

History is filled with individual battles and single campaigns longer than the war between Israel and the Arab states of Egypt, Syria, Jordan, and Iraq, which began on June 5, 1967, and ended with a cease-fire just 6 days later, on June 10.

Brief as the Six-Day War was, very few armed encounters have been more decisive—except that, in the Middle East, words like "decisive" are never simple. Israel's victory was absolute and huge. In military terms, it was certainly decisive. As far as its consequences for determining the outcome of the Middle East conflict, however, it was ultimately no more decisive than any other twentieth-century armed exchange in the region.

In This Chapter

- Background of the war
- Comparison of forces and initial mobilization
- Israel's Sinai victory
- The struggle for Jerusalem and the West Bank
- Taking the Golan Heights
- A total victory without permanent effect

In Brief

It is possible to describe this remarkably compact war with unremarkable brevity. Following the 1956 Suez Crisis, the UN attempted to stabilize the region by sending the United Nations Emergency Force (UNEF) to occupy the Sinai—the desolate desert peninsula from which Egypt frequently mounted military actions against Israel. In 1956, Israeli forces had taken control of the Sinai, but pursuant to a UN order, handed it over to the UNEF. Eleven years later, in 1967, Egyptian President and Prime Minister Gamal Abdel Nasser demanded the withdrawal of UNEF from Sinai, and the United Nations complied.

With UNEF gone, it did not take long for Nasser to act. He sought to strangle Israel by imposing a shipping blockade of the Straits of Tiran, the narrow seaway between the Sinai and Arabian peninsulas, separating the Gulf of Aqaba from the Red Sea. In addition to the blockade, Nasser effectively closed the major Israeli port of Eilat on the Aqaba gulf.

Having, as he saw it, wrapped his fingers around Israel's neck, Nasser ordered Egyptian forces and those of his ally Syria to mobilize along the border created by the UN-mediated armistice of 1949. Israel responded to this mobilization in kind.

The scenario appeared sickeningly familiar: two armed camps were braced for a spasm of guerrilla-style attacks in the border regions. To many, however, the situation appeared worse than ever for Israel, now menaced from three sides. With coordinated action, Egypt, Syria, Jordan, and Iraq could dismember Israel with multiple thrusts aimed toward the sea.

This time, however, Israel neither hunkered down nor contented itself with guerrilla assaults and small-unit operations. It mounted no defense, but instead immediately went on the offensive. On June 5, at the urging of Israeli Chief of Staff Itzhak Rabin, the Israeli Air Force launched a massive, preemptive aerial campaign that targeted some two dozen enemy airfields, destroying in short order more than 400 Egyptian, Syrian, Jordanian, and Iraqi aircraft—on the ground. This was the bulk of the Arab air power. The most powerful militaries of the Arab world had massed against Israel. Now they stood stunned by the instant ruin of their air assets.

It only got worse. Under the direction of Defense Minister Moshe Dayan, a one-eyed veteran of Suez, IDF ground forces swept over the Sinai Peninsula and seized Jerusalem's Old City, Jordan's West Bank, the Gaza Strip, and the Golan Heights, occupying all of these areas by the time a UN-sponsored cease-fire was declared on June 10, 1967.

Moshe Dayan

Moshe Dayan was born in 1915 in the first kibbutz Zionists established in Palestine. As a teenager, he joined the Haganah and served in the force patrolling the kibbutz perimeter.

Dayan first saw significant action during the Arab revolt of 1936–1939, serving with Yizhak Sadeh's guerrilla units. The Jewish settlers sporadically cooperated with the British during the revolt, and Dayan trained under the British General Orde Wingate, who specialized in guerrilla and small-unit tactics. Dayan's continued activity in the Israeli independence movement, however, provoked his arrest at the outbreak of World War II. He was imprisoned at Acre in October 1939 and not released until February 16, 1941. The exigencies of war in the Middle East again brought cooperation between the Haganah and the British, and Dayan became a scout, working in advance of the British invasion of Vichy French-held Syria and Lebanon during June 1941. In combat on June 8, Dayan lost his left eye and from that point on wore the black eye patch that became his trademark.

Dayan served on the Haganah general staff prior to the United Nations partition of Palestine in November 1947. In the Israeli War of Independence that followed, he fought against the Syrians in Galilee, successfully defending the Deganya settlements during May 19–21, 1948. Drawing on his Haganah training, as well as his experience with Wingate, he raised the 89th Commando Battalion, a highly mobile mechanized strike force, which participated in a series of lightning raids against Arab-held positions at Lod and Ramallah between July 9 and July 19, 1948. Following these successes, he was put in charge of the Jerusalem sector (1948–1949) and was instrumental in early settlement negotiations with King Abdullah of Jordan in 1949.

After Israeli independence was won, Dayan went to England in 1953 to study at the Camberley Staff College, returning to Israel later that year as chief of staff of the IDF. When the Suez Crisis erupted in 1956, Dayan planned and directed the Israeli campaign (October 29–November 5). Two years after the successful conclusion of the war, he resigned his commission to enter politics, gaining election to the Knesset on the Labor ticket in 1959 and serving as minister of agriculture from December 1959 to November 1964. In 1964, he broke with his party to join David Ben-Gurion in founding the Rafi (Labor List) Party and once again won election to the Knesset.

In June 1967, Dayan was appointed defense minister under Prime Minister Levi Eshkol. As defense minister, he directed operations during the Six-Day War.

Dayan stepped down from the Defense Ministry after Yitzhak Rabin succeeded Golda Meir as prime minister in May 1974, but returned to government in 1977, serving as foreign minister in the government of Menachem Begin through 1979. He was instrumental in creating the Camp David peace settlement U.S. President Jimmy Carter mediated between Israel and Egypt. However, growing differences with Begin over policy toward the Palestinian Arabs prompted Dayan's resignation as foreign minister in 1979, two years prior to his death, on October 16, 1981.

Order of Battle

Back in 1964, when Nasser presided over the first summit of the Arab League and the founding of the PLO, he counseled his Arab brethren to be patient when it came to military action against Israel. He warned that the Arab states were not yet ready for full-scale war.

By the late spring of 1967, Nasser led the Arab world into closer alliance and imminent confrontation with Israel. In the three years since 1964, Egypt and its allies, aided by the Soviet Union, had built formidable military forces.

 VOICES

> The rising tide of Soviet penetration, and the trends in Arab politics which that penetration encouraged and fortified, threatened major American and allied interests in the region … and … a continuation of the process, which could involve the Nasserization of Jordan, … Lebanon, Libya, Tunisia, Morocco, Saudi Arabia, and the Persian Gulf, would present … a security crisis of major, and potentially catastrophic proportions.
>
> —U.S. Department of State policy study, 1967

Egyptian Arms

Egypt, largest of the Arab states, had the biggest and most powerful armed forces, totaling 240,000 men, under the command of Field Marshal Abdel Hakim Amer. The army was amply equipped with tanks and artillery, mostly Soviet, and the air force, under the command of General Mahmoud Sidky, had an impressive 450 aircraft, of which 431 were operational—all of Soviet manufacture.

The Egyptian naval fleet was made up of about 100 ships, including 8 destroyers, 18 Soviet-built missile boats (armed with STYX surface-to-surface missiles), and a dozen submarines.

Jordanian Armed Forces

The Jordanian armed forces consisted of 58,000 men, all but 3,000 in the army. Its air force operated 22 British-made, 1950s-vintage subsonic Hawker Hunter *ground-attack* fighters, deployed in two squadrons. The problem was that King Hussein had just 16 pilots capable of flying the Hawkers.

 DEFINITION

Ground-attack aircraft are military aircraft specially designed for attacking ground (and sea) targets with greater precision than bomber aircraft. The best ground-attack aircraft are built to withstand low-level antiaircraft defenses. The Israeli air force made especially extensive use of such aircraft.

Syrian Military Forces

Syria was the third major Arab combatant and had 75,000 men under arms, 65,000 of whom were in the army. Syria's air force, 9,000 strong, had 127 aircraft, mostly MiG fighters.

 DID YOU KNOW?

> In 1967, the MiG-21 was the most advanced fighter aircraft used in the Middle East. Introduced in 1959, the MiG-21 was capable of a top speed of Mach 1.77 (1351+ mph, nearly 1.8 times the speed of sound). It was armed with a 23-mm cannon in addition to air-to-air missiles.

Iraq's Army

Although Iraq had a large army of 75,000 men and 630 tanks, it sent just one division to Jordan during the war, along with 106 of its air force's 220 fighter aircraft.

IDF

Against a combined deployed Arab strength of approximately 409,000 men, the Israel Defense Forces (IDF) had 264,000 regulars and first-line reservists available. Unique to the IDF army units was a 50/50 *tooth-to-tail ratio,* in which combat (tooth) personnel were evenly divided with support (tail) personnel. In most armies of the era, including the U.S., British, and Arab forces, the tooth-to-tail ratio was 20/80. The relative *combat* strength of Israeli versus Arab forces was therefore less unequal than the raw numbers suggest.

 **DEFINITION**

> The **tooth-to-tail ratio** in a military formation is the percentage of combat forces (forces intended to be in direct front-line contact with the enemy) versus the percentage of support forces (logistical, administrative, and other support troops in the rear echelons).

Israeli combat brigades were also highly flexible. They could be grouped into divisional-size task forces, called *ugdahs,* which increased efficiency of command as well as speed and flexibility of battlefield deployment.

The Israeli army was equipped with advanced weaponry from modern Western sources. Of the 450 aircraft in the Israeli air force, 286 were first-line combat-operational warplanes. Israel also had a modest navy, consisting of 3,000 sailors manning 24 vessels: 4 destroyers, 2 submarines, 3 landing craft, 12 torpedo boats, and 3 patrol boats.

The Air War

The greatest challenge to the Israeli air force was the presence of MiG-21s in the Egyptian, Syrian, and Iraqi arsenals. Only Israel's French-built Mirages and the Super Mystères could come close to matching these in air-to-air combat. Israeli air force commanders persuaded military Chief of Staff Yitzhak Rabin to authorize a go-for-broke preemptive air strike to destroy as many enemy aircraft as possible on the ground. Rabin reasoned that this approach would not only cancel out an Arab technological advantage, it would achieve an Israeli air superiority that would very likely ensure victory in the war.

Yitzhak Rabin

Born in Jerusalem in 1922 to Ukrainian emigrants, Yitzhak Rabin studied at the Kadoorie Agricultural College, from which he graduated with distinction. In 1940, he joined the Palmach, the elite unit of the Haganah fighting for the creation of an independent Israeli state. In the 1948–1949 War of Independence, Rabin commanded the Harel Brigade, which was deployed on the Jerusalem front, and for the first 20 years of Israel's existence as a nation he served in the high command of the Israel Defense Forces (IDF). As chief of staff (1964–1968), Rabin was in overall command of the IDF during the Six-Day War.

Rabin retired from the military on January 1, 1968, and was soon appointed ambassador to the United States, enhancing a period of especially close relations between the two countries. He returned to Israel in the spring of 1973, became active in the Labor Party, and was elected to the Knesset (the Israeli parliament) in December 1973. In April 1974, Prime Minister Golda Meir appointed him to her cabinet as minister of labor. After she stepped down in May, Rabin succeeded her as prime minister.

As prime minister, Rabin built up the IDF even as he welcomed U.S. mediation to conclude "disengagement" agreements with Egypt and Syria in 1974 and a more extensive interim peace agreement with Egypt in 1975. Later in the year, Rabin signed the first "Memorandum of Understanding" between the governments of Israel and the United States, which simultaneously strengthened the alliance between the two nations and pledged Israel to a course of constructive reconciliation with its Arab neighbors.

In June 1976, Palestinian terrorists hijacked an Air France airliner, holding 103 Jews hostage at Entebbe, in Idi Amin's Uganda. Rabin authorized a daring Israeli commando raid, which, against formidable odds, succeeded in liberating the hostages.

When the Labor Party lost ground in 1977, Rabin resigned as prime minister and was succeeded as party leader by Shimon Peres. In 1984, Rabin reentered the government as defense minister in a coalition government of the Labor and Likud parties. Late in the 1980s, he ordered a harsh crackdown against the First Intifada in the West Bank. Although controversial, the crackdown was effective, at least in the short term, and Rabin ousted Peres as Labor Party leader in 1992. He then led his party to victory in the national elections, becoming prime minister while continuing also to serve as defense minister.

With his credentials as a tough military leader long and well established, Rabin astounded the world by playing an active role in peace negotiations between Israel and its Arab neighbors. This culminated in 1993 with his endorsement of what many had believed unthinkable: a historic peace agreement with the Palestine Liberation Organization (PLO), which provided for mutual recognition and a transition to Palestinian self-rule in the Gaza Strip and West Bank. For this extraordinary achievement, Rabin shared with Peres and PLO leader Yasir Arafat the Nobel Peace Prize in 1994. That same year, he signed a peace treaty with Jordan, and the next year he expanded the PLO agreement to further enhance Palestinian self-rule.

In all of this, Rabin was well aware that he was taking grave political and indeed personal risks. Rabin was assassinated on November 4, 1995, by an Israeli law student with ties to Israeli right-wing extremist groups.

Air force General Mordecai Hod committed 183 combat aircraft in the first wave of the attack, followed by 164 in the second. This left behind a mere dozen combat-capable planes to defend Israel. The first attacking squadron took off at 7:45 on Monday morning, June 5, flying low enough to get beneath Egyptian defensive radar. Twenty-two Arab air bases were targeted for bombing. In the space of three hours, most of the enemy air fleets were blown up before they could take to the air. Refusing to let up, Israel launched a series of follow-up strikes the next day in an effort to make the destruction total.

In the raids of June 5–6, Egypt lost 309 of its 450 aircraft, including most of its dreaded MiG-21s. Syria lost 60 of the 127 aircraft in its air force. The toll on Jordan was 29 aircraft, and Iraq lost 17. Lebanon, which managed to get two British-made Hawker Hunters aloft for a raid over the Sea of Galilee (it would be Lebanon's only contribution to the war effort), lost one plane.

In total, 416 Arab aircraft were destroyed on days one and two of the war, 393 of them on the ground. In subsequent days there were some aerial dogfights between Israeli aircraft and the few fighters remaining to the Arabs, but the Arab performance in the air was unimpressive. Sixty-one Egyptian and sixteen Syrian or Jordanian aircraft were shot down before the armistice; 58 of these Arab craft were lost in dogfights. Israel's air losses for the entire war were 46 aircraft destroyed, of which just 10 were shot down in air-to-air dogfights and 16 by ground-based antiaircraft fire. Twenty-six Israeli pilots were killed, and 13 were captured.

The Israeli air campaign of the 1967 war is considered the single most successful combat air operation in history.

The War in the Sinai

The jet strikes were followed by an Israeli armored assault across the Sinai. The peninsula, some 25,000 square miles of desolate scrublands, was ideal ground for fast-moving modern tanks. Deployed throughout the Sinai and the Gaza Strip, adjacent to the east, were some 100,000 Egyptian soldiers, in seven divisions, with 930 tanks, all under the command of General Abdel Mohsen Mortagui.

Egypt's 20th Palestine Division was in the Gaza Strip, while the the 7th, 2nd, and 6th Infantry Divisions were arrayed along the Sinai frontier with Israel, running north to south. The 3rd Infantry and 4th Armored Divisions, along with the Shazli Force (4 tank battalions, 1 motorized infantry brigade, 1 commando battalion, and 3 artillery regiments) were positioned farther back in the desert.

The Israeli invasion force, under Brigadier General Yeshayah Gavish, was 70,000 strong and included 750 tanks. It struck hard and fast, entering from the Negev in three *ugdahs*. One ugdah, commanded by General Israel Tal and consisting of one airborne (paratroop) and two tank brigades (armed with 300 tanks, 100 half-tracks, and 50 field-artillery pieces), attacked the Gaza Strip and along the coast. Another ugdah, under Brigadier General Avraham Yoffe (1 mechanized and 2 tank brigades—200 tanks and 100 half-tracks) attacked the central Sinai, while the third ugdah, commanded by future Israeli Prime Minister Brigadier General Ariel Sharon, invaded the southern Sinai.

All three prongs of the Israeli ground offensive were closely supported by air power. They plowed through Egyptian armor and infantry, surging to the Suez Canal and to Sharm el-Sheikh at the southern tip of the Sinai Peninsula, which they reached on Thursday, June 8.

Egyptian forces suffered catastrophic failures of command. When one armored column was ambushed at the Mitla Pass, the chaos and panic made any attempt at effective defense impossible. Hit by aircraft and ground forces, the column was quickly transformed into a junkyard and a graveyard. Similarly, in Rafah, the entire Egyptian 7th Infantry Division was overrun, suffering 2,000 casualties, four times that among the Israeli infantry.

 DID YOU KNOW?

> A recent study of the Egyptian military during the Six-Day War reveals that field commanders were so fearful of reporting accurate estimates of unit capability that they routinely covered up widespread equipment failures and failures in training. The result was that the Egyptian leadership went into war with a catastrophically inflated self-image.

The defeat of Egypt in the Sinai was both swift and total. Seven hundred Egyptian tanks were lost, including 100 abandoned intact. A staggering 500 pieces of field artillery were destroyed or captured, along with no fewer than 10,000 trucks. At least 3,000 Egyptian soldiers were killed, 5,000 wounded, and 4,990 taken prisoner. Israeli casualties in the Sinai Campaign were 303 killed in action, 1,450 wounded, and 11 missing or made prisoner. One hundred twenty-two Israeli tanks were lost.

Jerusalem and West Bank Combat Operations

While Egypt, on paper the most formidable military power in the region, collapsed in the Sinai and Gaza Strip, the Jordanian Arab Legion (including a unit of Bedouin Arabs) proved a much tougher adversary on the central front, which encompassed the Jordanian-held West Bank and East Jerusalem.

Unlike the Egyptian forces in the Sinai, the Jordanians (under Egyptian General Abdul Munim Riad) assumed the offensive with a massive artillery barrage against Israeli-held West Jerusalem. This was subsequently expanded into an artillery bombardment against Tel Aviv, a mere 15 miles from the West Bank.

Fighting erupted all along the West Bank, reaching its fiercest intensity in Jerusalem itself. On Wednesday, June 7, following prolonged combat in which the Israeli paratroop brigade was most fully engaged at the appropriately named Ammunition Hill, the IDF achieved a breakthrough, and armored, infantry, and airborne brigades, all under the command of Brigadier General Uzi Narkis, prevailed against the defenders of East Jerusalem—the 5,000 men of Jordan's 27th Infantry Brigade, led by Brigadier General Ata Ali.

Following the victory, Moshe Dayan prayed at the Old City's Wailing Wall. The victory had cost the lives of 181 IDF soldiers and 14 Jewish civilian residents of Jerusalem. Jordanian losses were much heavier: 396 military personnel and 249 civilians were killed. The fall of Jerusalem precipitated the collapse of the rest of Jordanian Palestine. Armor belonging to the ugdah commanded by General Elad Peled overran the territory after sunset on Wednesday.

Along with Jerusalem, Latrun, a hilltop in the Ayalon Valley overlooking the main road to Jerusalem, was also taken on Wednesday evening. During the 1948 war, Israeli forces had repeatedly assaulted Latrun and had been repeatedly driven back with heavy losses. Now it fell, and on the following morning, Thursday, June 8, Ramallah, Nablus, Bethlehem, and Jericho also fell to the IDF, one after the other.

At this point, Jordan's King Hussein announced that his vaunted Arab Legion—certainly, the most effective fighting forces the Arabs fielded in the Six-Day War—had been defeated. Total losses for Jordan were 696 killed, 421 wounded, and 2,000 missing (of whom only 530 were later accounted for as POWs). Also lost were 179 Jordanian tanks. Israel incurred 553 killed and 2,442 wounded in action against Jordan. Tank losses were also heavy at 112 destroyed.

 DID YOU KNOW?

Jordan fielded a far smaller force than Egypt, but inflicted much heavier casualties on the Israelis: twice those suffered in the victory over Egypt. In the Sinai, Egyptian casualties were six times those of Israel—a catastrophic defeat.

Endgame: Golan Heights

When Friday, June 9, dawned, only one of the Arab armies originally arrayed against Israel remained in the field: the thirteen brigades of General Ahmed Soueidany's Syrian army.

During the first four days of the war, Soueidany had kept his forces dug in on the Golan Heights, at the point where the northeast border of Israel meets Lebanon to the west and Syria to the east. Throughout those days, he had directed artillery fire against Israeli kibbutzim in Galilee. With both Egypt and Jordan now out of the war, Israel turned to the Golan Heights.

The Syrians had stout fortifications, behind which were 40,000 troops. Israeli Brigadier General David Elazar attacked with just 20,000 troops and 250 tanks. By late in the day on Saturday, he had managed to completely destroy the Syrian defenses. When the principal town of the Golan Heights, El Quneitra, fell to the Israelis, Soueidany asked for a cease-fire.

Soueidany had 600 dead soldiers, 700 wounded, and 570 missing or taken prisoner. Eighty-six of his tanks were wrecked—although Israel had also suffered a severe loss of armor, with 160 tanks destroyed, mostly by detonated mines and fire from antitank guns. In personnel, Israel lost 127 killed, 625 wounded, and 4 missing.

DID YOU KNOW?

There was a naval dimension to the Six-Day War, but it was strangely uneventful. In fact, the only notable—and tragic—incident was the result of friendly fire. The USS *Liberty* was a World War II-vintage "Victory Ship," originally built as a transport and modified as a "technical research ship" (in reality, an "electronic intelligence platform," or spy ship). Israeli sea patrols mistook *Liberty* for an Egyptian vessel, and on June 8, Mirage fighters were dispatched to strafe and torpedo it. Thirty-four U.S. sailors were killed, and 70 wounded (out of a crew of 358). It was the worst casualties suffered by a U.S. Navy vessel since World War II. Damaged beyond repair, USS *Liberty* was decommissioned in 1968.

Outcome

By any military measure, Israel had triumphed in the Six-Day War. Military historians count it among the fastest and most complete victories ever recorded. Total Arab casualties (killed, wounded, captured, and missing) were 17,967. In addition, 965 tanks were destroyed, as were nearly 500 aircraft. Israeli casualties were 5,515, in addition to the loss of 394 tanks and 46 aircraft.

Israel's conduct of a three-front offensive showed the world the combat effectiveness of this tiny nation, even when faced with numerically superior enemies. In the near term, Israel made its precarious borders more secure and conquered 27,000 square miles of Arab territory.

In the near term, too, the ignominious defeat of Egypt prompted Gamal Abdel Nasser to appear on Egyptian television to announce his resignation. More significant than the tender of resignation, however, was the refusal of the mass of Egyptians to accept it. They took to the streets to demand that

Nasser withdraw his resignation—and he did. Moreover, although Jordan suffered severe economic setbacks as a result of the war, and although Palestinians were seemingly confirmed in their status as stateless refugees, subject to martial law on the West Bank, the Middle East stage was once again set for decades of renewed violence.

Without question, Israel had gained much—especially in the eyes of the world. Yet the six-day victory led the Israelis to underestimate the military capability of the Arabs. The failure in the Sinai was in part due to Nasser's strategic blunder in deploying troops in positions of passive defense and in the orders a panic-stricken Egyptian field marshal, Ali Amer, had issued on June 6 for a general withdrawal. To be sure, the Egyptian forces in Sinai were almost certainly doomed to defeat, but the disorderly withdrawal cost them the chance to retreat intact, turning what might have been a tactical retreat into a complete rout. The Israelis should have known that the Egyptians would not likely repeat these errors in future encounters. As a result, Israel very nearly lost the Yom Kippur War of 1973.

 VOICES

Israel has swallowed a serpent.

—Palestinian saying about Israel's conquest of the West Bank and Gaza Strip in the Six-Day War

Finally, in defeat, the Arab nations involved in the war were bonded more powerfully than they might have been even in victory. Lands, natural resources like the water-rich Golan, and loved ones had been lost. The several hundred thousand new refugees created by the Six-Day War added to Israel's security challenges. And the motives of recovery and revenge created common cause within the Arab world.

The Least You Need to Know

* After securing the withdrawal of UN forces from the Sinai Peninsula in 1967, Egypt's Gamal Abdel Nasser prepared to invade Israel, in concert with Syria, Jordan, and Iraq.

* Collectively, the Arab forces outnumbered and outgunned the Israel Defense Forces (IDF); however, Israeli commanders were more highly skilled and its military formations were both better trained and better organized.

* Israel's victory was virtually assured by the relentless preemptive air attacks in just the first two days of the war, which, for all practical purposes, neutralized the Arab air arm.

* Israel's victory against the Egyptians in Sinai was total and swift. In contrast, the contest with Jordan's Arab Legion for Jerusalem and the West Bank was hard-fought and harder won.

* The Six-Day War was a decisive Israeli victory, yet its long-term outcome was anything but decisive, in that it led only to renewed warfare, including the Yom Kippur War (1973), in which Israel came perilously close to defeat.

The Yom Kippur War, 1973

If proof were needed that there was no "quick fix" for the Arab-Israeli conflict, the Six-Day War (Chapter 12) supplied it. Few wars in history were quicker. Few victories were more complete. And yet the core issue—who owns the land?—remained unresolved. Israel had won possession of the Sinai, the West Bank, the Gaza Strip, and the Golan Heights, but Egypt wanted the Sinai returned, the Palestinians wanted autonomy over the West Bank and the Gaza Strip, and Syria wanted possession of the Golan Heights.

Anwar Sadat, who had become Egypt's third president on the death of Gamal Abdel Nasser in 1970, extended an olive branch to Israel in exchange for the return of all of the occupied territories. The 1967 war had been a triumph, but it had come at a cost to Israel of some 5,500 casualties. The government refused to withdraw to the pre-1967 armistice lines, which were less militarily defendable and occupied fewer water resources.

Sadat's peace feelers put him in a spot. If he simply backed down, he would lose credibility with the Egyptian people and the leaders of the rest of the Arab world. Egypt had lost honor in the 1967 war. Backing away now would (Sadat believed) sacrifice that honor beyond redemption. He therefore decided that starting a war—albeit with defined and limited objectives—was the only solution.

In This Chapter

- Causes of the war
- The new Arab alliance
- The Cold War context
- Action of the Syrian front—the Golan Heights
- Action on the Egyptian front—the Sinai
- The road to Camp David and the hope of a lasting peace

Falling into War

Sadat had a specific strategic reason for going to war. He wanted to force a return to the pre-1967 borders with Israel. Unspoken was the emotional motive shared by Egypt's allies in the 1967 war: a burning need to undo the shame of an ignominious defeat and legitimize their rule despite major foreign policy failures.

DID YOU KNOW?

> Some new scholarly studies allege that the wars of 1967 and 1973 were first and foremost about water resources. The 1967 conflict, they conclude, was sparked by planned dams upstream of Israel; the Yom Kippur War was provoked by Israel's extension of the hydrological resources of Tel Aviv, giving it what it has today: control over the water supply for the occupied Palestinian territories.

As for the Israeli leaders, they too allowed themselves to be ruled by emotion. It was a sentiment the authors of ancient Greek tragedy knew well: *hubris*—overweening confidence that can induce fatal complacence.

The Israeli general staff, usually the source of calls for constant vigilance and preparedness, assured the government that the nation was safe from Arab attack, and by the early 1970s, Israel was, for the first time since independence, ill prepared for an attack. The country's highly developed intelligence service, Mossad, which had kept it on the alert since 1948, now seemed blissfully unaware after 1967. Israeli commanders saw the buildup of Arab forces along the Suez Canal, but they chose to interpret it as nothing more than a military exercise.

Day of Atonement

Yom Kippur, the holiest day in the Jewish calendar, is called the Day of Atonement. For some 25 hours, observant Jews fast and pray, typically spending much of the day in the synagogue. It is the day on which God seals the verdicts that determine each person's fate for the year to come.

On the afternoon of Yom Kippur, Saturday, October 6, 1973, Syrian and Egyptian forces simultaneously attacked on the Golan Heights and on the *Bar Lev Line* along the Suez Canal, 300 miles to the southwest of Golan.

DEFINITION

> The **Bar Lev Line** was a chain of fortified positions Israel erected along the eastern side of the Suez Canal after capturing the Sinai during the Six-Day War. The elaborate fortification system ran for 100 miles.

The attack came as a stunning surprise—partly because of Israeli complacency, but also because it differed sharply from prior Arab tactics. It was the first time since the 1948 war that Arab states had seized the initiative with a major, coordinated offensive strike.

Most important were the highly realistic objectives of the offensive. In contrast to the implausible goal of both the 1948 and 1967 wars—the total destruction of Israel—the Yom Kippur offensive was aimed primarily at forcing Israel to negotiate the return of its 1967 conquests and thereby redeem Arab honor. Sadat and Syrian President Hafez al-Assad had reason to believe that these limited objectives would win some support from the rest of the world and might even induce the United States to coax Israel to the bargaining table.

Hafez al-Assad

Hafez al-Assad became president of Syria in 1971 and served until his death in 2000, when he was succeeded by his son Bashar al-Assad. That succession reflects the true nature of Assad's presidency, an absolute dictatorship, which he envisioned as the beginning of a dynasty.

Born in 1928 in Qardaha, Syria, to a poor peasant family named Wahsh ("wild beast"), the young man grew up determined to remake himself as a leader. Before enrolling in the Homs Military Academy, he changed his name to Assad ("lion") and graduated in 1955 as an air force pilot. Three years later, he was sent to Syria's longtime ally, the Soviet Union, to study night warfare techniques and was promoted to squadron leader in the Syrian air force, only to be summarily dismissed from the service in 1961 after he opposed Syria's secession from Egyptian President Gamal Abdel Nasser's United Arab Republic.

After his dismissal from the air force, Assad became a leader in the Ba'ath Party, which advocated pan-Arab unity under the banner of socialism. The Ba'ath Party assumed power in Syria in 1963, and on March 8, 1965, Assad was not only reinstated in the air force, but appointed its chief, becoming minister of defense the following February. He also led troops to crush the Black September uprising in northwest Jordan.

In 1969 and 1970, the civilian and military wings of the Ba'ath Party divided, and Assad, a member of the military wing, assumed control of the government in 1970, winning election as president the following year. He allied Syria with Egypt in the Yom Kippur War in October 1973, and though Syria was defeated, Assad nevertheless emerged as a national hero and as a hero in the Arab world. In 1976, claiming Lebanon as part of "Greater Syria," he sent a large occupation force into that strife-torn nation. As part of his effort to create a union or alliance among Syria, Jordan, Lebanon, and the Palestine Liberation Organization (PLO), Assad both openly and covertly financed a variety of terrorist organizations, including the PLO.

In 1979, Assad sought an alliance with Iraq, only to reassert his nation's traditional animosity towards Iraq in 1983, when he closed his border with that country. Far more dramatically, he joined the United States and other nations in a coalition opposing Iraq during the Gulf War of 1991. Indeed, the Gulf War came at a most propitious time for Assad, who had long aligned his nation with the Soviet Union. With the collapse of the USSR in 1991, he desperately needed to find some form of rapprochement with the United States. Joining the anti-Saddam coalition was the opportunity he needed.

Assad showed remarkable political agility during his long presidency, but his regime came under severe attack from dissidents, particularly the Muslim Brotherhood. His response to those he considered rebels was always harsh. In 1982, he virtually destroyed the city of Hamah, stronghold Sunni majority city, and, over the years, he killed some 20,000 dissidents. In addition to employing outright military measures to suppress opposition, Assad made extensive use of surveillance, detention, torture, and execution. Like many other Arab leaders, he deliberately fostered a personality cult, and his image was displayed prominently throughout Syria.

Beginning in 2011, his son and successor found himself challenged by a mass opposition movement, driven in part by the Muslim Brotherhood and the spirit of the "Arab Spring." As of this writing (spring 2014), Syria is locked in a horrific civil war marked by the Assad regime's brutal treatment of Syrian citizens.

Order of Battle

Although Egypt and Syria were the principal Arab combatants in the Yom Kippur War, combat support also came from Jordan and Iraq as well as Algeria, Morocco, and Tunisia, in addition to one nation far from the Middle East, Cuba. Numerically, the Arab armies were greatly superior to those of Israel. Including the 74,000 men Jordan potentially made available, Arab forces stood at 539,000, compared with the 300,000+ men and women of the Israel Defense Forces (IDF). Combined Arab air power consisted of 976 aircraft, mostly of Soviet manufacture, including the formidable MiG-21, capable of speeds close to Mach 2 (twice the speed of sound) albeit with a limited 350-mile range.

Israel's fully mobilized military strength was more than 300,000 men and women. The highly developed Israeli air force, the key to victory in 1967, was staffed by 10,000 regulars and an equal number of first-line reservists. Its cadre of 1,200 combat pilots was arguably the best in the world. Moreover, the IDF air force could field 2.4 pilots per combat aircraft, giving it a significant edge over the more limited Arab pilot pool. Israeli aircraft totaled 517, mostly U.S. and French made.

The men and women of the IDF army—275,000 in all—were anchored by a professional cadre of 75,000 regulars, who were some of the world's ablest and most experienced soldiers and officers.

Golan Heights Operations

Leading off with an hour-long, 300-gun artillery bombardment, the Syrians attacked along four axes across a 44-mile front early on the afternoon of October 6. The first wave consisted of three Syrian infantry divisions, with about 16,000 men in each division. Also in the first wave was a Moroccan brigade of 1,800 men.

Behind the initial wave were two armored divisions, with some 10,000 men each. The Syrians deployed nearly 1,500 tanks in the assault on the Golan Heights.

In all, Syria's General Youssef Chakour attacked with a force of 60,000 men. In addition to the tanks, Chakour had some 600 artillery pieces, 400 antiaircraft guns, and 100 batteries of SAM-2, SAM-3, and SAM-6 missiles—a total of nearly 500 launchers.

The Syrian objective was the so-called Purple Line, an Israeli defense-in-depth extending 12.5 miles before Israel's Golan Heights positions. The Purple Line included a minefield backed by an antitank ditch 18 feet wide and 9 feet deep. Behind these two defenses was a chain of 17 fortified positions, which included 112 pillboxes and blockhouses. Each of these posts was manned by 10 to 30 Israeli soldiers.

DID YOU KNOW?

> Although much of the effectiveness of the initial Egyptian/Syrian assault may be attributed to uncharacteristic Israeli complacency, the military leaders of both Arab nations must be given credit for having prepared their offensive with highly effective secrecy and for executing the opening moves with much professionalism and courage, both far above the levels demonstrated in the 1967 war. The Arabs had learned well from their earlier mistakes.

Hitting the Purple Line

Along the Purple Line were 12,000 Israeli troops under Brigadier General Rafael Eitan. They were equipped with 177 tanks and 44 field guns. Behind the Purple Line were three more brigades of 6,000 men each. An additional seven were ready reserves.

The first Israeli position overrun that afternoon was atop Mount Hermon, at the northern end of the Golan defensive line. It fell to an attack by Syrian commandoes brought in by helicopters. The Israelis attempted to retake the position two days later, only to be repulsed.

While the northern end of Golan was being overrun, to the south, on the rocky Golan plateau, a titanic tank battle roared into being. It was a brutal exchange of fire, with tanks destroying each other in great numbers as both sides employed advanced ammunition designed to pierce the thick armor and kill the tank crews inside.

The Israeli 7th Brigade fought a gallant holding action against Syria's superior numbers, losing all but 7 of its 100 tanks and managing to delay the Syrian advance by 2 days. Moreover, although the Israeli line was ultimately pushed back, it was never entirely broken. In the north, the attackers gained four miles; in the center, five miles. Only in the south did the Syrians achieve anything like a breakthrough, penetrating 12.5 miles into Israeli-held territory. It was the most significant success any Syrian force ever achieved over the armed forces of Israel.

Although the Syrian 5th Infantry Division and the 1st Armored Division came close to entering Galilee, and while these forces exacted a heavy toll on the Israelis, their own losses were devastating. More than 500 Syrian tanks and APCs were destroyed in 2 days. By October 9, as more Israeli forces joined the battle, the Syrian advance was completely halted, and another 200 tanks taken out of the war.

The Israeli Air Force in Golan

In 1967, the Israeli air force played a spectacular offensive role in the Sinai. At the Golan Heights, ground-attack aircraft did much to arrest the Syrian advance, but, flying at low levels, they also took heavy casualties from the enemy's surface-to-air missiles (SAMs) and antiaircraft artillery.

On the first day of combat, 34 Israeli planes were brought down; however, once the Syrian surge had been arrested, the Israeli air force mission changed from tactical defense to strategic offensive strikes in addition to retaliatory raids against Damascus, the Syrian capital, in response to FROG missile attacks on kibbutzim in Galilee. Targets in Damascus and other Syrian cities included refineries, power stations, and ports. Civilian residential neighborhoods were also bombed, resulting in at least 100 noncombatant deaths.

Golan Counterattack

On October 8, after absorbing two days of unremitting punishment, Israeli forces were finally positioned to counterattack. Divisions led by General Dan Laner and General Moshe Peled pounded back against the Syrians. In contrast to the slashing offensive of 1967, this action was a bloody slog for the Israelis, but by October 10, the attackers had been forced back across the Purple Line. In ruins on the field were 867 of the 1,400+ Arab tanks that had rushed the line on Yom Kippur.

Now the Israelis wholly seized the initiative, advancing into Syria—penetrating 6 miles in the north and 12.5 miles in the south. On October 13, Iraq rushed its 3rd Armored Division to the Syrian front in an effort to stiffen resistance there. The Iraqis counterattacked against Laner, whose troops threw them back, destroying 80 tanks in the process.

With the Syrian situation now desperate, King Hussein of Jordan sent his 40th Armored Brigade into the melee, and Saudi Arabia deployed a 1,000-man battalion to the battlefront. The reinforced Arab defensive position finally arrested the Israeli counteroffensive before the village of Sasa, on the road to Damascus.

The Arabs Counter the Counterattack

Because much of Israel's strength had to be devoted to halting the Egyptian advance in the Sinai, the counterattack in Syria bogged down.

On October 16, Arab forces hit the Israelis on the south flank of their *salient* into Syria. Jordan's 40th Armored Brigade (150 tanks) spearheaded this counter-counterattack, which the Israelis repelled, knocking out 28 Jordanian and 60 Iraqi tanks. The Arabs countered again during October 18–19, but were again rebuffed with heavy losses: 20 Jordanian and 60 Iraqi tanks destroyed.

 **DEFINITION**

In military parlance, a **salient** is a part of a battle line that extends into enemy territory so that it may have enemy forces on three sides, and may therefore be vulnerable.

At Mount Hermon

Although Arab forces kept harassing the salient, the Israelis held their position—and no more major tank battle occurred. There was, however, one final action on the Syrian front, during October 21–22. An Israeli airborne brigade was lifted by helicopter, in coordination with the overland advance of Israel's Golani Brigade, in an operation to eject the Syrians from the positions they had captured on Mount Hermon on the first day.

The assault was successful, prompting Syria to agree to a UN-ordered cease-fire on the evening of October 22. The net result at the time of the cease-fire was that Israel had taken another 300 square miles of Syrian territory—while also recovering the Golan.

Although the Syrian armies retired intact, they had incurred severe casualties. Destroyed were 1,200 tanks, 400 APCs, 250 artillery pieces, and 222 aircraft. Three thousand one hundred Syrian troops were dead, another 6,000 wounded, and 500 taken prisoner. Iraq lost 200 tanks and Jordan lost 54 in defensive operations following the assault on Golan. Of the 12,000 troops it had committed to combat, Iraq lost 278 killed, 600 wounded, and 20 captured. Out of 4,000 Jordanians, 28 were killed and 49 wounded—according to official Jordanian sources. (Some historians believe the true figures were much higher.) Morocco's 1,800-man brigade suffered at least 200 killed.

Israel lost 250 tanks in the Golan fight—although 150 were later repaired. Eighty aircraft were downed, and troop casualties included 772 killed in action, 2,453 wounded, and 65 taken prisoner.

Sinai and Suez Combat

The Egyptian military took great pains to avoid repeating the tactical and strategic errors it had made in 1967. The assault it mounted along the 110-mile Suez Canal in the Yom Kippur War was planned in detail and then rehearsed in the guise of routine maneuvers. Egyptian Minister of War Ahmed Ismail and the chief of staff, General Saad al-Shazli, were personally involved in the planning.

The assault stepped off at 2 P.M. on Yom Kippur. Two hundred forty MiGs bombed, strafed, and lobbed rockets into the Israel's Bar Lev Line along the canal. In addition, positions to the rear of the line were also hit by a 53-minute barrage from 1,850 cannons. Some 200 tons of high explosives were dropped onto 35 Israeli positions.

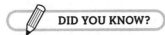 **DID YOU KNOW?**

> It has been estimated that the main Israeli defensive line along the Suez Canal, the Bar Lev Line, absorbed 10,500 artillery hits during the opening minute of the barrage. That is 175 high-explosive impacts per second.

The Israeli Sinai Defense Force consisted of 18,000 soldiers under Major General Avraham Mandler. They faced General Saad Mamoun's Second Army—110,000 men—in the north and General Abdel-Muneim Wassel's Third Army—90,000 troops—in the south.

Crossing the Canal

Following the opening barrage were waves of three infantry divisions from the Second Army and two from the Third. After the infantry, the troops and tanks of three mechanized and two armored divisions were to follow. In support of the attack were five independent tank brigades, a pair of parachute brigades, a brigade of marines, and 28 commando battalions.

The very first wave of the advance consisted of 8,000 infantrymen, armed with Soviet-made Snapper and Sagger antitank missiles, who paddled across the Suez Canal to land in the wide spaces between the Bar Lev fortifications. The initial forces quickly seized four major bridgeheads. Sadat had predicted that as many as 10,000 men would be killed in the effort to cross the canal. The surprise was so complete, however, that only 208 Egyptian troops died on the first day of the war.

Once the bridgeheads were established, Egyptian engineers threw 10 pontoon bridges across the canal. Fifteen Israeli posts on the edge of the canal were overrun that first day, with 10 more holding out for up to 6 days before surrendering. Another 10 were evacuated.

Commando Operations

While the main Egyptian force crossed the canal, elite commandos and paratroopers made deep penetration raids into the Sinai Peninsula to delay the arrival of Israeli reinforcements as long as possible.

The bold raids did not go well. Israeli jets shot down 14 helicopters carrying commandos, and an amphibious commando assault on Israeli-held Sharm el-Sheikh at the southern tip of the peninsula was repulsed, with heavy casualties on both sides. Nevertheless, the operation disrupted Israeli rear lines, and the commandos' antitank missiles took a toll on Israeli armor.

Arresting the Egyptian Advance in the Sinai

By the end of the first day of the war, five Egyptian divisions—80,000 troops, 500 tanks—were on the east bank of the Suez Canal. Israeli reinforcements were rushed to counter the advance, and on October 8 two armored brigades hastily counterattacked without vital air support. That was a grave error, as Egyptian antitank units destroyed most of the 190th Armored Brigade, 85 tanks.

Still, Israeli reinforcements continued to pour in, at last arresting the Egyptian advance. On October 14, with the Syrian situation in the Golan Heights deteriorating and the Egyptian advance stalled at the edge of their bridgeheads, Egypt launched a massive attack against the three Israeli divisions now arrayed on a line from north to south. The result was the biggest tank battle since the epic contest between the German and Soviet armor at Kursk, 280 miles southwest of Moscow, during July 1943.

On the flat scrubland of the Sinai, the Israelis rolled out 800 Pattons, Centurions, and Shermans to meet the Egyptian armored onslaught. Egypt suffered its first major defeat of the war. Not only were its armored forces hammered back to their bridgeheads, 264 tanks and 200 other armored vehicles were lost, and more than 1,000 troops were killed or wounded. Egyptian Second Army commander General Mohammed Saad Eddin Mamoun collapsed from a heart attack after receiving news of the devastating defeat. (He recovered, but was out of action for the rest of the war.) On the Israeli side, Major General Mandler was killed when an Egyptian shell hit his half-track.

Sinai Counterattack

With the Egyptian breakout arrested in the Sinai, Israeli high command commenced a massive counteroffensive. In the Cold War climate of the early 1970s, the Soviets were rushing to resupply the Arabs and the Americans were doing the same for the Israelis. A total of 935 cargo flights poured in from the USSR before the conflict ended, delivering 16,000 tons of materiel to Egypt and Syria. Americans flew 815 cargo sorties, delivering even more to the Israelis: 27,900 tons of munitions and equipment. The Soviets and the Americans also flew in fresh combat aircraft—206 planes for the Arabs and 68 for the Israelis, among these 32 F-4 Phantoms. The Americans delivered cutting-edge combat electronics and smart bombs, including new Rockeye cluster bombs, Walleye television-guided bombs, and brand-new laser-guided missiles.

His air support capability revitalized, General Ariel Sharon was tasked with leading his division in Operation Strongheart, advancing through the gap between the Second and Third Egyptian armies north of the Great Bitter Lake and then establishing a bridgehead on the *African* side of the Suez Canal.

The operation began on the night of October 15 with a brigade of paratroopers, supported by amphibious tanks, slipping through the gap and crossing over into Africa. In response, the Egyptian Second Army to the north and the Third Army to the south counterattacked, endeavoring to close the corridor the Israelis had opened on the east bank.

The most intense combat of the war exploded at Chinese Farm, where Sharon's forces fought off an armored onslaught from the 21st Armored Division of the Egyptian Second Army. In the meantime, even though the Egyptians worked to pinch off the Israeli salient in their territory and thereby isolate (and destroy) the Israeli units that had penetrated into Africa, Sharon boldly continued to send more brigades across the canal by pontoon bridge and ferry, always under heavy fire. It was an incredibly dangerous gamble, and at times it looked as if the bulk of Sharon's division would be cut off and lost. On the night of October 15–16 alone, Sharon lost 300 killed on either side of the Suez. In addition, 70 tanks were destroyed out of 280 engaged.

 VOICES

> He can best be described as a Patton-like, swashbuckling general, who rose in the ranks of the Israel Defence Forces, proved himself to have an uncanny feel for battle, but at the same time to be a most difficult person to command. Few, if any, of his superior officers over the years had a good word to say for him as far as human relations and integrity were concerned, although none would deny his innate ability as a field soldier.
>
> —Chaim Herzog, Israeli president from 1983 to 1993, on Ariel Sharon

On October 16 the Israeli 14th Armored Brigade slogged through a 12-hour battle to secure a vital crossroads on the east bank of the canal. Although victorious, the brigade lost 60 of its 100 tanks, along with 121 soldiers killed—a third of whom were officers.

On the next day, October 17, the Egyptian 25th Armored Brigade battled units from two Israeli brigades near the south end of the Great Bitter Lake. Israel lost four tanks while destroying 86 of the 96 Egyptian tanks engaged. With this victory, the precarious Israeli corridor to the Suez Canal held, and by October 20, it was enlarged to three miles wide. This allowed the Israelis to position more forces on both sides of the canal.

The Counterattack Intensifies

Having widened the corridor to the canal, the Israelis used it to strike both north and south, taking or destroying scores of SAM batteries along 50 miles of the canal. This created a gaping hole in Egypt's antiaircraft defensive umbrella, which the Israeli air force wasted no time in exploiting to provide close air support for Sharon's ever-advancing brigades. When Egypt sent planes to fight the Israelis in the air, the Soviet aircraft were quickly bested in dogfights. The U.S.-built Phantoms outflew even the MiG-21s, and, more important, the Israeli pilots handily outflew their Egyptian counterparts.

On October 22, additional Israeli units reinforced Sharon's division and enlarged the bridgehead into Egypt. The war suddenly accelerated in tempo as Sharon's division advanced to outskirts of Ismailia, key city of the Suez Canal. General Magen's division turned in the opposite direction, south, cutting off and isolating the Egyptian Third Army.

Cease-Fire

The UN had called for a cease-fire on October 22. Syria accepted it, but neither Israel nor Egypt heeded the call until October 24. By this time, Israel had extracted victory from what had looked, early on, like certain defeat. It held about 1,000 square miles of Africa, and Sharon and Magen were poised to destroy Egypt's hopelessly isolated Third Army.

Israel now agreed to the cease-fire. Many in the Israeli government wanted to push the victory further, but the international community, including the United States, applied pressure, and Israel quit on a high note.

The Naval War

The Yom Kippur War was fought primarily on the land and in the air, but it was also the first of the Arab-Israeli wars to include substantial naval action. Egypt had a navy manned by 17,000 sailors and equipped with 16 Soviet-built submarines, 6 destroyers or frigates, 19 missile boats, and 40 small torpedo boats. Syria's navy was much smaller—2,000 sailors manning 9 missile boats and 16 patrol craft. The Israeli navy was also small, consisting of 4,000 sailors and about 35 ships. Its combat craft included 3 submarines and 14 missile boats, capable of firing advanced Israeli-built Gabriel surface-to-surface missiles with a range of 12 miles. In addition, the navy had 9 patrol craft and 9 torpedo boats.

In contrast to the course of the rest of the Yom Kippur War, Israel prevailed on the water from the beginning. On the night of October 6–7, five Israeli missile boats used their Gabriels to sink three Syrian missile boats in the space of 25 minutes off Latakia, Syria. Two nights later, six Israeli missile boats attacked four Egyptian missile boats off Damietta, sinking three. The Israeli navy also carried out successful raids on the coast of Syria and on Egypt's Red Sea and Mediterranean coasts.

Vessels of the Israeli navy sank 19 enemy ships during the Yom Kippur War while suffering no losses, except for three sailors killed in action and 24 wounded.

Outcome

The Yom Kippur War was a dicey and bloody affair for Israel, but, in the end, there was no question as to the victor. Only after some months of negotiation did U.S. Secretary of State Henry Kissinger mediate a disengagement and partial Israeli withdrawal from the fronts as they existed on the day of the UN cease-fire, October 24, 1973.

Despite the Israeli victory, both Prime Minister Golda Meir and Defense Minister Moshe Dayan drew heavy criticism for the IDF's lack of readiness when the attacks came. Losses had been heavy—2,838 killed in action, 8,800 wounded, 508 missing, and 301 taken prisoner. Arab losses were 3,500 killed on the Syrian front and approximately 7,700 Egyptian personnel lost in the Sinai. Another 12,000 Egyptians were wounded, and 8,031 taken prisoner. Equipment losses were high on all sides.

The United States Pays a Price and Brokers a Peace

The United States paid a price for its aid to Israel when the Organization of the Petroleum Exporting Countries (OPEC) doubled its export oil prices, creating a severe gasoline shortage in the United States and contributing to a U.S. (and worldwide) economic crisis.

A Meeting at Camp David

As it turned out, both Egyptian President Anwar Sadat and his Israeli counterpart, Prime Minister Menachem Begin, wanted more than the peace Kissinger had brokered. Years of conflict had led Egyptian and Israeli leaders to conclude that the survival of one nation excluded the survival of the other. What changed in the perception of both Sadat and Begin was the realization that survival and prosperity were largely dependent on strong positive relations with the United States. The administrations of Richard Nixon, Gerald Ford, and Jimmy Carter made it clear to both men that the United States would not choose between Egypt and Israel; therefore, good relations with America became the common ground on which the two Middle Eastern leaders met.

Both leaders had to face down extreme opposition from within their own governments. Sadat made the first bold move when, on November 9, 1977, he abruptly departed from the written text of a speech to the Egyptian parliament and announced his intention to "go to the ends of the earth" to reach an accommodation with Israel. By this, he meant that he would travel to Israel to present his proposal for a peace settlement—provided that he was invited. Prime Minister Begin picked up the diplomatic hint and prompted the Knesset to present an invitation via a U.S. diplomat, Hermann Eilts. In response, on the evening of November 19, 1977, Anwar Sadat flew to Israel, landing at Ben-Gurion Airport outside Tel Aviv.

Sadat's address to the Knesset created both great hope and great uncertainty—and a kind of diplomatic gridlock in both Egypt and Israel. To resolve it, U.S. President Jimmy Carter invited the two men to a summit at Camp David beginning on September 5, 1978. For the next dozen days, President Carter kept the leaders talking. They ultimately issued the Camp David Accords, consisting of two agreements: a broad framework for achieving peace in the Middle East, and a more specific blueprint for a peace treaty between Egypt and Israel. The first document called for Israel to gradually grant self-government to the Palestinians in the Israeli-occupied West Bank and Gaza Strip and to partially withdraw its forces from these areas as a prelude to negotiations on their final status.

The second document called for a phased withdrawal of Israeli forces from the Sinai Peninsula, which Israel captured during the Six-Day War of 1967, and the return of that region to Egypt within 3 years of the signing of a peace treaty. In addition to guaranteeing the right of passage for Israeli ships through the Egyptian-controlled Suez Canal, the Camp David Accords included a concession both Nasser and Sadat had repeatedly sworn Egypt would never make: the documents affirmed Israel's right to exist.

The Last Casualties

The "final" casualty of the Yom Kippur War was Anwar Sadat. Having, even in defeat, redeemed the honor of Egypt in war, Sadat concluded the Camp David Accords. For this, he shared with Begin the Nobel Peace Prize, and much of the world considered him a hero—even as some in the Arab world deemed him a traitor.

On October 6, 1981, the eighth anniversary of the storming of the Bar Lev Line, he was gunned down by Islamic extremists while reviewing a parade commemorating the Egyptian victories of 1973. Five other dignitaries were slain, and 28 others were wounded.

The Least You Need to Know

- The Arab defeat in the Six-Day War left the major territorial issues unresolved and created a desire among the Arabs, especially Egypt and Syria, to redeem Arab honor lost in the humiliating outcome.

- Egypt and Syria (with support from other Arab states and Cuba) attacked on two major fronts during Yom Kippur 1973, making devastating inroads in the Golan Heights in northeastern Israel and in the Sinai on the south.

- The Arabs were armed by the Soviets, and the Israelis by the United States, making the Yom Kippur War a Cold War "proxy" conflict between the super powers.

- The Israelis recovered from surprise and early losses to regain control of occupied territory and even to conquer more Syrian ground, but both Prime Minister Golda Meir and Defense Minister Moshe Dayan were heavily criticized for having left Israel militarily vulnerable.

- The Yom Kippur War produced at least one extraordinary long-term result, the Camp David Accords of 1978, which ended the 30-year conflict between Israel and Egypt—at the price, ultimately, of Anwar Sadat's life.

Global Battleground

While the two world wars taught the political and military leaders of the United States and those of the rest of the West the global strategic and economic importance of the Middle East and its conflicts, it was OPEC's direct impact on the energy crisis of the 1970s that literally brought this importance home, especially to the American people. The chapters in Part 4 document the events that have chained the fate of the Middle East to that of the rest of the world.

Chapter 14 covers Iran's Islamic Revolution and its profound effect on American international policy and domestic politics. Chapter 15 shows how the aggression of Iraq's Saddam Hussein drew the United States into its first major war since the long disaster of Vietnam. Chapter 16 introduces global terrorism as a tactic of asymmetric warfare, by which small, relatively weak states and even stateless groups of people can wield deadly power with global impact.

The final chapter in this part, Chapter 17, is an overview of two of the longest wars in American history, that in Afghanistan (2001–present) and that in Iraq (2003–2011).

Iran's Islamic Revolution

Despite its greatness as an ancient empire and its modern importance in nineteenth and twentieth-century geopolitics, Persia—officially renamed Iran in 1935—had little place in the American popular consciousness prior to 1979, when the U.S. embassy in Tehran was breached by some 500 Iranian revolutionaries and 66 Americans were taken hostage, most of them destined to be held prisoner for 444 days.

If the Organization of the Petroleum Exporting Countries (OPEC) oil embargo of 1973 had brought the Middle East conflict into the everyday lives of Americans, the hostage crisis planted the Middle East even more powerfully in American hearts and minds.

The Iranian Backstory

There is some irony in the fact that the 1979 hostage crisis made Iran into the Middle Eastern state most visible to the United States and the West in general. The fact is that Iran is very different from the countries in the rest of the region. Although Americans frequently confused Iran and Iraq back in the 1970s (the difference between them apparently a single letter), Iran is much bigger than Iraq, with four times the territory and more than twice the population.

In This Chapter

- Iran's Persian heritage and Shiite identity

- Persian-European relations through history

- The Tobacco Revolt of 1891 foreshadows the Iranian Revolution of 1979

- The Pahlavi Dynasty

- The rise and fall of Mohammad Mosaddegh

- U.S.-Iranian relations and the hostage crisis of 1979-1980

Even more important, while Iraq is, like most of the Middle East, dominated by Sunni Islam, Iran is a Shiite country, which sets it apart religiously, culturally, and politically not only from the rest of the region, but from 90 percent of the Islamic world.

Finally, Iran is Persian, not Arab. The national language, Farsi, uses the same Arabic script and many Arabic loanwords, but Farsi and Arabic are nevertheless mutually unintelligible.

A large Middle Eastern state, Iran is isolated in the Middle Eastern region. What's more, even though so-called Islamic fundamentalism, which rose to its height in the 1970s, cut Iran off from the West, the country has struggled to "modernize" through much of the past 150 years, which has meant emulating many aspects of Western technology and culture. At various times, the two trends—toward conservative Islam and toward Western-style modernization—have created ambivalence and conflict within the country, with regional neighbors, and with the West.

Shiite Nation

One of the central conflicts of the Middle East is the clash between Sunni and Shia Islam. Recall that the origin of the dispute lay in the seventh century, when Muhammad died without having designated a successor to lead the new religion. The Sunni shared the opinion of many of Muhammad's companions, that the next leader should be elected from among those judged most capable, whereas the Shia believed that leadership should devolve on the Prophet's nearest male relative. In the course of time, official Islam became Sunni and one of the variant branches, Shia, manifested in Persia, came to dominate the antiestablishment Islamic sects, and absorbed many Persian cultural forms.

Through the centuries that followed Muhammad's death, the heart of the succession controversy lay at the very core of the Islamic faith. While Sunni and Shia have often coexisted cordially, the dispute has at times driven bloody conflicts.

Toward the end of the fifteenth century, as Persia was struggling to recover from the devastation of the Mongol invasions, competing dynasties vied for dominance. Among these, the Safavids gradually emerged triumphant. This tribe, however, soon faced a threat from the Ottoman Empire, adherents of Sunni Islam. The Savafid leader, Shah Ismail, acted to counter Ottoman influence in Persia by forcing a total conversion to Shia throughout the realm. In part, this was done through education, as Shiite *mullahs* were brought in from Lebanon and southern Iraq to open and operate Shiite mosques and schools. Much of the conversion, however, was forced. Safavid officials desecrated Sunni mosques and tombs and officially decreed that the annual *hajj* (pilgrimage) to Mecca be scrapped in favor of a hajj to Karbala, the southern Iraq city in which the martyred Shiite hero Hussein and his brother Abbas are buried.

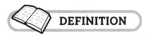 **DEFINITION**

> A **mullah** is a Muslim thoroughly educated in Islamic theology and sacred law; as such, the title is mostly used in Central Asia and in Shia cultures for Islamic clerics and the leaders of mosques.

Education and compulsion proved effective, but Persia still had many stubborn Sunni holdouts. Judging them beyond conversion, the Safavids massacred them. During the sixteenth and seventeenth centuries, entire Sunni towns were liquidated, and by the middle of the eighteenth century, Persia was, in fact, a Shiite kingdom.

East Meets West

Persia was long a center of trade, the nexus of key caravan routes, but by the middle of the eighteenth century, ships from Western Europe began arriving in Persian ports, and maritime commerce rapidly eclipsed overland trade.

The Safavid rulers were reluctant to open Persia to European commerce, but with caravan income drying up, they had no choice. Soon, they made significant concessions to European powers, especially to the British East India Company, a private trading enterprise intimately tied to the British ruling class and crown.

As the eighteenth century drew to a close, the Safavid Dynasty, weakened by corruption and inefficiency, fell to a Turkic tribe called the Qajars. Seeking to restore Persia to its former greatness, the Qajars invaded Georgia in 1804. Defeated there, they were forced to cede Persian territory in the Caucasus to Russia.

Caught in a geopolitical power struggle between Moscow and London, Persia's shah courted an alliance with Russia's rival, Britain. By an 1814 treaty, Persia opened itself to occupation by British troops and permitted British officers to train its native military forces. This created the basis for a strong and long-lasting British influence and presence in the country.

Unfortunately for the Qajars, the alliance failed to defeat the Russians. When Persia declared war on Russia in 1826, seeking at last to regain lost territory, Britain happened to be allied with Russia in Greece's war for independence from the Ottoman Empire, and was not about to join *Islamic* Persia in fighting a *Christian* ally in its own war against Muslim Ottomans. Russia therefore defeated Persia yet again. This not only confirmed the previous loss of Persian territory, but resulted in the levy of punitive war reparations against Persia.

Already economically anemic, Persia entered the nineteenth century saddled with a heavy war debt. What's more, the Industrial Revolution that shifted into high gear in Europe, transforming the Western nations into economic powerhouses, bypassed Persia. Demand for most handcrafted Persian goods declined, not only on the export market, but domestically as well. Persia found itself flooded with cheap European goods. Compounding this crisis was a fall in the global price of silver, on which the Persian dinar was based.

Tobacco Starts a Revolution

Desperate to save the Persian economy, in 1872 the shah hired Baron Julius von Reuter, a British subject, to take control of the nation's finances. It was inviting a wolf into the hen house. Reuter opened the door to preferential treatment of British imports and industries at the expense of domestic enterprises. Incredibly, the shah doubled down on this so-called Reuter Concession in the 1880s by expanding it to tobacco, turning over the entire Persian tobacco market to Britain's Imperial Tobacco Corporation. Ruinous to domestic farmers and merchants, the monopoly provoked the Tobacco Revolt of 1891.

Much as a tea monopoly and tax had been instrumental in the American Revolution, the Tobacco Revolt became a much larger rebellion against Western imperialism. Merchants outraged by the outright theft of their production led the revolt, which quickly brought in other Iranians and even some Russians disadvantaged by British economic control.

In the meantime, the Qajar shah pursued even closer economic ties with both Russia and Britain, securing huge loans from the czar and granting to the British an exclusive contract for the extraction of Persian oil.

Defeated in the financially ruinous 1905 Russo-Japanese War, Russia was forced to cut off loans to Persia, which pushed the tottering Persian economy off a cliff. The revolt that had begun years earlier over tobacco now intensified. Although some Persian clerics sought to put themselves into national leadership, the merchant class managed to force the shah to create something approaching a constitutional monarchy by establishing the *Majles*, a parliament modeled after the French system of government.

 **DEFINITION**

Majles is the traditional name for the Persian (later, Iranian) parliament, which is today more formally called the Islamic Consultative Assembly of Iran. After 1906 and up to the revolution of 1979, *Majles* was also the name applied to the lower house of the Iranian Legislature. The upper house was known as the Senate.

The death of the fifth Qajar shah, Mozaffar ad-Din Shah Qajar, brought his son Mohammad Ali Shah Qajar to the throne in 1907. Almost immediately, Mohammad Ali sought to undo the parliament, declaring martial law in Tehran in 1908 and seizing the Majles. This provoked the so-called Constitutional Revolution, which was a successful secular revolt of tribes, particularly the Bakhtiyari, and merchants against a corrupt autocracy, foreign subjugation, and rigid state-sponsored religious structures. In many ways, the 1908 revolution was the genuine predecessor of the 1979 Iranian Revolution. Thanks to foreign intervention and domestic corruption, both fell far short of their lofty goals of creating a constitutionally ruled Iran respectful of the diversity of the nation's many peoples.

Europe Marches In

Over the years, Britain and Russia had often contested control of Persia. In response to the chaos prevailing with ascension of Mohammad Ali, they concluded the Anglo-Russian Agreement of 1907. While the czar sent troops to counter the new shah's assault on the Persian constitutional forces, the British aided those forces with funding and materiel.

The Anglo-Russian aid was sufficient to allow the secular constitutional democrats to take control of the government. Yet no sooner were they in power than they began to regret having ceded so much influence to the Europeans. Looking now to defend Persia against Britain and Russia, the Majles voted to import military advisors from yet *another* European power, Sweden, and to supplement this with economic advice from another Westerner, an American expert in finance.

The British and Russians responded by invading northern and southern Persia, demanding that the Majles dismiss both the Swedes and the American. Moreover, they demanded that Persia reimburse the United Kingdom and the Imperial Russian government for the cost of the invasion! Not surprisingly, the Majles refused. The British and Russians had powerful Persian officials in their pockets, however. Instead of responding militarily to the refusal, they ordered their proxies to engineer the dismissal of the defiant Majles leaders. The will of the people notwithstanding, the Constitutional Revolution ended with Persia a vassal of Britain and Russia.

World War I

As discussed in Chapter 5, World War I (1914–1918) brought many changes to relations between the West and the Middle East. Persian oil resources now became critical strategic assets, and the country found itself caught between Britain and Russia on the one hand and the German-allied Ottoman Empire on the other. Both sides wanted control of Persian oil, and Persia became a field of battle between them.

The fighting from 1914 to 1918 damaged Persian agriculture and infrastructure, and the armies of occupation quite literally ate up local resources. This, coupled with continued economic crisis, contributed to a great famine that killed 2 out of 10 Persians before the war ended.

From 1917 to 1919, after Russian revolutionaries overthrew the czar, Persia saw yet more fighting on its soil, this time between the British and the Soviets. The Persian government was not pleased to have British soldiers on its soil, but its greater fear was the rise of Soviet communism and the prospect of the Red Army entering the country to "liberate" it from the British. For this reason, the shah once again embraced European power, concluding with Great Britain the Anglo-Persian Agreement of 1919, giving the UK a great deal of control over Persian finances, the military, and general policy—all in return for a promise to defend the country against a Soviet incursion.

America's Shah

The 1979 hostage crisis revealed to Americans the full extent of U.S. involvement in the government of Iran. Mohammed Reza Shah Pahlavi, shah from September 16, 1941, until he was overthrown by the Iranian Revolution on February 11, 1979, became widely known as "America's shah." The path to this identification was a long one.

Reza Shah

The father and predecessor of Shah Mohammed Reza Pahlavi was Reza Khan. The son of a Persian army officer, Reza joined the elite Persian Cossack Brigade when he was just 16. He rose within the Persian Cossacks to the rank of brigadier general, and in 1921 led a large contingent into Tehran, ostensibly to counter an imminent uprising against Ahmad Shah Qajar and his government.

Ordering his troops to arrest several Majles members on charges of conspiring against the shah, Reza quickly went on to seize the capital and force the dissolution of the government. He replaced the prime minister with his close friend Seyyed Zia'eddin Tabatabaee while he appointed himself *Sardar Sepah*—commander in chief of the army.

In all of this, Reza Khan was supported by the British, who feared Soviet aggression as much as the Persian government did. British authorities made no objection when, in 1923, Reza pushed Tabatabaee out of office and took over as prime minister, nor did Britain make any move three years later when the Majles, under Reza's leadership, overthrew the Qajar dynasty and declared him, Reza Khan, Reza Shah.

The new shah promptly named his new dynasty "Pahlavi." He had two immediate, if at times contradictory, goals. One was to diminish foreign influence—especially from Great Britain; the other was to modernize—in other words, Westernize—Persia by securalizing Persian government and culture.

 **DEFINITION**

> **Pahlavi** is a "throne name," a surname chosen when one ascends the throne. It also became the surname of a short-lived twentieth-century Iranian dynasty. *Pahlavi* is a word referring to the Persian writing system dating to the pre-Islamic era, thereby suggesting a foundation of secular authority independent of Islam.

Reza Shah moved toward his first goal by signing a treaty with the Soviet Union, securing the Red Army's withdrawal from Persia. With the Soviet presence eliminated, communist agitation diminished in Persia, and the need for British military protection ended. This moved Reza to rescind the Anglo-Persian Agreement of 1919 and to replace British concessions and monopolies in Persia with protective tariffs that favored the development of domestic Persian industries. Next, Reza Shah challenged the pre-World War I Anglo-Persian oil agreements, and by 1933 was able to negotiate far more favorable terms for divvying up the revenues flowing from the nation's oil.

In moving toward his second goal, modernization, Reza Shah reduced government waste and corruption in order to channel funds to building infrastructure, including modern roadways, bridges, and power plants. For his model, he looked to Turkey's great modernizer, Atatürk, who saw traditional Islam as the enemy of modernization and who therefore moved his country toward secularization. Reza Shah abolished *sharia* courts based on religious law, thereby taking legal and civil matters out of clerical hands. He founded a system of public schools to offer modern secular education as an alternative to the system of religious school that dominated Persia. He did much to elevate the status of women, compelling the nation's universities to admit them and outlawing the wearing of the *burka* in public.

Predictably, Reza Shah's secular reforms aroused vehement opposition from Muslim clerics and religiously observant Muslim laity. The shah responded by creating a huge secret police network, which used brutal tactics to suppress opposition from religious groups, as well as from communists, labor unions, and all other elements perceived as "dissident." As for the Majles, from which Reza himself had risen, the shah brought it to heel by placing it under the direct control of the military, which, in turn, answered to him and him alone.

Persia officially became Iran in 1935, pursuant to a letter Reza Shah submitted to the League of Nations. The shah insisted that *Iran* was the historically correct name, whereas *Persia* was the name of only one of Iran's cultural provinces.

Courting the Nazis

In the run-up to World War II, Reza Shah made no secret of his admiration for Adolf Hitler and the Third Reich. For one thing, the Nazi regime seemed to him the ideal of the hypermodern, hyper-efficient state, a model to which he believed Iran should aspire. For another, the shah took literally the Nazi doctrine of the superiority of the Aryan race—to which those of Persian, or Iranian, stock belonged.

Today rarely used in academic circles, *Aryan* formerly denoted a people who spoke an Indo-European language and who invaded northern India during the second millennium B.C.E. As used by the Nazis and their supporters, the word more narrowly described a racially "pure" Nordic variety of the Caucasian race, without Jewish, Slavic, Gypsy, or other ethnic heritage. Today, neo-Nazi white supremacists use the word simply as a synonym for "Christian Caucasian."

The shah thus reaped no benefit from his pro-Nazi leanings. Nevertheless, in August 1941, he declared neutrality and refused to allow the Soviet Union and Britain to use Iran as a corridor for shipping supplies and transporting troops. Fearing that Reza would align Iran—and its strategic supplies of oil—with the Nazis, the Soviets and British launched an air, sea, and ground assault on Iran and occupied it.

The shah's vaunted military did nothing to resist the invasion, a full 15 army divisions surrendering without a firing a shot. Having occupied the country, the British politely demanded that Reza Shah abdicate in favor of his son, the pliable Mohammed Reza Pahlavi.

 **VOICES**

Would His Highness kindly abdicate in favour of his son, the heir to the throne? We have a high opinion of him and will ensure his position. But His Highness should not think there is any other solution.

—Message delivered to Reza Shah, August 1941

After meekly abdicating, Reza Shah was taken by British forces to exile on the island of Mauritius off the coast of Africa and then moved to Durban and, later, Johannesburg, South Africa, where, a broken man, he succumbed to a heart ailment on July 26, 1944.

Ejecting the Soviets

As it did in many places it occupied during World War II, the Soviet Red Army refused to leave Iran after hostilities had ended. In addition, the Soviets sponsored an Iranian communist party, the Tudeh, which called large-scale labor strikes and other demonstrations in the aftermath of the war.

U.S. President Harry S. Truman put three combat divisions on alert in Austria and warned that, if necessary, they would compel the Soviet forces to leave Iran. Unwilling to fight the Americans, the Red Army withdrew in May 1946, but the Tudeh remained active. The new shah, however, was as fervently anticommunist as his father had been, a fact that prompted him to reach out to the United States for an alliance.

Postwar Iranian-American Relations

Mohammad Reza Shah Pahlavi also wanted American money—lots of it. Following the war, the United States was extraordinarily generous with aid, but while the Truman government did put together an Iranian assistance package, it was comparatively modest. The United States' first priority was helping out the nations in Europe and Asia most directly ravaged by the war. Nevertheless, despite the tight-fisted generosity, Iranian perceptions of the United States were mainly positive after World War II, as a majority of the population welcomed its anticolonial, pro-democracy traditions, and its public stance supporting liberation movements across the world.

In the late 1940s, a dispute developed between Iran and Great Britain over the division of Iranian oil revenues as they had been negotiated in 1933 by the Anglo-Persian Oil Company (APOC)—called, since 1935, the Anglo-Iranian Oil Company (AIOC). London threatened military intervention, and the wrath of both conservative Iranian clerics and communist secularists turned on Mohammed Reza Shah, who was believed to be in cahoots with the British. After surviving an assassination attempt in 1949, he cracked down hard on the religious conservatives *and* the communists, prompting the two disparate factions to find common cause against him. They were joined by a large portion of the liberal middle class to form the National Front under the leadership of Mohammad Mosaddegh.

Mosaddegh led an opposition to British—and *American*—"meddling" in Iran and, in so doing, drew popular support that enabled him to usurp much of the shah's authority. As we saw in Chapter 8, however, Britain embargoed the importation of Iranian oil, crippling the country's already precarious economy and turning the Iranian electorate against Mosaddegh and the National Front by 1952. Mosaddegh responded by attempting to rally Iran against the West. This prompted Winston Churchill (reelected as UK prime minister in 1951) to trade British support for America's prosecution of the Korean War (1950–1953) for U.S. support of Britain's position regarding Iran. Perceiving a new threat from the West and responding to pro-Mosaddegh popular demonstrations, the shah made Mosaddegh his prime minister and gave him more authority than ever.

Mosaddegh used his new position to declare martial law and suspend the Iranian constitution. Fearing that Iran would harden into an anti-West attitude that would open it once again to a Soviet takeover, Britain finally agreed to a 50/50 oil revenue split. But it was now too little, too late. Mosaddegh responded by demanding the 50/50 split *plus* $50 million in reparations—a proposal London angrily rejected.

 VOICES

> [I am] authorized by the will of the nation to share in the movement launched to protect the independence of the country, to sever the grip of the foreigners and to reestablish the prestige, the glory, and the honour of the Persia of ancient times ... the shattering of the chains of colonialism ... toppling the pillars of oppression.
>
> —Mohammad Mosaddegh, March 20, 1953

Ajax

At this point, 1953, Dwight D. Eisenhower was sworn in as the new U.S. president. Mosaddegh greeted his arrival in the White House with a stern warning. If Britain did not conclude a satisfactory oil deal, he would turn to the Soviets for aid. Eisenhower did not respond directly to this threat, but instead directed the CIA to work with MI6 (British military intelligence) to create and implement Operation Ajax, a covert scheme to replace Mosaddegh with a "friendly" leader handpicked by the two intelligence services. The principal weapon in this operation was CIA-MI6 control of Iranian newspapers, which were used to shape public opinion against Mosaddegh. At the same time, President Eisenhower abruptly cut off all U.S. aid to Iran.

The combination of a clandestine propaganda assault and induced financial hardship resulted in the ouster of Mosaddegh and his replacement by General Fazolla Zahedi, the CIA-MI6 candidate, as prime minister. Street violence accompanied the change of power, but confident that he had the backing of the United States (and Britain), Reza Mohammed Shah mobilized the military to put it down.

The United States had its shah, purchased at the price of enduring resentment from Iranians—liberals—on the one hand and religious fundamentalists on the other.

The White Revolution

After the fall of Mosaddegh, an emboldened shah personally took up the reins of government. As the Soviet threat receded, he recognized that the clerics and Islamic fundamentalists were his primary domestic enemy. Accordingly, in 1957 he took a leaf from his father's book and created a new, even more powerful secret police force, SAVAK (National Intelligence and Security Organization), which the CIA, together with the Israeli Mossad, helped to train.

SAVAK proved to be a highly efficient intelligence organization. Even more, it quickly earned a much-feared reputation for brutality in the service of the monarchy. Subject to no constitutional oversight, answering exclusively to the shah, SAVAK freely employed imprisonment, torture, and assassination. Opponents of the regime either converted or disappeared.

While Reza Mohammed ruthlessly eliminated all opposition, he resolved to pick up where his father had left off in the modernization of Iran. In 1963, he inaugurated what he called the White Revolution, which was partly designed by Western advisors and consisted of three main initiatives:

- **Land reform:** The members of the Iranian clergy were the major landowners in Iran. The shah high-handedly seized clerical properties and instituted a program of redistribution of land for individual ownership and for public use.

- **Women's suffrage:** The shah prevailed on the Majles to give women the right to vote—a rarity in any Muslim country, and a move that outraged the fundamentalists even more than the land seizure.

- **Educational reform:** Reza Mohammed's father had already created a system of secular public education side by side with the traditional Islamic schools. The new educational reform initiative purged all religion from the public schools and ensured that no government funding reached the religious schools.

Ayatollah Khomeini

Inevitably, the reforms of the White Revolution brought the faithful angrily into the streets while also politically radicalizing the Iranian clergy. Among them was Ruhollah Khomeini, a charismatic *ayatollah* and political activist, who criticized the White Revolution as a "Jewish-American plot" against Iran.

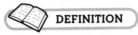 **DEFINITION**

> **Ayatollah** is a distinguished title conferred on Muslim clerics by the Shia denomination known as the Twelvers. An ayatollah is deemed an expert authority on Islam, especially as it applies to the law, matters of ethics, and philosophy. High-ranking ayatollahs in Iran control much of the country.

The shah acted quickly to suppress the rioting and arrest the clergy. Among these was Khomeini, who was arrested in November 1964, held for six months, and then released. Summoned to an audience with Prime Minister Hasan Ali Mansur, Khomeini angrily spurned Mansur's plea that he recant his opposition to the government. Frustrated by the cleric's recalcitrance, Mansur slapped Khomeini's face—a grave insult. Two weeks after this incident, Mansur was assassinated by a fundamentalist group supportive of Khomeini's position.

As for Khomeini, he went into exile, first to Turkey and then in the holy Shiite city of Najaf, Iraq. In 1978, Saddam Hussein, at the time Iraq's vice president, fearing the growing popular influence of the ayatollah, "encouraged" him to leave Najaf. Khomeini then reestablished himself in the Paris suburb of Neauphle-le-Château, from which he conducted a highly effective media war against the Pahlavi regime, recording exhortations on cassette tapes, which his followers smuggled into Iran.

The White Revolution Collapses

It was not as if Khomeini was going up against a popular regime. The White Revolution was proving a miserable failure. The bold land-redistribution scheme had been thoroughly corrupted by those connected to the Pahlavi family, who managed to preempt huge tracts of expropriated land— invariably the richest agricultural properties. As for the poor, even those who managed to acquire land lacked the money to farm it. They could not afford agricultural equipment, livestock, seed, or fertilizer and so ended up selling the property, at cut rates, back to the original owners. Thus land reform alienated the religious without benefitting the masses.

Thanks to renegotiated petroleum contracts with the West, petrodollars were flowing into the Iranian coffers. But just as quickly as the money came in, the shah spent it, mostly on extravagant purchases of military hardware from the United States, even though the Arab nations of the Middle East, preoccupied with Israel, offered few overt threats to Iran.

While the mass of the Iranian people received little benefit from the inflow of oil money, the volume of revenue meant that Iran, in the eyes of the U.S. government, was no longer a "developing country." For this reason, American development aid was cut off, leaving the people without an economic lifeline from abroad or from its own government.

A Regime in Decline

The shah alienated his people with his autocratic rule. While squandering vast sums on unnecessary military purchases, he refused to crack down on official corruption, which was rampant. Moreover, in the face of the failure of the White Revolution's land-redistribution scheme, he instituted wholesale agricultural collectivization in a badly misguided effort to increase food production. In the end, the program seized farms that had been given to struggling Iranian families in impoverished rural districts, yet failed to produce more food. And just when it looked as if the agricultural picture could not get any darker, the shah instituted price ceilings on agricultural commodities that made profitable farming, already difficult, impossible.

Another great failing of the land-redistribution scheme was its lack of any provision for new housing, which was a pressing need in Iran. Population grew, but the shah's government steadfastly refused to respond. The urban housing shortage was compounded by dispossessed farmers flooding into the cities.

Poverty and homelessness created political desperation, to which the Pahlavi regime responded not with sympathy but with renewed violent crackdowns on labor unions and opposition parties. SAVAK, it seemed, was everywhere.

Ruhollah Khomeini

Most sources agree that Ruhollah Musavi Khomeini was born on September 24, 1902, in Khomein, a town some 200 miles south of Tehran. His father, Mustapha Musavi, was the town's chief cleric, and was murdered when his son was just five months old. The child was raised by his mother, Hajar, and aunt, Sahebeh, until he was about 15 years old, when both women died.

From 1908 through 1962, Khomeini underwent Islamic education and became an ayatollah, an authority and teacher expert in Islamic subjects. During this period, he also wrote extensively. Late in his studies, in the holy city of Qom, he married and had two sons and three daughters.

During his years of scholarship, Khomeini lived a quiet life and was not politically active. He did, however, embrace the political activism shown by many of his fellow Iranian clerics, and beginning in 1962, he himself entered the political arena, launching a fight against the regime of Shah Mohammed Reza Pahlavi based on strict Shia principles. His voice was instrumental in the outbreak of a popular religious and political rebellion on June 5, 1963, which is widely regarded by Iranians today as the start of the Islamic revolutionary movement in Iran.

When the shah crushed the rebellion, Khomeini was arrested, jailed for 6 months, and sent into an exile that stretched over 14 years, first in Turkey, then in the Shiite city of Najaf, Iraq, and finally in a suburb of Paris. During his exile, he conducted a sustained media campaign against the shah's regime, Israel, and the United States—the "Great Satan" (he argued) who had made the shah its puppet.

On February 1, 1979, after Mohammed Reza Shah was overthrown, Khomeini returned to Iran. Just 10 days later, on February 11, revolutionary forces loyal to him seized power, elevating Khomeini to the position of "supreme leader" of what was now the Islamic Republic of Iran.

On October 22, 1979, U.S. President Jimmy Carter invited the deposed shah to the United States for treatment of his advanced cancer. Two weeks later, Khomeini exhorted Iranian university students to "expand with all their might their attacks against the United States" in order to compel the return of the shah to Iran. On November 4, 500 "students" stormed the U.S. embassy and took its skeleton staff hostage. They would remain captives for the next 444 days.

The revolution was characterized by multiple rifts between those whose veneration for Khomeini was absolute and those who differed with him on specific issues of policy. On June 22, 1981, Khomeini dismissed President Abul Hassan Bani-Sadr, who, he believed, interfered with the remodeling of Iran as the ideal Islamic republic. The internal strife was compounded by a ruinous war with Iraq, costly efforts to export the Islamic Revolution to the rest of the region, and—most disturbing to the West—growing relations with the Soviet Union.

Late in 1982, Khomeini seemed to retreat somewhat from his absolutist program by sharing some power with the nation's secular sphere. He also approved overtures to end Iran's self-inflicted status as a global pariah and supporter of terrorism. As it distanced itself from the Soviet Union—itself in steep decline—Iran expanded commercial relations with the West and even voiced a desire to reestablish relations with the Great Satan itself, the United States.

On February 14, 1989, Khomeini seemed to suddenly reverse the apparent move away from religious absolutism when he issued a religious edict or "fatwa" condemning the novelist Salman Rushdie to death because his novel *The Satanic Verses* was a blasphemous portrait of Islam. In the eyes of the West, this action eclipsed any gestures toward liberalism, and when Khomeini succumbed to cancer on June 3, 1989, his death was regarded outside of Iran as the end of an uncompromising Islamic theocrat. Within Iran, he is honored as the chief founder of the Islamic republic.

America Meets Iran

In 1977, the United States was emerging from its own era of collective political dissatisfaction and cynicism. In 1975, the Vietnam War had ended in a disturbing mixture of defeat, heartbreak, outrage, and relief when, after more than 10 years of war, American armed forces pulled out of the country, leaving it to the communists. Richard M. Nixon, having made some spectacular diplomatic strides toward ending the seemingly interminable Cold War, resigned from office in criminal disgrace on August 9, 1974. Gerald Ford (whom Nixon had appointed to the vice presidency after the resignation of Vice President Spiro Agnew, charged with extortion, tax fraud, bribery, and conspiracy) became the first nonelected president in American history.

For many Americans, Ford's avuncular personality was a welcome change after Nixon's polarizing presence, but Ford was never able to shake free of the public suspicion that his appointment as VP had been contingent on an understanding that, if Nixon resigned, Ford would pardon him to bar criminal prosecution relating to the Watergate scandal that had brought him down. Ford therefore failed to gain election in his own right in 1976, losing to a Washington "outsider," Jimmy Carter, Democratic governor of Georgia.

On March 17, 1977, the new president addressed the UN General Assembly, announcing that the foreign policy of his administration would give top priority to promoting and protecting human rights. It was, in effect, a repudiation of the manipulative international policies that had moved every president since Harry Truman to prop up distasteful, even brutal foreign regimes, including that of Reza Mohammed Shah, just because they were anticommunist.

Opportunity in Afghanistan

On December 25, 1978, the People's Democratic Party of Afghanistan (PDPA) overthrew the ruling regime of Mohammad Daoud Khan and proclaimed the Democratic Republic of Afghanistan (DRA) under Nur Mohammed Taraki, a Marxist supported by the Soviet Union. Immediately, opposition rose against the Taraki government, primarily among the Muslim mountain tribes, who formed the Mujahideen. The Soviet Union responded by sending more military aid, and as a bloody guerrilla war developed, President Carter secretly authorized U.S. aid to opponents of the pro-Soviet regime.

Eruption in Iran

Even as he exploited the situation in Afghanistan to weaken America's Cold War adversary, the Soviet Union, President Carter was confronted with the eruption of a full-scale revolution in Iran. In January 1979, rioting in the cities of Iran sent the shah seeking refuge in Egypt. Not only did he flee, he also named a "regency council" to rule during his absence. The flight and appointment were a double sign of weakness that the exiled Khomeini was quick to exploit. From Paris, the Ayatollah intensified his taped messages of revolution. Demonstrations now assumed spectacular proportions, sometimes massing more than a million participants. When the shah's army mutinied, refusing to fight the demonstrators, Khomeini ended his 14-year exile and returned to Iran.

By February 1979, the government of Reza Mohammed Shah Pahlavi was no more. In its place, Khomeini proclaimed Iran an Islamic republic, and he set up a Revolutionary Council through which he ruled. "Liberated" from the shah's incompetent, corrupt, and oppressive rule, Iran was plunged into a reign of revolutionary terror, in which thousands of people labeled as "subversives" and "counterrevolutionaries" were given show trials before being imprisoned or summarily executed.

The ayatollah's new regime created extremes of worshipful devotion and dissident protest. In the forefront of the protest were women who objected to being repressed by a return to Muslim fundamentalism. Various ethnic groups, most notably the Kurds, also rebelled. Khomeini answered the dissidents by pointing to the results of a popular referendum, which, he announced, showed that 99 percent of the people of Iran supported his revolution and reforms.

Yet the counterrevolutionary rebellion intensified, prompting the Revolutionary Council to create the Army of the Guardians of the Islamic Revolution on May 6, 1979. This new force moved even more vigorously against dissidents, and the tempo and volume of trials and executions intensified. Iran cut itself off not only from the West, but from the rest of the Islamic world in the Middle East. The nation became a global pariah.

The Embassy Falls

In the early days of the Iranian Revolution, the Carter administration saw its loss of a reliable ally through the familiar but narrow lens of the Cold War. The Soviets were on the run in Afghanistan, and at least the threat in Iran was Islamic rather than Marxist-Soviet. True, the new regime was intensely hostile to the United States, which Khomeini called "the Great Satan." Yet President Carter did not hesitate to extend a helping hand to the exiled shah when he disclosed that he was desperately ill with cancer. The president invited him to the United States for advanced medical treatment.

The gesture outraged at least one element of Iranian revolutionaries. On November 4, 1979, some 500 Iranians stormed the U.S. embassy in Tehran, being run by a skeleton staff who had stayed behind after the majority had been evacuated early in the revolution.

The embassy's invaders initially seized 90 hostages, including 66 U.S. nationals. The non-Americans and 13 American women and African-American hostages were released on November 19 and 20, leaving 53 U.S. nationals in captivity. As ransom, their captors demanded the return of the shah. President Carter refused, but the shah, hoping to end the crisis, voluntarily left the United States in early December, to no avail. The hostages remained in captivity. The Ayatollah Khomeini may or may not have explicitly ordered the assault on the U.S. embassy, but he subsequently approved of the action as well as the holding of hostages against the return of the shah.

Eagle Claw

As the hostages languished in captivity, the United States, with all its military might, learned its first lesson in *asymmetric warfare*: a small, weak nation—or regime within a nation, or faction within that regime—could hold a great power at bay, rendering it a helpless giant.

 **DEFINITION**

> **Asymmetric warfare** is war in which a relatively small, weak state or non-state entity (such as a terrorist organization) is able to effectively leverage some form of coercion or other power (such as terrorism) against the political and military assets of a larger, more powerful state.

Fearful that any major military response would promptly result in the deaths of the hostages, President Carter somewhat reluctantly authorized a secret rescue mission, Operation Eagle Claw, to be undertaken by an elite Delta Force unit.

On April 24, 1980, eight helicopters were launched from the aircraft carrier USS *Nimitz*. They carried a Delta team to a rendezvous in the Iranian desert with C-130 transport aircraft to refuel prior to flying into Tehran. The plan was to swoop in, storm the location at which the hostages were being held, liberate them, and airlift them to a soccer stadium on the outskirts of Tehran, where additional helicopters would fly them to freedom.

It was a desperate mission hastily conceived, and one of the variables that had escaped calculation was the harsh and unpredictable weather of the Iranian desert. At the rendezvous point, a severe sandstorm caused engine trouble in a C-130, and, in the reduced visibility of the sandstorm, one of the helicopters collided with the crippled cargo plane. Eight of the Delta operatives were killed, and the decision was made to abort Operation Eagle Claw.

The only good luck in the ill-fated mission was the fact that it did not result in retaliation against the hostages. Nevertheless, it seemed to many Americans like a culminating defeat.

 VOICES

What happened in Tehran was the diplomatic equivalent of Pearl Harbor. It was bad. We totally missed the significance of the revolution. We supported the shah much too long. We couldn't cut loose from him.... It was laziness, sheer intellectual laziness.

—Moorhead Kennedy, U.S. diplomat taken hostage in Iran

The Ayatollah's Revenge

President Carter ran for reelection in 1980 with the odds stacked against him. The nation's economy was still bogged down in a recession, compounded by an energy crisis aggravated by stringent OPEC limits on oil production.

This was bad enough, but overshadowing everything was the lingering specter of the embassy captives. Carter appeared weak. Not until after President Carter's landslide loss to Ronald Reagan did the Iranian parliament propose a set of definitive conditions for the return of the hostages. These included a U.S. pledge not to interfere in Iranian affairs, the release of Iranian financial assets President Carter had frozen in the United States, the lifting of all U.S. sanctions against Iran, and the return of the shah's property to Iran.

Prior to the inauguration of the new president, Jimmy Carter hammered out an agreement with Iran and the parties signed it, and yet the Ayatollah Khomeini delayed the hostage release until January 20, 1981, the very day Jimmy Carter left office and Ronald Reagan entered it.

The delay was unquestionably intended as one final humiliation for the leader of the nation that Khomeini at times referred to as "the Great Satan." And to be sure, the 444 days in which American diplomats were held captive were humbling not just for the president but for the nation. Nevertheless, the new American president refused to take the bait Khomeini offered. In an act that showed the

American democracy at its most noble, compassionate, and just—qualities often conspicuously absent from U.S. Middle Eastern policy—President Reagan delegated to the man he had defeated the honor of being the first to welcome the returning hostages when they landed at a U.S. Air Force base in West Germany.

The Least You Need to Know

- Iran, which shaped much of America's perception of the Middle East during the 1970s and 1980s, is unique in the region for its Persian rather than Arabic identity and its majority Shiite population in an Islamic world in which 90 percent of the faithful are Sunni.

- Beginning in the seventeenth century, Persia (called Iran after 1935) became increasingly entangling ties with European traders and governments, a situation that eventually compromised Persian sovereignty.

- The Tobacco Revolt of 1891 foreshadowed Persia-Iran's drift toward and struggle against domination by Western powers, which culminated in the Iranian Revolution of 1979.

- After World War II, the United States often treated Iran as a pawn in its Cold War with the Soviet Union, a circumstance that motivated the United States to bring about the downfall of Mohammad Mosaddegh and to prop up the repressive regime of Mohammed Reza Shah Pahlavi—circumstances that contributed to the hostage crisis of 1979-1980.

The Gulf War

During and after the Iran hostage crisis, many Americans tended to assume that all the countries of the Middle East—except for Israel—were enemies or at least potential enemies. Of course, the reality was—and remains—far more complex. The history of relations between the West and the Middle East has always been a story of shifting alliances and grudging accommodations. Throughout most of the 1980s, this was true of the United States and Iraq. Before America went to war with Saddam Hussein the first time, it helped him fight a war.

The Iran-Iraq War

Revolutionary Iran did not see the United States as its only enemy. For many years, it had disputed with neighboring Iraq over control of the Shatt al-Arab, a 120-mile-long tidal river flowing past the key Iraqi port of Basra and Iran's Persian Gulf port of Abadan. After the 1979 Iranian Revolution, the long simmering dispute exploded into a firefight pitting the new government led by Khomeini against Saddam Hussein, president of Iraq, a secular nation jostling for leadership of the largely Sunni Arab world. Sunnis held most Iraqi government posts, and Saddam was only the most recent postcolonial leader who persecuted his country's Shiites. For Shiite-majority Iran, this was reason enough for a holy war against its neighbor.

In This Chapter

- The United States aids Saddam Hussein against Iran

- Saddam Hussein invades and annexes Kuwait

- The United States leads an international coalition against Iraq

- From Operation Desert Shield to Operation Desert Storm

An Iranian terrorist group, Al Dawa ("the Call"), targeted Saddam for assassination, made an attempt on the life of Iraq's deputy premier, backed civil disturbances in Baghdad, attacked Iraq's embassy in Rome, and ultimately tried to stir Iraqi Shia to outright rebellion. In addition, the Iranian military shelled Iraqi border towns, killing civilians. On September 21 and 22, 1980, Saddam Hussein responded with a combined air and ground assault on Iran.

Brutal Futility

The Iraqi dictator anticipated a quick victory, and with it the downfall of the Khomeini regime. Instead, he ended up handing Khomeini what he sorely needed during the chaotic late stages of Iran's Islamic revolution: an enemy to rally the country around as he solidified his control over the republic. Khomeini called for an all-out military response to Iraqi aggression, and many Iranians rallied to his cause. The resulting conflict would be the longest-running conventional war in the twentieth century, with an enormous price tag of about $1.4 trillion and the sacrifice of hundreds of thousands of lives.

Although the deposed shah of Iran had squandered huge sums on military aircraft and other weapons, the military hardware had been neglected since his downfall and, in any case, the weapons were of insufficient quantity to adequately equip the country's military forces. Khomeini's call to arms mustered an army of two million—but the vast majority were poorly trained (if at all) and ill-equipped. In contrast, Iraq had modern Soviet-built tanks, missiles, and artillery, as well as French-made fighter planes, although its armed forces were at the beginning of the war just one-fourth the size of Iran's.

In effect, the disparity between the two militaries—one huge but inefficient, the other smaller but better trained and equipped—cancelled each other out. The war devolved into an extravagantly bloody stalemate stretching over nearly eight costly years.

Fanaticism and Attrition

Initially the aggressor, Iraq hunkered down behind fixed fortifications built across a 300-mile front. Iranian commanders sent against the fortifications wave after wave of troops, everything from regular army soldiers to teenage Revolutionary Guards and child soldiers. The attackers inflicted heavy losses, but they suffered far heavier losses in what amounted to one desperate suicide attack after another.

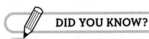 **DID YOU KNOW?**

> Although Iranian law prohibits recruiting children under 16 for military duty, child soldiers were widely used in the Iranian forces during the war with Iraq. Estimates suggest that some 95,000 Iranian troops were under age 16, and in March 1984, a reported 10,000 children were roped together and sent into an Iraqi minefield ahead of assault troops. Unmoved by the age of the human mine detectors, Iraq fired mustard gas shells against the children, a particularly heinous example of that nation's use of chemical weapons in the Iran-Iraq War.

Often, Iran seemed to gain the upper hand, but ultimately neither side proved capable of mounting a decisive offensive. For this reason, combat became a matter of attrition. And it was in attrition that Saddam Hussein found his most effective weapon. He and his people were willing to absorb terrible punishment while forcing the enemy to punch and punch to the point of exhaustion.

The United States Steps In

As the two combatants mauled each other on the battlefield, they also attacked each other's economy. For both sides, this meant hitting oil fields, refineries, pipelines, and especially shipping. Attacks on tankers plying the Persian Gulf threatened to expand the war beyond the Middle East by interfering with international trade as well as global oil shipments.

The U.S. was already inclined to hold Iran responsible for any bloodshed against Americans and American interests in the region. Saddam Hussein and his brutal tactics were repugnant, but the United States, memories of the hostage crisis still fresh, tilted toward Iraq. Pledging to allies that it intended to keep the Persian Gulf open to international trade and safeguard the main sources of oil for Western Europe and Japan, the United States trained Iraqi military personnel on home soil (many at Fort Bragg, North Carolina, home to Special Forces Operations) and supplied custom-made spare parts and ammunition for Iraq's Soviet-manufactured military hardware. Most disturbing of all, the U.S. Department of Commerce licensed the exportation of pathogenic (disease producing), toxigenic (poisonous), and other biological research materials to Iraq. Among these materials were eight strains of anthrax.

U.S. military assistance to Iraq was put to a severe test in May 1987 when an Iraqi fighter plane fired a French-made Exocet air-to-sea missile into the destroyer *USS Stark,* killing 37 sailors and injuring 21. President Ronald Reagan chose to accept Saddam's apology, but used the incident as a basis for reflagging Kuwaiti tankers, giving them temporary U.S. registry and thereby justifying the deployment of armed U.S. Navy escort vessels in local waters.

When the USS *Samuel B. Roberts,* escorting a reflagged Kuwaiti tanker, struck an Iranian mine on April 14, 1988, President Reagan authorized Operation Praying Mantis, an air-sea-land raid against Iranian oil facilities and military installations, which triggered a 10-hour naval battle in which Iran lost three of its major ships and suffered severe damage to a fourth.

 DID YOU KNOW?

> On July 3, 1988, a U.S. Navy cruiser, the USS *Vincennes,* allegedly misidentified an Iranian civil airliner (Iran Air Flight 655) as an Iranian F-14 Tomcat fighter and shot it down. All 290 passengers and crew perished. The U.S. government claimed that the *Vincennes* was operating in international waters and responded to what it feared was an attack. In a 1992 appearance on ABC's *Nightline* news program, U.S. Admiral William J. Crowe revealed that the *Vincennes* was actually in Iranian territorial waters. The American government never apologized for the attack.

Climax and End

After its April 1988 battle with the U.S. Navy, Iran lobbed 60 Soviet-made Scud MRBMs (medium-range ballistic missiles) into Baghdad. The attack did minimal damage and served only to prompt retaliation in kind, as Iraq unleashed more than 200 Scuds against Iranian urban targets. This was quickly followed on April 17, 1988, by a massive ground invasion of Iran. It proved to be the tipping point. Iran agreed to a cease-fire, and both sides, claiming victory, withdrew from the field.

Tactically, the long war ended inconclusively. Strategically, however, Iraq came out ahead. Both nations had suffered catastrophic losses, but Saddam Hussein was convinced that he had prevailed. Moreover, he now believed that the United States, though certainly no friend, saw Iran as a common enemy and would unite with Iraq against it, if doing so meant ensuring the continued flow of oil.

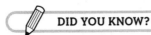

DID YOU KNOW?

Casualty figures vary wildly for the Iran-Iraq War. Iran claimed to have lost as many as 300,000 troops killed, whereas Iraq claimed to have killed 800,000. Iraqi losses have been put between 105,000 and 375,000 killed. Economic losses for Iran have been estimated at $627 billion and, for Iraq, $561 billion.

Saddam on the March

It did not take Saddam long to act on his newfound confidence. On August 2, 1990, he sent 100,000 Iraqi troops and some 500 tanks rolling across the border of Kuwait in an invasion quickly followed by the declared annexation of the country. Opposing the invasion was the entire strength of the Kuwaiti defense forces, just 25,000 men, many of whom withdrew into Saudi Arabia.

U.S. President George H. W. Bush and his Department of State assembled a coalition of armed forces from 28 countries, including Middle Eastern states and nations from all over the world, initially with the defensive purpose of containing further Iraqi aggression, particularly against Saudi Arabia, the richest oil producer in the region.

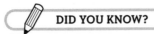

DID YOU KNOW?

Notably absent from the coalition was the United States' strongest ally in the Middle East, Israel. President Bush believed that the presence of Israel would have made it politically impossible for most of the Arab states to sign onto the coalition. At the president's request, Israel bowed out.

The United States took the lead in the coalition and contributed by far the most personnel and equipment. The entire defensive mission was code-named Operation Desert Shield and was assigned to the command of U.S. Army General H. Norman Schwarzkopf.

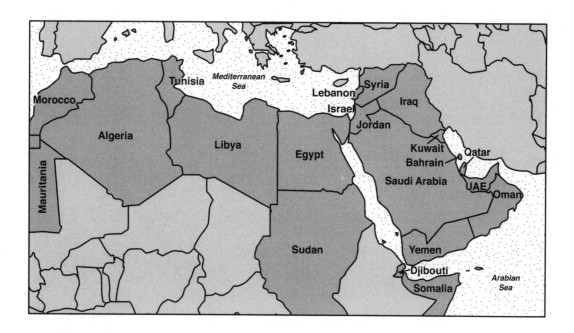

Desert Shield

In the initial onslaught and occupation, 2,793 Kuwaitis were killed and 605 went missing. The cost to Iraq was perhaps 200 soldiers—although many hundreds more were killed by forces of the Kuwaiti underground resistance as the occupation went on.

Build-Up

The United States acted quickly in the defense of Saudi Arabia, initially sending two squadrons of F-15E Eagle fighter-bombers, along with the 2nd Brigade of the 82nd Airborne Division, 2,300 men. Over the following three months, the rest of the 82nd was sent in, along with the 101st Airborne Division (Air Assault), the 24th Mechanized Infantry Division (with the 197th Mechanized Infantry Brigade attached), the 11th Air Defense Brigade (armed with Patriot antimissile missiles), and the 1st and 2nd Marine Divisions.

President Bush understood that most Americans looked upon the Desert Shield build-up with considerable anxiety. The United States military had not engaged in any major operation since the Vietnam War, a long, politically divisive, and demoralizing ordeal that had eroded public confidence in the U.S. military. With considerable persuasive skill, a president who had hitherto seemed colorless, even remote, reengaged the confidence of the American people.

In November, he put that confidence to the test by announcing that the defensive mission would be escalated to an offensive operation to liberate Kuwait if Saddam Hussein refused to end the occupation and renounce the annexation. With this, the president added additional Army and Marine units—the Marines arriving in the Persian Gulf aboard assault ships.

Together with support and logistical units, U.S. numbers reached a peak of 541,425, barely short of the 545,000 deployed at the height of the Vietnam War.

Coalition Forces

In addition to the more than a half-million U.S. personnel, their weapons, and equipment, the coalition included forces, totaling 254,000 personnel, from 24 other nations, some big and many small. Put under the unified command of General Schwarzkopf and designated the U.S. Third Army, the total force consisted of 793,539 troops, with 3,360 tanks, 3,633 artillery pieces, 4,050 APCs, 4,876 fixed-wing combat aircraft, 1,959 helicopters, and 120 warships.

Coalition Air Power

Of exceptional note was the air arm of the coalition forces, which included 80 B-52 bombers, 36 F-111F bombers, 44 F-117A stealth fighter-bombers, 72 F-15E fighter-bombers, 192 A-10 attack aircraft, 288 F-16 fighters, 144 F-15C fighters, and 48 F-4G Wild Weasel antiradar fighter-bombers, all from the U.S. Air Force (USAF). The U.S. Navy dispatched 6 aircraft carriers with a total of 144 F-14 fighters, 120 F-18 attack aircraft, 24 A-7 attack aircraft, and 60 A-6E bombers. The U.S. Marine Corps deployed 120 F/A-18 fighter/attack aircraft and 168 AV-8B attack *"Jump Jets,"* capable of vertical takeoff and landing. Also crucial was the U.S. complement of aircraft for reconnaissance, electronic combat, surveillance and control, tactical airlift, and in-air refueling. Saudi Arabia, Britain, France, and the Gulf States contributed significant air assets as well, making the coalition air armada the most powerful assemblage of aerial strike capability ever assembled.

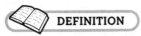 **DEFINITION**

Jump Jet is the nickname of the Harrier strike aircraft originally developed by the British Hawker Siddeley company in 1969 and repeatedly redesigned since. It is a V/STOL aircraft, equipped with directed thrust capability that enables "vertical/short takeoff and landing."

Iraqi Forces

In terms of raw numbers, Iraq had a formidable military. With 1.2 million men under arms in 1990, Iraq had the fourth largest armed force on the planet. In addition to the seven corps of the regular Iraqi army was the elite Republican Guard, consisting of one special forces, two armored, one mechanized, and four motorized divisions.

Iraqi armor totaled 5,500 tanks and included a thousand advanced Soviet-built T-72s and 1,600 T-62s. In addition, the army inventory included 1,000 infantry fighting vehicles, 1,000 armored reconnaissance vehicles, 7,000 APCs, 3,000 towed artillery pieces, 500 self-propelled guns, 200 multiple-rocket launchers, 4,000 antiaircraft guns, 350 long-range surface-to-air missiles (SAMs), 100 surface-to-surface missiles, and 160 armed attack helicopters.

The Iraqi navy had a modest fleet of 43 small warships, but the nation's air force was the sixth largest in the world, with 809 combat aircraft, including some 80 highly advanced MiG-29 fighters.

Impressive as the Iraqi military numbers were, at the moment Operation Desert Shield transitioned into Operation Desert Storm—the offensive phase of the Persian Gulf War—Iraqi personnel strength officially stood at approximately 350,000. Of this number, perhaps no more than 200,000 troops were actually present in the operational area at the outbreak of the coalition attack.

Desert Shield Becomes Desert Storm

The build-up of coalition forces was intended to serve two purposes. One was simply to position forces for war. The other was to intimidate Saddam Hussein into withdrawing from Kuwait. President Bush set January 15, 1991, as a deadline for the withdrawal. Back in August 1990, Saddam had proposed that "all cases of occupation ... in the region be resolved simultaneously" and called for Israel to withdraw from the occupied territories in Palestine, Syria, and Lebanon and for Syria to withdraw from Lebanon. When this was underway, Saddam promised an "arrangement" for the "situation in Kuwait." The United States did not accept this condition and, indeed, did not negotiate any compromise of the demand for Iraq's withdrawal from Kuwait. Thus, when the deadline came and went without Iraqi compliance, Operation Desert Shield became Operation Desert Storm. On January 17, the build-up became war.

 **VOICES**

> Prior to ordering our forces into battle, I instructed our military commanders to take every necessary step to prevail as quickly as possible, and with the greatest degree of protection possible for American and allied service men and women. I've told the American people before that this will not be another Vietnam, and I repeat this here tonight. Our troops will have the best possible support in the entire world, and they will not be asked to fight with one hand tied behind their back. I'm hopeful that this fighting will not go on for long and that casualties will be held to an absolute minimum.
>
> —President George Bush, address to the nation, January 16, 1991

The Air War

As in Israel's remarkably successful Six-Day War against Egypt and other Arab states in 1967, Desert Storm began with an air war. The very first shots were fired by Apache attack helicopters of the U.S. 101st Airborne Division against Iraqi radar posts. From the Persian Gulf, the cruiser USS *Bunker Hill* and the World War II-era battleship USS *Wisconsin* launched a barrage of Tomahawk cruise missiles. Before the first 24 hours of the operation had elapsed, nine naval vessels had launched 106 Tomahawks. Flying too low to be picked up on radar, the Tomahawks took out key Iraqi command and control systems and air defenses.

Coordinating with these strikes, Lieutenant General Charles Horner, the USAF's top commander in theater, sent an array of combat aircraft, ranging from massive B-52G bombers to agile A-10 Warthog tank killers into action. Tactical ground targets were also hit by more AH-64 Apache attack helicopters.

The volume and tempo of the air attacks were intense—about a thousand sorties (attack missions) in the first day, which set the pace for most of the rest of the air campaign, which ended on February 23, 1991.

Few Iraqi aircraft rose to challenge the Allied air assault, and no Allied aircraft was shot down by the Iraqi air force. Iraq lost 141 or more aircraft: 37 (five helicopters, the rest fixed-wing) in aerial combat, the rest on the ground. Saddam Hussein ordered 147 of his jets flown into internment in Iran. These never participated in the war.

The first objectives of the air campaign—achieving air superiority, degrading or suppressing ground-based air defenses, and disrupting command and control capability—were quickly achieved. The next targets were lines of communication and supply, SCUD missile sites, and chemical and nuclear production facilities. After this, the campaign focused on the Republican Guard—the elite core of Iraqi ground forces—and the Iraqi garrison occupying Kuwait.

> **DID YOU KNOW?**
>
> During the war, the United States and other coalition members touted the effectiveness of "smart" weapons in selectively hitting military targets while minimizing civilian casualties. In fact, during 43 days of bombing, the air campaign killed 2,300+ Iraqi noncombatant civilians, including 204 who had taken shelter in a Baghdad air raid bunker on February 13.

Between January 17 and February 23, 1991, coalition air strikes hit about 700 strategic targets in Iraq and Kuwait. As a result of the air campaign, 15 or more divisions of the Iraqi army were reduced by 50 percent each, through casualties and desertions. About half of the ordinance of these divisions was also lost. An additional 10 Iraqi divisions lost at least 25 percent of their strength during the air assault. In all, it is believed that 9,000+ Iraqi military personnel were killed in the air war and 17,000 were wounded. A staggering 153,000 men are believed to have deserted. These losses reduced Iraqi ground strength to 183,000 men as the air war transitioned to the ground campaign.

Scud Attacks

Iraqi armed forces were virtually powerless to defend against the air campaign. In all, just 41 coalition aircraft were lost in combat during 43 days of intensive bombing, and an additional 28 were lost in accidents. USAF Commander Horner had predicted losses of at least 200 aircraft.

The only meaningful response Iraq made to the air campaign was the firing of 40 of its Soviet-made Scud-B missiles against targets in Israel, and 51 against Saudi Arabia and Bahrain.

Like World War II-era German V-2 ballistic missiles, the Scuds were not guided weapons and had a very low accuracy rate. Many impacted without causing great damage. Nevertheless, a Scud hit on a U.S. barrack near Dhahran, Saudi Arabia, killing 28 service members and wounding 102. Those launched against Israel were potentially the most dangerous, since the objective of these attacks was clearly to produce civilian casualties and provoke an Israeli counterattack, which, Saddam hoped, would drive a wedge between the United States and its Arab coalition allies. Despite 4 deaths and the wounding of nearly 300 Israelis in the Scud attacks, Israel—for the first time in its history—declined to retaliate. The coalition held.

For its part, the United States claimed that its ground-based mobile batteries of Patriot antimissile missiles provided a highly effective defense against the Scuds. During the height of the Scud attacks, U.S. authorities claimed to have intercepted at least 50 percent of the missiles in flight. In fact, the number intercepted was certainly close to zero—and, quite possibly, zero.

The Battle of Khafji

The only ground offensive Iraq managed to launch came on January 29, when 2,000 men and 100 armed vehicles attacked Khafji, on the Saudi side of the border with Iraq. The initial attack overran the town, but a brigade of Saudi National Guard, assisted by a Qatari mechanized battalion and supported from the air by USAF A-10 Warthogs and USMC Cobra helicopter gunships and Harrier Jump Jets pushed the Iraqis out within 36 hours. Thirty-two Iraqis were killed, 35 wounded, and 463 taken prisoner. The Saudi counterattacking forces incurred 18 killed, 32 wounded, and 11 missing in action. Friendly fire from an A-10 hit two Marine LAV-25s (light armored vehicles), killing 12 Marines.

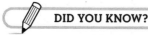 **DID YOU KNOW?**

> As Saddam Hussein failed to mount an effective military defense against the coalition, he resorted to environmental warfare, releasing a massive spill of millions of barrels of oil into the Persian Gulf and setting fire to 514 Kuwaiti oil wells. Managing the spill and putting out the fires required a massive international effort following the war.

100 Hours to Victory

The United States generally commands air superiority in combat, a fact that leads many politicians and much of the public to support air war but resist committing to "boots on the ground." Military commanders understand that air assault is only one component of a war-winning strategy. Typically, massive aerial attack is highly effective at preparing the way for a ground campaign, but rarely does an air war alone compel the enemy to surrender.

Even while the air war was under way, approximately 2,000 U.S. special operations troops—army, Navy SEAL teams, USAF Special Operations personnel, and a small unit of British SAS (Special Air Service) troops—conducted ground-level reconnaissance preparatory to the ground offensive, which began on February 24.

Hold the Enemy by the Nose

The iconic U.S. World War II General George S. Patton Jr. often characterized his favorite combat tactic with the earthy maxim, "Hold the enemy by the nose and kick him in the ass." A version of this describes the overall strategy of the ground campaign in the Persian Gulf War.

On February 24, 17,000 Marines of the 2nd Marine Expeditionary Force (MEF) positioned themselves for an amphibious assault on the Kuwaiti coast. As planned, they did not actually execute the assault, but their demonstration served as bait that diverted a full six Iraqi divisions, pinning them in place as the entire right wing of the coalition army swung forward at high speed against the so-called Saddam Line defending occupied Kuwait. Holding the enemy by its nose, the coalition hit him in the flank.

While the 2nd MEF remained off the coast of Kuwait, units of the 5th MEF and the Joint Forces Command-East (including troops from Saudi Arabia, the UAE, Oman, Kuwait, Qatar, Morocco, Bangladesh, and Senegal) attacked directly along the Kuwaiti coast. To the east, the 1st and 2nd Marine Divisions attacked three Iraqi divisions, which crumbled under the onslaught. North of this action, a combination of Marines, Kuwaitis, Saudis, and Syrians (all from the Joint Forces Command-North) joined the Egyptian II Corps to strike Iraqi defensive positions behind the sand berms of the Saddam Line. These defenses were breached on February 25.

Once the Saddam Line had been broken, Task Force Ripper—composed of the U.S. 2nd Armored Division's 1st "Tiger" Brigade, together with the Marines—stormed into the Kuwait International Airport, on February 27 destroying the 100 T-62 tanks of the Iraqi 3rd Armored Division. A short time later, Kuwait's 35th Armored Brigade triumphantly entered Kuwait City. The Iraqi forces—3 corps, a total of 22 divisions—garrisoning the Kuwait capital fled. Just 77 hours had elapsed since the beginning of the ground offensive.

And Kick Him in the...

While the Marines held the enemy's nose and Kuwait City was being taken back, coalition commander H. Norman Schwarzkopf, far to the west, launched the main attack against the forces of Saddam Hussein.

With stealth and speed, 1,500 tanks and 260,000 troops (VII Corps and the XVIII Airborne Corps) swung in an end run 100 miles beyond the original left flank of the coalition army. In a massive surprise attack, VII Corps wholly enveloped the Iraqi flank.

The enemy was simply rolled up. The combination of speed, intensity, and radar-guided counter-battery fire rendered Iraq's impressive array of artillery useless. Moreover, the Hammurabi Division of Iraq's elite Republican Guard was overwhelmed, its tanks no match for the U.S. Abrams tanks and Bradley fighting vehicles, which were supported from the air by A-10 Warthogs and Apache helicopters firing laser-guided Hellfire missiles.

While VII Corps dealt this hammering, the XVIII Airborne Corps (U.S. 3rd Armored Cavalry Regiment, 24th Mechanized Infantry Division, 101st Airborne Division, and 82nd Airborne Division, plus the French 6th Light Armored Division) hooked farther west and to the north, closing in on the Euphrates River, just 150 miles from Baghdad. This movement first cut off and then surrounded the Republican Guard divisions already under attack.

The 101st then executed the biggest helicopter assault in history, airlifting 2,000 troops, along with howitzers and supplies, 50 miles into the desert to Al Ubayyid, where they set up Cobra Base. From here, the 101st sent 1,000 troops in 60 Blackhawk helicopters to close off Highway Eight, the principal escape route for the Iraqi army between Basra and Baghdad. In the meantime, the French 6th Light Armored Division (with an 82nd Airborne brigade attached) defeated the Iraqi 45th Infantry Division, capturing 2,500 of the enemy and securing the coalition's left flank.

On the right flank of XVIII Airborne Corps attack, the 24th Mechanized Division (with the 3rd Armored Cavalry Regiment attached), under Major General Barry McCaffrey, rushed to Jalibah, turned sharp right toward Basra, and intercepted the Republican Guard 4th Motorized "Al Faw" Division. Two hundred Iraqi tanks were wiped out. By the end of the day on February 27, the VIII Airborne Corps sealed the Iraqi escape route north along the Euphrates. With this, the whole of the Iraqi army, left with nowhere to go, was doomed to defeat.

Saddam Hussein

Saddam (Tikriti) Hussein was born in Tikrit, Iraq, in 1937. Orphaned at nine months, Saddam was raised by an uncle, Khairallah Talfah, an anticolonialist who led an unsuccessful coup d'état and bid for independence in 1941. Without advantageous family connections, young Saddam was refused enrollment in the Baghdad Military Academy and turned instead to membership in the radical Ba'ath (Arab Socialist Renaissance) Party, which had been founded by Michel Aflaq in Syria. The party first supported Abdul Karim Kassim's attempt to overthrow the Iraqi monarchy in 1958, and then turned against Kassim. Saddam, having already killed a communist politician who ran against his uncle in a parliamentary election, volunteered to assassinate Kassim. The attempt failed, and Saddam, wounded in the leg, was forced to flee to Syria. From Syria, he went to Cairo, Egypt, where he studied law.

Saddam Hussein remained in Egyptian exile for three years and, in an effort to confound police files, dropped the name Tikriti (by which he was known at the time), taking as his last name his father's first, Hussein. He returned to Baghdad and organized a secret Ba'ath militia, which, in February 1963, at last succeeded in deposing and executing Kassim. One of Saddam's relatives, Ahmed Hassan Bakr, became the new premier. Five years later (July 17, 1968), Bakr overthrew President Abdul Rahman Arif (who had installed him), and a decade after that, in July 1979, stepped down himself in favor of Saddam Hussein.

Domestically, Saddam's regime was marked by police-state terror. He struggled particularly with the rebellious Kurds, against whom he used sarin nerve gas and other chemical agents on March 16, 1988. Regionally, he consistently behaved as a bellicose and blustering bully. Controlling the world's fourth-largest army, in September 1980 he began an 8-year war against Iran so costly that it nearly led to a military coup in Iraq. In 1990, he invaded and attempted to annex the small, oil-rich nation of Kuwait. His army, air force, and navy were quickly defeated by a United Nations-sanctioned coalition of 28 countries led by the United States (January 17 to April 10, 1991), and he was compelled to withdraw from Kuwait.

Varying degrees of civil unrest followed the ruinous war, especially in outlying provinces (particularly Kurdistan), but Saddam Hussein managed to maintain power and, throughout 1991 and 1992, exhibited bouts of defiance against sanctions levied by the United Nations.

In 2003, President George W. Bush presented a dubious case implicating Saddam Hussein in the 9/11 terrorist attacks against the United States and charging that he was stockpiling weapons of mass destruction (WMDs). Based on this, the American president authorized a military invasion of Iraq, Operation Iraqi Freedom, which became the Iraq War (2003–2011). Aimed at overthrowing Saddam Hussein, the war sent him into hiding. Captured by U.S. forces on December 13, 2003, he was tried by the Iraqi interim government for crimes against humanity and other offenses, found guilty on November 5, 2006, and hanged on December 30.

Cease-Fire

In the run-up to the Persian Gulf War, Saddam Hussein had promised to annihilate any forces arrayed against him. He spoke of emerging victorious from the "Mother of All Battles." In fact, almost everywhere, Iraqi forces offered little resistance and surrendered in such masses that handling the influx of prisoners became a major challenge.

On February 28, after 100 hours of combat, the ground war ended. Twenty-nine Iraqi divisions were knocked out of the war, and more than 63,000 Iraqis had become POWs. Kuwait was liberated. From start to finish, the Persian Gulf War took just 43 days.

 DID YOU KNOW?

> The coalition's greatest fear was that Saddam Hussein would employ chemical weapons, as he had in earlier conflicts. Fears extended to the possibility of biological warfare as well. Although the United States had supplied both chemical and biological materials to Saddam during his war with Iran, neither chemical nor biological weapons were ever used in the brief war.

Two days after the cease-fire, the 24th Mechanized Division encountered and fought a diehard division of Republican Guards at Ramallah. In a 5-hour battle that some have called a blatant exhibition of overkill, the 24th destroyed 600 Iraqi tanks, guns, and APCs. The United States lost a single tank.

An Unfinished Victory

Save for the Israeli victory in the Six-Day War of 1967, few armed exchanges have ended in such an overwhelming tactical victory as the Persian Gulf War. U.S. combat deaths numbered 146, wounded 467, and POWs 21 (all released following the cease-fire). One hundred fifty-one Americans were killed in noncombat accidents, more than were killed in combat—a first in U.S. military history. The other members of the coalition likewise suffered remarkably light casualties. The total of non-U.S. coalition combat deaths was 99, with 434 wounded and an additional 411 troops dying from noncombat causes.

Iraq suffered massive losses, although their precise extent, remarkably enough, remains uncertain to this day. Initially, the United States claimed that as many as 100,000 Iraqis had been killed in combat—yet U.S. forces buried a mere 577 enemy bodies. British estimates were much lower: 40,000 killed and 100,000 wounded. Independently, Greenpeace reported as many as 120,000 Iraqi military personnel killed, with perhaps as many as 15,000 Iraqi civilians killed by aerial bombardment and 4,000 to 16,000 succumbing to starvation, privation, and disease shortly after the war.

Anticlimax

If few victories have been as lopsidedly absolute as that of the U.S.-led coalition against Iraq, even fewer total victories have gained, relatively speaking, so little. The stated objectives of Operation Desert Storm were the liberation of Kuwait and the defense of Saudi Arabia. Both of these objectives were fully accomplished. Many Americans believed, however, that the coalition should have taken full advantage of its victory by removing Saddam Hussein from power.

It is clear that President George H. W. Bush, his national security advisor, Brent Scowcroft, and others believed that the defeat was so total, so costly, and so humiliating that Saddam would be removed by popular uprisings. Indeed, U.S. officials made a number of statements implying American support for such actions. No such support was ever forthcoming, however.

Bush and Scowcroft justified their moderate course in a 1998 memoir, *A World Transformed*, arguing the case that capturing Baghdad and precipitating a coup d'état would have torn apart the coalition, turning the Arab states against the United States and other Western powers, and would have created a war without a foreseeable end (see Chapter 17).

Some 400,000 foreign supporters of the Saddam Hussein regime were expelled from Iraq after the war ended, most of them Palestinians—Yasser Arafat and the Palestine Liberation Organization (PLO) having proclaimed solidarity with Saddam throughout the war.

 VOICES

> I would guess if we had gone in there, we would still have forces in Baghdad today. We'd be running the country. We would not have been able to get everybody out and bring everybody home.
>
> And the final point that I think needs to be made is this question of casualties. I don't think you could have done all of that without significant additional U.S. casualties.... And the question in my mind is, how many additional American casualties is Saddam worth? And the answer is, not that damned many. So, I think we got it right, both when we decided to expel him from Kuwait, but also when the president made the decision that we'd achieved our objectives and we were not going to go get bogged down in the problems of trying to take over and govern Iraq.
>
> —Dick Cheney, secretary of defense under George H. W. Bush, speaking in 1994

Abortive Rebellion

On February 2, 1991, a CIA-run radio station based in Saudi Arabia broadcast to the people of Iraq a message proclaiming that they would soon be liberated from the tyranny of Saddam Hussein.

The broadcast voiced support of the uprisings that accompanied the coalition's war against Saddam Hussein.

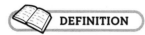

DEFINITION

> Kurds are an Iranian people who speak Kurdish. They number about 30 million and live in Western Asia, inside Iraq, Iran, Turkey, and Syria. Their historic homeland is divided with borders imposed by colonialism, so that they do not represent a majority in any of the countries they live in. The Kurds have fought many governments for increased autonomy and some dream of a viable independent Kurdistan. They have been brutally persecuted, especially by Turkey and Iraq.

In the north, leaders of the Kurds, long oppressed by the Hussein regime and long opposed to it, initiated an uprising in anticipation of U.S. support. Not only did the support fail to materialize, Saddam Hussein used attack helicopters to suppress the Kurds. In this, he exploited a condition of the peace agreement negotiated with the coalition allowing him to use the helicopters to maintain the integrity of his borders.

In the south, dissident Shiites also rose up in armed rebellion, only to be beaten down by Iraqi military forces using artillery and helicopters against major cities. With tragic irony, these urban areas had escaped damage from coalition action, but were now reduced (in some cases) to rubble. In his suppression of incipient rebellions, Saddam Hussein's forces killed an estimated 20,000 to 30,000 Kurds and Shiites by the end of March 1991.

The Least You Need to Know

- During the Iran-Iraq War of 1980-1988, the United States supplied military aid to Saddam Hussein.

- After Saddam Hussein invaded and annexed the neighboring oil-rich country of Kuwait, the United States, in 1990, led a coalition of 28 countries, including Arab states, initially to defend Saudi Arabia (and potentially other countries) against Iraqi aggression and ultimately to force the invaders to withdraw from Kuwait.

- The massive build-up of the coalition's military strength in the Middle East was called Operation Desert Shield and was followed, on January 17, 1991, by Operation Desert Storm, the Persian Gulf War.

- Operation Desert Storm, the Persian Gulf War, began with an air campaign of unprecedented scope and intensity, which essentially broke the Iraqi military, making it vulnerable to defeat in a ground campaign that consumed a mere 100 hours.

- Despite having achieved overwhelming victory, the coalition negotiated a peace that allowed Saddam Hussein to remain in power. His first act after the Persian Gulf War was the brutal suppression of Kurdish and Shiite uprisings against him.

Acts of Asymmetry

"War," the early nineteenth-century military theorist Carl von Clausewitz famously wrote, "is ... a true political instrument, a continuation of political intercourse carried on with other means." We can say nearly the same thing about terrorism: it is violence against civilians used for political purposes.

The Anticolonial Background

What some call terrorism, others consider asymmetric warfare. History is rife with examples. Consider the activity of the Jewish Zealots against the Roman Empire in Judea during the first century C.E. (see "The Jews Go to War Against Rome" in the Prologue). Some regard the Zealots and Sicarii as freedom fighters, whereas others, citing their indiscriminate slaughter of Roman civilians and of Jewish civilians who cooperated with the Romans, classify them as terrorists. The same can be said of the likes of South Africa's Nelson Mandela and Israel's Menachem Begin, both of whom sometimes used extreme violence for political purposes, yet both of whom fought for freedom, and both of whom advocated reconciliation and peace. What cannot be disputed is that they all practiced asymmetric warfare, leveraging whatever strength they had to prevail against a much stronger power.

In This Chapter

- Role of terrorism in politics and religion

- The evolution of terrorist skyjacking

- Suicide terrorist acts

- Osama bin Laden and al-Qaeda

- The 9/11 attacks combine suicide terrorism with skyjacking

- The War on Terror and associated wars begin

The Zealots and Sicarii, like Mandela and Begin, fought against colonial domination by an imperial power. For the early Jews, it was Rome; for Mandela, it was a white-supremacist South African government that treated indigenous blacks as second-class citizens; for Begin, it was the British administration of Palestine.

Indeed, most asymmetric warfare, including that which most people would regard as terrorism, has been waged against colonial domination of one sort or another. This has been especially true in the recent past and most especially among groups centered in the Middle East.

Religious Terrorism or Geopolitical Terrorism?

Many religious groups have employed terrorism in an effort to coerce political change. In 1605, for example, Robert Catesby, an English Catholic, plotted with Guy Fawkes and others to blow up the House of Lords in a scheme to depose the corrupt English monarchy. During much of the twentieth century, Northern Ireland was torn by religious terrorism in acts of violence between Protestants and Catholics. Jews have been both the victims and perpetrators of terrorism. Even Buddhism has spawned the likes of Aum Shinrikyo, the terrorist cult infamous for attacking the Tokyo subway with deadly sarin gas in 1995, resulting in 13 deaths.

Although some so-called religious terrorism is based on strong spiritual belief, much of it has a powerful geopolitical component. In seventeenth-century England and twentieth-century Northern Ireland, for example, Catholics vied with Protestants for political power. In Palestine, Zionist Jews vied with Britain as well as Palestinian Arabs for control of territory on which to create a national homeland.

Numerous events in the recent past—including the attacks against New York and Washington on September 11, 2001—have made the phrase "Islamic terrorism" all too tragically familiar. As with other forms and instances of so-called religious terrorism, terrorism committed by Muslims typically has a powerful geopolitical dimension. This is due in no small part to the fact that Islam was founded as both a religion and a form of political governance. For many modern Muslims, religion is inseparable from politics and from their nation or national aspirations. Moreover, the geopolitical dimension of Islam has made both Islamic revolution and terrorism a means of overcoming colonial domination by non-Muslim foreign imperialist powers. In any case, the overwhelming majority of Muslims denounce terrorism, even—perhaps especially—when applied in the name of Islam. They often brand such acts as "Islamist terrorism"—the word *Islamist* describing a political interpretation of Islam at odds with the majority Muslim perspective, whereas *Islamic* is simply the adjectival form of *Islam*.

Islamist Terrorism

As with most religious terrorism, Islamist terrorism is intended to achieve certain political ends in the name of religion. Acts of Islamist terrorism have occurred worldwide, but the most intense activity in the post-World War II era has occurred in or has emanated from the Middle East and may therefore be considered an integral aspect of the Middle East conflict.

It is possible to find apparent sanction for terrorism in the Quran's "*Sword verse*," which calls on Muslims to "fight those who do not believe in Allah." But it is equally possible to find calls to war and violence in the Jewish Torah and the Christian Bible. Context is everything, and while the Sword verse has been used to justify terrorism as well as to impute to Islam an ethos of violence, the historical context of this passage of the Quran is that the *musharikeen*—polytheists, idolaters, pagans—are a tribe at war with the early Islamic community. The verse calls for nothing more or less than just retribution after an attack. Some Islamist terrorism is the product of a specific interpretation of Islamic doctrine—an interpretation rejected by the majority of Muslims. Most, however, is rooted not in religion but in revolt against imperial, colonial, or quasi-colonial domination by foreign powers.

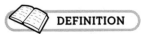 **DEFINITION**

> The **Sword verse** (Ayat al-sayf) is the fifth verse from the *sura* (chapter) of the Quran known as At-Tawba (The Repentence). The verse calls on Muslims to kill "idolaters" or "pagans" or "polytheists" (translations vary) wherever they are found. In some translations, the non-Muslims are to be spared if they repent and convert to Islam. In others, the conversion is to be coerced. The Sword verse is often abused—taken out of context as a blanket call to violence in the name of Islam.

Western Foreign Policy, Islamist Terrorism

Although the early history of Islam was rife with wars of conquest for the purpose of growing the faith, most terrorism perpetrated by modern Muslims is a revolutionary response to acts of imperialist Western foreign policy.

In the late 1940s, Egypt's Muslim Brotherhood attacked British policemen and soldiers, who were part of the apparatus by which the UK occupied Egypt. In Palestine, before the UK ended its mandate, British troops and officials were targeted for terrorist acts by both Arabs and Jews.

The rise of the Palestine Liberation Organization (PLO) and its constituent organizations in the 1960s and 1970s, has been associated with numerous acts of terrorism, including the lethal hostage-taking at the 1972 Summer Olympics in Munich (Chapter 11). Many of these acts (including Munich) had very specific political motives, often including efforts to compel Israel or some other power to release Muslim militant prisoners. That the acts are more political than religious in motivation does not make them any less violent or horrific, especially when perpetrated against children and other noncombatants.

Skyjacking and Suicide

The PLO and its constituents have explicitly sanctioned terrorist acts not in the name of Islam or against Jews, but for nationalist reasons, namely the liberation of their homeland from foreign occupation. The Popular Front for the Liberation of Palestine (PFLP) was founded in 1967 by George Habash, not a Muslim, but a Palestinian Christian, whose politics were Marxist-Leninist. The PFLP specialized in armed attacks against and *skyjacking* of airliners, beginning with the skyjacking of an El Al flight from Rome to Tel Aviv on July 23, 1968, and ending with the skyjacking of a Lufthansa flight from Palma de Mallorca to Frankfurt on October 13, 1977.

Death over Scotland

Whether you call asymmetric tactics guerrilla warfare, insurgent warfare, unconventional warfare, or terrorism, a key advantage practitioners enjoy is the ability to change approaches unexpectedly. The element of surprise—of shock—is often the most terrifying aspect of terrorism.

During the 1960s, skyjacking became an eerily familiar feature of the nightly news. A sign of changing times, the word *skyjacking* was first used in print in 1961. Between 1958 and 1967, there were 48 skyjackings, an average of five per year. In 1968 alone, there were 38 skyjackings, and in 1969, 82, a record that still stands. Between 1968 and 1977, the annual average was 41. Most often, the destination was Fidel Castro's Cuba, to which the United States and a number of other noncommunist nations had prohibited travel. In the single month of January 1969, eight airliners were skyjacked to Cuba.

Skyjacking became very nearly routine. Pilots and flight crews were trained not to resist, but to fly to the destination the skyjacker(s) demanded. The Cubans always returned the aircraft, passengers, and crew. Violence was threatened, but seldom carried out.

Law enforcement, the public, and the media were also trained, albeit inadvertently, to see skyjacking as something of an inconvenience more than a matter of life and death. This is one of the reasons why the detonation of a bomb in baggage aboard Pan Am Flight 103, over the village of Lockerbie, Scotland, on December 21, 1988, was so profoundly terrifying. It violated what had come to seem the prevailing rules of airborne terrorism.

 DID YOU KNOW?

> The sabotage of Pan Am Flight 103, called the Lockerbie Bombing, killed everyone onboard the Boeing 747-121, 243 passengers and 16 crew, while fire and debris resulting from the crash killed 11 people on the ground. The aircraft was en route from Frankfort to Detroit via London and New York City.

The Pan Am bombing created so powerful an effect worldwide that a number of groups rushed to claim responsibility. Among these was the Guardians of the Islamic Revolution (a kind of private Iranian armed force of about 120,000 persons), which said that the bombing was in retaliation for the U.S. Navy shoot-down of Iran Air Flight 655 the year before. Another group, Islamic Jihad Organization (based in Beirut and Baalbek, Lebanon, and closely associated with the Guardians of the Islamic Revolution as well as with Hezbollah), claimed the bombing had been intended to commemorate Christmas. There were two additional claims, including the Ulster Defence League, a purported militant Northern Irish group, and an anonymous claim that Israeli intelligence, the Mossad, had planted the bomb. Authorities tended to believe that the Guardians of the Islamic Revolution were likely perpetrators, although the Popular Front for the Liberation of Palestine-General Command (PFLP-GC) was also suspected.

In 2003, 15 years after the event, Libyan dictator Muammar Gaddafi admitted Libya's responsibility and paid the victim's families a settlement, but denied having personally ordered the bombing. Some believe that Gaddafi actually decided to take the blame in place of Iran, whose government (some assert) was the actual perpetrator.

Martyrdom Weaponized

Skyjacking can be seen as a particularly compelling political leveraging of asymmetrical tactics. Large jet airliners are symbols of national economic and cultural power. To seize an airliner is to expose the limits and vulnerability of that power—to humiliate it. Moreover, because the aircraft and the lives of its occupants are of tangible value, skyjacking can be an effective means of compelling a specific political action, such as freeing political prisoners or delivering ransom money to fund other political or terrorist acts. Finally, because skyjacking attacks more or less random members of the public, it sends a message that a great and powerful nation may be geographically remote from a disputed area (such as Palestine), but its citizens are nevertheless vulnerable to the violence, injustice, and oppression suffered by the people or faction the skyjackers purport to represent.

While most Westerners can understand skyjacking as an effective, if deplorable, asymmetric weapon—in its way, a supremely rational tactic—the suicide attacks that have characterized much Islamist terrorism since the 1980s seem fundamentally irrational and are readily dismissed (if greatly feared) as fanaticism.

In fact, suicide has sometimes been a highly effective political device. The self-immolation of a Buddhist monk, Thich Quang Duc, in the middle of a major Saigon intersection on June 11, 1963, forced South Vietnam's President Ngo Dinh Diem to end at least some of his persecution of Buddhists.

Combining suicide with terrorism can be even more politically effective. Tactically, an assassin or a soldier willing to die in order to achieve his or her objective is very difficult to defeat. Moreover, the emotional effect of giving one's life to a cause can be very powerful. As a political statement, suicide attacks are intended deliver a powerful message in the strongest possible terms: *We will kill your people and ourselves if you do not withdraw from our land.*

In a sense, the suicide attack is the ultimate asymmetric weapon. No matter how powerful a state may be, it can do little or nothing to prevent a person from killing himself or herself, even with explosives that also cause the deaths of many others. And even though the purpose of the suicide attack may be political, the added religious dimension can do much to motivate the doomed attacker. In a religious context, suicide in pursuit of a strategic or political objective is also martyrdom, as many faithful see it, the ultimate act of spiritual devotion.

 DID YOU KNOW?

> The Western media has popularized the belief that suicide attackers (mostly young men) are in part motivated by the belief that, as martyrs to Islam, they will be rewarded in heaven by the gift of 72 virgins. This is a reference to a predominantly Sunni concept of a garden-like heaven, in which (among many other things) men are not only accompanied by their earthly wives, but enjoy the companionship of *houris*, supernaturally beautiful female beings with fair skin and very large eyes. Because they neither menstruate nor become pregnant, they are regarded as virgins. The Quran does not mention the beings, and Sunni tradition holds that they represent divine knowledge rather than carnal gifts for a well-lived Islamic life.

The Path to 9/11

As the bombing of Pan Am Flight 103 was a terrible shock in part because it deviated from the "customary rules" of skyjacking, the devastating attacks of September 11, 2001, were not unimaginable, but *unimagined*. Even though President George W. Bush received on August 6, 2001, 36 days before the attacks, a President's Daily Brief (PDB) headed "Bin Ladin [*sic*] Determined to Strike in U.S.," warning that the al-Qaeda leader posed a threat, no one in the U.S. law enforcement or military community apparently anticipated the possibility that skyjackers would be suicide attackers who would commandeer commercial airliners to use as human-guided cruise missiles, their destructive force a combination of velocity, mass, and highly volatile jet fuel, and their targets including the largest commercial buildings in the world, the headquarters of the U.S. military, and (unsuccessfully) the U.S. Capitol Building or the White House.

Osama bin Laden and al-Qaeda

In more than 255 Islamist terrorist attacks between 1970 and 2014, more than 12,000 people have been killed by a variety of individuals and organizations. From an American perspective, the highest-profile among individual terrorists was that of Osama bin Laden, and the most infamous terrorist organization was the group he founded, al-Qaeda (an Arabic word meaning, roughly, "the Base").

The son of a billionaire Saudi construction magnate, bin Laden was hardly a typical terrorist. But bin Laden's story is a story of religious fanaticism crafted to achieve political purposes by leveraging available resources against the greatest superpower on the planet. It is representative of how terrorism allowed one Saudi Arabian Muslim to project hugely destructive force far beyond the Middle East.

A Terrorist Comes of Age

Osama bin Mohammed bin Awad bin Laden was born in 1957 in the capital of Saudi Arabia, Riyadh, the son of an influential construction magnate with close ties to the Saudi royal family. Of the roughly $5 billion his father made in the construction industry, Osama was destined to inherit about $30 million.

Although young Osama was educated at the Al-Thager Model School, a modern, secular, elite institution catering to the children of wealthy Saudis, and went on to study economics and business administration at King Abdulaziz University, he was raised in the conservative *Wahhabi* Islamic tradition. Even as he took business courses, his consuming interest was the interpretation of the Quran and jihad. He had a particular interest as well in military history and the biographies of military leaders.

 **DEFINITION**

> **Wahhabi** Islam, or Wahhabism, is a branch of Sunni Islam that aspires to reform Islam in order to return it to the fundamental or historical purity associated with the origins of the religion. Wahhabism became a revivalist movement as a result of the teachings of Muhammad ibn Abd al-Wahhab (1703–1792), a Muslim theologian from Najd, in what is now Saudi Arabia.

In the course of his development, bin Laden came to believe that the foreign policy of the United States was responsible for the oppression and killing of a large number of Middle Eastern Muslims. Michael Scheuer, the CIA analyst who long led the hunt for him, believed that bin Laden and his followers "hate us for what we do, not who we are." In short, Scheuer concluded, bin Laden's motives were not chiefly religious, but political and geopolitical. Nevertheless, bin Laden believed that only conservative, fundamentalist Islam would raise the Muslim world above the oppression it suffered. He called for a revival of the caliphate and the restoration of sharia law throughout the Muslim world. Bin Laden rejected modern political solutions for productively uniting Muslims, including pan-Arabism, communism, socialism, and democracy, in favor of what he regarded as a pure form of Islam.

Osama bin Laden's beliefs were hardly new. As we saw in Chapter 6, the Egyptian poet and Islamic theorist Sayyid Qutb, an early leader of Egypt's Muslim Brotherhood, advocated the same position, a combination of Wahhabi Islam applied with the force of jihad, a position often called "Qutbism."

In addition to his political opposition to Americans, Osama bin Laden was an anti-Semite who regarded Jews not merely as political enemies but as morally corrupt, money grubbing, and generally treacherous. A Sunni, bin Laden ranked Shia Muslims with Americans, Jews, and "heretics" as the four great enemies of Islam.

Bin Laden Goes Militant

Osama bin Laden left college in 1979 and moved to Peshawar, Pakistan, on the border with Afghanistan. Living here at the time was Abdullah Azzam, a Sunni scholar who had been among bin Laden's teachers and who became known as the Father of Global Jihad for his advocacy of holy war. Azzam was a supporter of the mujahidin fighting the Soviet occupation of Afghanistan. With Azzam, bin Laden established an organization to fund the mujahidin and to recruit, from around the world, fighters for the struggle in Afghanistan.

The war against the Soviet occupiers was bin Laden's introduction to politically motivated jihad. It also introduced him to Ayman al-Zawahiri, an Egyptian physician who was a member (and, later, leader) of the Egyptian Islamic Jihad and who, together with Osama bin Laden, would found al-Qaeda.

In the late 1980s, the CIA funded Osama bin Laden as part of Operation Cyclone, a covert program to arm and aid mujahidin in their efforts to oust the Soviets from Afghanistan. Britain's former foreign secretary (1997–2001), Robin Cook, has asserted that al-Qaeda itself was actually assembled and trained by the CIA.

The Founding of al-Qaeda

Osama bin Laden went beyond organizing, funding, and recruiting for the Muslim jihad in Afghanistan. He also actively fought in the war, briefly, but long enough to earn a reputation as a hands-on fighter. He disagreed with Azzam over the role of Arab fighters in Afghanistan. Azzam wanted them fully integrated into the Afghani mujahidin, whereas bin Laden wanted them to operate as a separate force under Arab command. He ultimately split with Azzam over this issue and returned to Saudi Arabia in 1990, hailed as a hero of jihad.

No sooner had he returned to Saudi Arabia, however, than he was faced with the royal family's decision to collaborate with the Americans (and other Western powers) in defending Saudi Arabia against the aggression of Saddam Hussein, who had just invaded and annexed Kuwait (Chapter 15). Appalled by the prospect of U.S. troops defiling sacred Saudi territory, Osama bin Laden had an audience with Prince Sultan, the Saudi minister of defense. Bin Laden pledged 100,000 fighters in 3 months, assuring Prince Sultan that he did not need Americans or any other non-Muslim forces. When Prince Sultan asked how his troops would deal with Saddam's missiles and chemical and biological weapons, bin Laden replied, "We will fight him with faith."

Spurned by the Saudi leadership, Osama bin Laden denounced Saudi Arabia's reliance on the U.S. military. The denunciation, in turn, stirred Islamist militants opposed to the Saudi government. Bin Laden was on the verge of arrest when a dissident member of the Saudi royal family arranged for him to go to Pakistan, where he established al-Qaeda as "the Base" for what is best described as a multinational yet stateless paramilitary organization. In 1992, bin Laden and al-Qaeda moved to Khartoum, Sudan.

In Sudan—and Out

In June 1989, a coup in Sudan installed an Islamist government, led by National Islamic Front (NIF) leader Hasan al-Turabi. Turabi had visions of making Sudan the center of a new Middle Eastern caliphate. In the wealthy bin Laden, he saw not only a proven jihadist and a fundamentalist Muslim, but a source of funding.

Initially, bin Laden funded several major infrastructure projects in Sudan, including a much-needed central highway, and was embraced by Turabi. But bin Laden's close association with Ayman al-Zawahiri eventually alienated the Sudanese leader, however. Bin Laden funded Zawahiri's Egyptian Islamic Jihad in various acts of terrorism, culminating in several attempts against the lives of high-ranking Egyptian government officials in 1993. This provoked government reprisals against the Egyptian Islamic Jihad, including the round-up and trials of some 100 members. Undaunted, Zawahiri plotted the assassination of Egyptian President Hosni Mubarak. The collapse of this plot made Zawahiri a hunted man and sent him fleeing to Sudan in 1994.

Mubarak sent undercover agents into Sudan to capture or kill Zawahiri and his top lieutenants. The agents managed to lure the 13-year-old son of an Egyptian Islamic Jihad member into a car, where he was drugged and then sodomized by the agents, who took lurid photographs of the event. In Islamic culture, homosexuality is a grave sin and legal offense. When the agents threatened to send the incriminating photographs to the boy's father, he agreed to cooperate with them. They promptly recruited another 13-year-old boy by the same means and sent both youngsters to spy on Zawahiri and his associates. This assignment was soon escalated to a mission of assassination. The agents armed the boys with a suitcase bomb, which they were to deliver to Zawahiri's quarters, where it would be detonated. Sudanese intelligence agents discovered the bomb, however, and arrested the boys, who were turned over to Zawahiri in return for his promise not to harm them.

In fact, Zawahiri hastily convened a sharia court, tried them, convicted them, and videotaped their execution by shooting. Outraged by the shooting of mere boys, Sudanese officials expelled Ayman al-Zawahiri from the country.

Bin Laden Moves to Afghanistan

A pariah, Ayman al-Zawahiri wandered from place to place, unable to find permanent sanctuary. In the meantime, the Saudi Arabian government at last lost patience with Osama bin Laden. From Sudan, he had been funding not only the Egyptian Islamic Jihad, but also terrorism in Algeria and Yemen. Before the end of 1994, the Saudis revoked his citizenship and ordered his family members, who still lived in Saudi Arabia, to cut off his access to the family fortune. This brought about severe cuts in his own funding of al-Qaeda as well as various projects in Sudan. When the United States applied pressure to Turabi to expel bin Laden from Sudan, the Sudanese leader complied.

Like Zawahiri, spurned throughout the Arab world, Osama bin Laden found a welcome in Afghanistan.

After the Soviets were expelled and the communists defeated, a coalition government was formed, but dissolved by 1992 into lawless chaos amid warring mujahidin factions. In 1994, a group called the Taliban, led by Mullah Mohammed Omar, rose to power in the Kandahar region by subduing the warlords and their warring gangs. The influence of the Taliban—the word comes from the students (*talibs*) originally recruited by Mohammed Omar—grew rapidly, and it became the de facto government of much of Afghanistan.

The strict fundamentalism of the Taliban drew many followers, mostly young men, into Afghanistan. The Taliban ideology meshed with Osama bin Laden's ultra-conservative variant of Wahhabism. He found in Omar a protector, and Omar found in him a well-connected fundraiser.

The child of Saudi wealth and privilege, bin Laden now withdrew into the rugged mountains and caves of Afghanistan's Tora Bora region. Here he reestablished al-Qaeda, setting up camps and extensive training facilities for a new army.

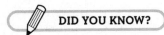 **DID YOU KNOW?**

> For Osama bin Laden, the caves of Tora Bora not only offered practical concealment for himself and for al-Qaeda, it recalled the cave in which the Archangel Gabriel appeared to Muhammad with the revelation from God.

KSM

Ayman al-Zawahiri was a longtime associate of Osama bin Laden. Khalid Sheikh Mohammed met bin Laden in Afghanistan, to which he fled in 1996 to avoid capture by U.S. authorities, who referred to him by his initials, KSM.

Born in Pakistan in 1965, KSM joined the Muslim Brotherhood at 16 and after graduating from high school, came to the United States, where he earned a degree in mechanical engineering at the North Carolina Agricultural and Technical State University in 1986. In 1987, he went to Peshawar, Pakistan, where he joined the mujahidin and attended Azzam's jihadist training camp. After earning a master's degree in Islamic Culture and History from Punjab University in Pakistan in 1992, he moved to Qatar, where he worked as a civil engineer.

He traveled to the Philippines and Bosnia in 1994 and 1995. In the Philippines, he and his nephew, Ramzi Yousef, hatched Operation Bojinka, a plot to destroy a dozen airliners flying between the United States, East Asia, and Southeast Asia. The idea was to coordinate airline timetables so just five men could board a dozen flights in a single day, plant a time bomb on each, and blow them up—with the loss of about 5,000 people. In addition, the pair planned to rent or buy a single-engine Cessna, load it with explosives, and crash it into CIA headquarters.

Yousef tested the plan on December 11, 1994, using a very small explosive device on Philippines Airlines Flight 434, a Boeing 747, bound from Manila to Tokyo. The resulting explosion killed one Japanese passenger but left the aircraft intact, and it was able to make an emergency landing in

Okinawa. As for Yousef, he was apprehended on February 7, 1995. In addition, a warrant was issued in the United States for KSM.

When the fugitive KSM arrived at the Tora Bora headquarters of Osama bin Laden, he spoke not only about the Bojinka idea—the mass destruction of airliners—but also revealed that his coconspirator, Ramzi Yousef, had made the truck bomb used on February 26, 1993, in an attack against Tower One of the World Trade Center in New York City. Loaded with a 1,336-pound explosive device packed with nitrate fertilizer enhanced with hydrogen gas, the bomb was detonated in an underground parking garage and was intended to bring down the tower. The tower did not fall—not in 1993—but the explosion did kill six people (including a pregnant woman) and injured more than a thousand others.

Bin Laden's imagination was stirred by KSM's narrative of the Bojinka and World Trade Center plots. Bin Laden also noted that he also had in mind the U.S. naval bombardment of Lebanon, which knocked down a pair of towers. He and KSM formulated a plan in which, on a single day, skyjackers would commandeer airliners departing from the east and west coasts of the United States and crash them into large symbolic landmarks. Original targets included Chicago's Sears Tower (renamed the Willis Tower in 2009), the densely populated financial district of San Francisco, the White House, the Pentagon—and the World Trade Center. Al-Qaeda, bin-Laden told KSM, would train the required jihadist skyjackers.

 DID YOU KNOW?

> All 19 of the 9/11 terrorists were indeed affiliated with al-Qaeda, but the key operatives received their most important training not in an al-Qaeda camp but in U.S. flight schools, where they learned enough about large passenger aircraft to pilot them into their intended targets. Of the 19 young men, 15 were Saudi citizens, two were citizens of the United Arab Emirates, one was an Egyptian, and one a Lebanese. They were divided into four teams, each led by a skyjacker trained as a pilot. The other team members were given tactical training to aid in subduing crew and passengers. The terrorists were sent into the United States between January 2000 and the early summer of 2001.

Going Public

As the new airliner plot jelled, bin Laden emerged from hiding in Tora Bora. Early in 1997, he granted interviews to a number of London-based newspapers, and in March he was interviewed on television by CNN's Peter Arnett. In these interviews, he accused the Saudi royal family of having renounced and betrayed Islam—an action (in his view) that made them eligible for assassination—and he openly declared war on the United States for crimes against Muslims, including support of Israel and defiling the land of the Prophet with troops during the Persian Gulf War. Bin Laden promised that his war would drive the United States out of the Middle East, and he made it clear that American civilians were legitimate targets in the coming conflict.

Later in 1997, bin Laden funded the so-called Luxor massacre, a November 17 attack on Deir el-Bahri (Hatshepsut's Temple), a major archaeological site and tourist attraction near Luxor, Egypt, in which 62 people, mostly tourists, were killed.

The media exposure and the Luxor attacks were too much for Mullah Mohammed Omar, who feared reprisals. Bin Laden assured him that the publicity was at an end.

In fact, it had just begun. In May 1997, Ayman al-Zawahiri rejoined Osama bin Laden, this time in Afghanistan, and in February 1998, the pair jointly signed a *fatwa* declaring the killing of North Americans and their allies a duty for every Muslim. In publicly announcing the fatwa, bin Laden added that Americans would prove to be "very easy targets." Early in the summer of 1998, bin Laden and Zawahiri openly organized an al-Qaeda conference, and on August 7, 1998, al-Qaeda operatives detonated truck bombs in U.S. embassies in Dar es Salaam, Tanzania, and Nairobi, Kenya, killing a total of 224 and injuring more than 4,000. The bombings earned Osama bin Laden a place on the FBI's Ten Most Wanted list.

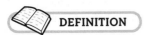 **DEFINITION**

> A **fatwa** is a legal opinion issued by a recognized jurist or mufti (Sunni scholar qualified in Islamic law) relating to Islamic law. Since bin Laden was not recognized as a jurist or mufti, the vast majority of Muslims regarded his fatwas as illegitimate.

In December, a month after the embassy bombings, the CIA's Counterterrorist Center reported to President Bill Clinton that al-Qaeda was preparing to attack the United States itself, directly, and was training personnel to skyjack aircraft. Late in 2000, Clinton security advisor Richard Clarke announced that bin Laden had planned a triple attack, which was to be carried out on January 3, 2000, against a hotel and tourists in Jordan, against the U.S. Navy destroyer *The Sullivans* in Yemen, and against an unnamed target in the United States itself.

The so-called Millennium Plot was detected and foiled before it could be carried out. Later in the year, however, on October 12, 2000, suicide attackers maneuvered a small craft close to the port side of the guided-missile destroyer USS *Cole* as it was being refueled in the port of Aden, Yemen, and detonated the explosives loaded aboard their boat. The resulting blast blew a 40-by-40-foot gash in the hull of the 505-foot, 8,900-ton *Cole*, killing 17 sailors and injuring 39 others. Al-Qaeda quickly claimed responsibility.

A Bright Blue Morning

At 8:45 A.M. (EDT) on the morning of September 11, 2001, a Boeing 767 passenger jetliner (later identified as American Airlines Flight 11 out of Boston) exploded into the north tower of New York's World Trade Center.

Within three minutes, television news images of the catastrophe had interrupted all regular broadcasting. Millions were drawn to television screens, and so millions bore witness at 9:03 to the impact of a *second* 767 (United Airlines Flight 175), this time into the World Trade Center's south tower.

President George W. Bush was not watching television during the attacks, but was in a Sarasota, Florida, classroom reading aloud from *The Pet Goat*. The president's chief of staff, Andrew Card, entered the classroom and whispered news of the second impact into the president's ear. TV news video from the Sarasota classroom show the change in his expression, but the commander in chief continued the reading lesson as Card withdrew.

In the meantime, at the White House, Secret Service agents were evacuating Vice President Dick Cheney and his staff. It was 9:30 before the president appeared on television to announce that the nation had suffered "an apparent terrorist attack."

There would soon be more.

Just 13 minutes after the president's announcement, at 9:43, a Boeing 757 (American Airlines Flight 77) tore into the Pentagon, and 22 minutes later, the south tower of the World Trade Center collapsed into itself, 110 stories of steel, concrete, and humanity seemingly swallowed into the earth itself. Five minutes later, another 757, United Airlines Flight 93, ploughed into the soil of rural Somerset County, Pennsylvania. Eighteen minutes passed, and the north tower of the World Trade Center gave way. TV news anchor Brian Williams managed a laconic epitaph: "The World Trade Center is no more."

 VOICES

> Clandestine, foreign government, and media reports indicate bin Laden since 1997 has wanted to conduct terrorist attacks in the U.S. Bin Laden implied in U.S. television interviews in 1997 and 1998 that his followers would follow the example of [1993] World Trade Center bomber Ramzi Yousef and "bring the fighting to America."
>
> —Presidential Daily Briefing, August 6, 2001, titled "Bin Laden Determined to Strike in U.S."

The Enemy Identified

The perpetrators of the horrific crimes of September 11, 2001, seemed well on their way to exposure even before the day was over. The media reported that the aircraft downed in Pennsylvania had been targeted on the White House or the United States Capitol. (It was later surmised that passengers rushed the skyjackers, who either lost control of the plane or deliberately crashed it.) Shortly after this, it was revealed that all four planes had been seized by suicide attackers, members of al-Qaeda, led by Osama bin Laden, and already well known to the U.S. intelligence community.

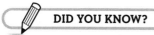 **DID YOU KNOW?**

> Casualties in the World Trade Center attack were 2,893 killed. An additional 189 were killed in the attack on the Pentagon, and 44 passengers and crew members died in the Pennsylvania crash. The attacks were condemned by most of the world's governments, including those of Islamic nations, and triggered anti-Bin Laden protests among millions of Muslims in mass memorials in Tehran, Cairo, Islamabad, Jakarta, and Istanbul.

New Wars, New World

President George W. Bush never called the attacks of 9/11 crimes or even crimes against humanity. Instead, in a speech on September 12, he called them "the first war of the twenty-first century" and on September 20, in an address to a joint session of Congress, proclaimed the United States to be on a war footing, pledging that the battle would now be taken to the terrorists.

In his address, the president characterized al-Qaeda as "a collection of loosely affiliated terrorist organizations" and compared its role in terrorism to that of the mafia in crime. But al-Qaeda's goal, he said, "is not making money; its goal is remaking the world—and imposing its radical beliefs on people everywhere…. The terrorists' directive commands them to kill Christians and Jews, to kill all Americans, and make no distinction among military and civilians, including women and children."

In his September 20 address, President Bush identified Osama bin Laden as al-Qaeda's leader, explained that al-Qaeda personnel "are linked to many other organizations in different countries, including the Egyptian Islamic Jihad and the Islamic Movement of Uzbekistan," and that there "are thousands of these terrorists in more than 60 countries … recruited from their own nations and neighborhoods and brought to camps in places like Afghanistan, where they are trained in the tactics of terror. They are sent back to their homes or sent to hide in countries around the world to plot evil and destruction."

 **VOICES**

> If inciting people to do that is terrorism, and if killing those who kill our sons is terrorism, then let history be witness that we are terrorists.
>
> —Osama bin Laden, October 2001

What immediately came to be called a "War on Terror" quickly spawned two additional wars. "The leadership of al-Qaeda has great influence in Afghanistan and supports the Taliban regime in controlling most of that country," President Bush told Congress and the American people. With this, he addressed the Taliban directly, demanding the delivery "to United States authorities all the leaders of al-Qaeda who hide in your land"; the closure of "every terrorist training camp in Afghanistan"; the surrender of "every terrorist, and every person in their support structure"; and full U.S. "access to terrorist training camps, so we can make sure they are no longer operating." The president warned the Taliban that they must "hand over the terrorists, or … share in their fate."

This was the beginning of the U.S. war in Afghanistan, to which would be added, beginning in 2003, a new war in Iraq.

They were three new wars, wars fought in what many people called a "new world," a "post-9/11 world," a world in which new laws quickly passed in the name of defending American freedom and security posed stern new challenges to those very things.

The attacks of 9/11 transformed the cityscape of lower Manhattan and forever changed the lives of some 3,000 families who had, in a matter of seconds, lost loved ones. The attacks also changed the American political, ideological, and diplomatic landscape. For how long, we do not yet know.

The Least You Need to Know

- Although many Westerners dismiss Islamist terrorism as religious fanaticism, it is more accurately a variant of asymmetric warfare with Islamic cultural motifs and is used to achieve political purposes, usually directed against Western powers perceived as imperialist as well as anti-Islam.

- Skyjacking and suicide attacks emerged as the hallmarks of Islamist terrorism; in the 9/11 attacks on the United States, these two tactics were combined in a new form of attack, one entirely unanticipated by American authorities.

- Although Osama bin Laden and his al-Qaeda organization are not "typical" of Islamist terrorism, they are—for Westerners, and for Americans especially—representative of the most extreme terrorist tactics employed against the perceived spiritual and political enemies of Islam.

- The 9/11 attacks motivated three American wars—the War on Terror, the anti-Taliban war in Afghanistan, and a new war in Iraq—and prompted sweeping legislation to expand the surveillance and investigative powers of the federal government, as well as the discretionary military authority of the president.

The Wars in Afghanistan and Iraq

President George W. Bush did not hesitate, the day after the 9/11 attacks, to define them as "the first war of the twenty-first century." And almost immediately, politicians and political pundits drew parallels with December 7, 1941, when the Japanese navy bombed Pearl Harbor, Hawaii.

Both attacks caught the nation unawares, but the 1941 attack was by the armed forces of a sovereign nation, whereas the 2001 attacks were carried out by 19 men at the behest of a Saudi-born millionaire running a terrorist organization from an Afghan cave. President Franklin D. Roosevelt asked Congress to declare war on Japan, while President Bush was obliged to declare war not on a nation, but on "terror."

Afghanistan, 2001: The Case for War

The problem with declaring war on "terror" is that "terror," unlike a nation, is difficult to identify and define. In his September 20, 2001, speech to Congress, President Bush defined the Taliban of Afghanistan as the protector, ally, and enabler of Osama bin Laden and al-Qaeda, both of which constituted a source and nexus of terrorism. In this way, the president sought to identify a quasi-national entity against which to wage war.

In This Chapter

- Afghanistan and Iraq: wars of choice or necessity?

- The role of the Northern Alliance

- The path to war in Iraq

- Saddam is toppled and Iraq descends into civil war

- Uncertain outcomes after 13 years of war in Afghanistan and Iraq

In terms of planning and executing a war, the Taliban, a political entity, made a better target than "terror." But the U.S. military still faced a major problem. Afghanistan was a rugged, forbidding, and underdeveloped country. The economic might of the United States had built a military equipped with weapons capable of ending civilization itself. In Afghanistan, most people lived in isolated villages.

"The United States respects the people of Afghanistan—after all, we are currently its largest source of humanitarian aid," President Bush explained, "but we condemn the Taliban regime." But that regime was in hiding, and the terrorists it supported, like bin Laden, were likewise lodged in caves and other all-but-invisible places. In planning a military campaign against the Taliban, the biggest problem the U.S. military faced was how to avoid what President Bush and his advisors called "pounding sand," making an ineffective show of force.

Goliath Gets Help

In responding to the 9/11 attacks, the United States found itself starting down the problem Goliath faced when he confronted the young shepherd David. Goliath was a giant, elaborately armed and armored. David was a lad with a slingshot. The Old Testament story may be the first account of the leverage possible in asymmetric warfare. Sometimes, a giant's strength is no asset and may even be a liability.

In the days following 9/11, while U.S. military forces were being deployed to strategic positions from which to enter Afghanistan, Bush administration officials were highly successful in securing the support of many nations in prosecuting a "war on terror."

From all appearances, the 9/11 attacks, remarkably successful from a tactical point of view, were nevertheless a strategic failure in that they turned the world—even much of the Islamic world—against the attackers. Even Pakistan, which shares a border with Afghanistan and had supported the Taliban regime there, agreed to allow U.S. aircraft to fly over its air space and to use certain air-base facilities. Yet more remarkable, Iran, implacably hostile since the fall of the shah and the hostage crisis of 1979–1981, likewise permitted flyovers and even offered to accept emergency military landings. Of all the nations in the region, only Saddam Hussein's Iraq refused cooperation.

President Bush justified the war against the Taliban primarily as a means of attacking terrorists where they lived and trained. On September 17, 2001, he told a television interviewer, "I want justice. And there's an old poster out West, I recall, that says, 'Wanted: Dead or Alive.'" The point of the war, it seemed, was very simple: kill or capture Osama bin Laden and his "gang." If this meant destroying the Taliban, so be it.

Big Weapons

The war did not start out looking like a manhunt in the Old West, however. It began with an air attack against Taliban targets on October 7, the United States using B-1 bombers and the even more advanced B-2 stealth bombers in addition to veteran B-52s. The heavy bombing attacks were supplemented by cruise missile launches.

The air attacks continued over several nights, until it was certain that Afghan's air defenses had been destroyed, giving U.S. and British aircraft—for the British had agreed to contribute major military assets to the war—absolute air supremacy. Once ground-based antiaircraft defenses had been neutralized, the B-1s, B-2s, and B-52s, all of which flew at altitudes above the range of these defenses, were replaced by strike aircraft capable of operating much lower. The low-altitude raids were also conducted by day rather than under cover of night, so that aircrews could actively seek and destroy tactical targets—*targets of opportunity*—including vehicles, aircraft on the ground, and troops.

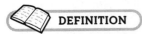 **DEFINITION**

> **Targets of opportunity** are those enemy personnel, vehicles, and weapons encountered in the course of operations and attacked wherever and whenever they are encountered. The attacks are executed ad hoc, rather than planned in advance.

The Anglo-American campaign took great pains to target military objectives exclusively, including al-Qaeda terrorist camps and Taliban installations. Not only were efforts made to avoid inflicting civilian casualties, U.S. Air Force (USAF) cargo transports flew over villages to drop food packages and other aid supplies—life-sustaining basics often unavailable under Taliban rule. The Anglo-American objective was not only to demonstrate both care and concern for the Afghan people, but to destabilize the Taliban by eroding popular support for it.

By destroying the Taliban, or at least driving it out of Afghanistan, President Bush and his advisors hoped to remove Afghan-based support for al-Qaeda and other terrorist enterprises. Cut off and exposed, Osama bin Laden and his followers would become more vulnerable targets.

Fighting an Asymmetric War

As was not always true during the Vietnam War in the 1960s and 1970s, U.S. military leaders understood that, in Afghanistan, they were fighting an asymmetric war. Without question, the U.S. military was far more powerful than the Afghan military, whose conventional forces consisted of no more than an estimated 45,000 poorly equipped troops. The far more formidable adversaries were the irregular forces associated with the terrorists. American leaders were well aware that the Afghani mujahidin had defeated the might of the Soviet Union. Those among these leaders who were readers of history also knew that Afghan resistance had, in the nineteenth century, defeated British imperial efforts to expand its Indian empire into Afghanistan. In fact, Afghanistan had long been known as the "Graveyard of Empire."

The initial air strikes were solely intended to prepare the way for action on the ground, and the Americans grasped that this ground war would have to be unconventional. On October 20, a mere 100 U.S. Special Forces troops raided Taliban facilities and obtained intelligence-rich Taliban documents. It would be the first of many similar operations—small, precisely targeted, aimed at disrupting and unraveling a network of individual terrorists.

The Special Forces leveraged their presence in-country by making common cause with the so-called Northern Alliance. A loose military front originally organized in the late 1990s to oppose the Taliban, the Northern Alliance consisted of ethnic groups, including Tajiks, Uzbeks, Hazaras, and Pashtuns. In forging a partnership with this assemblage, the Special Forces operators recognized that Afghanistan was far less a modern nation-state than a collection of tribal and ethnic groups, whose trust and partnership would have to be earned. In 2001, the Northern Alliance fielded a guerrilla army of about 15,000, which the United States helped to supply and sustain.

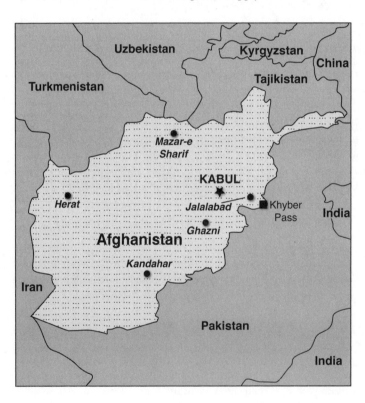

Overthrowing the Taliban

During November, U.S. and Northern Alliance attacks against Taliban positions made encouraging progress. On November 12, Mazar-e Sharif was captured. Home of the Blue Mosque—a sacred Muslim site—the city was also a strategic gateway between Afghanistan and Taliban sympathizers in Pakistan as well as a supply route into Uzbekistan.

The nature of the American troops participating in this victory is telling. They were a collection U.S. Special Forces, CIA paramilitary operators, and a USAF Combat Control Team (forward controllers who coordinate precision air strikes from the ground). The battle for Mazar-e Sharif used advanced close-support aircraft as well as warriors mounted on horseback.

The Taliban's loss of Mazar-e Sharif was a severe blow to its power, opening the way to the occupation of the Afghan capital city of Kabul by Northern Alliance troops on November 13, followed by the fall of Kunduz, a northern Taliban stronghold, on November 25–26.

 DID YOU KNOW?

> Ostensibly a U.S. ally, Pakistan frequently acted against American interests in the Afghanistan war. Shortly before the Taliban surrendered at Kunduz, Pakistani aircraft flew into the city to evacuate Taliban troops and intelligence personnel stationed there. Allegedly, this "Airlift of Evil" (as Americans called it) evacuated 5,000 people, Taliban members as well as al-Qaeda fighters.

By the end of November, only Kandahar remained in Taliban hands. It fell to U.S. Marines in December. Yet despite these rapid victories, Osama bin Laden and many other significant al-Qaeda figures remained at large, pursued into mountainous Tora Bora by a combination of Northern Alliance-affiliated tribal militia, U.S. Delta Force troops, and members of British Special Forces. By January, the militarized caves of Tora Bora had been cleared by a combination of air strikes and ground operations, and some 200 al-Qaeda fighters were captured. But the leadership, including bin Laden, remained at large.

On December 20, 2001, the United Nations created the International Security Assistance Force (ISAF), which was initially tasked with stabilizing Kabul and the surrounding area. Consisting of troops from 46 countries—the U.S. supplied half the force—ISAF was commanded by an American general. As a UN-sanctioned coalition, ISAF did much to keep the war in Afghanistan from looking like a mission of specifically American vengeance.

The Anaconda Strikes

After the removal of the Taliban from Kabul and other strongholds, a pro-Western interim government was installed in Afghanistan under the "chairmanship" of Hamid Karzai, a prominent Afghan political figure selected by a committee (a *loya jirga*) of Afghani leaders.

Recognizing that the Taliban, though on the run, was regrouping in the Shahi-Kot Mountains southeast of Gardez, a combination of U.S. and Afghan forces launched Operation Anaconda on March 2, 2002. These were hit-and-run raids on individual Taliban caves and bunkers. Anticipating that the mission would involve mopping up an essentially defeated (that is, retreating) force, the Americans and their allies were shocked to discover that the numbers of Taliban guerrillas in the mountains were actually increasing because of a stream of reinforcements flowing in from Pakistan and the tribal areas of Waziristan.

As of summer 2014, Operation Anaconda is still ongoing, with U.S. troops augmented by a full complement of ISAF units and by NATO forces.

 **DEFINITION**

> **Loya jirga** is a Pashto word meaning "grand assembly" or "grand council." In traditional Afghan tribal politics, such a mass meeting is convened whenever a major collective decision must be made.

Taliban Resurgent

Was the Taliban on the run in 2002? Absolutely. Was it in on the ropes? No. In fact, a number of Taliban bases were reconstituted throughout the country, and the Taliban guerillas radically changed their tactics. Instead of mounting major offensives, they now focused on attacking isolated ISAF and NATO outposts using very small units armed with rockets. Roads were mined with improvised explosive devices (IEDs).

A Change in Priority

After making significant inroads into the Taliban presence, the Bush administration shifted priorities in 2003. The initial justification for Operation Enduring Freedom, as the war effort in Afghanistan was originally called, was to "get" bin Laden and to eliminate Taliban sources of terrorists. But even after dislodging the Taliban government and scattering its forces, the Islamist terrorist presence not only persisted, it was steadily reinforced. What's more, Afghan government forces repeatedly proved unreliable, and instances of so-called *green-on-blue fratricide*—attacks by regular Afghani military forces on Americans fighting side by side with them—became distressingly frequent. Also frequent were disputes with Hamid Karzai, who was (understandably) eager to avoid being seen as an American puppet.

 **DEFINITION**

In a military context, **fratricide** is an attack on one's ally, comrade, or "brother in arms." In the Afghanistan war, green-on-blue fratricide referred to attacks on U.S. Army troops (whose dress uniforms are blue) by Afghani soldiers (clad in green uniforms) supposedly allied with them. By 2012, green-on-blue fratricide accounted for 15 percent of coalition deaths.

All of these difficulties tended to reduce U.S. public and political enthusiasm for the war in Afghanistan and helped prompt a turn to another combat theater, another country, another enemy.

Purple Thumbs

In 2005, Afghanis could measure their success against the Taliban by proudly holding up their thumbs, purpled by ink used to mark those who had voted (and were therefore ineligible to vote a second time) in the country's first free elections ever. The elections returned Karzai to office, now as a popularly elected president.

Despite having conducted the first free, democratic elections in its history, Afghanistan continued to be roiled by war, as no U.S., ISAF, or NATO tactical victory proved strategically decisive.

Hamid Karzai

Hamid Karzai was born in 1957, in Karz, a village near Kandahar, Afghanistan. The grandson of Khair Mohammad Khan, who had fought in Afghanistan's war of independence (the Third Anglo-Afghan War, 1919) and had served as deputy speaker of the senate, Karzai was the son of Abdul Ahad Karzai, a tribal elder prominent on the national political scene. Abdul Karzai served as the deputy speaker of the parliament during the 1960s.

Hamid Karzai was educated through high school in Afghanistan, and then traveled to India in 1976 as an exchange student, where he earned a master's degree in international relations and political science from Simla University in 1983.

After obtaining his degree, Karzai traveled to Pakistan, where he joined the mujahidin resistance against the Soviet occupation of Afghanistan. In 1985, he traveled to Lille, France, where he took a three-month journalism course before returning to Peshawar, Pakistan, as director of information and, later, deputy director of the Political Office of Afghanistan's National Liberation Front.

In 1989, after a transitional mujahidin government was formed in Afghanistan, Karzai was appointed director of the Foreign Relations Unit in the Office of the President of the Interim Government. In 1992, following the establishment of the permanent mujahidin government, he became deputy foreign minister.

After civil war commenced among rival mujahidin factions in 1994, Karzai resigned and worked to create a national Loya Jirga (Grand Council). In the meantime, in August 1999, his father, Abdul Ahad Karzai, was assassinated in Pakistan by the Taliban. This determined Hamid Karzai to work to coordinate efforts to overthrown the Taliban.

Karzai's leadership in the anti-Taliban movement prompted United Nations members participating in a conference on Afghanistan held in Bonn, Germany, to elect him chairman of the Interim Administration of Afghanistan on December 5, 2001. He continued to lead the interim government until October 9, 2004, when he was officially elected to a five-year term as president. He was reelected for a second term in 2009.

A personally distinguished figure, fluent in Pashtu, Dari, Urdu, and English, Karzai has often differed with U.S., NATO, and ISAF leaders in his country. Some have accused him of nepotism—he has six brothers and one sister—and his family of corruption.

Iraq, 2003: The Case for War

The United States commenced its second war against Iraq on March 19, 2003, with an air strike on a Baghdad bunker believed to be sheltering Saddam Hussein. A few months later, on September 6, with the new war well under way, *The Washington Post* published the result of a poll in which nearly 7 out of 10 (69 percent) Americans expressed their belief that Saddam Hussein was "personally involved" in the 9/11 attacks. The majority included Democrats as well as Republicans, and, most important, the majority included President George W. Bush.

While he and his administration (most enthusiastically, Vice President Dick Cheney) based the case for war on Saddam Hussein's supposed involvement in 9/11, even more important was the president's assertion that Hussein and Iraq were sponsors of terrorism who posed an ongoing threat to the world because of a secret stockpile of "weapons of mass destruction" (WMDs), a category that includes nuclear (fission- or fusion-based), radiological (a conventional bomb loaded with radioactive material), biological, and chemical weapons or, indeed, any weapon capable of inflicting mass casualties.

Yet, the evidence for Saddam's involvement in 9/11 was always slim and any WMD stockpiles ultimately proved nonexistent. Even more than a decade after the war began, it remains impossible to declare with certainty just what moved the Bush administration to go to war against a country that had, in truth, committed no overt act of war against the United States.

Many journalists have nevertheless tried. Seymour Hersh (in *Chain of Command: The Road from 9/11 to Abu Ghraib*, 2004) and Bob Woodward (in *Plan of Attack*, 2004) are among those who believe that the administration of George W. Bush entered the White House in 2001 determined to "finish" the war with Iraq that (in the administration's view) had been left incomplete in 1990–1991 by the administration of Bush's father, George H. W. Bush. Whatever the motive, most critics of the Iraq War condemn it as a war of choice rather than a war of necessity, and they question whether choosing to go to war with Iraq produced any net benefits.

The Neocon Influence

George W. Bush and his inner circle—including Vice President Dick Cheney; Secretary of Defense Donald Rumsfeld; Douglas Feith, under secretary of defense for policy from July 2001 to August 8, 2005; and Paul Wolfowitz, deputy secretary of defense from May 2001 to December 2004—were often labeled neoconservatives—"neocons" for short. At the time, this label described advocates of a strongly interventionist foreign policy, which extended to the use of military force to remove and replace autocratic regimes with democratic ones. The theory was that democratic regimes would necessarily be friendly to the interests of the United States. A maxim popular at the time was, "Democratic countries do not go to war with democratic countries."

Woodward, Hersh, and many others claim that the 9/11 attacks provided the neocons with a pretext for a war they had actually wanted for some time to fight. Some, including journalist James Bamford (*A Pretext for War: 9/11, Iraq, and the Abuse of America's Intelligence Agencies,* 2004) argued that the administration manipulated intelligence information (especially intelligence concerning Iraq's purported possession of WMDs) to make the case for war. Others have argued that the war grew out of a more positive and even imperative vision of American global moral and political leadership. Such authors as the late Christopher Hitchens (*A Long Short War: The Postponed Liberation of Iraq,* 2003) asserted that the democratization of the Middle East was vital to the stability of the region and the world and was necessary for the survival of democracy itself.

The Religious Dimension of the Iraq War

In prosecuting the War on Terror and the war in Afghanistan, the Bush administration was careful to imply no religious agenda of any kind, other than a respect for all faiths, Islam among them. It is nevertheless true that President Bush, stepping off Marine One (the presidential helicopter) on September 16, 2001, described the war on terrorism to reporters as "this crusade." The word *crusade,* of course, was freighted with religious connotations, evoking the medieval wars fought between European Christians and Middle Eastern Muslims. Almost certainly, it was a slip of the tongue; in the many centuries since the Crusades, the word has lost its religious overtones for most Westerners. But many in the Middle East seized on the word as proof that the American president was intent on fighting a *Christian* jihad. This interpretation was undoubtedly enhanced by President Bush's self-proclaimed identity as a born-again Christian and the fact that his election had been enthusiastically supported by America's conservative Christian right.

For his part, President Bush portrayed both the wars in Afghanistan and Iraq as a "preemptive strike." He frequently spoke of fighting the terrorists "over there" so that Americans would not have to fight them "here," in the United States. The administration never advanced a religious agenda, but promoted the Iraq war as a means of ensuring America's security, a way to avoid future 9/11s. Yet, doubtless, many who supported both the president and the war did see it as a religious struggle, a defense of Christianity against Muslim terrorists bent on destroying it. Like it or not, the United States was embarking on a new war of religion.

States like these [Iraq, Iran, and North Korea], and their terrorist allies, constitute an axis of evil, arming to threaten the peace of the world. By seeking weapons of mass destruction, these regimes pose a grave and growing danger.... The price of indifference could be catastrophic.

—President George W. Bush, State of the Union Address, January 29, 2002

The President Addresses the UN

President Bush repeatedly expressed his willingness to go to war in Iraq, even if the United States had to act alone. Nevertheless, he appeared before the United Nations General Assembly on September 12, 2002, to present to the world his case against Saddam Hussein's Iraq. Ultimately, he secured approval of Resolution 1441 (November 8, 2002), directing Iraq to comply with its disarmament obligations and to prove it had divested itself of all WMDs.

The president did not wait for passage of the resolution before he obtained from the U.S. Congress, on October 11, 2002, authorization to use military force against Iraq.

WMDs

The appeal to the United Nations was by no means a mere formality. We may think of the United Nations as primarily a peacemaking and peacekeeping organization, but it is also a body founded to uphold the right of all nations to sovereignty and self-defense. If the president could persuade the General Assembly that Iraq presented a threat to U.S. as well as collective security, war against Iraq would be justified by international law.

Saddam Hussein had already shown himself willing and able to use mustard gas on a mass scale. He had deployed a chemical WMD against his own people in the 1980s. By making the case that Iraq *currently* possessed a stockpile of chemical, biological, and/or nuclear weapons, the Bush administration would present a prima facie case for self-defense in attacking Iraq preemptively.

When he addressed the UN in September 2002, the president had no hard evidence to support his case. On January 28, 2003, however, when he delivered the State of the Union Address to a joint session of Congress, he declared that the "International Atomic Energy Agency confirmed in the 1990s that Saddam Hussein had an advanced nuclear weapons development program." He went on to declare: "The British government has learned that Saddam Hussein recently sought significant quantities of uranium from Africa."

This 16-word sentence was *the* show stopper in the address. Initially shocking and compelling, it subsequently came under intense scrutiny from the press and from government officials outside of the Bush administration. These skeptics pointed out that the British "evidence" cited had actually been discredited by U.S. intelligence agencies—and not *after* Bush delivered the State of the Union Address, but before. In fact, critics revealed evidence that the 16 words were supposed to have been stricken from the speech, but were somehow included.

DID YOU KNOW?

The "infamous 16 words" remained a contentious issue until July 8, 2003, when President Bush himself admitted that the sentence had been included in the speech by error. At this point, however, the United States was already fighting in Iraq, and critics of the administration claimed the sentence was yet another instance of the willful manipulation of intelligence used to build a case for a war.

Pursuant to the General Assembly resolution President Bush had secured, the UN sent a team of weapons inspectors to Iraq in search of WMDs, including nuclear weapons. They found nothing. Undaunted, the Bush administration continued to assert its conviction that Iraq possessed the weapons, and, on February 5, 2003, sent Secretary of State Colin Powell to present its evidence to the UN Security Council.

In contrast to the president, a polarizing figure both nationally and internationally, Powell had been universally respected as chairman of the Joint Chiefs of Staff during the Persian Gulf War and was highly regarded in his new role in the Bush cabinet. He was not identified with the neocons, and his nonpartisan integrity was above reproach.

In a televised presentation to the Security Council, he presented images, diagrams, an audio recording of an intercepted conversation between Iraqi military officials, and even held up a vial of simulated weaponized anthrax spores, all intended to bolster his effort to persuade the Security Council of the imminence of the Iraqi threat.

In fact, most of the international community remained unconvinced and was reluctant to give its approval to a war against Iraq.

VOICES

When I made that presentation in February 2003, it was based on the best information that the Central Intelligence Agency made available to me. We studied it carefully; we looked at the sourcing in the case of the mobile trucks and trains [supposedly mobile chemical and biological weapons laboratories]. There was multiple sourcing for that. Unfortunately, that multiple sourcing over time has turned out to be not accurate. And so I'm deeply disappointed. But I'm also comfortable that at the time that I made the presentation, it reflected the collective judgment, the sound judgment of the intelligence community. But it turned out that the sourcing was inaccurate and wrong and in some cases, deliberately misleading. And for that, I am disappointed and I regret it.

—Colin Powell, interview on television's *Meet the Press*, May 16, 2004

A "Coalition of the Willing"

With or without the blessing of the Security Council, the Bush administration diligently assembled what it called a 49-member "coalition of the willing" to oppose Iraq. The echo of the coalition the president's father had assembled in 1990 was unmistakable. Yet the new coalition was quite different.

Before the war began, Costa Rica bowed out, bringing the roll to 48 members. Of this assemblage, 47 of them, together, contributed just 2 percent of the troop strength. The rest, 98 percent, was American: 133,000 men, initially. Great Britain contributed the next largest share, 8,361 men, followed by South Korea (3,300), Italy (2,600), and Poland (900). Twenty-two coalition members contributed from 130 to 830 each, and 17 nations withdrew by spring 2006.

Two major powers, allies of the United States, pointedly declined to join. Among these were France and Germany, which actively opposed any war with Iraq. Spain, another U.S. ally, chose to withhold direct military support, but pledged logistical and humanitarian assistance. Practically speaking, in contrast to the Persian Gulf War, the United States faced Iraq all but alone.

Ultimatum

In the United States, as among the nation's allies, debate was bitter over the prospect of war with Iraq. Some felt that the evidence Powell had presented to the Security Council—and, even more, the fact that it was Powell who presented it—was a compelling, if not altogether conclusive, justification for war. But there was little sense that a tipping point had been reached.

Then, quite suddenly, on March 16, 2003, President Bush made a televised speech from the Cross Hall in the White House. "Today," he began, "no nation can possibly claim that Iraq has disarmed. And it will not disarm so long as Saddam Hussein holds power. ... [S]ome permanent members of the Security Council have publicly announced they will veto any resolution that compels the disarmament of Iraq…. The United Nations Security Council has not lived up to its responsibilities, so we will rise to ours."

With this, the president postulated a reason to do what his father had declined to do 12 years earlier, after victory in the Persian Gulf War: remove Saddam Hussein from office. Moreover, the president now presented his reason for breaking with the United Nations Security Council to achieve this end.

"In recent days, some governments in the Middle East have been doing their part," President Bush continued. "They have delivered public and private messages urging the dictator to leave Iraq, so that disarmament can proceed peacefully. He has thus far refused. All the decades of deceit and cruelty have now reached an end. Saddam Hussein and his sons must leave Iraq within 48 hours. Their refusal to do so will result in military conflict, commenced at a time of our choosing…."

It was the equivalent of a declaration of war. On March 19, the 48-hour deadline having come and gone, the president authorized a "decapitation" attack, sending bombers over Iraq to destroy a bunker believed to shelter Saddam. It was the opening blow in Operation Iraqi Freedom.

Shock and Awe

The bombing of the Baghdad bunker, which failed to kill, injure, or force the surrender of Saddam Hussein, was the first in a series of carefully targeted air strikes, using satellite-guided Tomahawk cruise missiles fired from American warships in the Red Sea and Persian Gulf and "smart bombs" dropped by manned aircraft.

The strikes were surgical, in that they employed prewar intelligence to pinpoint military and government targets while avoiding civilian structures wherever possible. Still, the effect was meant to achieve what Harlan K. Ullman and James P. Wade, authors of a 1996 report on military doctrine prepared for the United States National Defense University, called "shock and awe." Whatever tactical effect the attacks might have on military and government targets, they were intended to intimidate the Iraqi population and thereby achieve rapid dominance. The hope was to minimize resistance.

Even as the air attacks were under way, ground operations began on March 20, as U.S. Army and Marine units took control of key oil fields. During the Persian Gulf War, Hussein had created an economic and environmental catastrophe by setting fire to Kuwaiti oil fields and production facilities. The U.S. military acted swiftly to forestall this in Iraq.

The American public had great anxiety that Saddam Hussein would not hesitate to respond to the invasion of his country by attacking U.S. troops with chemical and biological weapons. The fears quickly proved unfounded—for the very good reason that these WMDs, which the administration cited as the principal provocation to war, simply did not exist.

Battles for the Cities

On March 25, ground forces began operations to capture the southern town of Najaf and the southern port city of Basra. On the next day, U.S. airborne troops were deployed in northern Iraq, and on March 28, U.S. Marines began a fierce battle for Nasiriya.

The conquest of Karbala, a central Iraqi city holy for Shia Muslims, began on April 2. Since Karbala was just 50 miles from Baghdad, the Iraqi capital, it was considered the commencement of the Battle of Baghdad. Karbala fell on April 3, after a single day of fighting. U.S. Special Forces troops then advanced against the Thar Thar presidential palace, on the northwest outskirts of the capital. Simultaneously with this assault, U.S. ground forces attacked Baghdad's Saddam International Airport.

While these battles were in progress, members of the U.S. 101st Airborne Division took the city of An Najaf, on the Euphrates, due south of Baghdad. On the day after this, April 4, the heavily defended Saddam International Airport was secured, and the Americans instantly and unceremoniously renamed it Baghdad International Airport.

Occupying Baghdad

The airport was rapidly transformed into the U.S. base of operations from which the campaign to take and occupy Baghdad was launched. It began on April 6 as American and British units maneuvered at will to surround the Iraqi capital. In position by April 7, U.S. forces advanced into the city. Their initial objectives were its numerous presidential palaces.

U.S. command identified a nondescript building in the city as a place harboring Saddam Hussein. Instead of storming it, commanders called in an air strike. As with the earlier attack on a building identified as Saddam's bunker, this strike failed to kill the Iraqi leader. While American forces rode through Baghdad in strength, the British cleared Basra in the southeast corner of the country.

On April 9, Western television cameras captured video images of massive statues of Saddam Hussein being pulled down, not only in the capital, but in cities throughout Iraq.

DID YOU KNOW?

In the run-up to the war, U.S. Secretary of Defense Donald Rumsfeld famously predicted that American troops would be greeted by the Iraqi people as liberators. Indeed, in some places, U.S. and British soldiers were greeted warmly, but elsewhere they were met with resistance that included sniper fire and explosive encounters with "improvised explosive devices" (IEDs). In an effort to undermine Saddam Hussein, the United States had imposed economic sanctions on Iraq. Between 1991 and 2003, Iraq suffered nearly a half-million deaths attributable to critical shortages created by U.S.-imposed embargoes on manufactured goods. While the sanctions were intended to hurt Saddam, they created severe hardship for the ordinary Iraqi. Many of the U.S. "liberators" of Iraq now received the blowback from this policy.

On to Tikrit

Baghdad was the biggest political, demographic, and military prize in the invasion of Iraq, but it was not necessarily the most compelling symbolic objective in the overthrow of Saddam Hussein. After Baghdad was occupied, U.S. forces turned their attention to Tikrit, Saddam's hometown and the bastion of his Ba'ath Party.

DID YOU KNOW?

One of the more bizarre things U.S. command did during Operation Iraqi Freedom was to print and distribute decks of playing cards, standard in every way, except that each card bore the photograph and name of one of 55 members of the Iraqi leadership considered the regime's most-wanted tyrants. The decks were issued to American troops in the field and were meant to aid soldiers in identifying the senior members of Saddam Hussein's government.

"Mission Accomplished"

On April 11, U.S. military spokesmen announced that Baghdad had been secured. This was true, perhaps, in a narrowly military sense. But the city was hardly orderly. Looting and violence were rampant. When reporters questioned Defense Secretary Rumsfeld in an April 12 press conference about the civil chaos, he denied the crisis in Baghdad was significant and calmly observed, "Freedom's untidy, and free people are free to make mistakes and commit crimes and do bad things," adding: "They're also free to live their lives and do wonderful things. And that's what's going to happen here."

 **VOICES**

Stuff happens.

—Secretary of Defense Donald Rumsfeld, response to a reporter's question about the widespread looting and civil disorder in Baghdad under U.S. occupation, April 12, 2003

On April 12, the city of Al Kut fell. U.S. forces subjected Tikrit to very heavy attack on April 13, and on April 14 the Pentagon, despite some continued fighting in and around Tikrit, issued a statement that "the major combat phase of Operation Iraqi Freedom" had ended.

President Bush delayed his own official response to the Pentagon's pronouncement until May 2, 2003. On that day, the former Texas Air National Guard pilot was flown on a Lockheed S-3 Viking antisubmarine jet to a landing on the deck of the aircraft carrier *Abraham Lincoln* off San Diego, California. The president emerged from the plane clad in a full flight suit, helmet and all, and waved to the sailors assembled on deck. Later, after changing into a business suit, he stood at a podium set up on deck in front of a huge banner strung across the carrier's lofty superstructure. "Mission Accomplished" was emblazoned across it.

"Admiral Kelly, Captain Card, officers and sailors of the USS *Abraham Lincoln*, my fellow Americans," he began. "Major combat operations in Iraq have ended. In the Battle of Iraq, the United States and our allies have prevailed. And now our coalition is engaged in securing and reconstructing that country."

The image was supposed to be triumphant—a president declaring victory below a banner proclaiming it. And it is true, the invasion of Iraq had proceeded with astounding speed and at relatively little cost in terms of U.S. and British casualties. The problem was that the war was neither over nor won. Iraq roiled. The country was torn by insurgent attacks, and a state of chronic civil insurrection prevailed. Often, in the months and years to come, it would verge on outright civil war.

Immediately after "major combat" had been declared over, a retired army lieutenant general, Jay Garner, was sent into Baghdad to lead U.S. occupation and reconstruction efforts throughout Iraq. These efforts fumbled so badly that, on May 11, 2003, Garner was unceremoniously replaced by a new administrator, diplomat L. Paul Bremer, former U.S. ambassador to the Netherlands (1983–1986) and coordinator for counterterrorism under President Ronald Reagan (1986–1989).

End of a Dictator

At the time of President Bush's "Mission Accomplished" speech, Saddam Hussein and his two sons were still at large. The young men, Uday and Qusay, did not live long. Both were killed in a July 22 raid. Five months later, on December 14, 2003, Saddam Hussein himself was captured. The scene was both squalid and ignominious. The dictator was found in a farmhouse cellar—really little more than a hole in the ground—10 miles south of Tikrit. U.S. authorities bound him over to Iraqi provisional authorities for trial on charges of war crimes.

Insurgency? Civil War?

After "major combat" had been concluded, the country was swept by what some described as an "insurgency" and others as a "civil war." U.S forces were targeted by hardline Saddam loyalists and so-called "foreign fighters," who specifically targeted American forces and U.S.-trained Iraqi forces, for the most part using IEDs planted along roadsides. Sectarian violence, especially between rival Shiite and Sunni factions, took its toll among the Iraqi civilian population.

L. Paul Bremer, administrator of the Coalition Provisional Authority of Iraq from May 12, 2003, to June 28, 2004 (when sovereignty of Iraq was officially transferred to the Iraqi Interim Government), came under withering criticism for contributing to the civil chaos by having summarily disbanded the old Iraqi army, thereby creating a security vacuum filled by thousands of embittered, jobless, and armed ex-military troops. Bremer also banned former Ba'ath Party officials from returning to the Iraqi government, a decree that deprived the nation of experienced administrators.

In 2007, a "surge" of 21,500 more U.S troops were brought in to counter the rising civil war. The extra troops proved effective, and at the end of 2008, the United States concluded an agreement with the Iraq government to withdraw U.S. combat forces by the end of 2011. The withdrawal was accomplished, and the war ended. As of the summer of 2014, it remains to be seen how stable the Iraqi government will prove.

Afghanistan

Although U.S combat involvement in the Iraq War officially ended on December 15, 2011, the United States and NATO, as of summer 2014, continue to formulate their withdrawal from Afghanistan. They do so having finally achieved the objective of killing Osama bin Laden, who was successfully targeted in Pakistan in Operation Neptune Spear by U.S. Navy SEAL Team Six. Moving in by stealth-equipped helicopters, the SEALs descended on bin Laden's compound in the city of Abbottabad, Pakistan, shortly after 1 o'clock in the morning of May 2, 2011. They killed bin Laden, his family, and others in the operation.

The fate of both Iraq and Afghanistan remains deeply uncertain. In 2008, presidential candidate Barack Obama criticized the Bush administration for having neglected the war in Afghanistan, a proven nexus of terrorism, to fight a costly war in Iraq, a nation largely unconnected with terrorist activity and never directly connected with the 9/11 attacks.

Yet the greater troop strength President Obama allocated to the Afghanistan conflict has not left the nation stable, and there is much doubt about its fate once the bulk of U.S., NATO, and ISAF forces pull out.

In all the regions associated with the Middle East conflict, Afghanistan may in the long term prove the least stable and least predictable. The U.S. role in this region already qualifies as the longest war in American history. What good, if any, this involvement will have accomplished is far from certain. Indeed, what the United States achieved in Iraq and Afghanistan—for its own security, the security of the region, and that of the world—is difficult to determine and will probably remain so for some time.

And what legacy have the wars in Iraq and Afghanistan created for the United States? The response to the attacks of 9/11 included such domestic legislation as the USA PATRIOT Act of October 26, 2001, widely criticized for infringing on constitutionally guaranteed rights of privacy and freedom from unreasonable search and seizure. In 2002, a massive detention camp was erected in the Guantanamo Bay Naval Base in Cuba, intended to hold "unlawful combatants" captured in Afghanistan, Iraq, and elsewhere. Ever since, the international community has condemned torture of prisoners held there, the denial of Geneva Convention protections, and the open-ended captivity of individuals without charge, let alone trial. In Iraq, where President George W. Bush hoped that images of Saddam's statues being toppled would serve in collective memory as the symbol of a U.S.-led "liberation," it is the grotesque photographs of detainees in the U.S.-run Abu Ghraib military prison, subjected by American soldiers to sexual humiliation and other abuse, that are destined to live, perhaps for generations, in Middle Eastern memory.

The Least You Need to Know

- Most historians currently believe that America's early unconventional small-force approach to the war in Afghanistan was effective in suppressing Taliban activity, but that the tactical and strategic initiative was lost when the military turned to the war in Iraq.

- America's path to war in Iraq was laid out by a combination of neoconservative political advisors in the administration of George W. Bush and fears (based on faulty or deliberately misleading intelligence) that Saddam Hussein was hoarding an arsenal of WMDs to loose upon targets in the Middle East and perhaps the United States. U.S. military intervention in Iraq has been heavily criticized as a misguided war of choice rather than a war of necessity.

- Begun on October 7, 2001, and (as of summer 2014) ongoing, the war in Afghanistan is the longest war in U.S. history, while the one in Iraq (March 20, 2003-December 15, 2011) is among the longest. What enduring outcomes the United States has achieved in these wars remains an unanswered question.

Risings and Revolutions

In January 1968, following the election of politician Alexander Dubček to the post of first secretary of the Communist Party of Czechoslovakia, reforms were introduced that ushered in a liberating period in Iron Curtain history the world dubbed the "Prague Spring." It ended abruptly in August, when the Soviets and its Warsaw Pact satellites invaded Prague, but the idea of a popular movement against an oppressive regime remained, and when a wave of mass demonstrations and protests (as well as riots and civil wars) swept the Arab world beginning in December 2010, the Western media collectively referred to the events as the "Arab Spring." This is the central topic of the final part of this book.

Chapter 18 begins with a dark overture to the Arab Spring, the Second Lebanon War (2006) and the War in Gaza (2008–2009), both of which illustrate the aspirations and the seemingly intractable problems that have alternately fueled hope and despair in the Middle East.

Chapter 19 presents the principal popular movements of the Arab Spring, in Tunisia, Egypt, Libya, and Yemen, while Chapter 20 takes the movement into its bloodiest and most tragic theater, Syria, in which civil war has created a humanitarian crisis in which the world seems powerless to intervene.

Borderlands

Until the birth of Israel in 1948 and the resulting conflict between Israel and the Arab states, modern Americans tended to think of the Middle East as distant, remote, and unconnected with their lives. Since the end of World War II, however, the Middle East has loomed progressively larger in the Western consciousness. The Organization of the Petroleum Exporting Countries (OPEC) oil embargo of 1973, Iran hostage crisis of 1979–1981, Persian Gulf War of 1990–1991, and the 9/11 attacks, and the wars that followed have given the Middle East a vast global dimension, especially for Americans.

Americans now realized the global consequences of events in the Middle East, and this has sometimes made it difficult to appreciate the intensely intimate origins of so many of the region's conflicts.

The Middle East is a comparatively compact place. Its most densely populated areas are small. As in Europe, a tight and complex political geography often promotes conflict, forcing peoples of different ethnicities, faiths, traditions, and needs to confront one another at close quarters. It is no wonder that Israel, a nation of little over 8,000 square miles, bordered by Egypt, Jordan, Syria, and Lebanon, and containing the separate Palestinian territories of the West Bank and the Gaza Strip, continues to be both the target and engine of so much of the Middle East conflict.

Party of God

The cosmopolitan makeup of Lebanon has long been one of the nation's greatest assets and most persistent source of conflict. Leading religious groups include the long-established Maronite Christians, the Druze (a monotheistic group with beliefs rooted in Shia Islam), and Sunni Muslims. The religious, ethnic, and political constituents within the country agreed to a constitution, the National Pact of 1943, which established a dominant role for the Christian Phalange Party.

Christian political power within Lebanon was something of a holdover from the Ottoman era, during which the Sublime Porte (Ottoman government) empowered Christians to serve as mediators among European traders, Ottoman provincial governments, and local merchants and politicians. Soon after the establishment of the state of Israel, Prime Minister David Ben Gurion and his advisor Moshe Sharett quietly promised to help the Lebanese Christians establish a separate state, to be allied with Israel. Israel supplied and trained the Phalange in the hopes of creating a friendly neighbor on its northern border. But Shia and Sunni Lebanese were not inclined to vacate their historic homes to accommodate a breakaway Christian state. This became a frequent source of violence between the relatively affluent and influential Christian minority and the poorer, often marginalized Muslim majority.

A Background of Civil War

Camille Chamoun, candidate of the Maronite (Eastern Catholic) Party, was elected president of Lebanon in 1952. He quickly established close ties with the West, especially the United States, a policy that further alienated Lebanon's Muslims, who wanted the nation to identify with its Arab neighbors, many of which were openly hostile to the West. Between May 9 and 13, 1958, Lebanese Muslims staged several violent demonstrations against Chamoun. Riots erupted in the capital, Beirut, and in Tripoli. The disturbances were apparently organized and supported by the United Arab Republic (the union, under Gamal Abdel Nasser, of Egypt and Syria that was created in January 1958). The UAR endorsed the militant Kamal Jumblatt, a Druze chieftain, pro-Muslim, anti-Christian, who had already led successful confrontations against the Lebanese army.

When Lebanese Muslims called for Chamoun's immediate resignation, he appealed to U.S. President Dwight D. Eisenhower for military aid. The president responded, on July 15, 1958, by landing marines at Khalde Beach in Lebanon. The next day, these forces were joined by an airlift of additional marines, and, on July 19, U.S. Army troops arrived. The total peak U.S. military presence was 14,000 soldiers and marines.

The U.S. presence facilitated a tenuous cease-fire, during which Undersecretary of State Robert Murphy negotiated an agreement for a new election, which brought into office another Maronite Christian, General Faud Chehab. After his September 23, 1958, inauguration, U.S. troops withdrew.

Throughout the 1960s, Lebanon, interfered with by Israel and the United States and torn by internal strife, descended into chronic conflict. As often happens when states implode, when they become *failed states,* outsiders rush in to fill the power vacuum. Palestinian refugees and the Palestine Liberation Organization (PLO), hounded out of territory within Israel, established settlements within Lebanon as well as bases from which the PLO could operate against Israel.

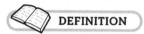 **DEFINITION**

> A **failed state** is a nation that cannot meet some or all of the basic responsibilities and functions of a sovereign government. It is, in fact, a nation in name only.

The presence of the PLO exacerbated the long-standing Christian/Muslim conflict within Lebanon, and, on April 13, 1975, four Christian Phalangists were killed in an attack by assassins targeting Phalange founder-leader Pierre Jumayyil. Christian Phalangists are members of the Lebanese Phalanges Party, often simply called "the Phalange." Although aligned with the Maronite Christians, the Phalange, founded in 1936, is secular. Assuming that the failed assassins were Palestinian, Phalangist forces retaliated on April 14 by attacking a bus carrying Palestinians through a Christian neighborhood. Twenty-six passengers died, and before the end of the day, fighting was widespread, though largely disorganized, throughout Lebanon.

For the next several months, the Lebanese government could not stem the violence, and a bloody pattern of aggression and retaliation developed among Christian and Muslim militia groups. Inexorably, the violence escalated into outright civil war, not only between Christians and Muslims, but also among various Christian and Muslim factions. If there was any unity to be discerned in the bloody melee, it was that those who favored upholding the existing government gathered under the umbrella of the Lebanese Front, while those opposed to the status quo organized under the Lebanese National Movement, which was loosely led by Kamal Jumblatt.

As 1975 drew to an end, no side was clearly emerging as victorious, but it was nevertheless apparent that the pro-government Lebanese Front had performed miserably against the rebel Lebanese National Movement. Prepared to exploit the anti-Western, anti-Israel, anticolonial, pro-Muslim, pro-nationalist lead, the Palestine Liberation Army (principal military wing of the PLO) acted to establish a strong political and military presence in Lebanon.

Syria, neighbor both to Lebanon and Israel, intervened on February 14, 1976, guiding the creation of a reform program called the "Constitutional Document." In part, Syria wanted to support the Muslim gains in the Lebanese government. Feeling that colonialism had divided Syria into isolated enclaves readily exploited by Western powers, the Syrian leadership was also bent on creating a "Greater Syria," to restore the territorial extent and integrity Syria had enjoyed under the Ottomans. During the days of that empire, Syria included present-day Jordan, Syria, Lebanon, Palestine, and Israel.

Syria's efforts failed. In March 1976, mutiny swept the Lebanese Army and many troops joined the Lebanese National Movement, forming the Lebanese Arab Army. Neither Israel nor Syria wanted this degree of instability, and when the Lebanese Arab Army stormed into Christian-controlled Beirut, forcing President Franjiyah to flee to Mount Lebanon, Syrian President Hafiz al-Assad sent troops into Lebanon. This forced all sides to meet at a peace conference convened in Riyadh, Saudi Arabia, on October 16, 1976.

Israel Invades, Withdraws, and Reenters

Although the civil war officially ended as a result of the conference, the Lebanese Arab Army suddenly turned against the Syrian occupation forces. Into this renewed chaos, in March 1978, the Israel Defense Forces (IDF) marched, invading southern Lebanon to retaliate against the PLO's Fatah faction, which had attacked an Israeli bus in the March 11 Coastal Road Massacre.

Bowing to a United Nations call, Israel withdrew from Lebanon to make way for a UN peacekeeping force—which proved no more effective in restoring or keeping the peace than the Lebanese government had. When the PLO backed an attempt on the life of Israel's ambassador to the UK, Israeli forces retaliated by reentering Lebanon on June 6, 1982, and arming and cooperating with the Phalange. Israel's immediate objective was to force the PLO out.

In August, an agreement was hammered out calling for the withdrawal of Syrian troops as well as PLO fighters from Beirut. The withdrawal was to be enforced by a three-nation Multinational Force (MNF) consisting of U.S., French, and Italian military units.

Hope and the Militias

Amal is the Arabic word for "hope," and in 1974, a new "movement of the dispossessed" was formed. Consisting of Lebanese Shiites, it called itself the Amal Movement—the Hope Movement.

Amal was primarily a political movement, which came into being amid a collection of Muslim militias. Early in the 1980s, these militias began to consolidate into an organization that called itself Hezbollah, meaning "the Party of God."

The Hand of Iran

After Israel succeeded in driving the PLO out of Lebanon, the IDF withdrew to the Lebanese margin of that country's southern border with Israel, establishing the area as a buffer zone held by a militia called the South Lebanon Army (SLA), which was armed and supported by Israel. The Israeli invasion and the action of the SLA took a terrible toll on those living in southern Lebanon. At this point, Syria's Hafiz al-Assad quietly invited some 1,500 Iranian Revolutionary Guards to establish bases in Lebanon. The Iranians backed both the organization and the rapid expansion of Hezbollah, which was intent on driving the MNF and the Israelis out of Lebanon. For their part, both Syria and Iran were bent on destroying Israel.

As narrated in Chapter 11, the United States mediated negotiations between Lebanon and Israel for total Israeli withdrawal, but when Syria refused to even discuss the withdrawal of its forces, the negotiations were suspended. The suspension brought terrorist attacks, some traced to Hezbollah, against U.S. interests in Lebanon, including the bombing of the U.S. embassy on April 18, 1983. When terrorists made a suicide attack against the MNF headquarters in Beirut on October 23, 1983, killing 298, mostly U.S. Marines, U.S. Secretary of Defense Caspar Weinberger blamed what he called Syrian-sponsored Iranians. More likely, they were members of the still-emerging, as yet officially nameless, Iranian-sponsored Hezbollah.

The 2006 Lebanon War

Hezbollah was clearly active by 1983, but it wasn't officially founded until 1985, when it publicly declared its intention to end the Israeli occupation of Lebanon once and for all. At this point, however, the Lebanese civil war came to a pause—less a declaration of peace than an admission of mutual exhaustion. The warring factions agreed to disarm—with the notable exceptions of Hezbollah and the SLA.

Months and then years passed, in which the two forces faced each other down along the border with Israel. At last, Lebanon and Israel agreed to a so-called Blue Line, dividing the two countries. The United Nations published the Blue Line on June 7, 2000, declaring that it was not a legally settled international boundary, but that it would serve as the agreed-upon withdrawal line between Lebanese territory and Israel as well as the Israeli-controlled Golan Heights.

With the agreement in place, Israel withdrew to its side of the Blue Line. No sooner was this done than the SLA, no longer backed by Israel, simply folded, and Hezbollah, unopposed, took control of what had been the borderland buffer between Israel and Lebanon. Both sides, Hezbollah and Israel, ratcheted up cross-border attacks.

Resistance by Abduction and Rocket Fire

In a bid to coerce Israel into freeing political prisoners, Hezbollah forces operating along the Golan Heights Blue Line attempted three times late in 2005 to abduct IDF soldiers so as to prompt a prisoner exchange. Each time, the attacks were defeated.

The next year, on July 12, 2006, Hezbollah launched Soviet-made Katyusha rockets in the direction of Israeli coastal military positions close to the border village of Zar'it. They fired rockets on the Israeli town of Shlomi as well as six smaller villages. The Katyushas were small and inaccurate, and the attacks inflicted just five civilian injuries and none among the military, although Blue Line surveillance cameras were knocked out. Under cover of the attacks, however, Hezbollah fighters managed to cross into Israel and strike two Humvees patrolling the border near Zar'it, killing three soldiers, injuring two, and—most important of all—capturing First Sergeant Ehud Goldwasser and Sergeant First Class Eldad Regev.

IDF commanders quickly responded to the loss of the Humvees by sending a rescue force, followed by an armed probe into Lebanon. In this expedition, an Israeli tank struck a mine and the explosion kill its four-man crew. Another Israeli soldier was killed and two others wounded by mortar fire.

Israel Strikes Back

In the long and tragic history of Middle East war, the border exchanges of July 2006 were limited in scale. Israel's Prime Minister Ehud Olmert, however, responded with a warning that Lebanon would "bear the consequences of its actions" and declared that those consequences would be "very painful and far-reaching."

What is significant here is that Israel now asserted a policy of holding Lebanon itself responsible for the actions of Hezbollah on its soil. Much as the United States had done in the post-9/11 war in Afghanistan, Israel now blamed the "host" state for all attacks originating from it. Israel's Chief of Staff Dan Halutz warned that "if the soldiers are not returned, we will turn Lebanon's clock back 20 years," and other officials declared all Lebanese targets fair game.

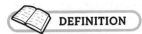 **DEFINITION**

Non-state actor is a phrase often used to describe a political, military, or terrorist organization, ostensibly unaffiliated with any nation, that attacks an established state.

On the first day of Israel's response, the IDF launched more than 100 attacks, mostly targeting identified Hezbollah bases in south Lebanon. Five bridges across the Litani and Zahrani rivers were destroyed to prevent Hezbollah from transporting the abducted soldiers farther north. Over succeeding days, the IDF hit Hezbollah headquarters in the outskirts of Beirut itself, along with buildings identified as the homes of the Hezbollah leadership. In addition, key TV and radio stations were destroyed, as were all runways and fuel depots at Beirut's international airport. Infrastructure in south Lebanon believed to be of use to Hezbollah was destroyed, as were very specific military targets, most notably 59 rocket launchers scattered throughout south Lebanon.

Flown on July 13, the Israeli air strikes consumed little more than a half hour, but were the product of six years of meticulous intelligence gathering. The strikes neutralized most of Hezbollah's medium-range missile capability. Shortly after the initial strikes, Hezbollah's long-range missiles were also targeted. Neither strike operations, however, did much to suppress fire from short-range Katyushas, which were fired from mobile launchers. Easily concealed, the launchers could also be moved immediately after an attack, making it impossible to trace the launches to their source.

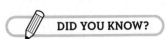 **DID YOU KNOW?**

Between July 12 and August 14, 2006 (when a cease-fire was declared), Israel's air force flew an astounding 11,897 combat missions into Lebanon.

Hezbollah Capability

The United States and other Western powers classify Hezbollah as a terrorist organization. Its performance against the IDF during the 2006 war, however, showed it to be a sophisticated military force, well-armed, well-trained, and highly capable of engaging the IDF in guerrilla actions. Although these engagements consistently proved more costly to Hezbollah than to the IDF, they also demonstrated Hezbollah's willingness to suffer disproportionate casualties in order to further the cause of resistance.

Although attacks on military targets were guided by careful Israeli intelligence, the destruction of civilian infrastructure was extensive and included some 400 miles of highway, a total of 73 bridges, much of the Beirut airport, electric power and other utilities, and many schools. At least 900 commercial buildings and 15,000 homes were totally destroyed, with an additional 130,000 homes damaged.

 **VOICES**

> No country in Europe would have responded in such a restrained manner as Israel did.
>
> —Israel's Prime Minister Ehud Olmert, August 2006, defending against media criticism that Israel's response to Hezbollah rocket attacks was "disproportionate"

Hezbollah also targeted civilians and civilian structures, including the Haifa railroad depot (in which eight Israeli railroad employees were killed in a July 16 attack). In all, Hezbollah fired some 4,000 rockets during the war, about 100 a day, the vast majority 122-mm Katyushas. Of these, somewhat less than a quarter hit urban areas in northern Israel. Israel reported 44 civilian deaths as a result of the war, in addition to two foreign civilians killed. The Lebanese civilian death toll is unknown but estimated at between 1,100 and 1,200, one third of the victims under the age of 13.

Outcome

After weeks of fruitless negotiation, a UN-sanctioned cease-fire was put into effect on August 14, 2006. As they stood down, both sides claimed victory.

Without question, Hezbollah suffered far heavier losses than the IDF—probably some 500 killed, compared to 119 IDF killed. Both Hezbollah and Lebanon suffered disproportionately extensive and costly material losses in infrastructure, buildings, and military equipment. Yet many Israelis did not feel like victors. Many Israelis took to the streets to protest the war, and an August 25 poll revealed that 63 percent of Israelis wanted Prime Minister Olmert to resign.

Some Israelis believed the war created excessive death and destruction in Lebanon. Others protested that it did not go far enough in eliminating Hezbollah as a threat. On the contrary, they argued, Hezbollah had gained in stature and perceived legitimacy by thwarting—not defeating, but successfully resisting—the most powerful and feared military in the Middle East.

Such organizations as Amnesty International and Human Rights Watch accused both Israel and Hezbollah of committing war crimes because both failed to distinguish civilian from military targets. While the reputation of Hezbollah was elevated in the Arab world, Israel's allies, most notably the United States, defended Israel's actions, pointing out that Hezbollah, after all, had started the war (while failing to note that the war had been provoked by an Israeli invasion). Yet President George W. Bush, in his 2010 memoir *Decision Points,* observed that Israel's military performance in the war had been "shaky" and had therefore reduced its military credibility in both the region and the world.

As for the two IDF soldiers whose abduction played a central role in starting the war, both were confirmed as having been killed, and in accordance with UN Resolution 1701, Hezbollah returned the bodies in exchange for a Palestine Liberation Front prisoner and four Hezbollah prisoners, in addition to the bodies of some 200 slain Lebanese and Palestinian militants.

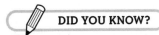

DID YOU KNOW?

> The Israeli government assigned a retired judge, Eliyahu Winograd, to chair a commission to report on the war. The Winograd Commission's report, issued on January 30, 2008, was scathing, calling the war a "missed opportunity," a conflict that had been allowed to end "without a defined military victory." The Winograd Commission did conclude, however, that the IDF had committed no war crimes.

Hezbollah Since 2006

As some see it, Lebanon in 2006 had become a failed state, in which Hezbollah, ostensibly a non-state actor whose paramilitary wing has been linked to many acts of terrorism, functioned as a state within a failed state. To be sure, Lebanon had proved fertile soil to the small Iranian-backed militia of the 1980s, allowing it to grow into a more powerful military force than the Lebanese state military. Currently (summer 2014), Hezbollah controls 11 of 30 seats in the Lebanese cabinet, giving it the ability to veto virtually any proposed government action. Even more important, Hezbollah has replaced the PLO as a movement representative of the resistance impulse throughout the Arab and Shiite worlds. A non-state power based in a state, Hezbollah is a transnational political presence and military force.

Since the 2006 Lebanon War, Hezbollah has been implicated in a May 2011 bombing attack in Istanbul, Turkey, apparently targeting Israel's consul there. The attack wounded eight Turkish nationals, but Turkish intelligence has disputed Israel's claim that it was the work of Hezbollah. The next year, however, a Lebanese man was arrested by Cyprus police officials on suspicion of planning Hezbollah attacks against Israeli interests in that country. Although no plot was actually executed, the suspect, Hossam Yaakoub, a Lebanese-born citizen of Sweden, was tried in a Cypriot court in 2013 and found guilty of participating in a criminal organization, planning to commit a crime, and money laundering. He was sentenced to four years in prison.

On July 18, 2012, a suicide bomber attacked a bus carrying Israeli tourists in Bulgaria's Burgas Airport. Five Israelis and the bus driver, a Bulgarian, were killed, and 32 other passengers, all Israelis, were injured. Bulgarian officials concluded that the attack was the work of Hezbollah, and Israel's Prime Minister Benjamin Netanyahu called it one of many either executed or planned in places across the globe.

Wars in Gaza

Hamas (an Arabic word meaning "zeal" and constituting an Arabic acronym translated as "Islamic Resistance Movement") was founded in 1987 as a Sunni Palestinian faction of the Egyptian Muslim Brotherhood with the express objective of creating a Palestinian Islamic state in Israel's West Bank.

As Hezbollah emerged as a major power in Lebanon, Hamas developed into a major power in the occupied Palestinian territories of the West Bank and the Gaza Strip, the 139-square-mile coastal Mediterranean tract bordering Egypt and Israel and now functioning as a de facto Palestinian state. In 2006, Hamas won a majority in the Palestinian parliamentary elections and acted to suppress its rival, Fatah. While many nations, including most of the Arab world as well as Iran, China, Russia, and Turkey recognize Hamas as a legitimate political party, Israel and the United States, along with Jordan, the European Union, and Japan, regard it as a terrorist organization.

The Intifadas

In 1989, two years after coming into being during the First Intifada, Hamas abducted and subsequently killed two IDF soldiers. In response, Israel arrested and tried Ahmed Yassin, the Muslim Brotherhood leader in Gaza who was the principal founder of Hamas. Israel also deported 400 Hamas members to Israeli-occupied south Lebanon, where they found opportunity to establish ties to Hezbollah. Beginning in 1993, the military branch of Hamas, called the Izz ad-Din al Qassam Brigades, carried out a series of suicide attacks in the West Bank and also identified, captured, and summarily executed Palestinians accused of collaborating with Israeli authorities.

Israel responded to the suicide attacks with more deportations and a program of assassinations targeting Hamas leaders. Mossad killed a Hamas bomb maker, Yahya Ayash, in 1996, but failed the next year in an attempt to assassinate Khaled Mashal, a Hamas leader.

Hamas and its military wing were active in the Second Intifada, the uprising against Israeli occupation of the West Bank, that spanned 2000 to early 2005 and that resulted in approximately 1,000 Israeli deaths and the deaths of more than 3,000 Palestinians. In January 2004, Ahmed Yassin, who had resumed leadership of Hamas after he was released from an Israeli prison in exchange for two Mossad agents who were being held in Jordan, offered to end the Second Intifada if Israel would agree to the establishment of a Palestinian state in the West Bank, Gaza Strip, and East Jerusalem. Abdel Aziz al-Rantissi, another leading figure in Hamas, added more specific terms, offering a 10-year truce but demanding, in addition to Palestinian nationhood, Israel's withdrawal from all territories captured in the 1967 Six-Day War. Denouncing both offers as shams intended to buy time for a Hamas military build-up, Israel launched an air strike on March 22 that targeted and killed Yassin. On April 18, another air strike killed al-Rantissi.

Hamas and Fatah Go to War

As Hamas and Israel battled one another, so did Hamas and Fatah. In 2006, Hamas beat Fatah, the largest PLO faction, for control of the Palestinian parliamentary government. The Palestinian Authority, which backed Fatah, had lost credibility on account of widespread corruption and nepotism. Many consider the 2006 election less a vote *for* Hamas than *against* Fatah, and far from settling the question of Palestinian leadership, the election ignited bloody clashes between Hamas and Fatah adherents, which moved Saudi Arabia to sponsor a mediation that resulted in an agreement, signed by PLO leader Mahmoud Abbas and Hamas leader Khaled Mashal in February 2007, to create a coalition government for Palestine.

A national unity government was officially proclaimed the following month, but in June Hamas and Fatah fell to fighting again, and Hamas ousted Fatah officials from the Gaza Strip administration. In response, Abbas, who not only headed the PLO but was also president of the State of Palestine, dissolved the Hamas-led Palestinian Authority government and outlawed the Hamas military wing. In May 2014, Hamas and Fatah announced agreement on the names of ministers to serve in a new Palestinian unity government. As of this writing (early summer 2014), the viability and durability of such a government remains to be seen. While Fatah has acknowledged the right of Israel to exist, Hamas does not recognize this right, prompting Israel's Prime Minister Benjamin Netanyahu to denounce any Palestinian regime that includes Hamas.

Mahmoud Abbas

Mahmoud Abbas replaced Yasser Arafat as chairman of the PLO in 2004 and succeeded him as president of the State of Palestine in January 2005. Born in Safed, Galilee, in 1935, Abbas fled with his family to Syria during the Arab-Israeli War of 1948. In Syria, he graduated from the University of Damascus, studied law in Egypt, and later traveled to Moscow, where he earned the equivalent of a PhD from Patrice Lumumba University, having written a dissertation on the secret relationship between Nazism and Zionism.

During the 1950s, Abbas became active in covert Palestinian politics and joined Fatah in 1961 while living in Qatar. Abbas played a key role in securing funding for Fatah from successful Palestinian exiles, some of which was used to finance the 1972 massacre at the Munich Summer Olympics. Alongside his support of asymmetric warfare, Abbas also attempted to lead Fatah in talks with Israeli moderates. By the 1980s, he was thus identified as a Palestinian moderate even as he fled to Yugoslavia to avoid prosecution under international law for terrorism.

In 1993, Abbas, on behalf of the PLO, signed the Oslo Accords with Israel and, with Israeli diplomat Yossi Beilin, drafted the Beilin-Abu Mazen Agreement, which was intended to serve as a framework for a permanent Israeli-Palestinian peace treaty. (Neither Israel nor the Palestinian leadership has accepted it.)

Although Abbas is the highest-profile Palestinian political leader, his authority is not universally accepted by Palestinians. Elected president of the State of Palestine with a term set to expire on January 9, 2009, he announced a one-year extension of his term during a period of intense internal conflict in the Palestinian leadership. After the extension—never voted on—expired, Abbas simply continued to serve. This prompted Fatah's rival, Hamas, to refuse recognition of Abbas as president. This promises to change if the "unity" government of Palestine, which includes both Fatah and Hamas and which was announced in May 2014, is actually installed and proves viable.

Abbas's authority has been further challenged by allegations of embezzlement of public funds, an accusation that had also been leveled against his predecessor and mentor, Yasser Arafat. In 2012, the U.S. Congress heard testimony that Abbas presided over a chronic kleptocracy. As of this writing (summer 2014), Mahmoud Abbas continues to serve as president of the State of Palestine.

Cast Lead

While Hamas and Fatah continued to fight, Egyptian mediators announced on June 17, 2008, that a six-month truce had been reached between Hamas and Israel. In exchange for Hamas's pledge to stop firing rockets into Israel, Israel partially lifted its blockade of Gaza.

The 6-month truce was punctuated by spasms of violence, and when it expired, on December 19, Hamas fired as many as 70 rockets and mortars shells into Israel between the December 19 and 21. On that day, Hamas announced its willingness to renew the truce, provided that Israel opened all border crossings. Instead of accepting, however, Israel commenced Operation Cast Lead on December 27 with air strikes against police stations, suspected weapons stores, suspected rocket-launching sites, and political and administrative structures. All targets were in Gaza, Khan Yunis, and Rafah, each a densely populated urban area, which meant that civilian casualties were inevitable. Israel justified its action as the only certain way to end the rocket assaults and to pinch off the stream of illegal weapons flowing into the Gaza Strip.

Initially, far from stopping the rockets, Operation Cast Lead only provoked an increase in the volume of attacks. This prompted Israel to begin ground operations on January 3, coordinating them with ongoing close-air support as well as naval operations. IDF ground units advanced into the city of Gaza on January 5, and beginning the following week, specifically targeted Palestinian rocket-launching units.

For its part, Hamas, though taking significant casualties, ratcheted up the volume of rocket launches and mortar attacks against Israeli civilian targets, the cities of Beersheba and Ashdod chief among them. In the end, it was Israeli leaders who blinked first. Although the Israeli military leadership was willing and able to strike deeper into Gaza, the Israeli government announced, on January 18, a unilateral cease-fire. Hamas responded within 12 hours by announcing a weeklong cease-fire. On January 21, 2009, in a demonstration of good faith, the IDF withdrew from Gaza. By that time, Cast Lead had killed 273 Palestinians in the Gaza Strip, 113 of whom were noncombatants.

> **DID YOU KNOW?**
>
> Operation Cast Lead was a lopsided tactical victory for Israel, which lost just 13 troops while inflicting over 1,000 (perhaps as many as 1,417) deaths among Palestinian forces. Both sides heavily targeted civilians and both sides were accused of war crimes. The United Nations Human Rights Council ordered Israel to fund repairs, but little rebuilding has occurred.

Pillar of Defense

Frequent Hamas rocket fire punctuated the cease-fire that ended Operation Cast Lead. Not all of the attacks came from Hamas. Rocket attacks from another group, Islamic Jihad, were chiefly responsible for breaking the truce, despite attempts by Hamas to suppress the most extreme anti-Zionist groups in Gaza. Nevertheless, the attacks provoked Israeli retaliatory raids. By November 2012, 797 rocket hits had been counted. For its part, Hamas promised to stop the rockets as soon as Israel lifted its naval blockade of Gaza's coast. For its part, however, Israel noted that Hamas was now using Iranian-made Fajr-5 rockets, whose increased range enabled penetration farther north into Israeli territory. The Gaza-based Palestinian Centre for Human Rights (PCHR) claimed that Israel was making frequent attacks against Palestinian fishermen, significantly reducing a source of food and livelihood. Some of the "attacks" were arrests, while others involved gunfire.

During October and early November 2012, the pace of cross-border incidents increased until November 12, when Hamas and Palestinian Islamic Jihad spokesmen proposed discussing a cease-fire. Yet, that very day, Palestinians launched a dozen rockets into Israel.

Two days later, at about four in the afternoon of November 15, an Israeli air force strike killed Ahmed Jabari, head of the Hamas military wing. At the same time, IDF units struck 20 other Hamas targets in the Gaza Strip, including Fajr-5 missile launchers and storage facilities. This was the start of a new Israeli offensive, Operation Pillar of Defense.

The Israeli attacks, intended to preempt a Hamas response, only spurred retaliation as rockets targeted Beersheba, Ashdod, Ofakim, and other Israeli targets. Israel's newly developed Iron Dome mobile air defense system, designed to intercept rockets and even artillery shells in flight, proved highly effective, shooting down 130 incoming missiles.

DID YOU KNOW?

> The campaign officially known as Pillar of Defense was called in Hebrew "Pillar of Cloud," in reference to a great cloudlike pillar God raised to guide the Israelites in their exodus from Egypt during Egypt's 18th Dynasty. (At night, the Pillar of Cloud became a Pillar of Fire.) The Palestinians called their response to Operation Pillar of Cloud Operation Stones of Shale, a reference to the Al-Fil sura in the Quran (105:4), in which Allah saves Mecca from attack by sending a flock of birds that pelted the attackers with stones, driving them away.

On November 16, a three-hour cease-fire was declared to allow Egyptian Prime Minister Hisham Qandil to visit the Gaza Strip in a show of solidarity with the Palestinians. Each side accused the other of taking advantage of the interval to launch attacks, and that evening a massive barrage of 500 rockets was launched from Gaza, overwhelming Iron Dome, which was able to intercept only 184. Israel retaliated the next day by expanding its official target list from military sites to government structures and facilities. The office building housing Ismail Haniyeh, prime minister of Hamas, was destroyed by IDF air strikes. Palestinian civilian casualties rapidly multiplied, swamping Gaza's limited hospital capacity. At this point, Eli Yishai, interior minister of Israel and member of the far-right Shas party, said that the Israeli objective had now become sending "Gaza back to the Middle Ages." A report by the UN High Commissioner for Human Rights found that the IDF had "failed in many instances to respect international law," and Human Rights Watch has condemned at least one Pillar of Defense airstrike, which killed 12 noncombatant civilians, not only a "disproportionate" response but a "war crime."

Still, the rockets flew. On November 18, the Israeli navy joined the air force in firing on the Gaza Strip. For the first time, media outlets were targeted, including buildings known to house international journalists. The IDF explained that Hamas was using the communications equipment, especially rooftop antennas, for their military communications. IDF accused Hamas of effectively using the journalists as human shields.

Even as Israel began allowing trucks with medical supplies and food to enter Gaza, the government announced preparations to expand Pillar of Defense into more neighborhoods throughout Gaza. One airstrike hit the Jabalia Refugee Camp, killing two children.

Several attempts were made to initiate a cease-fire before Egypt's foreign minister, Mohamed Kamel Amr, and U.S. Secretary of State Hillary Clinton jointly announced a cease-fire to take effect at 9 P.M. on November 21. In accepting the cease-fire, both sides claimed victory. Almost immediately, both sides also violated the cease-fire, but the region, while continuing to simmer, has not boiled over in the wake of the 2011 Arab Spring. Rockets occasionally leave Gaza, and missile strikes continue to explode in Gaza as drones fly overhead.

The Least You Need to Know

- Hezbollah, the "Party of God," arose amid the chaos of Lebanese civil war to become a shadow state within a failed state.

- Although Hezbollah was created as an anti-Zionist Lebanese Shia political and guerrilla organization dedicated to national sovereignty, it was financed by Iran and given political support by Syria.

- While Hezbollah was based in Lebanon, where it became a strong military and political power, Hamas, a hardline religious Palestinian nationalist organization, took root in the Gaza Strip. It soon contended with the Fatah faction, essentially the established political elites, for political control of the occupied Palestinian state.

- Despite attempts at creating Palestinian/Israeli coexistence, beginning with the 1993 Oslo Accords, the conflict between Palestinians and Israelis remains, as made tragically evident in Operations Cast Lead (December 27, 2008–January 18, 2009) and Pillar of Defense (November 14–21, 2012).

Storms of the "Arab Spring"

"It is the policy of the United States to seek and support the growth of democratic movements and institutions in every nation and culture, with the ultimate goal of ending tyranny in our world," George W. Bush proclaimed in his second inaugural address, on January 20, 2005. "Tyranny," he said, creates "resentment" and "ideologies that feed hatred and excuse murder." In places ruled by tyrants, "violence will gather, and multiply in destructive power, and cross the most defended borders, and raise a mortal threat."

Both "events and common sense," he said, lead "to one conclusion: the survival of liberty in our land increasingly depends on the success of liberty in other lands. The best hope for peace in our world is the expansion of freedom in all the world."

And so, in his second term, President Bush continued the wars in Afghanistan and Iraq, bolstered by an argument other presidents made at other times when the issue was fighting a war or rendering aid in a part of the world remote from the United States. The argument for unconditionally supporting democracy is the lens through which many Americans have observed the uprisings against a variety of leaders in the Middle East, events Westerners have called the "Arab Spring."

In This Chapter

- The influence of the Democratic Peace Thesis

- The "Jasmine Revolution" in Tunisia

- The "Lotus Revolution" in Egypt

- Revolution and civil war in Libya

- The Yemeni Revolution

- Other uprisings of the "Arab Spring"

The Democratic Peace Thesis

When war engulfed the nations of Europe, together with their global colonies, beginning in the summer of 1914, the people and politicians looked on from across the Atlantic at what they called "the European War" and congratulated themselves that they and their sons would not be fighting and dying in it. Actual German aggression combined with British and French propaganda over the years to influence American popular opinion, which painted Germany and its allies (called the "Central Powers") as driven by "autocratic tyranny" that was in and of itself a menace to democracy in America and the rest of the world.

When President Woodrow Wilson asked Congress for a declaration of war against Germany in 1917, he declared that the "world must be made safe for democracy." And most Americans agreed with him. The idea that only autocratic nations, nations ruled by tyrants, made war was an unspoken but powerful assumption of most Americans. Its corollary was likewise a compelling article of faith: democracies don't make war on one another.

Historians and scholars called it the "Democratic Peace Thesis," and they traced its origin to such eighteenth-century philosophers as Montesquieu, Rousseau, and especially Immanuel Kant, whose 1795 essay *Perpetual Peace: A Philosophical Sketch* lays out the political conditions by which nations might govern themselves in ways that promote peace rather than war. Paramount among these conditions is a government that is constitutional, representative, and republican. Building on the liberal political ideas of the Age of Enlightenment, the idea of democracy as essentially peaceful gained traction through the nineteenth and twentieth centuries, becoming an assumption that has informed much of American foreign policy through the twentieth century and now into the twenty-first.

 DID YOU KNOW?

> Although Kant's *Perpetual Peace* is widely seen as the source of the Democratic Peace Thesis, the essay does not simply identify democracy as the leading condition for world peace. In fact, Kant specifies the need for republican, not democratic, government. A republican government is representative, but that representation is not necessarily democratic because it need not be the product of universal suffrage. Moreover, Kant also specified moving beyond national government to create a world government based on a "federation of free states" and a "law of world citizenship" founded on a concept of "universal hospitality."

This world view is noble, but it may also distort regional and local realities by imposing a Western cultural and political vision on places, circumstances, and people who are driven by their own sets of deeply held beliefs. The wars in Afghanistan and Iraq, as well as the events of what many Westerners call the "Arab Spring," have put the Democratic Peace Thesis to a hard test, exposing it as both simplistic and naïve.

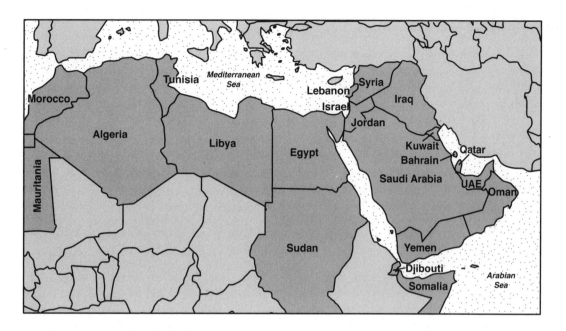

A Burning in Tunisia

Eight relatives depended for support on Mohamed Bouazizi, age 26, who sold vegetables from a cart in Sidi Bouzid, a town 190 miles south of the Tunisian capital of Tunis. He had managed, somehow, to make a living with his cart for seven years, until December 17, 2010, when an encounter with a police officer suddenly changed all that.

It had happened to him once before. He operated his cart without a license, for which the fine was 10-dinar, equivalent to seven U.S. dollars, a full day's wages for a working man like Bouazizi. This time, however, the policewoman—allegedly—spat out an insult to Bouazizi's dead father and slapped him across the face. (The unarmed policewoman later claimed she did not insult Bouazizi, who, she said, assaulted her.) When his cart and merchandise were confiscated, Bouazizi went to the local administrative authorities in an effort to get them returned. The officials refused to see him, however. With that, Bouazizi left the administrative building.

A short time later, the young man returned to the building, poured an unidentified flammable liquid over himself, and set himself ablaze.

Mohamed Bouazizi, gravely burned, lingered in the local hospital. Seeking to reverse the decline of his beleaguered popular image, President Zine el Abidine Ben Ali visited him on December 28. He hoped his demonstration of concern would quell the riots that rocked Sidi Bouzid and soon spread to Tunis and other cities. By the time Bouazizi died on January 4, 2011, Internet social media had broadcast video of the uprising throughout the Arab world and the world beyond it.

The Jasmine Revolution

On the face of it, the demonstrators were powerless. The police were armed with tear gas, clubs, and guns. The people had nothing but their will to resist, to endure police assault, and, in some cases, like Bouazizi, to end their own lives in their own way. On December 22, a demonstrator named Lahseen Naji electrocuted himself by climbing a high-voltage power transmission pylon. Another man killed himself over the hopeless debt imposed by a government-sponsored micro-credit scheme. Many others were killed or wounded by police.

Everything that happened, it seemed, was captured by cellphone video and shared online with the world. Soon, labor strikes brought the country to a standstill, and what was now being called the "Jasmine Revolution" spread from the margins of the lowest classes upward as the nation's 8,000 lawyers joined the general strike.

 VOICES

> The United States stands with the entire international community in bearing witness to this brave and determined struggle for the universal rights that we must all uphold, and we will long remember the images of the Tunisian people seeking to make their voices heard.

—President Barack Obama, January 15, 2011

On January 14, 17 days after Bouazizi's self-immolation, President Zine el Abidine Ben Ali fled Tunisia after 24 years of dictatorship. When his plane was denied permission to land in France, it touched down at Jeddah, Saudi Arabia, where King Abdullah granted asylum to him and his family—on condition that he renounce politics forever. It is unlikely that Ben Ali will ever leave Jeddah. At the request of the interim Tunisian government, the international police agency Interpol issued a warrant for Ben Ali's arrest for money laundering and drug trafficking. A Tunisian court sentenced him and his wife, in absentia, to 35 years in prison for theft and unlawful possession of cash and jewelry and, subsequently, also sentenced Ben Ali to life imprisonment for inciting violence and murder.

From Protest to Democracy

The flight of Ben Ali was sudden, leaving both rejoicing and disorder in its wake. Citing Article 57 of Tunisia's constitution, a Constitutional Court certified Fouad Mebazaa, president of the country's Chamber of Deputies, as the nation's acting president. An interim caretaker government, consisting of members of the Constitutional Democratic Rally (RCD)—Ben Ali's own party—and a variety of opposition leaders, was put in place pending the outcome of elections, which were set to take place in 60 days.

The opposition leaders were not content to allow a coalition with the RCD and resigned as quickly as they were appointed, thereby touching off new street protests throughout the country. From the people themselves, a cry arose to disband the RCD and to permit none of its former members from serving in a new government. In response, Prime Minister Mohamed Ghannouchi, on January 27, removed from office all RCD members—save himself—and, days later, the interior minister ordered the suspension of all RCD activities. The party was officially dissolved on March 9, 2011.

In the meantime, despite his purge of RCD officials, Ghannouchi himself bowed to ongoing public protests and stepped down on February 27. With the interim government free of everyone associated with Ben Ali, Acting President Mebazaa announced on March 3, 2011, elections for the Constituent Assembly to be held on October 23.

The moderate Islamist Ennahda Party won a plurality, and on December 12 the Constituent Assembly elected Moncef Marzouki, a physician and human rights activist, interim president of Tunisia.

Miracle and Model

The Jasmine Revolution had taken 27 days, from the first demonstrations on December 18, 2010, to the departure of Ben Ali on January 14, 2011. The dead numbered 338, with more than 2,000 injured—given the scope and effect of the revolution's success, a relatively modest toll.

The Constituent Assembly had been put in place through free and democratic elections, and the result was a genuine coalition of moderate Muslims (the Ennahda Party) and center-left secularists (the Congress for the Republic Party), in addition to a minority of frankly leftist members of the Ettakatol Party.

The transformation seemed a miracle, and it served as an inspiration and a model for the overthrow of other repressive regimes in the Arab world. Yet the process and results of change would not be nearly so "miraculous" elsewhere.

Revolution in Egypt

Americans shared in Tunisia's celebrations, and when, beginning on January 25, 2011, the democratic momentum appeared to spread to Egypt, they shared the hopes of demonstrators in Cairo's Tahrir Square. At issue was the one-party, one-man rule of Hosni Mubarak, who had succeeded Anwar Sadat when he was assassinated in 1981.

The fourth president of Egypt, Mubarak served for 30 years, longer than any of his three predecessors. His Egypt suffered from high unemployment, abysmal minimum wages, and inflated food prices. During his administration, he engaged in electoral fraud, used police to suppress dissent, exercised political censorship, presided over high-level government corruption, and used state-of-emergency laws to exercise absolute power.

State of Fraud

To much of the world, and to Westerners in particular, what had been different about Tunisia's Jasmine Revolution was its political character, which seemed quite different from the religious motives that often drove popular uprisings in the Middle East. What was happening in Egypt looked to be following Tunisia's lead. Hosni Mubarak was, theoretically, the president of a constitutional republic. In fact, however, he governed a police state through a kind of low-level martial law and enjoyed power so absolute that his many critics referred to him as a latter-day pharaoh.

Because Mubarak was friendly to the West, especially the United States, and because he maintained the fiction of democracy, America generally supported the Mubarak regime, which was content to continue the policy of peaceful coexistence with Israel begun by Sadat, and which, for political reasons, acted to suppress Islamic militants, especially the Muslim Brotherhood, within Egypt.

Hosni Mubarak

Born in the fertile Nile delta region on May 4, 1928, to an official of the Ministry of Justice, Hosni Mubarak attended local schools before enrolling in the Egyptian Military Academy, graduating in February 1949. He then attended the two-year course at the Air Force Academy, where he stayed on as a flight instructor until 1959. After receiving advanced bomber training in the Soviet Union and attending the elite Frunze General Staff Academy there, Mubarak returned to Egypt and, during the early 1960s, commanded the Egyptian bomber force during the Yemeni civil war.

In 1967, President Gamal Abdel Nasser named Mubarak director of the Air Force Academy and tasked him with rebuilding the Egyptian air force, which had been largely destroyed by the Israelis during the Six-Day War.

Promoted to air force chief of staff, Mubarak became a close associate of President Anwar Sadat, who named him commander in chief of the air force in 1972. With the air force as rebuilt by Mubarak, Sadat launched the Yom Kippur War on October 6, 1972, beginning with an air strike Mubarak himself had planned. Although the Egyptian air arm was still undermanned and was equipped with planes inferior to those of Israel, Mubarak's pilots nevertheless destroyed over 90 percent of the Israeli installations they targeted. While Egypt was ultimately defeated in the 1972 war, the air campaign was one of the greatest victories in Egyptian military history.

When Islamic fundamentalists assassinated Sadat on his reviewing stand during a parade in October 1981, Mubarak, though wounded in the attack, succeeded him as president. Immediately following his accession, he rounded up 2,500 radical Muslims, crushing an Islamic uprising. He ordered the execution of those directly implicated in the assassination and sentenced many others to long prison terms. He vowed to carry on Sadat's programs, particularly the momentous strides Sadat had made toward bringing peace between Egypt and Israel. Mubarak's diplomatic savvy personally restored Egypt's standing in the Arab world without repudiating the Arab-Israeli treaty.

And yet, over the years, against a background of economic crisis, the Mubarak government was characterized by corruption, including financial malfeasance. Criticism of the government was dealt with severely, through a network of secret police. By the time of the January 25 Revolution, Mubarak had clearly lost touch with a majority of the Egyptian people. He resigned as Egypt's president on February 11, 2011, having served 30 years, longer than any previous president. He was arrested and brought to trial on charges of corruption, abuse of power, and negligence for failing to give orders to stop the killing of peaceful protestors. Military prosecutors also began investigating the possibility of Mubarak's complicity in the assassination of Anwar Sadat.

Mubarak was sentenced to life imprisonment on June 2, 2012, but an appeals court overturned his sentence and ordered a retrial on January 13, 2013. On August 20 of that year, another court ordered his release from prison, but the country's interim prime minister ordered his confinement under house arrest.

Nights in Tahrir Square

Poverty, corruption, and tyranny can masquerade as democracy for only so long. Despite all dangers, anti-Mubarak opposition groups formed and coalesced. A combination of high-level corruption—a cozy relationship between prominent Egyptian tycoons and the Mubarak regime—and a failing economy plus accumulating incidents of sometimes lethal police brutality created the critical mass sufficient to sustain a popular uprising. All that was required to set off a chain reaction was some precipitating event. The Mubarak government could control broadcast media, but not the Internet and social media—at least not completely. Like the rest of the world, Egyptians saw the Jasmine Revolution unfold in Tunisia.

January 25 was National Police Day in Egypt. Opposition groups used this official holiday as an occasion for protest, in which tens of thousands of individuals took part. The next day, demonstrations spread from Cairo to Suez and other places. Friday evening, January 28, saw the ranks of demonstrators in Cairo and elsewhere swell to the hundreds of thousands in what was called the "Friday of Anger." The escalation was confirmed by the Mubarak government itself, which withdrew the police from the streets and sent in the military.

 DID YOU KNOW?

Tahrir Square is an enormous traffic roundabout and urban space in downtown Cairo long used as a place of demonstration and protest and was the central gathering place of the popular protests that led to the overthrow of President Hosni Mubarak. Called Ismailia Square after Khedive Ismail, who ruled Egypt from 1863 to 1879 and reshaped central Cairo in the image of Paris, the square was informally renamed Tahrir—"Liberation"—Square after the 1919 revolution, a name officially confirmed after the revolution of 1952.

But the military showed restraint, and, on Friday night, the violence that erupted in Cairo's Tahrir Square was not between the army and demonstrators, but between anti-Mubarak protestors and those Egyptians who still supported the government.

By the next day, January 29, more troops were in the streets of Cairo, and the government declared a curfew. Many thousands of protestors simply ignored the curfew and continued to gather in Tahrir Square. It was a mass spectacle that could not help but attract the attention of worldwide media. When Mubarak ordered the military to use live ammunition to clear the square, the army refused.

Mubarak Falters—and Falls

Now that he could no longer rely on the military for unquestioning obedience, Mubarak appeared on Egyptian television on February 1 to offer concessions, including a promise to implement a slate of political reforms and not to run for reelection in September.

The protestors were unconvinced, and the day after Mubarak's televised address, clashes between pro- and anti-Mubarak demonstrators increased in intensity, culminating in a camel charge through Tahrir Square. Mubarak supporters, wielding sticks, rode camels and horses into the anti-Mubarak crowd. When the protestors stood their ground, violence was turned instead against reporters—clearly a desperate effort to suppress images of revolt.

On Sunday, February 6, Tahrir Square became the site of a remarkable interfaith mass, in which Muslims and the country's ancient and sizeable community of Coptic Christians participated together. This demonstration of solidarity, crossing the lines of faith, was powerful. At this point, too, it was becoming apparent that the military was not about to turn against the protestors, but was functioning to provide security for everyone in the streets, while protecting from damage and looting the great Egyptian Museum of Antiquity, in which the ancient heritage of the nation was housed. Perhaps for the first time in 30 years, the mass of the Egyptian people saw the military serving to protect them and to preserve the heart and soul of the nation.

Indeed, the military seemed poised to launch a coup d'état, and on February 10, when Mubarak once again appeared on television, many Egyptians expected that he was about to announce his resignation. Instead, he announced that he was turning over some of his authority to his vice president, Omar Suleiman. If this gesture was an attempt at appeasement, it failed miserably. Following the broadcast, the pace and intensity of protest increased throughout Egypt.

 **VOICES**

The sooner Mubarak leaves, the better it is for everybody and the quicker we can restore normality and stability in Egypt and establish the cornerstone of democracy in the Middle East.

—Mohamed Elbaradei, Nobel laureate and former acting vice president of Egypt, quoted in *The Guardian*, February 2, 2011

The Friday of Departure

Through the night of February 10, the protests only grew, spilling over into Friday, February 11, 2011. At 6:00 that evening, Vice President Suleiman—not Hosni Mubarak—appeared on Egyptian television screens. He announced that the president had resigned and had turned over governing authority to the Supreme Council of Egyptian Armed Forces.

The world now watched Tahrir Square erupt into celebration, and the world celebrated alongside them and their successful nonviolent democratic movement

An Absence of Certainty

In the immediate aftermath of Mubarak's resignation, the Supreme Council of Egyptian Armed Forces dissolved parliament and suspended the Egyptian constitution—both actions taken in response to the demands of the demonstrators. The military announced its intention to retain power for six months or until elections could be held, and a spokesman pledged that that the military would not put forth a presidential candidate from its ranks.

In March, protestors raided buildings that housed Egypt's State Security Intelligence offices, in search of documents that would provide evidence of Mubarak's crimes against the Egyptian people.

On April 1, demonstrators participated in a "Save the Revolution Day," a protest aimed at urging the military to move faster in tearing down the vestiges of the Mubarak government. They also called for the trials of Mubarak and other deposed government officials.

April 8 was proclaimed the "Friday of Cleaning," with Tahrir Square erupting in protests demanding speedier action from the Supreme Council. On May 27, in a "Second Friday of Anger," tens of thousands of demonstrators again filled Tahrir Square, along with sites in other cities, still seeking definitive action to speed the transition from military to civilian government.

Another Friday demonstration, the "Friday of Retribution," took place on July 1, 2011. This time, hundreds of thousands gathered in Tahrir Square, Suez, and Alexandria to condemn the sluggish pace of reform and voice their fears that the military would never relinquish power. These demonstrations were repeated three more times in July, culminating in a violent clash at the Defense Ministry on July 23, when protestors were assaulted by a mob wielding sticks, stones, and Molotov cocktails.

On August 1 and 6, the military itself attacked and arrested protestors. The fact is that many Egyptians sided with the military and supported these actions—an indication that popular patience with ceaseless protest was wearing thin. In an even more disheartening development, thousands of protestors stormed the Israeli embassy in Cairo, prompting a major confrontation with the Egyptian military. Egypt's information minister assured Israel and the international community that the nation remained committed to all of its treaty obligations and was also determined to ensure the safety of foreign diplomats.

Elections and a New Uprising

The autumn of 2011 saw further clashes between security forces and protestors in Tahrir Square and elsewhere, all leading up to parliamentary elections, which spanned November 28, 2011, to January 11, 2012. At the end of this process, no party won a clear majority, but the Freedom and Justice Party, a political front for the Muslim Brotherhood, secured the most seats, 235 (255 were needed for a majority).

On January 23, Egypt's first democratically elected parliament (called the People's Assembly) convened, and the Supreme Council of the Armed Forces officially and peacefully handed over legislative authority. On the following day, Egypt's state of emergency, in force throughout most of the Mubarak regime, was partially lifted. It would totally expire on May 31, 2012. In the meantime, Egyptians cast their votes in the first round of presidential elections during May 23–24.

Mubarak's Fate

By the time of that first round, Hosni Mubarak and both of his sons had been questioned about corruption and abuse of power, Mubarak was bound over for trial on charges of negligence for not giving orders to stop the killing of peaceful protestors during the revolution. The trials began on August 3, 2011, and dragged on until June 2, 2012, when the deposed president was sentenced to life imprisonment.

Age and stress took their toll, and Mubarak suffered several bouts of illness. His sentence, however, was overturned on appeal on January 13, 2013, and he was released from prison on August 20. On the next day, Interim Prime Minister Hazem el-Beblawi intervened to order Mubarak to be placed under house arrest.

President Morsi

The victory of Mohammed Morsi in a presidential runoff election was announced on June 24, 2012. He had defeated Ahmed Shafik, who had been prime minister under Mubarak, garnering 51.7 percent of the vote. Morsi was inaugurated on June 30.

Having won the right to democratically elect their president, Egyptians, like Palestinians in Gaza, had elected a leading member of the Muslim Brotherhood, an organization hostile to the West generally and to the United States in particular. This was hardly the vision of "democracy" either George W. Bush or his successor, Barack Obama, had imagined.

The irony deepened on November 22, when the democratically elected Morsi granted himself unlimited powers so that he could protect the democratically elected People's Assembly from what he said was its planned dissolution by order of the Mubarak-era judges who still held their posts in the new government.

But the people were not buying it. After Morsi empowered himself, tens of thousands again gathered at Tahrir Square and elsewhere to protest the decree. Most of the demonstrators were secularists, liberals, leftists, and Christians, all profoundly uncomfortable with the idea of a Muslim Brotherhood leader as president. Soon, battles broke out between Morsi supporters and anti-Morsi protesters. The street combat turned ugly and resulted in scores of deaths and hundreds of injuries.

When some 200,000 anti-Morsi demonstrators marched to the presidential palace, they were confronted by Republican Guard tanks and some 100,000 Morsi supporters. Yet even as large numbers rose in Morsi's defense, his young administration was already beginning to fall apart, as numerous advisers and officials resigned in protest of the president's assumption of absolute power.

Hoping to stave off a coup d'état, Morsi annulled his own decree on December 8, 2012, yet continued to act as if the decree were in force. He wielded unchecked power. Days later, on December 22, the draft of the new Morsi-endorsed constitution was approved in a national referendum by a margin of 64 percent. Instantly, cries of fraud arose, and President Morsi found his government paralyzed by protests ongoing and new.

June 30, 2013, the anniversary of his inauguration, was observed by mass protests in Tahrir Square, outside the principal presidential palace, and throughout Cairo and elsewhere. Millions took to the streets, and an organization calling itself the Egyptian Movement for Change announced that it had collected 22 million signatures on a petition demanding Morsi's immediate resignation.

Coup d'État

On July 1, the Egyptian military stepped in, calling for Egypt's political parties to "meet the demands of the people" within 48 hours, after which the military would take charge. On July 3, with the deadline passed, a military spokesman quietly announced that the presidency of Mohammed Morsi had come to an end. Accordingly, the spokesman continued, the constitution was suspended, but a new presidential election would be held soon.

The military leadership did not offer one of its own as interim head of state, but announced that the chief justice of the constitutional court, Adly Mansour, was to be acting president and that a transitional government would be formed, pending new elections.

The anti-Morsi demonstrations were replaced by protests against military rule and, as of this writing (summer 2014) those protests continue. Yet, as noted in Chapter 6, the nation has not exploded into anything like full-scale revolution or civil war. On January 18, 2014, a new constitution, supported by 98.1 percent of the 38.6 percent of eligible voters who cast ballots, was put into force, and, in May, Abdel Fattah el-Sisi won election to the presidency by a landslide in what was, however, a low-turnout election.

Revolution in Libya

If the narrative arc of Egypt's January 25 Revolution fell far short of Tunisia's inspiring rise to democracy, there was early hope that the brewing revolution—or was it civil war?—in Libya would make more gratifying progress.

Whereas Tunisia's deposed dictator, Zine El Abidine Ben Ali, was little known in the West, and Hosni Mubarak was at least palatable to the United States as a pliable secular leader in a region known for fiery religious ideologues, Muammar Muhammad Abu Minyar al-Gaddafi, "Brotherly Leader and Guide of the Revolution of Libya" since 1969, was infamous—feared and despised in the West and throughout most of North Africa and the Middle East. A terrorist and supporter of terrorism, a tyrant who always seemed to dwell just beyond the edge of rationality, Gaddafi was forever linked to the 1988 bombing of Pan-Am Flight 103 over Lockerbie, Scotland. In a complex region where Americans and other outsiders too often made the mistake of simple-mindedly demonizing leaders, Muammar Gaddafi consistently looked and acted like a demon.

 **VOICES**

> There is a tendency in Washington to refer to the Libyan dictator, Muhammad [sic]
> Gaddafi, as a crazy man. Armchair psychologists justify this glib label by pointing to
> his fanatic extremism, his failure to put realistic limits on boastful pronouncements,
> and his periodic fits of deep depression when he retreats to the desert and broods in
> his tent.
>
> —U.S. columnist Jack Anderson, March 1982

From Protest to Revolution

The anti-Gaddafi protests began in Libya on February 15, 2011. As in Egypt, they took inspiration from the protest movement in Tunisia, but in Libya they seemed to move much faster. Within three days, antigovernment forces seized control of most of Benghazi, Libya's second-largest city. The Gaddafi government sent elite regular army troops, augmented by loyal militia, to retake Benghazi, but they were quickly forced into retreat.

Gaddafi, who rose to power in the Libyan military, often wore outlandishly elaborate uniforms and portrayed himself as a military strongman, but in a matter of days a ragtag cadre of rebels had bested Gaddafi's army. The spectacle inspired a general uprising throughout much of Libya, and by February 20 protests and demonstrations were being staged in the capital city of Tripoli.

It was the Tripoli manifestations that prompted a television address by Saif al-Islam Gaddafi, second son of the Libyan leader, holder of a PhD from the prestigious London School of Economics and an unofficial spokesman for his father. Saif warned that the civil unrest could quickly escalate into bloody civil war.

It turned out to be an accurate assessment, as protest indeed quickly morphed into war. In contrast to Tunisia, where bloodshed was relatively limited, the toll of injured and dead rose rapidly in Libya. Gaddafi's failure to seek a peaceful end to the violence prompted many of his closest advisers and other officials to resign. Some even called for his resignation and, with it, the immediate dismantling of the government. Onlooker nations, both within and outside of the Arab world, were virtually unanimous in their condemnation of the regime. Already an outcast among world leaders, Muammar Gaddafi was now an irredeemable pariah.

A Reversal of Fortune

While the rebels used an array of improvised weapons and jerry-rigged vehicles to wage a battle for the capture of Tripoli, opposition leaders proclaimed an interim government in Benghazi, challenging the established government in Tripoli.

Initial news coverage that reached the West tended to portray the rebels as skilled insurgents fighting poorly led government forces. It soon became apparent, however, that after suffering early losses, those government forces were making gains and retaking lost territory, including most of Libya's Mediterranean coastline.

Gaddafi made no attempt to spare the lives of the people he had long ruled. He fought the internal rebels as if they were external enemies, ruthlessly and without making any distinction between combatants and noncombatants. For their part, however, the rebels lacked cohesive central leadership and, when it suited them, resorted to inflicting terror on communities identified as loyal to Gaddafi.

The UN Acts

On March 17, the United Nations Security Council passed Resolution 1973, which declared a no-fly zone over Libya and ordered measures to be taken for the protection of civilians. Acting on the resolution, France, the United States, and the United Kingdom launched a bombing campaign beginning on March 19, exclusively targeting government forces, both Gaddafi's regular army and loyalist militia units.

Such was the magnitude of the humanitarian crisis and the universal international contempt for Gaddafi that, very quickly, 27 nations from Europe as well as the Middle East formed a coalition to "protect" the people of Libya. What this meant, in effect, was to support the rebels. Yet "the rebels" were a very diverse lot, ranging from those who sought a military victory to those who sought vengeance and were willing to terrorize, torture, and kill anyone who got in their way. As in many of history's civil wars, there was no neatly defined opposition between one "side" and another. The combatants were factionalized, with many groups, both pro- and antigovernment, pursuing their own agendas and taking violence to horrific extremes.

Backed by coalition air support and armed with coalition-supplied weapons, the rebels were able to force Gaddafi's troops out of Benghazi. This accomplished, the rebels launched a new offensive, moving rapidly from one small coastal town to another, capturing and occupying each.

Despite the outside assistance and the momentum regained, the offensive petered out. Once the movement stalled, Gadaffi responded with a large-scale counteroffensive that rapidly reclaimed most of the coast.

Bloody Stalemate

As the government counteroffensive slowed, the war settled into a gruesome stalemate between forces centered in government-held Brega and rebel-controlled Ajdabiya. While the fighting raged there, government forces and loyalist militia laid siege to Libya's third-largest city, Misrata, which was tenuously held by the rebels. Only after coalition air strikes were called in did the siege break and government forces withdraw.

Tripoli Falls

On June 11, Gaddafi and his son Saif al-Islam offered to hold elections, and Gaddafi pledged to step down if he was defeated. The rebels as well as the coalition supporting them—which was now led by NATO—spurned the offer. In July, NATO aircraft began bombing Tripoli in preparation for a rebel offensive aimed at capturing the capital. This commenced on August 20, 2011, and on August 21, the rebels reported that they had arrested Saif al-Islam and were now surrounding Gaddafi's compound.

On August 22, rebel forces entered central Tripoli and set up a base in the city's Green Square, which they renamed Martyrs' Square to honor those who had fallen in the fight to overthrow Gaddafi.

It now seemed that a rebel victory was imminent; however, on August 23, Saif al-Islam gave the lie to rebel claims that he was a prisoner by appearing at the Rixos Hotel, which was controlled by the government, to announce that his father was still very much in charge. When, later that afternoon, the rebels overran the fortified Bab al-Azizia barracks in downtown Tripoli, where Gaddafi was reported to be holed up, they found neither the dictator nor any of his family.

The End of Gaddafi

On August 24, Gaddafi himself broadcast a radio address, acknowledging that he had indeed made a "tactical" withdrawal from Bab al-Azizia. Even as fighting—disorganized on both sides—continued to rage in Tripoli, it became apparent that Gaddafi and what remained of his government had fled. The rebels therefore pushed northwest toward the city of Sirte, engaging and destroying loyalist militia and regular army forces along the way. As the endgame of the civil war played out, Gaddafi announced that Sirte was Libya's new capital.

As numbers of his lieutenants fled to other towns as well as to remote refuges in the vast Libyan Desert or to whatever neighboring countries would accept them, Gaddafi stubbornly remained in his "new capital."

On October 20, 2011, rebels identifying themselves with the National Transitional Council closed in on Sirte. At this point, Gaddafi took flight in a combined civilian-military convoy, headed for the Jarref Valley. Observing the convoy, NATO aircraft attacked, hitting 14 or more vehicles and killing 53 or more persons. In surviving vehicles or on foot, the members of the convoy scattered.

Gaddafi and some of his innermost circle took refuge in a local house, which the rebel militia immediately shelled. Seeking to escape this onslaught. Gaddafi and others hid in sewer pipes and culverts stored at a nearby construction site while the dictator's loyal bodyguards shot it out with rebels.

Disabled by a head wound suffered in a grenade blast, Gaddafi was captured by rebel Misrata militiamen. They beat him mercilessly and, in an act of sadistic humiliation, stabbed him in the rectum. All the while, they recorded the episode with a mobile phone video camera. Gaddafi's body—he may still have been alive at the time—was draped across the hood of a pickup truck, as if it were a slain deer. The video shows it falling off as the truck begins to move. At this point, he was picked up and loaded into an ambulance, which carried him to Misrata. By the time the ambulance arrived in the town, Gaddafi was dead.

Outcome

The end of Gaddafi was not the end of war in Libya. Diehard loyalists continued fitfully to engage rebels. The National Transitional Council (NTC) emerged as an interim legislature as the country struggled—and (as of summer 2014) continues to struggle—to reconstitute itself.

Initially, most of the legislation the NTC enacted granted legal immunity to all rebel fighters for any acts committed during the war and ordered the speedy trial of pro-Gaddafi prisoners. All criticism of the revolution was banned, as was any praise of Muammar Gaddafi, his family, or his government.

Although Libyans voted for members of parliament (called the General National Congress) on July 7, 2012, and the NTC handed over power to the General National Congress on August 8, sectarian violence and economic crisis have continued to plague the country. In a climate of lawlessness, oil production, virtually the sole driver of the Libyan economy, has ceased.

 DID YOU KNOW?

Americans were swept up in Libyan the violence on the night of September 11, 2012—anniversary of the terrorist attacks of 2001—when militants stormed the U.S. consulate in Benghazi. The U.S. ambassador to Libya, J. Christopher Stevens, along with Foreign Service Officer Sean Smith and two security team members, Glen Doherty and Tyrone S. Woods, died in the attack.

Revolution in Yemen

Yemen, January 27, 2011. Half the people of this Arab nation at the southwestern end of the Arabian Peninsula, live below the $2-a-day poverty line. Only a small minority of Yeminis have access to anything like modern sanitation, and although the country has roads, fewer than 1 in 10 is paved.

It would be fair to describe Yemen as a failed state. Its central government, headed by President Ali Abdullah Saleh, is riddled with corruption and exercises barely any positive control outside of the capital city of Sana'a. Rural districts are at the mercy of violent gangs, and Yemenis now flood Sana'a and other urban areas in search of employment and a semblance of security, neither of which exists. What little income Yemen receives comes from oil exports. Experts predict that the nation's oil fields will run dry sometime in the early 2020s.

Clearly, Yemenis had an abundance of reasons to be desperately dissatisfied, and calls for President Saleh to step down had been coming as early as 2009, including from members of his own inner circle. But on January 27, the 16,000 or so students and other activists who gathered in protest at Sana'a University made no secret of their inspiration. It was, as in Egypt and Libya, the revolution in Tunisia. "Oh, Ali," they shouted, "join your friend Ben Ali"—a reference to Zine el Abidine Ben Ali, the ousted Tunisian president.

The January 27 demonstration was the culmination of a series of more modest protests specifically targeting the generally abysmal economic conditions, desperately high unemployment, and the government's culture of corruption. An especially sore point, and one that put Saleh in the crosshairs, was the president's proposal to modify the national constitution to allow his son to inherit his office, as if he were a prince. Bolstered by the Tunisian experience, this proposal escalated the protest into a demand that Saleh resign. At this point, the military, along with top administration officials, voted with their feet. They deserted the president in droves.

Days of Rage

President Saleh sought to placate the rebellion on February 2 by announcing that he would neither run for reelection in 2013 nor pass the presidency down to his son. Emboldened, the people responded with an even bigger protest in Sana'a on February 3. Twenty thousand gathered in the capital, and several thousand protested in the southern port city of Aden. It was dubbed a "Day of Rage."

Countering the antigovernment demonstration was a pro-government rally of loyal soldiers and armed civilian members of the General People's Congress. To this, the antigovernment forces replied on February 18 by staging a "Friday of Anger" in Sana'a as well as in Aden and Taiz. On March 11, in what was billed as a "Friday of No Return," protestors clamored for the immediate overthrow of Saleh. The protest turned violent, and three demonstrators were killed.

Protests soon spread to other cities, and on March 18, government forces fired live ammunition into a crowd of demonstrators in Sana'a. Fifty-two died in a massacre so shocking that police, soldiers, and government officials resigned en masse.

The Persistence of Ali Abdullah Saleh

In late April 2011, President Saleh accepted a deal brokered by the Gulf Cooperation Council (GCC), which called for his resignation and the transfer of power to an interim government. On three separate occasions, he agreed to sign the deal, only to back away at the last minute. At last, a frustrated GCC announced that it was suspending its role as mediator.

On May 23, one day after the GCC walked away, Sheikh Sadiq al-Ahmar, leader of Yemen's powerful Hashid tribal federation, declared his group's support for the anti-Saleh movement. This provoked an armed confrontation between his supporters and Saleh loyalists. Soon, Sana'a was embroiled in bloody street fighting. Into the melee, both sides threw artillery and mortar fire.

On June 3, an explosion devastated a mosque within the presidential compound. It was—and remains—unclear whether the explosion was the result of an artillery barrage or the detonation of planted bomb. In either case, five government officials were killed and others were wounded, President Saleh among them. He flew to Saudi Arabia for medical treatment, and, on June 4, in his absence, Vice President Abd al-Rab Mansur al-Hadi took over as acting president.

Masses of protestors celebrated what they assumed was the longed-for transfer of power, but government officials announced that President Saleh intended to resume the presidency. Indeed, early in July, the government rejected a demand for the creation of a transitional council and a caretaker government to supervise the first democratic elections in Yemen's history.

Undaunted by this rejection, a partial coalition of opposition groups proclaimed its own transitional council on July 16, but failed to attract a clear majority of the opposition factions. Nevertheless, on November 23, President Saleh at last signed the GCC-brokered power-transfer agreement. Saleh was obliged to transfer presidential power to the vice president within 30 days and then leave office entirely by February 2012. In return, he was promised immunity from prosecution.

Election Day

On January 22, 2012, Saleh reportedly left Yemen for medical treatment at a New York City hospital. A month later, he left the United States and landed in Ethiopia on February 24. Three days earlier, on February 21, Yemen had conducted its first democratic presidential election. Sixty-five percent of eligible voters turned out at the polls, 99.8 percent of them voting for the man who had served as the country's vice president, Abd al-Rab Mansur al-Hadi. He ran uncontested.

Hours before Hadi took the oath of office on February 25, Saleh arrived in Yemen to attend the inauguration, officially resign his office, and formally transfer power. He had been president for 33 years.

AQAP and Others

Hadi's candidacy was officially uncontested, but on the very day of his inauguration, February 25, 2012, a suicide attack on the presidential palace killed 26 Republican Guards. A group calling itself al-Qaeda in the Arabian Peninsula (AQAP) claimed credit.

Currently, AQAP remains a threatening presence in Yemen, and while Saleh, granted immunity, has left politics, his son, General Ahmed Ali Abdullah Saleh, commands a substantial following among segments of the Yemeni military.

Hadi currently presides over a unity government, which includes a prime minister from the party opposed to his, and is overseeing the creation of a new constitution. From time to time, AQAP commits acts of terrorism on the streets of Sana'a and elsewhere, and the United States has stationed a contingent of CIA operatives and Special Forces soldiers in the country, part of an effort to curb the AQAP attacks. As of this writing, in the summer of 2014, the situation in Yemen remains fluid. The nation is still desperately poor, but a majority now has reason to hope for some measure of improvement in their lives.

The Problem with Metaphors

In addition to the major revolutions discussed here, the Arab Spring has seen an uprising in Bahrain and major and minor protests throughout the Arab world, in Algeria, Iraq, Jordan, Kuwait, Morocco, Sudan, Mauritania, Oman, Saudi Arabia, Djibouti, Western Sahara, and Palestine. The most bitter and violent rebellion of all has morphed into a nightmarish stalemate of monumental civil war in Syria, the subject of the next chapter.

All of these events, from the remarkable degree of success seen in Tunisia to the horrors of Syria, and everything in between, point to the critical problem with the poetic metaphor of the Arab Spring.

 DID YOU KNOW?

In February 1993, historian James Lee Ray published an influential essay ("Wars between democracies: Rare or nonexistent?" International Interactions, 18:3, pp. 251–276) in which he enumerated at least 19 major wars between democracies, including the American Revolution, the American Civil War, and the Arab-Israeli War of 1948. And, Ray pointed out, if one considers the chronic warfare among Native American tribes (whose governments are often cited as models of democracy) or goes back to the ancient world, the volume of democracy-on-democracy wars increases considerably.

Spring, of course, is a time of rebirth and new growth. It is a time of great beauty, relief from winter's long oppression, and an affirmation of new life. Coined in the West, the phrase "Arab Spring" is not used by Arabs, who refer instead to the "Arab Uprisings." Many, both in the Middle East and elsewhere, criticize the spring metaphor because it implies that the Arab peoples were dormant, hibernating during the long years of dictatorship, when in reality they struggled under powerful oppression. Moreover, spring is a season. A function of planetary motion, it is destined to return year after year. A political-cultural-military movement cannot know such certainty, and while the period of uprisings suggests great promise, much also reveals the fragility of change in a region long abused by colonial powers, by individual tyrants, by religious intolerance, and, in so many places, by an unforgiving climate and a paucity of vital natural resources.

The Least You Need to Know

- No sooner were revolutionary forces victorious than the United States and other Western powers pronounced the events an "Arab Spring," interpreting it as a popular aspiration to Western-style democracy.

- The remarkably rapid "Jasmine Revolution" in Tunisia, which has brought an ample measure of democracy to the country, inspired popular uprisings against a host of "strongman" dictators throughout the Arab world. So far, none has been as successful as the Tunisian Revolution.

- Because of Egypt's large population, military power, and geopolitical importance, the world has followed the January 25 Revolution there with intense interest and anxiety as the people overthrew an autocratic and corrupt regime, elected a president with strong ties to radical Islam, and then supported a military coup against him.

- Uprisings in both Libya and Yemen quickly morphed into bitter civil wars, the ultimate outcomes of which remain unsettled.

Civil War in Syria

The uprisings in Syria began on March 15, 2011, as protests clearly aligned with what much of the world (outside of the Middle East itself) was calling the "Arab Spring." By this time, the "Jasmine Revolution" in Tunisia was over after less than a month, and Tunisia looked to be well on its way toward full democratic government. Loss of life, always tragic, was just 338 persons. There was hope that Syrians would enjoy a similar miracle.

As of summer 2014, the Syrian civil war continues. More than 100,000 Syrians have been killed, more than 2 million have become refugees (75 percent of them women and children), and more than 4 million have been displaced from their homes within Syria, which has a population of about 22 million.

In This Chapter

- Modern Syria's background of turbulence and tyranny

- The Assad "dynasty" is established

- The presidency of Bashar al-Assad initially offers hope of a "Damascus Spring"

- Bashar al-Assad turns tyrant

- An anti-Assad protest movement quickly expands into civil war

- Involvement of foreign powers in Syria's civil war

- The Syrian Civil War as representative of the Middle East's uncertain future

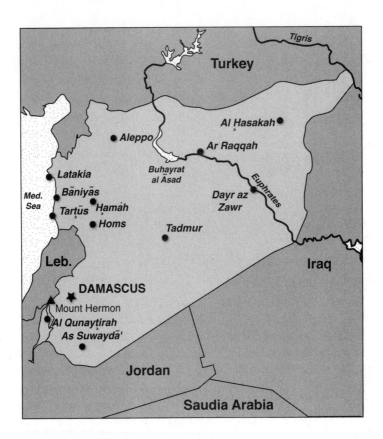

Syria Before Assad

Syria forms part of the so-called cradle of civilization. Here, archaeologists have found the remains of a Neolithic culture dating to 10,000 B.C.E. As noted in the Prologue, the land that is now Syria passed through many rulers before 1516, when the Ottoman Sultan Selim I defeated the Mamluks and annexed it to the Ottoman Empire. It remained under Ottoman governance until 1920, when, thanks to the dissolution of the Ottoman Empire brought by World War I, Syria gained independence in 1920 as the Arab Kingdom of Syria.

 **VOICES**

The whole of it, and forever!

—Premier Alexandre Millerand, proclaiming French possession of Syria, July 26, 1920

French Mandate

Almost as quickly as it was established, however, the Arab Kingdom came to an end as a result of the brief Franco-Syrian War, which resulted in the French Mandate of Syria officially ratified by the League of Nations in 1923. Following a 1925 rebellion known as the Great Syrian Revolt, Syria progressed toward independence as the Republic of Syria, which was proclaimed on May 14, 1930. Six years later, a Franco-Syrian Treaty of Independence was signed, but remained unratified by the French legislature. After France fell to Germany in World War II, the German puppet French Vichy Government took control of Syria until July 1941, when Free French and British forces invaded the country and liberated it. Syria once again proclaimed itself independent, a status that was not internationally recognized until January 1, 1944.

Turbulent Independence

On May 29, 1945, days after World War II ended in Europe, France, which had never ratified the Franco-Syrian Treaty, bombed the Syrian capital, Damascus, in an effort to recover its mandate. Backed by the newly founded United Nations, Syria responded by pressing its claim to independence, and in April 1946, the French, under pressure from Britain and the United States, evacuated the country.

In 1946, Syria finally and formally became independent. The government, however, was unstable. Syria's unrelenting opposition to Israel led the United States CIA to back a military coup d'état against the Syrian national government in 1949. The new leader, Ussni al-Zaimy, was quickly overthrown by one of his top lieutenants, Sami al-Hinnawi, who was himself deposed months later by Colonel Adib al-Shishkali. A veteran of the French Mandate Army, Shishkali opposed Hashim Bay Khalid al-Atassi, Syria's president during 1936–1939, 1849–1951, and 1954–1955, who proposed an Iraqi-Syrian merger as a way of restoring the Greater Syria of Ottoman days.

Shishkali made no pretense of championing democracy and supplanted the civilian government with military control. By 1951, he was functioning as absolute dictator. In 1954, however, a coalition of Syrian communists, Druze military officers, and members of the Ba'ath Party—quite possibly backed by Iraq—overthrew Shishkali, restoring Atassi to the presidency.

Even more intense instability followed the 1954 coup, but the coup had nevertheless given both the Ba'ath Party and the communists a firm foothold in the government. In November 1956, in the wake of the Suez Crisis, Syria concluded a pact with the Soviet Union, which equipped its military with modern aircraft, tanks, and artillery.

UAR

Seeking greater stability and with the Iraqi merger a nonstarter, Syria merged with Egypt as the United Arab Republic (UAR) on February 1, 1958. In a single stroke, all Syrian political parties lost standing—communists and Ba'athists included.

The UAR proved short lived, however. On September 28, 1961, a military coup created the Syrian Arab Republic. This triggered a series of coups followed by counter-coups, until March 8, 1963, when the Syrian military joined with civilian leaders of the Ba'ath Party (also known at this time as the Arab Socialist Renaissance Party), which installed a Cabinet controlled by Ba'athists.

The House of Assad

Ba'athism advocates Arab nationalism, to be expressed ultimately in a single unified Arab state. When the Ba'ath Party assumed control in Syria, the Syrian government proposed an alliance or league with Nasserist Egypt and Iraq (which was also controlled by Ba'athists), but negotiations came to nothing, and in November 1963 they collapsed entirely after the Ba'ath Party was overthrown in Iraq.

In the meantime, in 1964, Syria formed a coalition government that attempted to provide wide representation of many interests within the country. Despite the rationality and good intentions of this coalition, however, the military staged another coup on February 23, 1966, imprisoning President Amin Hafiz, dissolving the Cabinet and the National Council of the Revolution, and tearing up the constitution. The Ba'ath Party was reinstated, however, and gained control of the government on a regional level. Just as its struggle toward stability began to look hopeful, however, Israel captured and occupied the water-rich Golan Heights during the Six-Day War. The defeat shook the nation.

The Rise of Hafez al-Assad

Hafez al-Assad, whom we met in Chapter 13, was the son of a local official in Qardaha, in north-western Syria. An *Alawite*, Assad's father initially opposed French occupation during the mandate, but then cooperated with the French (who used the Alawites in their minority-rule colonial system) and resisted integration into the independent Syrian state. As Alawites, the Assads found themselves distrusted and even persecuted by the Sunni majority and so gravitated toward Ba'athism, which espoused secularism and pan-Arabism rather than Sunni-dominated government.

 **DEFINITION**

> **Alawites** are followers of a branch of Shia Islam that also integrates belief in elements of Gnosticism, Platonism, and Christianity. Centered in Syria, with communities in Turkey and Lebanon, the faith currently has perhaps three million adherents.

During the late 1940s, Assad rose within the Ba'ath movement, earning a reputation as a recruiter and organizer while he was still a teenage student. Too poor to pursue the medical studies that were his ambition, he joined the Syrian Armed Forces and entered air force flight school. By 1955, he graduated, with a trophy naming him best aviator. He was sent to Egypt and then to the Soviet Union for advanced flight training.

Despite his distinguished and promising early career, Assad was not content to remain a military officer. He became politically active and played roles in the military coups culminating in that of 1966, which resulted in his appointment as minister of defense under the Ba'athist "strongman," Salah Jadid.

The humiliating Arab defeat in the Six-Day War nearly cost Assad his cabinet post as well as his position in the Regional Command, the Ba'ath Party's highest decision-making body. This brush with failure drove him to build a network to oppose Jadid and thereby undercut his power. Whereas Jadid sought to insulate and isolate Syria from much of the Arab world and opposed the creation of a coalition government with elements outside of the Ba'ath Party, Assad reached out, both to other states and to members of other parties.

Exploiting Black September

On September 18, 1970, during the Black September crisis, in which the Palestine Liberation Organization (PLO) challenged the Hashemite monarchy of Jordan for control of the country, Hafez al-Assad, the de facto power behind Syrian government (still *officially* dominated by Jadid) and, as defense minister, in absolute control of the Syrian military, moved to intervene on behalf of the PLO.

The intervention failed, crushed by Jordanian air strikes. This should have fatally weakened Assad's position. But Jadid's criticism of Assad came across as abject defeatism. So even though the forces Assad had sent into Jordan were beaten, and even though the Emergency National Congress Jadid convened stripped Assad of his government posts, he refused to concede defeat. Instead, on November 12, 1970, Assad ordered his loyalists in the military to round up key members of Jadid's regime. The coup was total, yet totally bloodless.

 **VOICES**

If I ever take power, you will be dragged through the streets until you die.

—Syrian leader Salah Jadid, after being overthrown and arrested by Hafez al-Assad in November 1970

Assuming Power, Holding Power

Once at the helm, Hafez al-Assad moved swiftly to ensure that there would be no further drift in Syria's government. He immediately put into place a Ba'ath-dominated legislature, the People's Council, and the party itself quickly elected a new 21-member Regional Command with Assad at its head.

In March 1971, Assad sanctioned a national referendum that confirmed him as president for a term of seven years. The following year, in March 1972, Assad created the National Progressive Front, a coalition of political parties with the Ba'ath Party out front. One year after this, a new constitution went into effect, followed soon after by elections for the People's Council—the first popular elections since 1962.

Hafez al-Assad exercised a remarkable combination of political agility, ideological flexibility, quasi-European manners, and harsh autocratic rule to bring to Syria a degree of stability unknown in its modern history. While he opened government to a coalition—though always Ba'ath dominated—he gave no latitude to the Muslim Brotherhood or other conservative or radical Islamic groups. Critics of the regime were automatically branded as rebels and dealt with very harshly. In 1982, Assad attacked the city of Hamah, stronghold of the Muslim Brotherhood, substantially wiping it out. During the 30 years of his rule, he killed at least 20,000 dissidents.

Hafez al-Assad never hesitated to use the Syrian military to suppress dissent. In addition, he employed a secret police force to detain, torture, and sometimes summarily execute those he identi-fied as his enemies. In parallel with this repression, he relentlessly fostered a cult of personality that was reminiscent of the old Soviet Union under Joseph Stalin. Visitors to Damascus and other major Syrian cities could not help but note the ubiquity of billboard and banner images of Assad.

Son and Heir

Hafez al-Assad was not a very old man by the late 1990s, but he was a diabetic afflicted by severe heart disease and bouts of phlebitis. Although only just past his middle 60s, he began to dodder and fail. His workdays became briefer and briefer—down to about two fully functional hours before the decade was over. Formerly a hands-on leader, he now absented himself from routine affairs of state. At last, on June 10, 2000, while speaking on the telephone with the prime minister of Lebanon, he suffered his second massive heart attack. This one killed him. He was 69.

His chosen successor had been his eldest son, Bassel al-Assad. A former Special Forces officer and a commander of a Republican Guard battalion, he was handsome and charismatic—dubbed the "Golden Knight" because of his prize-winning equestrianism. If there was one thing he liked more than fast horses, it was fast cars. On January 21, 1994, he drove his prized Maserati at high speed through dense fog. He failed to see a looming motorway roundabout, hit a part of it, and was killed. Bassel's death left the younger son, Bashar al-Assad, next in line. He himself had never anticipated succeeding to the presidency.

DID YOU KNOW?

> Before designating Bassel al-Assad as his successor, Hafez al-Assad had settled on his brother Rifaat al-Assad. In 1983-1984, however, Hafez al-Assad suffered his first heart attack. Rifaat publicly announced that his brother's health would never be restored and that he would be unfit to rule. He therefore proclaimed his own candidacy for president. But Hafez did recover, and one of his first acts was to remove his brother from all offices and from the succession.

Bashar al-Assad did not look like a political leader, let along an autocratic one. His eyes were close-set, his mouth small, his chin weak, and he spoke in a soft voice, with a marked lisp. Indeed, he had not prepared for a political career, but rather for the career his father had been too poor to pursue. He graduated from the medical school of Damascus University in 1988, practiced as an army doctor, and then went to London's Western Eye Hospital to become an ophthalmologist.

Upon his brother's death, he was summoned back to Syria to begin preparations to rule. He attended the national military academy, and in 1998 was given command of the Syrian occupation of Lebanon.

"Damascus Spring"

His father's anointed heir, Bashar al-Assad faced only one obstacle to succession: the legal requirement that presidential candidates be at least 40 years old. Bashar was just 34, but the parliament obliged by voting to lower the minimum age. Official vote counters claimed that the young man garnered 97 percent of votes cast—an achievement rendered less impressive when it is understood that he ran unopposed. (When he stood for reelection in 2007, Bashar al-Assad actually improved his 2000 results slightly, polling 97.6 percent of the votes cast. As in the earlier race, he ran unopposed.)

Bashar al-Assad was by no means pro-Western, save for the cordiality he has often extended to France. Yet the fact that his wife had been born in Britain and that his French and English were fluent persuaded some that he was a reformer who intended to steer Syria on a secular course toward a willingness to compromise and coexist with the West. Moreover, he cooperated with the American post-9/11 War on Terror, relaxed restrictions on Western investment in Syria, and generally courted the West.

In contrast to his father, Bashar actually opened Syria to public political dialogue, so that the period from July 2000 to August 2001 was dubbed the "Damascus Spring." Lively debate and discussion were carried out in thousands of well-educated homes. Yet the spring proved fleeting. When the debate turned toward genuinely free and open elections and the espousal of true democracy, the regime surrounding Bashar, which had developed during his father's reign, asserted itself. In August 2001, Bashar, to a significant degree a figurehead for these men, sent government police forces to arrest the nation's 10 principal liberal political activists. With their imprisonment, the Damascus Spring came to an abrupt end, as did hopes that the new regime would be progressive.

A Well-Polished Image

Despite the crackdown on dissent, Bashar al-Assad continued to portray himself to the outside world as a cultivated and enlightened leader who saw in democracy a means of improving Syrian life. He cautioned, however, that democratic change would have to move slowly, very slowly. In fact, the human rights record of his regime has always been poor. A variety of human rights organizations have documented the imprisonment, torture, and even execution of political opponents. Those branded as dissidents are routinely watched by the secret police, and their travel both within and outside of Syria is strictly regulated.

 **VOICES**

> [In Syria,] the military, ruling elite, and ruthless secret police are so intertwined that it is now impossible to separate the Assad government from the security establishment.... [T]he government and its loyal forces have been able to deter all but the most resolute and fearless oppositional activists.
>
> —Michael Bröning, "The Sturdy House That Assad Built," *Foreign Affairs*, March 7, 2011

As a Ba'athist, a member of a party that espouses secularism in government, Bashar al-Assad generally avoids religious references in policy statements and speeches.

If Westerners took comfort in anything about Bashar al-Assad, it was his secular orientation. He might well be an autocrat, even a tyrant, but at least he was not an Islamist. Yet the United States, European Union, and Israel have jointly accused Assad of providing material support to militants and such political groups as Hezbollah, Hamas, and Islamic Jihad, who share the ideology that Zionism is a wrong that must be forcibly rectified. Thus, while his own internal politics may be secular, his regime has aided violent anti-Zionist organizations the United States and others have labeled as terrorist.

The Syrian Economy Under Bashar al-Assad

Thanks to oil, the Syrian economy has been more prosperous than the economies of the poorest Middle Eastern nations. But the tight state control of industry and an over-reliance on petroleum exports for income have slowed development and made foreigners wary about investing in Syria.

Among the nation's poor, who are predominantly Sunni, economic woes are just one more reason to hate the Assad government. In recent years, discontent over socioeconomic inequality has become increasingly intense, especially among largely unemployed Sunni youth. That Bashar al-Assad, like many other political leaders in the Middle East, is financially corrupt has further eroded his popularity and credibility. The Assad family fortune, as of 2012, was estimated at some $1.5 billion.

Uprising, Insurgency, Civil War

The regional uprisings that began in 2010 swept into Syria during January 2011, with minor protests erupting in Damascus and elsewhere and a truly large-scale protest breaking out in Daraa, a city in the nation's south.

The Assad government acted quickly, with mass arrests and police brutality. Some of those taken into custody were abused, even tortured. The strong-arm crackdown succeeded only in escalating the protests, however. Anti-Assad activists took to burning public buildings, including Ba'ath Party headquarters in Damascus.

Suddenly, in May, Assad took a new tack, announcing the release of a large number of political prisoners, including ardent Islamists. But instead of appeasing the protestors, the gesture only provoked them further. Worse, the released political prisoners now became key leaders of the anti-government forces.

From Civil Uprising to Civil War

By this time, Assad, in his effort to stem protest, had largely withdrawn the police cadres and replaced them with the manpower and firepower of large-scale military deployments. But by June, many soldiers were deserting, defecting to the side of protestors. On July 29, 2011, army officers who had defected announced the formation of the Free Syrian Army (FSA). It was at this point that the civil uprising escalated into a civil war, and while the rebel forces consisted of numerous factions, the FSA remained the largest and most professional insurgent force. It became *the* opposition army, and it would grow to a strength of about 40,000 men by June 2012.

The Nightmare Begins

Many in the West wrongly predicted that the military defections would quickly spell the end of the Assad regime. Far from seeking conciliation, Assad cracked down by redoubling military offensives and sieges. The "Ramadan Massacre" of July 31, 2011, for example, killed 142 opposition fighters and injured many more. Where forces loyal to Assad managed to blockade and cut off towns and cities, bringing all transportation to a halt, famine hit war-torn communities especially hard. The continued support of Moscow and Tehran kept the Syrian regime solvent as it expanded its efficient and brutal military into an increasingly disjointed rebel force.

VOICES

The future of Syria must be determined by its people, but President Bashar al-Assad is standing in their way. For the sake of the Syrian people, the time has come for President Assad to step aside.

—President Barack Obama, written statement on the Syrian crisis, August 18, 2011

With the war outrunning the rebels, a number of the disparate opposition groups met in Turkey to create the Syrian National Council in an effort to coordinate the effort against Assad. But unifying the factions soon proved hopeless, and, badly fragmented, the rebels soon reeled under the relentless blows of Assad's forces.

The FSA continued to show itself the best-organized among the rebel forces and attempted to press the offensive against the government during September 2011. Beaten back by Assad's troops, the FSA made a tactical withdrawal across the Syrian border into Turkey, which, in October, extended aid to it in the form of supplies and base facilities. From the Turkish side of the border, FSA units launched attacks against Syrian government-held positions and gained footholds in several border towns.

Escalation

By the end of 2011, the intensity of the war increased, especially in the city of Homs, a Ba'athist stronghold that nevertheless became one of the centers of opposition to the regime. At the same time, the FSA hit Syrian military and Ba'ath facilities in and around Damascus. This led to Assad's decision to use artillery on a large scale, beginning in January 2012.

From this point forward, destruction of homes and other civilian structures and infrastructure became virtually indiscriminate, especially after Assad's forces supplemented ground-based artillery bombardment with aerial bombardment. Particularly cruel were so-called *barrel bombs*. Large barrels filled with high explosive (sometimes nitrate fertilizer) and shrapnel, these improvised devices were deployed from helicopters and have been especially lethal in Syria's largest city, Aleppo.

A United Nations attempt to implement a cease-fire early in 2012 collapsed during negotiations, and fighting actually intensified during the summer of 2012.

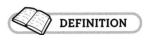 **DEFINITION**

> The **barrel bomb**, a barrel packed with high explosives (such as nitrate fertilizer) combined with shrapnel and sometimes shrapnel plus oil, is a nonstandard or improvised explosive device (IED) introduced by the Syrian Air Force during the Syrian civil war. Low-tech munitions, barrel bombs are typically dropped from helicopters simply by pushing them out the door of the aircraft.

Other Countries, Other Agendas

As has been the case with many modern conflicts in the Middle East, foreign countries have hijacked a regional civil war and exacerbated it to further their own geopolitical objectives. Syria has become a violent landscape where regional and global alliances are fighting for dominance in the Middle East.

Both during and after the Soviet period, Russia has been an ally of Syria and maintains a naval base in the Syrian port city of Tartus—the Russian navy's only base outside the territory of the former Soviet Union. Eager to maintain a foothold in the Middle East, Russia has supplied Syrian government forces with weapons and equipment as well as training. Russia has even injected currency directly into Syria's economy, which is faltering badly under the strain of civil war.

Iran, a longtime ally of Syria, has not only sent the Assad regime financial and technical support, but has actually deployed troops in combat.

Hezbollah, which has strong Ba'athist ties, has successfully fought to keep the Lebanese supply lines of the Syrian regime open. In 2014, Israeli intelligence sources stated that Hezbollah was working to raise and unite the country's disparate loyalist militias into a 100,000-man irregular army under unified command.

Supporting the Opposition

Having ended a seven-month campaign in Libya, NATO announced in November 2011 that it would take no part in the Syrian civil war. The announcement prompted some 600 Libyan fighters to enter the conflict in Syria on the side of the rebels.

The United States, UK, and France began supplying rebel forces with non-lethal military equipment and supplies, and the UK shared with rebel commanders intelligence gathered from its bases and listening posts in Cyprus. According to *New York Times* reporting, CIA operatives based in Turkey funneled weapons to the opposition. Together with non-lethal supplies, these originated in the Persian Gulf, where Qatar and Saudi Arabia vied for influence in the region. Using oil wealth to buy guns, food, and medicine, the Gulf kingdoms even paid opposition military salaries directly and became the largest suppliers of aid to the anti-Assad forces. In April 2013, the European Union lifted an embargo on all Syrian oil to allow imports directly from rebel groups.

A "Red Line"

Early in 2013, the United Nations received reports that Assad's forces were using chemical weapons in the war. UN weapons inspectors confirmed the use of *sarin* on at least four occasions, and on August 21, 2013, chemical attacks on Ghouta, a collection of opposition-controlled Damascus suburbs, killed between 281 and 1,729 persons, according to widely varying estimates.

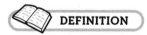 **DEFINITION**

> Although often referred to as a poison gas, **sarin** is actually an odorless, colorless liquid that is weaponized as an aerosol dispersed by artillery shells or aerial bombs or as a vapor. It is an extremely potent nerve agent, 26 times more lethal than cyanide.

A year earlier, in August 2012, President Barack Obama announced that any attempt by Syrian government forces to use or to move its chemical weapons would cross a military, moral, and political "red line," which (the president implied) would possibly move the United States to a more direct military intervention. Although reports from the UN and from Ghouta seemed unquestionably to confirm the chemical attacks, additional reports suggested that rebel forces also used chemical weapons.

In August 2013, Britain's Prime Minister David Cameron supported a motion in Parliament to supply direct military aid to the opposition in Syria, but Parliament voted the motion down. On September 19, 2013, French President François Hollande dropped broad hints that France was ready to supply lethal military aid to rebel forces, but took no action.

As for the United States, President Obama finally acted on his "red line" warning. He authorized the shipment of a limited quantity of lethal aid, including small arms and ammunition in addition to antitank weapons. He declined to send the antiaircraft hardware the opposition had most urgently requested, however. As of the summer of 2014, the president had not yet made a decision on whether to declare and enforce a no-fly zone in southern Syria—a move that would give rebel forces a place to organize and train without fear of air strikes.

VOICES

> We have been very clear to the Assad regime, but also to other players on the ground, that a red line for us is we start seeing a whole bunch of chemical weapons moving around or being utilized. That would change my calculus. That would change my equation…. We're monitoring that situation very carefully. We have put together a range of contingency plans.
>
> —President Barack Obama, news conference, August 20, 2012

Al-Qaeda Enters the Conflict

During 2012, it had frequently appeared that the Assad regime was on the ropes. By the spring of 2013, however, Hezbollah entered the Syrian civil war in full earnest and breathed new life into the Assad government's campaign against the opposition.

Worse for that opposition, early in 2014, ISIS—the Islamic State of Iraq and the Levant—entered the war, ostensibly on the side of the rebels. ISIS came into being during the Iraq War, when it was known as "al-Qaeda in Iraq." The radically anti-Western, anti-secularist Islamist agenda ISIS espoused soon led to armed conflict with the more moderate Syrian rebel groups, especially the FSA, the Islamic Front, and the Army of the Mujahidin. By early 2014, ISIS was in control of territory in Aleppo and Idlib provinces in the northwestern corner of Syria. Assisted by the Turkish air force, the moderates expelled ISIS from these strongholds and thereby managed to push ISIS/al-Qaeda out of the country, at least for the time being.

Future Imperfect

Fighting among rebel forces diluted the opposition's fight against Syrian government forces precisely when Hezbollah, fighting alongside Assad's forces, assumed a greater role in the war. As of this writing, the Syrian Civil War continues. It would be easy to characterize the war, now entering its third year, as a bloody stalemate, but the situation is far more dynamic than that.

The democratic impulse behind the uprisings in the Middle East is a noble one that has produced results ranging from tragic to disappointing to hopeful to remarkable. In the case of Syria, however, the principal outcome appears to be a juggernaut of destruction. Therefore, alongside the hopes and aspirations of peoples who trace their heritage to the very dawn of civilization, the Syrian Civil War is a bloody reminder of the kinetic potential of the Middle East. Its descent into intercommunal violence and rapidly shifting alliances may be indicative of at least some of a dark future for the region.

The Least You Need to Know

- After the dissolution of the Ottoman Empire following World War I, Syria fell under a French mandate, struggled to achieve independence, then lurched from one unstable government to another until Hafez al-Assad became president in 1971.

- Hafez al-Assad used repressive police-state measures to enforce a stable government on Syria and to create a dynastic regime within a quasi-republican form of government.

- Syrians, together with much of the world, looked upon Bashar al-Assad's succession to the presidency in 2000 with the hope that he would introduce a significant measure of genuine democracy to the country. For some seven years, Bashar did reduce the state repression that marked his father's regime, but in the face of increasing opposition, resorted to a greater degree of brutality and dictatorship.

- Inspired by the events of the Arab Spring, an anti-Assad movement came into being in 2011 and rapidly expanded into an increasingly bloody civil war, ongoing and with no end in sight as of the summer of 2014.

- The mixture of hope and horror presented by the Syrian Civil War not only embodies much of the history of the Middle East, it suggests a future of great uncertainty.

Additional Resources

Books

Allawi, Ali. *The Occupation of Iraq: Winning the War, Losing the Peace.* New Haven: Yale University Press, 2007.

Anderson, Scott. *Lawrence in Arabia: War, Deceit, Imperial Folly and the Making of the Modern Middle East.* New York: Doubleday, 2013.

Asbridge, Thomas. *The Crusades: The Authoritative History of the War for the Holy Land.* New York: HarperCollins, 2010.

Baer, Robert. *Sleeping with the Devil: How Washington Sold Out Our Soul For Saudi Crude.* New York: Crown Publishers, 2003.

Bass, Warren. *Support Any Friend: Kennedy's Middle East and the Making of the U.S.-Israel Alliance.* New York: Oxford University Press, 2003.

Ben-Ami, Shlomo. *Scars of War, Wounds of Peace: The Israeli Arab Tragedy.* New York: Oxford University Press, 2006.

Braude, Joseph. *The New Iraq: Rebuilding the Country for Its People, the Middle East and the World.* New York: Basic Books, 2003.

Congressional Quarterly. *The Middle East.* 9th Edition. Washington, DC: CQ Press, 2000.

Edelhelt, Abraham, and Hershel. *History of Zionism: A Handbook and Dictionary.* Boulder: Westview Press, 2000.

Emerson, Steven. *American Jihad: The Terrorists Living Among Us.* New York: The Free Press, New York, 2002.

Esposito, John L., ed. *The Oxford Encyclopedia of the Modern Islamic World.* New York: Oxford University Press, 2001.

Gilbert, Martin. *Historical Atlas of the Arab-Israeli Conflict, 7th Edition.* New York: Routledge, 2002.

Golan, Galia. *Israel and Palestine: Peace Plans and Proposals from Oslo to Disengagement.* Princeton: Markus Wiener, 2006.

Goldziher, Igantz. *Introduction to Islamic Theology and Law.* Princeton: Princeton University Press, 1981.

Herzl, Theodore. *The Jewish State.* Reprint, New York: Dover Publications, 1989.

Hourani, Albert. *A History of the Arab Peoples.* Cambridge: Harvard University Press, 1991.

Karsh, Efraim. *Islamic Imperialism: A History.* New Haven: Yale University Press, 2007.

Kepel, Illes. *Jihad: The Trail of Political Islam.* Cambridge: Harvard University Press, 2002.

Kimmerling, Baruch, and Joel S. Migdal. *The Palestinian People: A History.* Cambridge: Harvard University Press, 2003.

Laqueur, Walter, and Barry Rubin, eds. *The Israel-Arab Reader: A Documentary History of the Middle East Conflict, 7th Revised and Updated Edition.* New York: Penguin Books, 2008.

Laqueur, Walter. *No End to War: Terrorism in the Twenty-First Century.* New York: Continuum, 2003.

Lewis, Bernard. *Cultures in Conflict: Christians, Muslims and Jews in the Age of Discovery.* New York: Oxford University Press, 1995.

———. *What Went Wrong? Western Impact and Middle Eastern Response.* New York: Oxford University Press, 2002.

Madden, Thomas F. *The New Concise History of the Crusades:* Lanham: Rowman and Littlefield, 2010.

Morris, Benny. *1948: A History of the First Arab Israeli War.* New Haven: Yale University Press, 2008.

———. *Righteous Victims: A History of the Zionist-Arab Conflict, 1881–1999.* New York: Alfred A. Knopf, 2000.

O'Ballance, Edgar. *Civil War in Lebanon, 1975–92.* New York: Palgrave Macmillan, 2002.

———. *Sudan, Civil War and Terrorism,* 1956-99, New York: Palgrave Macmillan, 2000.

Oren, Michael B. *Power, Faith, and Fantasy: America in the Middle East 1776 to the Present.* New York: W. W. Norton, 2007.

———. *Six Days of War: June 1967 and the Making of the Modern Middle East.* New York: Oxford University Press, 2002.

Pipes, Daniel. *Militant Islam Reaches America.* New York: W. W. Norton, 2003.

Rabinovitch, Itamar. *Waging Peace: Israel and the Arabs, 1948–2003.* Princeton: Princeton University Press, 2004.

Rubin, Barry, and Judith Rubin, eds. *Anti-American Terrorism and the Middle East: A Documentary Reader.* New York: Oxford University Press, 2006.

Rubin, Barry. *The Truth about Syria.* New York: Palgrave Macmillan, 2007.

Tibi, Bassam. *The Challenge of Fundamentalism: Political Islam and the New World Disorder.* Berkeley: University of California Press, 2002.

Websites

Avalon Project—The Middle East 1916–2001: A Documentary Record
avalon.law.yale.edu/subject_menus/mideast.asp

BBC News: Middle East Conflict
bbc.co.uk/news/special_reports/middle_east_crisis/

Foundation for Middle East Peace
fmep.org

Frontline: Muslims
pbs.org/wgbh/pages/frontline/shows/muslims/

Global Connections: The Middle East
pbs.org/wgbh/globalconnections/mideast/index.html

Heritage: Civilization and the Jews
pbs.org/wnet/heritage/index.html

Internet Islamic History Sourcebook
fordham.edu/halsall/islam/islamsbook.asp

Palestine Daily
palestinedaily.com/#/videos

TimeLine of Israeli-Palestinian History and the Arab-Israeli Conflict
mideastweb.org/timeline.htm

Washington Post: Middle East
washingtonpost.com/world/middle-east/

Films

Argo (2012). The CIA and Hollywood join forces to free U.S. Embassy hostages during the 1980 hostage crisis in Iran. Directed by Ben Affleck.

Dirty Wars (2013). Critical documentary of journalist Jeremy Scahill's investigation into U.S. involvement in the Middle East conflict. Directed by Rick Rowley.

Ghosts of Abu Ghraib (2007). Documentary examining the prisoner abuse scandal in Iraq. Directed by Rory Kennedy.

House of Saud (2005). PBS documentary about the rise and power of Saudi Arabia and its royal leadership. Directed by Jihan El-Tahri.

In the Valley of Elah (2007). The dehumanizing toll of the Iraq War on U.S. soldiers. Directed by Paul Haggis.

Incendies (2010). Story of Europeans searching for their Middle Eastern roots in a time of conflict. Directed by Denis Villeneuve.

Iraq in Fragments (2006). Documentary collection of stories as told by Iraqis living in war. Directed by James Longley.

Rendition (2007). A CIA analyst has doubts about U.S. detainment and interrogation of terrorism suspects. Directed by Gavin Hood.

Syriana (2005). Influence of oil on U.S. policy and actions in the Middle East. Directed by Stephen Gaghan.

The Hurt Locker (2008). The Iraq War through the eyes of a U.S. bomb disposal specialist. Directed by Kathryn Bigelow.

The Square (2013). Documentary of the Arab Spring in Egypt. Directed by Jehane Noujam.

The War You Don't See (2010). Documentary about the media's role in the wars in Iraq and Afghanistan and the Israel-Palestine conflict. Directed by John Pilger.

Zero Dark Thirty (2012). The hunt for Osama bin Laden. Directed by Kathryn Bigelow.

Index

S

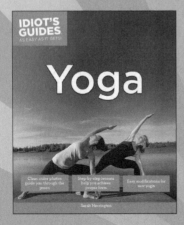

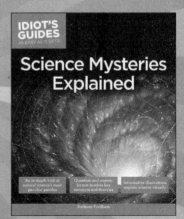
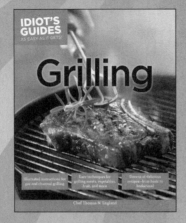
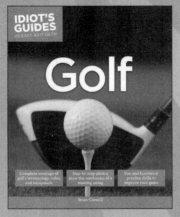
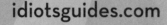